The World's Richest Indian

The World's

TANIS C. THORNE

Richest Indian

The Scandal over Jackson Barnett's Oil Fortune

OXFORD
UNIVERSITY PRESS

OXFORD
UNIVERSITY PRESS

Oxford University Press, Inc., publishes works that further
Oxford University's objective of excellence
in research, scholarship, and education.

Oxford   New York
Auckland   Cape Town   Dar es Salaam   Hong Kong   Karachi
Kuala Lumpur   Madrid   Melbourne   Mexico City   Nairobi
New Delhi   Shanghai   Taipei   Toronto

With offices in
Argentina   Austria   Brazil   Chile   Czech Republic   France   Greece
Guatemala   Hungary   Italy   Japan   Poland   Portugal   Singapore
South Korea   Switzerland   Thailand   Turkey   Ukraine   Vietnam

First published in 2003 by Oxford University Press, Inc.
198 Madison Avenue, New York, New York 10016

www.oup.com

First issued as an Oxford University Press paperback, 2005

Oxford is a registered trademark of Oxford University Press

Library of Congress Cataloging-in-Publication Data
Thorne, Tanis C.
The world's richest Indian: the scandal over Jackson Barnett's oil fortune / Tanis C. Thorne.
     p. cm.
Includes bibliographical references and index.
ISBN-13 978-0-19-516233-2; 978-0-19-518298-9 (pbk.)
ISBN 0-19-516233-1; 0-19-518298-7 (pbk.)
1. Barnett, Jackson, 1856–1934. 2. Creek Indians—Biography. 3. Indians of North America—
Legal status, laws, etc. 4. United States. Bureau of Indian Affairs—History. 5. Indians of North
America—Oklahoma—Government relations. 6. United States. Commission to the Five
Civilized Tribes. 7. Baptists—Oklahoma—History. I. Title.
E99.C9B377 2003
976.6004'973—dc21   2002193171
[B]

Printed in the United States of America
on acid-free paper

For my parents,

Robert and Ingibjorg Chapman

Rabbit and Wolf were friends, they say. Rabbit used to drink out of a well, but he would stir up the water 'til it was muddy. Then they wanted to kill him for it. To catch him they made a man image out of pitch and set it where he came along. The rabbit saw the image of the man. He came up close, and said, "Get out of my way!" It did not move. "Out of my way, I told you; I'll kick you!" he said. But it did not move. He went up and kicked it. Then his foot got stuck. "Let go of me!" he said. "I'll kick you with my other foot!" He kicked again with the other foot. It got stuck, too. "Turn me loose, or I'll hit you with my hand!" said he. He hit him, and his hand got stuck. "Turn me loose, or I'll hit you with my other hand!" he said. He hit him with that, and it stuck. Then he said, "I'll butt you again with my head, that is left me, if you don't turn me loose!" The image of the man did not loose him. He struck him with his head, and that got stuck. Then he was caught.
—AFRICAN-MUSKOGEE FOLKTALE

Acknowledgments

My acquaintance with Jackson Barnett began in 1994 with the discovery of a tiny newspaper clipping in the Rupert and Jeanette Costo Collection at the University of California, Riverside. The clipping, dated March 13, 1929, from an unidentified newspaper, reported the resignation of Commissioner of Indian Affairs Charles Burke in the wake of a Department of Justice report of illegal action in the Jackson Barnett case. Who was this Jackson Barnett? What gross mismanagement had caused the commissioner of Indian affairs to resign in shame? As I explored other California archival collections in pursuit of other research interests, more references to Jackson Barnett appeared. My curiosity increased, and I began collecting a file of information on Barnett. Then in June 1995, while doing research in the Mission Indian Agency records at the federal archives center in Laguna Niguel, archivist Suzanne Dewberry mentioned that there were several boxes of Jackson Barnett materials in their holdings. Just a stone's throw across Aliso Creek from where I was then living was an unexpectedly large and rich Jackson Barnett cache. Though Barnett was a Creek Indian born in Indian Territory, he lived the last decade of his life in Los Angeles, which explains why such volumes of Barnett materials are in a southern California repository. As my interest developed into a book project, new Jackson Barnett sources were uncovered, but I could find little secondary literature.

Jackson Barnett's case generated a marathon of litigation, multiple congressional investigations, and much national publicity in the 1920s. Why had so little been published about this remarkable story? Why wasn't it included in Native American history textbooks as standard fare? After years of concentrated research and study of the many mysterious aspects of the case, the answers to these questions gradually became clearer. The Jackson Barnett saga is large and complex with evidence scattered in different archives across the nation. And while Barnett's story is important, it is also profoundly convoluted, laden with paradox, ambiguity, and the self-serving and hidden agendas of those who left records about him and his fortune. There is a warped, cartoonish character to this rags-to-riches story that belies the deadly serious and seemingly intractable issues of American Indian policy underlying it. These very qualities of paradox and ambiguity made the Jackson Barnett case enigmatic to Barnett's contemporaries and even more difficult for later generations to comprehend. This book aims to present the full story of Jackson Barnett's life as a window through which we may see Indian policy in crisis and transition. Tellingly, we still grapple with the difficult and unresolved problems raised by the Jackson Barnett scandal more than eighty years ago.

In the effort to place Barnett in historical context, I owe a great debt to historian Angie Debo for her meticulous research and her peerless analysis of the Five Civilized Tribes in her classic work, *And Still the Waters Run,* and also to Princeton University Press for allowing me to liberally quote from it and to reproduce two tables. I also want to give due credit to Benay Blend for her pathbreaking but little known 1978 master's thesis, "Jackson Barnett and the Oklahoma Indian Probate System," completed at the University of Texas at Arlington. An encouraging sign that Jackson Barnett's story is beginning to receive the scholarly attention it deserves is the chapter "Jackson Barnett and the Allotment of Muscogee Creek Lands" written by Donald Fixico in his 1998 book, *The Invasion of Indian Country in the Twentieth Century.* Fixico gives the Jackson Barnett story its due as a nationally prominent case epitomizing the exploitation of Indian people.

The American Baptist Historical Society, Valley Forge, Pennsylvania, kindly gave permission to quote from a number of personal letters in its collection, principally from the correspondence of Charles White and George Hovey. The quote from Will Rogers that serves as the epigraph to chapter 10 is credited to the Will Rogers Museums, Claremore, Oklahoma.

I feel fortunate for having had the opportunity to write this book. It has been a privilege to study the remarkable Creek people. To them, I owe the deepest debt of gratitude. I hope I have faithfully recorded the horrific injustices they suffered and the experiences of their endearing native son, Jackson Barnett, and I hope I have shown due respect and honor to their culture and history.

A host of people have made this book possible. Doing research and writing this book have absorbed much of my time in the last eight years, and along the way, many made invaluable contributions. Heading the list of people whom I want to thank are Lance Hall and Fred Schoemehl. Lance Hall is a great-great-great–half nephew of Jackson Barnett by Jackson Barnett's half sister Hannah. Lance has assiduously researched family genealogy and many other aspects of the Barnett case, publishing much of this scholarly research on his excellent Web pages. He has cheerfully and competently helped me at various stages in the manuscript production: doing research in Oklahoma newspapers, sharing generously of his knowledge, obtaining photographs (including the book's cover image), and reading and correcting parts of the manuscript in its final drafts. Friend and colleague Fred Schoemehl—now completing his Ph.D. at the University of California, Irvine—has not only aided me in the conceptual development of the book in innumerable conversations over the years but has edited and improved the manuscript at different stages. Sincere thanks also go to Bill Graff, a great-grand–half nephew of Jackson Barnett, and his mother, Tunney Litsey Graff, who have shared family stories and photos and have warmly supported this book project. Another descendant of one of the principals, Mary Petersdorf, granddaughter of Carl O'Hornett, Barnett's guardian, has also been generous with her family memories and photographs.

A number of scholars have read parts or the whole of the manuscript and offered their constructive criticisms and encouragement. In particular, I wish to thank Martin Ridge, David Wilkins, Daniel F. Littlefield, Jr., Donald Fixico, Joan Pinkvoss, Charles Roberts, and Thomas Clark. The Huntington Library legal research discussion group at San Marino reviewed and commented on a chapter in the spring of 2000, as did the UC, Irvine, women's faculty reading group two years earlier. Colleagues in the history department at UCI—Tim Tackett, Helen Chenut, Steve Topik, Bob Hine, and James Given—have been very supportive. The Office of Academic Affairs, Humanities Center, at the University of California provided a faculty development award in 1998 for research and travel for this project. A number of students have also done research and made thoughtful comments that have enriched this work, namely, Barnaby Montgomery, Steve Morrison, Maria Sanchez, and Carole Autori.

I am also grateful to the many archivists and librarians—some of whom are not mentioned here by name—who have furthered my research efforts. Suzanne Dewberry, National Archives and Records Administration (NARA), Southeast Region, Atlanta; and Paul Wormser, NARA, Pacific South Region, Laguna Niguel, helped launch this study; Fred Romanski, Joe Schwarz, and Michael Pilgrim from NARA, College Park, and Barbara Rust from NARA, Southwest Region, Fort Worth, provided invaluable aid in finding Barnett materials. Thanks also go to Greg Plunges, NARA, Northeast Region, New York; Beverly Carlson, Betty Layton, and Deborah

Van Broekhoven from the American Baptist Historical Society Archives Center, Valley Forge, Pennsylvania; William Welge, director of the Oklahoma Historical Society, Oklahoma City; John Johnson of the Okmulgee County Historical Society, Okmulgee, Oklahoma; Carolyn G. Hanneman, archivist at the Carl Albert Center, Congressional Archives, University of Oklahoma, Norman; Kay Collins, UCI government information librarian; and Carolyn Kozo Cole, curator of photographs at the Los Angeles Public Library. Mike Miller and Dwayne Pack of UC Irvine's Instructional Technology Center (with an assist from Jeff Holtzman) created the map, offering their expertise generously, as always.

Susan Ferber, my editor at Oxford University Press, saw the promise in the manuscript, for which I am greatly appreciative. She and Stacey Hamilton facilitated production of the manuscript and handled my many queries in a thoroughly professional manner.

This gratitude list would not be complete without thanks to my friends and family, whom I have regaled with stories of Jackson Barnett for years and who have invariably shown patience, encouragement, and often warm interest and enthusiasm. These include Chuck Anderson, my parents, my son, Galen, my brother, Leif, Beverly Mathias, Nan Yamane, Judy Raftery, and—in Gold County—Erin and Debi Alders, Chris Nielsen, Tim Cleary, and Jim and Susan Pyle.

Contents

Chronology

1830	Removal Act
1836–1837	Creek Trail of Tears
c. 1856	Jackson Barnett born
1861–1865	Civil War
1866	Creek Treaty cedes half of territory and permits railroad right-of-way
1870s	Creek Golden Age
1881	Anna Randolph born
1887	Dawes Allotment Act
1898	Curtis Act
Mar. 1901	Creek Compact
1890s–1909	Chitto Harjo (Crazy Snake) uprising
1903	Jackson Barnett allotment issued
1905	Convention for state of Sequoya
Apr.–May 1906	McCumber Amendment and Burke Act
1906	Creek government dissolved; Oklahoma Enabling Act
1907	Oklahoma statehood; Senate investigation in Oklahoma
May 27, 1908	Oklahoma Closure Act ("Crime of 1908")

Mar. 1912	Tom Slick discovers Cushing field; Jackson Barnett signs oil lease for drilling on his property
Apr. 30, 1912	Barnett declared incompetent by Okmulgee County court
May 1, 1912	Carl O'Hornett appointed as guardian; second oil lease signed
Sept. 1912	Superintendent Dana Kelsey approves compromise lease; Henryetta farm purchased for Barnett
1913–1921	Cato Sells's administration
1917	Barnett's oil wells yield $45,000/month royalty; he's dubbed "World's Richest Indian"; $640,000 in Liberty Bonds purchased; Secretary of the Interior Franklin Lane's New Policy
Sept. 1919	Barnett donates $25,000 to Henryetta church construction fund
Nov. 1919	Barnett's allowance raised to $650/month
Jan. 1920	Anna Randolph Lowe meets Jackson Barnett; first marriage attempt
Feb. 23, 1920	Jackson Barnett and Anna Lowe married
Mar. 1, 1920	Anna Barnett contracts with Harold McGugin and William Keith to defend the marriage
Apr. 1920	Bowie Report submitted to Commissioner Sells
May 1920	Kansas court ruling sustains marriage on trial basis
1921–1929	Charles Burke's administration
July 1921	Interior rejects Sells's pledge of $200,000 to Southern Baptist Convention
Sept. 1921	McGugin and Anna Barnett maneuver to circumvent O'Hornett; Burke decides to give money to Bacone
Dec. 18, 1921	Anna and Jackson move to Muskogee
July 1922	Ward, Mott, Burke, and McGugin meet to discuss donation
Aug. 2, 1922	Solicitor Edwin Booth's opinion submitted to Interior
Oct. 7, 1922	Amendment to Indian bureau regulations to allow Interior to circumvent the local Oklahoma guardians in "individual cases"
Jan. 31, 1923	Fall approves $1.1 million distribution to Northern Baptists and Anna Barnett
Feb. 1, 1923	Creation of $750,000 Barnett trusts at Equitable and Riggs banks
Feb. 1923	Barnetts move to Los Angeles
Mar. 1923	O'Hornett files suits to block disbursement of allowances and trust annuities to Barnetts and sues trust companies Riggs and Equitable

May 1923	Barnetts purchase Brentwood home
Nov. 1923	O'Hornett resigns as guardian and is replaced by Elmer Bailey
Jan. 1924	*Oklahoma's Poor Rich Indians* published
June 1924	House of Representatives demands full investigation of Burke and BIA
July 1924	Jackson declared incompetent in Los Angeles Superior Court; Security Bank named guardian
Dec. 9, 1924	Judge Hugh Murphy alleges Burke's wrongdoing before Congress
Feb. 1925	Security Bank resigns as Barnett guardian and Leslie Hewitt appointed; Attorney General Harlan Stone says distribution unauthorized
Mar. 1925	Snyder's House subcommittee recommends court review of $1.1 million donation; suit filed to challenge Bailey's guardianship
Apr. 1925	Department of Justice supports Interior's action in creating the trusts
Dec. 1925	Justice charges wrongdoing by Interior; Parmenter confirmed as assistant attorney general
Mar. 4, 1926	Frear attacks Burke in Congress
Apr. 1926	Harreld-Hastings Act authorizes Justice to pursue Barnett litigation
July 1926	Oklahoma appeals court validates guardianship; Justice Branson dissents
1926	Barnetts move into Hancock Park mansion; Barnett brought to Oklahoma for grand jury hearing, which is cancelled
Oct. 1926	Attorney General Sargent opines that the Interior secretary's actions cannot be questioned "unless there is an abuse or arbitrary exercise of that discretion"
Nov. 1926	*Equitable* trial begins in New York; Oklahoma Supreme Court nullifies the Oklahoma guardianship
Dec. 1926	Congressman Frear renews call for congressional investigation
Feb. 1927	Barnett oil leases challenged in court; King resolution in Senate to make full investigation of bureau
May 1927	Jelliffe examines Jackson Barnett
Aug. 1927	Judge Knox's decision in *Barnett v. Equitable Trust*
Feb. 1928	Meriam Report
Mar. 1928	Hearings on creation of trust estates for rich Indians
May 10, 1928	Congress extends restrictions for Five Civilized Tribes

June 1928	Attorney general intervenes to cancel second grand jury in Muskogee
July–Aug. 1928	Federal judges Pollock and Kennamer uphold Interior's authority in creating the trusts in *McGugin* and *Mott* cases
Oct. 1928	Knox decision upheld due to procedural error in appeal
Nov. 1928	Senate subcommittee hearings begin in Riverside
Mar. 1929	Butler report leads to Burke resignation
May 1929	Federal judge Pollock upholds Interior's authority in *Mott*
1931	In *Mott v. United States,* the U.S. Supreme Court declares Barnett donation illegal
Mar., 1934	Federal district court ruling by Judge James in *Barnett v. United States* annuls the Barnett marriage
May 29, 1934	Jackson Barnett dies
Feb. 1935	*United States v. Riggs* decided; $200,000 in Anna's name in trust account returned to Interior
Jan. 1938	U.S. Supreme Court refuses to hear appeal in *United States v. Anna Barnett*
Oct. 30, 1938	Anna Barnett and daughter evicted from Hancock Park mansion
Dec. 1939	Judge Williams rules regarding determination of Barnett heirs
1940	*United States v. McGugin* requires McGugin to return legal fees

The World's Richest Indian

Introduction

Upon its facts the case was so strange and amazing as to tax credulity.
—HENRY RAMEY

In 1911, a self-trained geologist and oil speculator named Tom Slick arrived in Creek County, Oklahoma. Though there weren't any known oil deposits in the vicinity, Slick followed his instincts, and in early March 1912 he struck oil on a hardscrabble farm he'd leased. Immediately, there was a mad scramble to secure oil leases from nearby property owners. Slick had opened up the world-renowned Cushing field, the source of the best high-grade crude yet found west of the Alleghenies. Within a year there were 150 wells and in a little over two years more than 890 wells in the Cushing field. Several wells had a daily production greater than all of Pennsylvania's oil fields. By 1917 the eighteen-mile-long Cushing field was producing 17 percent of all oil marketed in the United States and 3 percent of total world production. The prolific Drumright pool, which included Slick's original well, was in the center of the Cushing field.[1]

In the heart of the Drumright pool were 160 acres owned by Jackson Barnett, a middle-aged and illiterate Creek Indian. Six to eight wells were drilled on his property after the Department of the Interior approved an oil lease in 1912. From January 1913 to May 1917, Jackson's monthly royalty income averaged $14,536. After the United States entered World War I in 1917, a spike in oil demand coincided with the discovery of a deep and seemingly bottomless pocket of oil on Barnett's land. Barnett's wells alone

3

produced 14,000 barrels of oil a day. (This site is on the National Register of Historic Places: #820003681.) The Drumright oil well known as Jackson Barnett No. 11 became the world's first well to produce a million barrels of oil in a year. Barnett's income skyrocketed to $47,082 per month.[2] The enormity of the wealth possessed by this unassuming man dwarfed any normal scale of measure and staggered the imagination. His wells produced $24 million worth of oil, garnering him a 12.5 percent royalty of $3–4 million during his lifetime, the equivalent of $30–40 million in 2002.[3] Newspapers crowned him the "World's Richest Indian." Jackson Barnett was a one-man Creek emirate.

Barnett displayed a marked indifference toward his windfall. Indifference or incomprehension: it was difficult to read Jackson Barnett. A man of simple needs and humble ways, he continued to wear rough clothing and remained unshaven, sporting a straggling beard and mustache. Having been freed from the need to labor, he went fishing with the neighborhood children. Though he was a shy, quiet man, he liked the hustle and bustle of human activity. He frequented the nearby town of Henryetta two or three times a week, traveling in his wagon or on a horse. He liked to order malted milks at the drugstore and then loiter on a street corner until sundown. Many approached him for donations. Kind and generous, he would often acquiesce if he liked the person. On one occasion, he even gave his approval for a $1 million donation. Even after Barnett had apotheosized into the World's Richest Indian, he was strangely immune to the excitement—bordering on gold fever—his wealth inspired in others. Jackson Barnett appeared to have no idea how to spend this fortune, and in point of fact, he had limited access to it. Prior to 1920, Barnett received direct payments of only a few hundred dollars per year. The rest was managed for him by the Department of the Interior and by the Okmulgee County court.[4] The World's Richest Indian was locked into this state of genteel poverty until 1920, when he eloped with a woman he had just met.

A widely shared explanation for Barnett's oddities—and the legitimacy of delegating control of his vast fortune to others—is that he was simple-minded, an incompetent. In his youth, Barnett had suffered a head injury when he fell from a horse. The facile allegation that Jackson Barnett was mentally impaired, however, should be treated with some skepticism for a number of reasons. Those that advanced it did so for self-serving purposes: to gain and maintain legal control of his money. Jackson Barnett's so-called lassitude may be attributed to an eccentric personality, his advanced age (he was approaching sixty when oil was discovered on his property), or his understandable ignorance of modern ways. Moreover, one must be skeptical about judgments made by non-Indians about Barnett because they were highly colored by ethnocentrism and the turn-of-the-century racial ideology that all Indians were mentally inferior.

Jackson Barnett's temperate and generous ways, when placed in the context of Creek cultural values and worldview, do not appear aberrant.

Earliest known photograph of Jackson Barnett, c. 1912–1915. In a clearly posed photograph emphasizing his "Indianness," a slender, dubious-looking Jackson—with a fresh haircut and wearing a tie—holds a bow as he sits on a fence surrounded by arrows. Courtesy of the Still Photo Archive, National Archives, College Park.

Acquisitiveness, greed, and self-aggrandizement were condemned, and open-handed generosity to the less fortunate was expected among Indians. The practice of redistributing surpluses within the kin networks was socialized into the Creek individual from an early age and became second nature. If Jackson Barnett viewed his changing fortunes matter-of-factly or with disinterested grace, this too can be attributed to his cultural predispositions. In the Creek worldview, reality was a "convergence of contraries,

Jackson, a bewhiskered and happy bachelor in his sixties, c. 1918. One of the earliest photos of "Jackson Barnett, Millionaire Indian." Courtesy of the National Archives, Southwest Region, Fort Worth.

without a final synthesis."[5] Philosophically, the Creeks had an approach to life that accommodated conflict and change as inevitable features of existence. The sacred principle of balanced opposites pervaded the worldview of the "Five Civilized Tribes"—the Creek, Cherokee, Choctaw, Chickasaw, and Seminole. This philosophical approach inspired the creation of ideological frameworks and tribal institutions that were flexible and resilient. Repeatedly, the Creeks were torn asunder by civil war and suffered staggering hardships, but they showed a remarkable ability to recover their equilibrium.[6] Throughout the tribulations of his life, Jackson Barnett displayed such resiliency.

Those who did not appreciate Creek culture were apt to fall into the error of underestimating Barnett's capabilities, for aspects of Indian culture and personality were subtle, elusive, and enigmatic to outsiders. One had to know Jackson Barnett well to appreciate his character. Jackson held firm to certain choices and values and displayed a lively sense of humor. Constantly harassed about his marriage, Jackson declared, "Indians get married like other people. Why don't you let us alone?"[7] Though affable and unaffected, he could not be persuaded to do what he did not wish to do (nor to undo what he had done in marrying Anna Lowe). Those who smugly assumed that Barnett could be easily manipulated were surprised when they discovered otherwise. For example, when Barnett was in his mid-seventies, he was called before a U.S. Senate subcommittee to testify. Senators Burton Wheeler and William B. Pine plotted to show Jackson Barnett to be a simpleton, but under their patronizing questioning, Wheeler and Pine were the ones who were embarrassed.

Jackson Barnett's spectacular hour in the public limelight arrived in 1920 with his sensational elopement at age sixty-four with femme fatale and gold digger Anna Laura Lowe. A tangle of litigation and political civil war followed. The jockeying for control of the Barnett estate was played out in a national political arena that pitted federal power against local control and the U.S. Department of the Interior against the Justice Department. Because the battle reached a level of contention equivalent to its prize, Jackson Barnett's fabulous wealth brought the legal exploitation of Indian resources into the national spotlight. The Barnett political scandal sent shock waves through the U.S. Congress, spurring numerous investigations. The scandal was a great political embarrassment to the U.S. Bureau of Indian Affairs. Litigation reached the nation's highest tribunals and shook the structures of power. Jackson and Anna Barnett played pivotal roles in a convulsive struggle that eventually drove Charles Burke, commissioner of Indian affairs, from office.

The grand tragicomedy of Jackson Barnett's life as the World's Richest Indian has been almost totally lost to historical memory, eclipsed in large part by the glamorous and aristocratic Osage. The Osage oil wealth rose spectacularly after 1919 as Jackson's royalties waned. As the new world's richest Indians, they amassed a legendary fortune from oil—an estimated $252 million from "black gold" between 1902 and 1936. Because of their unique legal agreement with the federal government, the Osage collectively owned their subsurface mineral rights and received per capita quarterly payments for their leases. Each man, woman, and child of the original 2,229 on the tribal roll had a share, or "headright," which in 1923 was worth $13,200. An average Osage family of four collected $60,000 in royalties annually during the peak years of the 1920s. An Osage was roughly four times richer in property and per capita income than the average non-Indian American of the 1920s and fifty times richer than the average Indian.[8]

Unlike Jackson Barnett, whose access to his own funds was limited, the Osage were able to spend their free-flowing money with "Olympian indifference" (in John Joseph Mathews's phrase), bedazzling the American public and commanding national attention.[9] Osage County was drenched in prosperity during the 1920s. Popular magazine articles with such titles as "Lo, the Rich Indian" and "Richest Indians in the World" gleefully reported the excesses and eccentricities of America's Indian nouveau riche. Non-Indians were both amused and envious that this wealth was suddenly raining down upon what to them seemed like an unlikely and undeserving population. The "primitive" Indian buying and misusing modern luxury items was a staple source of racist humor, while wastefulness and frivolity were piously condemned. The American public was both fascinated by the rags-to-riches stories of the wealthy Oklahoma Indians and appalled by the trespass on the Protestant work ethic values of industry, frugality, and simplicity.

Jackson Barnett's experiences as a wealthy Indian closely parallel that of the Osage in many ways. George Vaux, Jr., of the Board of Indian Commissioners, stated it succinctly in 1917: the "problem of the Indian is the problem of poverty. With the Osages the problem is the problem of riches."[10] As with the Osage, many opportunists were eager to carve out shares for themselves from Barnett's enormous "surplus" wealth. Oilmen, lawyers, churchmen, politicians, bootleggers, and gold diggers all volunteered to lend a helping hand and do the "right thing" with his money. Barnett's compliant personality, his Creek worldview, and his alleged intellectual defects made him the target for dozens of schemers who tried to appropriate his wealth for themselves. As a federal judge saw it, Jackson Barnett was the "shuttledore in a game of battlecock, in which the stakes were high."[11]

In Jackson's simplicity lies the tale. If Jackson Barnett had not been so elemental, his story would not be so elegantly enigmatic and emblematic. Like Dostoevski's Idiot or Capra's Mr. Deeds, Jackson's innocence and purity illuminate the motivations and methods of those around him.

The World's Richest Indian is a biography of Jackson Barnett, but it is also an emblematic study of a Native American as an economic and political pawn. A case study of a power struggle among many parties seeking to control a rich Indian's estate, it illuminates the broader principles of law that gave authority to certain individuals and governmental agencies to manage Indian property. It thus elucidates the political structures and legal vehicles available to transfer Indian wealth to non-Indians once treaty rights and tribal institutions were undermined and tribal property individualized. Prophetically, a California senator, Eugene Casserly, commented on the cupidity that motivated Congress's action in 1871 to end treaty making, saying, "It was the first step in a great scheme of spoliation" and dishonor.[12] The Dawes Allotment Act, which followed shortly thereafter in 1887, called by Teddy Roosevelt "a mighty pulverizing engine to break up the Tribal mass,"[13] delivered Indian estates to non-Indian hands. Two-thirds of the Indian treaty lands were so transferred by the 1930s. The damage that the Dawes Act did to Native America cannot be underesti-

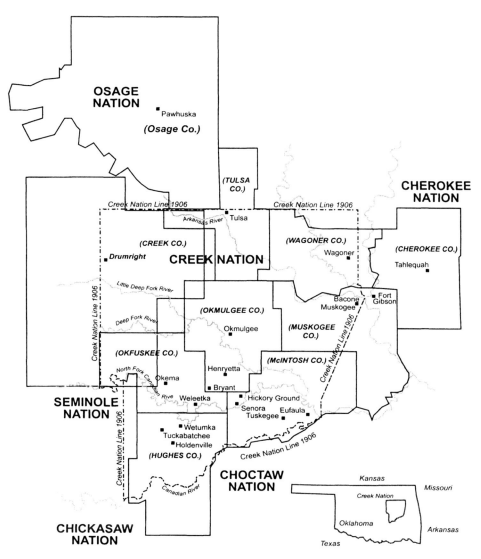

Map: *Five Civilized Tribes Territory/Eastern Oklahoma, 1866–1920.* This map highlights the locations of the Five Civilized Tribes in Indian Territory after post–Civil War cession treaties reduced holdings; also shown are the new political boundaries of counties after the Creek lands were folded into the state of Oklahoma in 1907. Produced by Mike Miller and Jeff Holtzman.

mated. By promoting the division of communally held reservations into individually held allotments, the Dawes Act paved the way for the legalized robbery of the twentieth century. Conspicuous examples of unconscionable episodes of large-scale swindling were the Five Civilized Tribes' experiences following statehood and the White Earth tragedy, in which the Minnesota Anishinaabe lost their lumber. Loss of land and resources were routine features of life for twentieth-century Indians. What made the otherwise commonplace tale of legalized theft of Indian resources remarkable in this instance was, of course, the outrageous size of Barnett's individual fortune.

To be understood, the uproar over Jackson Barnett's personal affairs and the Indian bureau's questionable dealings in allegedly mismanaging his estate must be cast against the twisted historical development of Indian policy and law. Jackson Barnett's case illustrates what Sharon O'Brien and Tom Holm aptly describe as an era of "confusion" in Indian policy. Such a perplexed state of affairs was frankly admitted by Secretary of the Interior Franklin Lane in 1914: "That the Indian is confused in mind as to his status and very much at sea as to our ultimate purpose toward him is not surprising. . . . Manifestly the Indian has been confused in his thought because we have been confused in ours."[14] Initially, the bureau's responsibility was to fulfill treaty promises, specifically to aid Indians in their progress toward economic and cultural adjustment to the dominant culture. The U.S. Supreme Court's *Cherokee v. Georgia* decision of 1831 defined the federal government's relationship to Native Americans as resembling that of a guardian to a ward. The federal government was thus committed to a paternalistic role in defending Indians from abuse, guiding them, and protecting treaty-held lands from intruders. This is the "federal trust" relationship. In 1886 the U.S. Supreme Court decision in *United States v. Kagama* codified the principle of Indian wardship into law. With the passage of the Dawes Act, this federal-Indian relationship was radically redefined. The Dawes Act inaugurated a policy of assimilation with the vision of all Indians becoming U.S. citizens once their tribal institutions and cultures had been eradicated. On their 160-acre allotments, Indians were expected to become self-sufficient farmers. Once the bureau had accomplished its task of educating Indians to the responsibilities of citizenship and farming, it would have worked itself out of a job.

When it became apparent by 1900 that the Dawes Act was falling far short of its humanistic goals, Congress tried ineffectually to turn back the clock and correct the defects of the allotment policy. Experience had shown that those Indians who had been given titles to their individual properties, and thus were no longer under federal trust protection, were quickly dispossessed. They lacked business skills, fell prey to fraud and intimidation, and could not pay their taxes. The removal of restrictions on the sale of allotments proved to be premature and disastrous even for the Five Civilized Tribes, which were considered more advanced than other

Indians by their white contemporaries. Progressive congressmen determinedly pushed legislation that would protect the weak and defenseless and stall the process of "liberating" unprepared Indians from federal control. This well-meaning corrective created the peculiar legal status of the "restricted" Indian. As defined by a federal judge, an Indian was "restricted," or incompetent, by virtue of "racial weakness, lack of education, and business training" and needed federal supervision, protection, and guidance during the pupilage to self-reliant citizenship.[15] As a restricted Indian, Jackson was among the people whose allotments (and royalties from grazing and mineral leases) were held in trust by the federal government.

In large part, the contradictions that the bureau found itself straddling in the 1920s were the paradoxical legacy of the Progressive Era. (Alluded to here as progressives are the adherents of the broad reform movement to bring honesty and efficiency to government, which spanned the decades from the 1890s to the 1920s.) As Holm observed, this was an era of ambiguity and turmoil in the way the dominant culture thought about Indians and in the legal status of Indians. Liberalism clashed with reform impulses and individualism with social-mindedness.[16] Jackson Barnett, who liked to watch and later direct traffic in front of his mansion in the star-studded Hancock Park neighborhood of Los Angeles, found himself at a busy crossroads: where private property intersected with public interest and where the machine-age ideologies of the late nineteenth century (Andrew Carnegie's gospel of wealth, Henry George's "unearned increment," and Herbert Spencer's Social Darwinism) collided.

In its accommodations to the revolutionary changes in public policy, the bureau went through a strange metamorphosis; simultaneously, American Indian law became more prolix, and the status of Native Americans became ambiguous. The progressives promoted an activist government to fight economic and political ills, but they had strong antidemocratic impulses, believing the common people could not be trusted. Contrary to the expectation that the Indian bureaucracy within the Department of the Interior would be gradually phased out of existence, it expanded rapidly to manage the millions of acres of restricted Indian lands. In the progressives' thinking, such an important responsibility could only be entrusted to trained professionals. Congress was stingy in its allocations to the Indian bureau to protect and educate Indians, but it did grant the Interior Department nearly unlimited discretionary power to manage Indian affairs. Significantly, this broad federal power extended over "surplus" funds of Indians.

The exercise of federal power with its undemocratic overtones was resented by both whites and Indians, but for different reasons. The Indian bureau found itself in an adversarial relationship with local politicians and businessmen, who wanted greater access to Indian resources and a dominant position in dealings with local Indian populations. Oklahomans, for

example, vigorously contested what they perceived as carpetbagging federal government policies. In federal legislation passed in 1908, called the
"Crime of 1908" by its critics, Oklahoma established its jurisdiction over
some Indian probate matters within the state. The federal government's resolve to protect Indians was continually compromised because the official
national policy was rapid assimilation of Indians into the general population by removal of all federal restrictions. Resource-hungry lobbyists demanded the liberation of Indians from federal control.

While appreciative of some federal protections, Indians suffered under
the bureau's arrogance and the flawed allotment policy to which the bureau was committed. As mixed-blood John Joseph Mathews wrote in his
autobiographical novel, *Sundown*, the Indian bureau always seemed to the
Osage people "a very whimsical and at times unreasonable power."[17] Indians were caught in the cross fire between locals touting democratic ideals
(while aiming to pillage their resources) and the federal government,
which demanded total subordination to its fallible judgment as the price
of protection. Jurisdiction under state law stripped Indians of their land
and wealth, and jurisdiction under federal law stripped them of their right
to make decisions for themselves.

In the first decades of the twentieth century, the unpopular and un-
derfunded Indian bureau valiantly struggled to find a way between the
treacherous polarities of liberation and protection. It attempted to steer a
clear course through the shifting tides of public opinion with only the stars
for guidance. Its reference points were an idealistic commitment to protecting a "weaker" race, an unflagging faith that instilling the Protestant
work ethic was the key to Indian salvation, and an unquestioning belief in
the superiority of federal bureaucratic management. Indian policy became
more inscrutable because of its complexity and convolutions, mystifying
all but an inner circle of bureau professionals. By the early 1920s, bureau
practice regarding lifting restrictions became decidedly conservative; the
management of Indian lands and resources hardened institutionally as a
permanent fixture of bureau responsibility. Thus, the Indian bureau's
covert policies and practices were jarringly out of step with the official national policy of rapid assimilation. The bureau had to resort to innumerable compromises, subterfuge, and raw power to continue its course. In
its thankless work, the bureau's strongest allies were Christian missionary
organizations.

The "problem of riches" in Oklahoma brought a precariously balanced Indian policy to a crisis because it exacerbated the tensions between
local and federal power. Oil wealth dramatically raised the stakes. The
management—mismanagement, in the opinion of many—of Jackson Barnett's estate fired the tinder that erupted into a conflagration of conflict.
Those who preyed upon Jackson Barnett, the Osage, and other wealthy
Oklahoma Indians used every conceivable avenue, legal and illegal.
One legal method by which Indians were victimized was the Oklahoma

guardianship system. Though restricted Indians' property was under federal trust protection, the county courts exercised the prerogatives granted
under the authority of the Crime of 1908 legislation to appoint local
guardians as well. This county court jurisdiction cost the estates dearly in
unnecessary and unwanted legal services. To counter the many ways Indians were being defrauded, the bureau was forced to take strong measures,
including drafting legislation to close loopholes and bringing the full
weight of federal power down upon those who exploited Indians. A disproportionate percentage of the bureau's resources was committed to defending the large estates of people like Jackson Barnett, while the vast
majority of poorer Indians was neglected. Trying to preserve the wealthy
Oklahoma Indian estates and to find a way out of this conundrum, Commissioner Burke used Jackson Barnett as his test case, thereby incurring
the wrath of Oklahomans. The contest over the Barnett estate epitomized
the struggle between the state of Oklahoma and the Interior Department
for jurisdiction over the restricted Indians of the Five Civilized Tribes.

A seminal issue in the Barnett controversy was Jackson's status as a restricted Indian under federal guardianship. Barnett's land and money were
under federal jurisdiction, but he also came under the jurisdiction of a
county court–appointed guardian. An epic struggle ensued when Commissioner Burke attempted to destroy the corrupt Oklahoma guardianship
system by asserting full federal control over Barnett's property. The bureau's
well-meaning decision to transfer Barnett's "surplus" wealth to the Baptist
Bacone College as an educational endowment for Indian people and the remainder to his wife, Anna, brought heavy criticism of the bureau's alleged
high-handedness in the administration of Indian wards' property.

Jackson's great wealth combined with his status as a restricted or incompetent Indian made for a volatile brew of legal complications. The
question of whether Jackson was of sound mind when he married Anna
was a sensational issue that drove the litigation forward. Litigation over
Jackson's estate put the question of his competency and the very definition
of the competency of Indians under intense scrutiny and into public dis-
course. How did the bureau differentiate between incompetent and competent Indians? What was the constitutional basis for the paternalistic authority the bureau exercised over restricted Indians, and what were its
limits? To what extent was federal jurisdiction over incompetent Indians
limited by the Okmulgee County court jurisdiction over this alleged mental incompetent? Did the bureau's authority extend as far as the right to
"give away" Jackson Barnett's estate to Bacone and to Anna Lowe Barnett,
and had Congress granted the bureau the discretionary authority to make
this distribution? Did Barnett's Creek relations have a superior claim on
the estate? Since it took nearly a half century and prolonged litigation in
dozens of courts, a large share of the Barnett estate was ground to dust in
trying to answer these questions.

The intractable problems of the rich Indians brought the best and worst aspects of the paternalistic policies of the bureau toward all Indians into clearer focus. The vast majority of Jackson Barnett's Indian contemporaries were quietly dispossessed and impoverished with little public outcry (since non-Indians reaped the advantage of the redistribution). But Jackson Barnett was fated to become the prototypical rich Indian. His wealth captured the popular imagination, producing a "distorted popular impression . . . of the extraordinary wealth attained by Oklahoma Indians through the production of oil on their land."[18]

The good-natured Creek was the joyful affirmation of the American dream: Jackson was the person least likely to succeed. He was a hapless, unassertive underachiever from a marginalized, impoverished racial minority. He was also simple, virtuous, and astoundingly lucky. He was the Greek Croessus, the European Cinderella, and the African-Muskogean Brer Rabbit rolled into one. Jackson only fell upward. Public fascination with the scandalous exploitation of one prominent, wealthy Indian in the end helped raise public awareness about the plight of Jackson's less-fortunate contemporaries. Representative of a people whose historical experience is unremittingly tragic, Jackson Barnett provides comic relief and cosmic justice.

Barnett enjoyed a brief but glorious reign as a wealthy Indian. He was the Indian whose estate was micromanaged rather than neglected. He was happily married to a harridan. His chief benefactor was his gold-digging wife. Though he was the consummate victim, he was happy rather than pathetic or disillusioned. He remained serene and self-possessed though publicly labeled a moron. Everyone had a hand in his pocket, but he freely gave his wealth away. Perhaps the richest contradiction of all was that Jackson Barnett—in the bureau's convoluted logic—was a competent "incompetent" Indian.

One of the great ironies of the story of the World's Richest Indian is that Jackson Barnett supported Chitto Harjo, or Crazy Snake, who refused to accept individualized shares of the Creek domain as an act of political resistance. An Indian agent once facetiously commented that Jackson Barnett could not be too stupid if he realized allotment was not in the Indians' best interests. Over a thousand of Chitto Harjo's Creek followers, called Snakes, were arbitrarily assigned allotments in the barren and rocky lands of Creek County in violation of their political convictions and their wishes. Seventy to eighty Snakes held roughly half of the lucrative oil leases in the Cushing field. These recalcitrant Snakes, who opposed the partition of Creek communal lands with every means available, garnered immense fortunes from their individual allotments, an irony that one author acknowledged by titling a chapter on this subject "Indians Have the Last Laugh."[19]

As Jackson Barnett's case illustrates, the architects of the allotment policy displayed a shameless ignorance of Indians' needs, values, skills, or preferences. The human cost of illegally dissolving the Creek nation and partitioning its lands against the people's will was incalculable. The U.S. government betrayed its treaty with the Creek. The Creek institutions were crushed and the nation's resources stolen. The elderly and harmless Jackson Barnett became the unlikely instrument of revenge on the American legal system. His case contributed to the cessation of the allotment policy in a bizarre and unexpected manner.

Protracted litigation over and U.S. political attention on this one extraordinary fortune brought long-postponed national awareness of the evils of allotment. The Barnett scandal added impetus to the reform movement that led to the Indian New Deal. The symbol of a diseased national Indian policy, Jackson Barnett's case illuminates the intricacies and paradoxes of Indian policy in the early twentieth century.

I

Please Pass the Injin Territory

Well so the preacher bow his head and say, "O Lord, we was mighty thankful for this feast. Please pass the possum." Same way Oklahoma was pray to Congress, saying, "We was mighty thankful for statehood. "Please pass the Injin Territory."
—ALEX POSEY'S "HOTGUN"

Traveling through the Creek nation on his way to Edward's Trading Post on the Canadian River in early February 1842, Ethan Allen Hitchcock beheld from the summit of a hill a most breathtakingly beautiful prairie, timbered hills, and valleys. Some of the hills, broken from their connection with a range, presented "isolated objects of beauty." Descending from this summit, he arrived at the homestead of "Old Man" Conner, a mixed-blood Creek trader married to a Creek woman, Conner and his family lived apart from the Creeks. The family of eight or ten had small outbuildings for storage, two mud-chinked log houses, and a corn mill with saddles, bridles, lariats, and a great variety of other things hanging from the rafters. Rail fences enclosed the houses and the horse pen. Hitchcock found specimens of pottery along with tools, such as augers and chisels, and, to his great relief, a bedstead. For his meal, Hitchcock enjoyed good coffee with sugar, fried pork and eggs, and native corn bread.[1]

Jackson Barnett, alleged to be Old Man Conner's grandson, was born around 1856 in the Creek Nation in Indian Territory, in what is today McIntosh County in eastern Oklahoma. His life began inauspiciously as the child of a transient union between Siah Barnett and Thlesothle (or Betty). Though Jackson Barnett is usually typed as a traditional Creek full-blood, this label glossed a hybridized genetic and cultural identity not uncommon among the Creek. While his mother was a full- or mixed-blood Creek, Jackson Barnett's father Siah was a freedman; Siah's father, Tom Barnett, was a Scottish-Creek mixed-blood who had three children with his African-Creek cook, Hannah Sullivan. Hannah is listed on the 1860 federal census as an Alabama-born farmer. The notation "B" after Siah's and Hannah's names in the census records identifies them as having African ancestry.[2]

Little is known of the courtship of Jackson's father and mother, except that they were soon parted. Siah, in his twenties in the 1850s, was characterized as having many love interests. He formed a lasting union with Mary Beams (an African-Choctaw woman of the Bear Clan), and they had five children. Their eldest child, David Barnett, was born between 1854 and 1858, quite possibly before the birth of his half brother Jackson. Jackson had a weak connection with his father in early life and was brought up by his mother's family, primarily because the Creek were matrilineal. He drew his town membership, Tuckabatchee, from his mother who had three sons with different fathers. In the 1857 and 1859 Tuckabatchee Town payrolls, Jackson was listed in a family group headed by Thlesothle and including older brothers Tecumseh (Cumsey Antrew) and Haryaryeche (aka Jim Lowe). Jackson's lack of contact with his biological father may also have been rooted in the Creek law that barred a freedman from marrying an Indian woman.[3]

There are many unknowns in Jackson Barnett's genealogy, which complicated the determination of heirs after Jackson's death and demonstrated how imprecise the Indian bureau's blood quantum distinctions were, though decisions vitally important to Indians' lives were based on the crude and proximate data in its files. Jackson's paternal grandmother, Hannah, may have been pure African, one of the British "gifts" of slaves to the Creek after the American Revolution, or she may well have been a *zambo,* the child of a union between an African and an Indian. Such unions were common in the eighteenth century in the Southeast. Old Man Conner was perhaps the son of Jack Kinnaird, a well-to-do Scots "half-breed" trader and slave owner, and was either one-half or three-quarters Creek. It was customary among traders to marry either full-blood women of important clans in which they were trading or *mestizas,* the term for European-Indian "half-breeds."[4] Rather than being the daughter of Old Man Conner, much evidence suggests that Thlesothle was the sister of "Uncle" John Leecher, who was born around 1790 and operated a ferry conveying supplies and travelers across the Arkansas above Fort Gibson. Leecher was a venerated conjurer and prophet, who could stun wild animals with his powers. Jackson spent his early years working as a ferryman for Uncle Leecher. Jackson had no memory of any of his Conner kin or, for that matter, his half brothers, Tecumseh and Haryaryeche. Whether Jackson Barnett's maternal grandmother was the mother of the remarkable Uncle Leecher cannot be determined with finality, but what is known with certainty is that Thlesothle's mother was a Tuckabatchee. In simplified terms, Jackson was predominantly Muskogee, part Yuchi, and approximately equal amounts of white and black ancestry. Jackson is identified on a 1914 disbursement document as "3/4 Creek" and on allotment documents as a full-blood Creek. On a 1920 census, he is listed simply as an Indian.[5]

Jackson Barnett's ancestry underscores Creek pluralism and the historical pattern of frequent unions among Indians of different towns and tribes, Africans, and Indian-white trader families. On at least one side of his family, and perhaps both, Jackson's ancestors included white traders who married Indian women and held African slaves. Because of the matrilineal nature of Creek clans, a trader who married a Creek woman was not categorically different than a Creek marriage partner. The children of these unions were fully integrated into Creek society under its matrilineal system as members of their mothers' clans and towns. The Barnetts, including the African-Creek Barnetts, were mixed-bloods who resided within the Creek Nation, identified as Creeks, spoke Creek, and were entrepreneurial in merchandising and in developing herds of livestock and plantations. The economic ambitions, material culture, religious leanings, and co-residency with blacks accentuated trader families' affiliation with the acculturative or progressive changes in Creek national life. Jackson's family background thus situates him within the sphere of entrepreneurial, mixed-blood families of the Creek Nation, though later in life he was affiliated with the Creek traditionalists.

Dualisms like progressivism and conservatism dissolve in the dynamic syntheses of Creek culture and identity as the example of Uncle Leecher, conjurer and ferry operator, graphically illustrates. The Creek were both ancient and modern. In the mid–nineteenth century, their material culture closely resembled that of white southerners, yet their beliefs and ceremonial practices dated back to the chiefdoms of the Moundbuilders. The Creek held to ancient philosophies, institutions, and a staple food, sofkey (or boiled corn), while seamlessly integrating European clothing and tools, domesticated animals, and African-American slaves into their society. Hitchcock described what to him appeared to be the eclectic Upper Creek dress of the 1840s: shirts of calico belted at the waist, buckskin leggings, and moccasins. More prominent Creeks wore turbans and shirts of fine broadcloth.[6]

Pluralism was a defining characteristic of the Creek, an aggregation of diverse peoples fused into one nation. More accurately understood as a confederacy of politically autonomous towns rather than as a tribe, the Creek— a Muskogean-speaking people—displayed a remarkable ability to absorb new peoples, ideas, and technologies to strengthen their economy, culture, and confederacy. Jackson Barnett's paternal great-great-grandmother was a Yuchi (or Euchee). A once-powerful chiefdom that joined the Creek confederacy in the early eighteenth century, the Yuchi had a language in-

comprehensible to the Muskogean-speaking Creek. Within the Creek confederacy, the Yuchi maintained their distinct language, customs of patrilineal descent, and other cultural traditions in their own politically autonomous communities. The Muskogee absorbed many non-Muskogean
peoples into their confederacy in this manner, including Hitchiti, Alabama,
and smaller decimated or refugee groups, like the Natchez and the Shawnee.
Early in its history of alliance formation with non-Muskogean towns, the
Creek Nation divided into two broad groups (halves or moieties): Musko-
gees and foreigners. This moiety division is one expression of the governing
principles of dualism and opposition that permeated the Creek world view
and shaped the tribe's philosophies and institutions. The dialectic between
paired opposites—white (peace) and red (war) principles, male and female,
Muskogee and non-Muskogee—was central to the way the Creek viewed
the world. The Creek accommodated different peoples and lifeways, and yet
rivalries and conflicts were an endemic part of Creek life.[7]

While the Creek Nation selectively integrated foreigners and their cultural contributions, Creek identity remained grounded in town organization. The *talwa,* or town, encompassing a number of surrounding villages,
was the foundational economic, political, and ceremonial unit in Creek
life. The matrilineal clans were affiliated either with white or red moieties,
creating a balanced but oppositional social structure. An aristocratic *micco,*
or king, was the town ruler, while subchiefs, or "lawyers," executed the
law. Surrounding the town were fenced fields, a communal field, and privately tilled lands. Each town had its square grounds and ball fields. The
major public celebration was the annual Green Corn ceremony, four days
of thanksgiving in which the Creeks fasted and purified themselves with
an emetic called the "black drink," hunted, stomp danced, relit the sacred
fire, then feasted. In the ball games, the women of the town squared off
against the men—or towns or moieties competed against one another—in
vigorous bids for supremacy.[8]

The two grand geopolitical divisions in the Creek Nation in the nineteenth century were the Lower and Upper Creeks, and Jackson Barnett's
ancestors included both. Before the Creeks relocated to Indian Territory in
the 1820s and 1830s, the Lower Creeks occupied towns along the Flint and
Chatahoochee rivers in what is now south-central Georgia. The Upper
Creeks lived along the Coosa and Tallapoosa branches of the Alabama
River to the west. These divisions reflected ethnic differences and separate
cultural orientations. The Upper Creek towns tended to adhere to older
Muskogean institutions, customs, and religious practices, while the Lower
Creeks were more racially and ethnically complex and included many
non-Muskogean peoples of the Creek confederacy. In the eighteenth century the Lower Creeks lived in close proximity to Spanish and English At-
lantic seaboard settlements, participated in the deerskin trade, and assimi-
lated African-American runaways and Euro-American traders into their
communities.

While both of Jackson Barnett's parents are identified as members of Tuckabatchee Town, the ceremonial center and capital of the Upper Creeks, Siah Barnett's paternal ancestors were Lower Creeks. Siah Barnett was the great-grandson of Timothy Barnard, a Scotsman with English citizenship who traded for a British firm, Leslie, Panton, and Company. He later served as an interpreter for the U.S. government. Timothy Barnard married a Yuchi woman, and they had eleven children. In addition to carrying on trade, the Barnards had a plantation with large herds of livestock, fruit trees, and other crops. African slaves did the labor, including spinning cotton. Timothy Barnard's son, Timpoochee Barnard, fought alongside Andrew Jackson during the War of 1812 to deliver a devastating defeat to the Creek Red Sticks at the battle of Horseshoe Bend. The Red Stick War, as the Creek called it, was a civil war: white factions favored accommodation with the Americans whereas the red factions, or "sticks," were militantly anti-American. Admiration for Andrew Jackson as a warrior accounts for the popularity of the name "Jackson" in later generations within the Barnard family. ("Barnett" was a corruption of "Barnard.") That Jackson Barnett, an African-Creek, was named for a white man who both owned slaves and dispossessed Indians was one of the many ironies of Jackson's life.[9]

By the nineteenth century, the Creek had a powerful confederacy of many towns, notable for its many mixed-race citizens and for its acculturation to European-American lifeways. African-American slaves or fugitives, Euro-American traders, missionaries, and non-Muskogean Native Americans were all agents of change in Creek life. For example, as Indian agent Benjamin Hawkins observed: "Where [Africans] are, there is more industry and better farms."[10] At the instigation of President Thomas Jefferson, who was promoting an assimilation policy in the early 1800s, Hawkins helped the Creek to form a national council based on town representation, to develop a written law code, and to adopt Anglo-American crops, tools, and farming methods. In imitation of the mixed-bloods' example, the Creek began adopting domesticated animals and manufacturing their own cloth once the supply of wild game declined.

Because of the marked success in mirroring the cultural forms of Euro-Americans, the Creek and their neighbors in the Southeast—the Cherokee, Choctaw, Chickasaw, and Seminole—acquired the collective label of the "Five Civilized Tribes." Following the War of 1812, the tribes faced a crisis. If they accelerated their progress toward "civilization," they could hope to remain on their lands in the southeastern United States. If they did not, they would be resettled west of the Mississippi River. Under the leadership of a literate mixed-blood planter elite, the Five Civilized Tribes adopted certain aspects of the dominant political culture in order to preserve their homelands. The Cherokees' crowning achievement in 1827 was the ratification of a constitution with a tripartite division of powers, giving undeniable proof of their ability to govern themselves. The Five

Civilized Tribes met the conditions for coexistence within the American legal system. Their growing political sophistication, however, did not prevent the loss of their aboriginal homelands in what would become the rich areas of cotton cultivation in the deep South, but it postponed and complicated the process. Following the Removal Act of 1830, the Five Civilized Tribes were coerced into surrendering their lands in treaties and were colonized in the Indian Territory west of the Mississippi River. In their removal treaties, however, the Five Civilized Tribes secured relatively high payments for their eastern lands, lands of comparable size and value in the West, and strong guarantees of federal protection for their sovereign rights in Indian Territory.[11]

Twenty years before Jackson Barnett's birth, his Upper Creek relations suffered scarring tragedy and bitter disillusionment on the Creek Trail of Tears. During the removal crisis, the leader of the Lower Creek, mixed-blood William McIntosh, capitulated to the pressure to relocate and signed a land cession treaty. Approximately 3,000 Lower Creeks moved to the lands in the northeastern part of the Creek Nation, West, in the late 1820s. Many Creeks, including Tuckabatchee Opothleyahola, viewed McIntosh as a traitor and adamantly opposed surrendering their homelands. Resistance leaders among the Upper and Lower Creeks were compelled to sign a treaty in 1832 surrendering all Creek lands east of the Mississippi, but only after they had been given verbal promises by U.S. Secretary of War Lewis Cass that lands in Indian Territory would be theirs "as long as the grass grows and the rivers run."[12] An important concession in the 1832 treaty was that those Creeks who chose to remain in the home territory in Alabama could do so if they took up individual allotments and submitted to state jurisdiction. The brief experiment in assimilation via allotment was a fiasco. Intrusion, fraudulent land transfers, intimidation, violence, and ultimately homelessness drove some desperate Creeks to retaliate, triggering the forced deportations in 1836–1837. After these hostile Creeks were removed in manacles, the rest of the Creeks followed in separate parties. One experienced disaster in a steamboat accident, while others traveled across Arkansas in the winter to reach Indian Territory. Jackson's grandmother Hannah, her young son Siah, and other children were probably among the freezing, starving, bedraggled, and heartbroken Creeks on the ice- and snowbound roads. After they arrived at Fort Gibson on the Arkansas River, rations were short due to profiteering by contractors, and Creeks were cheated out of their annuities. Suffering and failing health reduced the Creek women's ability to reproduce, and few infants were seen in the nation for two years after this tragically mismanaged deportation. Estimates place the total Creek deaths from disease, exposure, natural disasters, and hunger at 7,000–10,000 or 33–45 percent of the people. By 1857, 14,888 people were enumerated. Opothleyahola ultimately accepted the McIntosh family's leadership in Creek Nation, West, but he remained bitter and suspicious.[13]

The conflicts between the Upper and Lower Creeks were carried over from the Creek Nation, East, as the Creeks reestablished their towns and institutions in the new Creek Nation, West. The Lower Creeks settled in the northeastern part of the nation along the Arkansas and were joined by 4,000 of the later immigrants. The more affluent mixed-bloods in the McIntosh faction abandoned the town organization, built log homes, fenced their fields, and enjoyed a high standard of material comfort based on slave labor. Many of the Upper Creeks moved to the Canadian River and settled in the fertile region near Eufaula, eventually spreading out to the south and west of the Lower Creeks along the forks of the Canadian. The Upper Creek capital of Tuckabatchee, with its great *tcokofa,* or round house, where the sacred fire was housed, was rebuilt near the Canadian River. Most Creeks resumed their town farming methods and their political and ceremonial practices. Each of the forty-five towns sent its *micco* to the upper House of Kings and one or more secondary chiefs to the lower House of Warriors in the two-chamber Creek National Council.[14]

The Creek reproduced their polity to the best of their ability in Indian Territory, but the removal era's violent disruptions and population losses set changes in motion. Towns became political rather than geographic divisions. The ethnic, racial, and cultural distinctions between the Upper and Lower Creeks progressively eroded due to intermarriages and migrations of families within the nation. Dualistic notions of clearly demarcated full-blood Upper Creek "traditionalists," who adhered to orthodox religious practices and farming methods, and Lower Creek mixed-blood "progressives," who owned slaves and embraced Anglo-American economic and religious values, fail to reflect the complex reality of the pluralistic Creek Nation at midcentury. In the vanguard of those leaving the towns were African-Creeks and freedmen, such as Siah Barnett's family, who bucked the concept of communal lands and wanted to carve out family farms. Religious beliefs and practices also underwent a change after 1848 as Baptist and Presbyterian missionaries proselytized and made many converts. Those anchored in the town structure and those innovating with more individualistic lifeways became receptive to Christianity as a flood of alcohol into the Creek Nation disrupted Creek ceremonies and other public events. This threatened community order and blocked demographic and economic recovery. Christian principles and practices were welcomed because they were constructive socially. For many if not most Creeks in the last half of the nineteenth century, Christianity reinforced rather than displaced older practices and beliefs; they continued to celebrate the Busks, or Green Corn, ceremony.[15]

Jackson Barnett's experience is representative of the many Creeks susceptible to the forces undermining town identities and transforming Creek culture at midcentury. Though he drew his legitimacy as a member of the Creek Nation from his mother's membership in Tuckabatchee Town, he never lived within the communal town structure of Tuckabatchee in Creek

Nation, West. Jackson had no known clan or moiety affiliation. He embraced neither Christian nor Creek religions but attended ceremonies of each on occasion. Though Muskogee was his native tongue, he learned English at an early age and was bilingual.

Jackson's earliest years were difficult ones for the Creek. The resilient Creek rebounded with a "miracle of reconstruction" in the 1840s and 1850s only to plunge into war again in the 1860s.[16] Like the removal era a generation earlier, the Civil War brought bitter factionalism, material losses, population decline, and displacement. The McIntosh faction, which included Jackson's cousin Timothy Barnett—slave-owning entrepreneurial mixed-bloods who dominated Lower Creek politics—favored the Confederacy. To stifle the opposition of powerful men like Opothleyahola, who were neutral or loyal to the Union, pro-Confederate Creeks put a bounty on their heads. As a result, approximately 8,000 Creeks—more than half of the Creek population, including many African-Creeks and slaves—fled to Kansas early in the war. Most of these "Loyal" (or pro-Union) Creek refugees returned during the course of the war and sought protection at Fort Gibson, a Union stronghold on the Arkansas River on the eastern edge of Creek territory. While these refugee Creeks suffered from starvation, disease, and exposure in Kansas and later at Fort Gibson, pro-Confederate Creeks also were driven from their homes. Union and Confederate forces counted on Creeks for both loyalty and provisions from cattle herds and farms. Multiple catastrophes—war, dispossession, ruined farms, and lost stock—struck the Creek Nation, and fratricidal violence claimed many lives.[17]

Like many others, Jackson's family was violently split by war loyalties. Tecumseh, Jackson's half brother, went to Kansas in the war years. The dislocations of the Civil War years attenuated Jackson's contact with his father during his early childhood. Siah, his mother, and brother Jim were among the Loyal Creek refugee group, and Siah sought reimbursement from the federal government for the material losses sustained during the war. Jackson retained few memories of his childhood or early adulthood and remembered neither his mother nor father. His earliest memory was of a "horse and a cow."[18]

Jackson became a refugee and orphan during the war years. In the summer of 1863, the Union commander at Fort Gibson ordered Jackson's maternal grandfather and his family to come to the fort, perhaps because he wanted to oversee the activities of Confederate sympathizers. Jackson Barnett and his mother presumably joined his grandfather Conner and other maternal relatives in their move to Fort Gibson. A more likely explanation is that the Conners, like most Creeks, fled to Fort Gibson for food and military protection. By the war's end, nearly 20,000 desperate Indians were living around Fort Gibson, but they were inadequately provisioned because of the activities of bushwhackers (raiders), congressional stinginess, and the fraudulent practices of suppliers. Thlesothle died at this refugee camp when Jackson was seven or eight. "Jackson was an orphan of the Civil war," recalled Billy McCombs, a Creek Baptist preacher, years later. "[A]s is always the case in such camps," said McCombs, "there were epidemics which carried off many people."[19] Aunt Jennie Conner and her husband, Jeffrey, took in Jackson and his cousin, but the couple had a hard time providing for their nephews. Jennie, according to McCombs's account, approached the McCombs family to take eight-year-old Jackson, and the McCombs cared for Jackson for five or six years until Uncle Leecher and other maternal kin claimed him. Jackson was persuaded to go with these "strangers" to the ferry northwest of Muskogee (located where the Spaulding bridge was later built), said McCombs. "He received wages, and that kept him satisfied."[20] While McCombs faithfully recalled the Creeks' brutal wartime experiences at Fort Gibson and his report about the Conners' travails has the ring of truth, Jackson himself had no memory of living with the McCombs family as a child. McCombs perhaps embellished the truth to get remuneration for aiding Barnett during his lean youthful years and to support the Conner family's claim to kinship.

For several years spanning adolescence to early adulthood, Jackson worked alongside his maternal half brother Tecumseh transporting goods across the Arkansas and Verdigris rivers north of Muskogee on ferries owned and operated by Uncle Leecher. Jackson put down the boards so the wagons could roll onto the ferry and then poled the ferry across the river. Jackson remembered this ferrying work vividly as well as driving horses and cattle. Life on the Arkansas River between the Cherokee and Creek nations was lawless with contraband whiskey being brought into Indian Territory. In the postwar period, a vicious community of horse and cattle thieves and bootleggers lived in the vicinity where Jackson Barnett worked as a ferryman. Circumstantial evidence and some suspect testimony given at court proceedings years later suggest that Jackson drank heavily and engaged in bootlegging during his years in this vicinity. He allegedly married a teenage African-American girl whose sister ran a sporting house. Jackson remembered his work ferrying and ranching, but not the drinking, bootlegging, or marriage.[21]

In addition to his work as a ferryman, Jackson also worked as a cowboy during his early adulthood. Several sources verify that Jackson worked for a rancher, Colonel William Robison, a mixed-blood Creek who served as a Confederate colonel. While herding cattle for Robison, Jackson sustained a serious head injury. He recalled that his leg became hung up on a strap when he was riding with the colonel's son, Fred Robison. In a later court appearance, Jackson initially denied that he received a head injury, but when asked, "Where was your head hurt?" he answered, "Hurt right through here," placing his hand on his forehead. That he received a head injury appears true; its severity is debatable. Jackson reputedly rode his horse into town after the accident, according to another kinsman, William Sullivan.[22]

While Jackson passed over the accident as insignificant, other witnesses magnified the seriousness of the injury as the cause for Jackson's alleged mental weakness, including his rather sketchy recall of the events of the first sixty years of his life. A Creek woman, Mary Fields, testified that the accident left Jackson incapacitated with constant pain and blindness, injuries requiring a year's care by Fields's grandmother and Jackson's stepmother, Mary Beams Barnett. Fields's opinion was that Jackson was not "right in the head" after this incident. She said that he was abnormally shy with women. He would repeat whatever was said to him, and he talked about people who were long dead. Later in life, Jackson occasionally identified himself as a deceased cousin, Josh Asbury (Siah's sister Lizzie's son), with whom he lived and worked and with whom he formed a very close emotional bond. Another Creek witness, Jack Dunsey, verified the details of the injury. Dunsey said Jackson was injured while he was drunk and afterward was unusually reclusive.[23]

If Jackson Barnett were mentally damaged enough to affect his behavior and mental capabilities, he nonetheless maintained a self-sufficient lifestyle, supporting himself as an unskilled laborer during his adult life. Though he did many types of jobs in his lifetime, he never became an entrepreneur, business owner, or master of any skill. He knew how to use a hammer and saw, for example, but he denied any claim to being a carpenter. "I just knocked around different places," Jackson recalled, plowing, hoeing, cutting wood, working for wages, and making up to $2–3 a day.[24]

Though Jackson Barnett was a confirmed bachelor and rather shy and slow, to say he was an antisocial misfit would overstate the case. Jackson was continually included and supported in a social web of Creek friends and relations. He made regular visits to his relatives, who welcomed his labor as a field hand during extended stays. Sympathetic Creek kinfolk fed and clothed him in times of sickness. Whether he was considered eccentric or even crazy is highly debatable. Jackson was a gentle and amiable man who enjoyed affection and care in the communal society of the Creek people.

Jackson Barnett's life underwent a change for the better as the Creek regained their social cohesion and their economic stability in the postwar period. Many Creeks remembered the brief interlude after the Civil War as a golden age, a time of peace and prosperity after violent upheaval. Prosperity returned as they rebuilt their homes and reestablished lives on the resource-rich, well-watered, and fertile land of the Creek Nation. The Creek had lost half of their territory (more than 3 million acres) as the price for the disloyalty of a Creek minority during the Civil War, but they still enjoyed a large landed estate for their population of roughly 14,000. Under pressure from mixed-bloods, the Creek after the war created a constitutional government but retained the town system of representation. More ambitious and entrepreneurial people grazed large herds on the communally owned Creek domain. The average Creek farmer owned a wagon and plow, farm tools, several horses, cattle, hogs, and fowl. Domesticated animals fed on the ample Creek range, which held an abundance of wild game, berries, honeybees, and other resources. The African-Creek slaves freed after the war, as well as mixed-blood and full-blood Creeks, enjoyed well-being as food was plentiful. During this time, according to Creek man of letters Alex Posey, the Indians were "happy with a cabin, sofkey patch, plentiful game, horses, and domestic herds."[25] More conservative Creeks enjoyed security in their towns. With some effort, one could accumulate material wealth, or one could simply subsist comfortably on nature's bounty. Wealthy Creek Pleasant Porter recalled the "idyllic conditions" of his boyhood, saying that the Creeks "always raised enough to eat and that was all we wanted. . . . The country was prosperous. In fact in my early life I don't know that I ever knew of an Indian family that were paupers. . . . They were all prosperous and happy and contented in their way."[26]

In this golden age, the Creek engaged the new frontiers of industrial progress, Christianity, and education. In particular, education and Christianity were viewed by many as a means to national security and prosperity. The Five Civilized Tribes provided financial support for educational institutions run by missionaries, who taught in the Indian languages. Literacy rates rose. Creek optimism was due in part to the great strides in education within the democratic framework of the Baptist religion. A case in point is the establishment of Bacone Indian University at Muskogee in the Creek Nation. Founded by northern Baptists with a vision of a first-class Christian university for Indian people that would provide theological training for a native ministry, Bacone received land from the Creek National Council in the early 1880s at the urging of Billy McCombs, a mixed-blood Baptist preacher. John D. Rockefeller donated the money for the first magnificent building—an English-style edifice made from home-manufactured bricks. Institutions providing primary education—like Tahlequah in the Cherokee Nation—sent their graduates to Bacone. With high academic standards and bilingual teachers, Bacone trained a generation of tribal leaders, professionals, and ministers. One of the most remarkable Bacone graduates was Alex Posey, son of a Tuskegee woman and a Baptist minister. Posey became an acclaimed poet and humorist. His *Fus Fixico* letters in Indian vernacular is a classic of Indian satirical humor.[27] Posey and other educated and Christianized leaders of this generation, particularly mixed-bloods, were eager to shake off the dominant culture's stigmatization of Indians as backward, communal, and racially inferior. A number competed capably with white people in their endeavors.

What sabotaged the Creek Nation was the migration of overwhelming numbers of African Americans and Euro-Americans, concomitant with the intensifying external pressures to integrate Creek resources into the American economy. The demographic and economic transformations in the Creek Nation became a cancer that the Creek had no power to arrest. The expansion of the cattle industry stimulated the building of railroads across Creek country. The Creek Treaty of 1866 gave a right-of-way across Creek land. New York stockholders J. Pierpont Morgan, John D. Rockefeller, and others of the Missouri, Kansas and Texas Railway lobbied Congress to open the Five Civilized Tribes' reservations to white settlement. Beginning with a rail link to Muskogee in the early 1870s, the railroad system extended farther and farther into Creek territory. Rail towns became beachheads for noncitizens, who were eager to profit by exploiting the resources of the Creek Nation. The construction of the railroad was like "a devastating pestilence" as it passed through the country, wrote Grant Foreman.[28] Prostitutes, gamblers, and land speculators arrived with the railroad workers. The railways encouraged the invasion of intruders by announcing in Missouri newspapers that Indian Territory was open to white settlement, though such entry was unlawful. Six thousand whites infiltrated eastern Indian Territory—the domain of the Five Civilized Tribes—in 1880. The railroads provided access to national markets, and cotton and hides became important Creek exports. African Americans from older areas of the South were attracted to the Creek Nation by work in cotton cultivation, free access to land and resources, and the markedly tolerant social and political climate. Newcomers did not conform to Creek ways nor defer to Creek institutions. The rapid rise in the unassimilated, non-Muskogean-speaking, colored population alarmed the Creek. Black immigrants combined with African-Creeks comprised approximately one-third of the population in the Creek Nation in the 1890s. Pleasant Porter, who served as chief executive of the nation, told a Senate committee in the 1890s: "We have striven in our own way for our elevation and uplifting, and for a time it seemed that we were actually going to evolve a sort of civilization that would suit our temperament; and we probably would have if it had not been for this white and black invasion."[29]

With the coming of the railroads, the Creek and their resources were drawn into the market economy. Among the immediate changes were the disappearance of game and hunting grounds, the presence of traveling salesmen, the growing indebtedness of Creek citizens, the rapid expansion of the ranching industry, and the clearing of forests. Porter became one of the Creek cattle barons who used Creek law to monopolize thousands of acres of Creek land for his personal use. Town lots were bought and sold. Grazing lands were leased, the range was fenced, Creek leaders were corrupted through bribery. Each was an irreversible sign of "progress." A minority of entrepreneurial and educated Creeks welcomed such changes while the majority of Creeks were bewildered and sporadically resisted. As Porter remarked approvingly in 1891, the Creek had made steady progress and "unconsciously passed over from a system of communism to that of individualism."[30]

By 1890, there were 210,000 non-Indians and 140,000 Indians in the Five Civilized Tribes domain of Indian Territory. Creek towns had become small islands engulfed in an ocean of foreigners. The new arrivals were covetous of Indian resources and impervious to Indian customs and laws. Theoretically, non-Indians were permitted to reside temporarily in the Creek Nation only after obtaining work permits from the tribal governments. But such political control was fragile at best. Because the Creek had no legal jurisdiction over U.S. citizens, control of crime became a problem. Cattle rustling, the rule of guns and whiskey, and violent personal vendettas were visible signs of what some perceived as rampant lawlessness. Adding to the perceived chaos, civil war broke out between two Creek factions. Historian Angie Debo comments, "The tribe waged a losing battle with cattlemen, intruders, increasing crime, and most of all, with the United States."[31]

The pressure to privatize and individualize the Indians' landed estate and tribal assets via allotment was the political issue that brought the demographic and economic developments to a head. During the 1880s, momentum was building in Congress to pass the Dawes Allotment Act, which unilaterally imposed allotment on all communally held lands of American Indian tribes. Allotting each Indian head of family a 160-acre farm to be held in fee-simple title (as private property was legally held among the non-Indian population), it was believed, would speed Indians from a state of barbarism to civilization. Conformity to American ideals of private property ownership would eliminate the legal, cultural, economic, and political obstacles to full assimilation. The purpose of the national reform movement foisting allotment on Indians was to achieve equality under the law. Equality and full citizenship in the American republic, once tribalism and communalism were destroyed, was the idealistic goal. While ideology was a source of the Dawes Act's appeal, the driving engine behind allotment was economic. Once in place, the act would facilitate private entrepreneurs' access to the considerable wealth of the Five Civilized Tribes, which was vested in land, trust funds, and resources (see appendix I). Railways in particular pressured Congress to make the Indians of the Five Civilized Tribes citizens, because their ventures would only be profitable if non-Indian commercial farmers and ranchers populated the region.

Although the tribes argued that forced allotment was an infringement of their treaties, the Five Civilized Tribes' well-guarded sovereign rights were destroyed. Beginning in the early 1880s the Creeks organized politically, hoping the changes undermining their way of life could be halted or reversed by gaining control of the Creek Council. One Creek, Isparhecher, led a revolt in the early 1880s and drew the support of many Upper Creek, who had no illusions about allotment. Isparhecher remembered the calamitous experiences of the Alabama Creeks, who had opted for allotment of their lands as an alternative to removal to Indian Territory in the 1830s. He correctly predicted a repeat of their experience: taxation leading to confiscation, wasting litigation over clouded land titles, and, ultimately, homelessness for the allottees.[32]

Using their treaty contracts and political skills, the Creek, Cherokee,

Chickasaw, Choctaw, and Seminole succeeded in winning an exemption from the 1887 Dawes Act mandating allotment. But this victory won them only a temporary reprieve from allotment and destruction of their nations. Determined to break the legal roadblocks presented by these tribes, the federal government authorized the Dawes Commission to negotiate with the Five Civilized Tribes. The commission set out to mobilize public opinion against these Indians, claiming to have found lawless conditions in Indian Territory, great inequalities in wealth, and treatment of blacks as second-class citizens. Senator Henry Dawes presented these unsubstantiated claims at a meeting at Lake Mohonk that was attended by prominent citizens who played an influential role in shaping Indian policy in Congress. Relentless federal pressure forced the tribes into negotiations on the allotment issue. Realizing in 1892–1893 that allotment was inevitable, leaders of the Five Civilized Tribes sent out circulars to their people warning that Congress would abrogate their treaties and liquidate their republics.[33] Meanwhile, the Dawes Commission began surveying Creek lands in anticipation of allotment.

The Creek were shocked into temporary paralysis by the "bold effrontery" of the U.S. government's actions, wrote one Creek, George Washington Grayson.[34] The Indians had treaties that guaranteed their land rights, but these legal contracts afforded no protections if the political will of the U.S. citizenry turned against them. A Cherokee delegation to Washington wrote home to their chief in 1895:

> It did seem as if the world was about to rise in arms against us. We saw that even the press had been largely subsidized in favor of the dissolution of our government and invasion of our rights. . . . [E]ven benevolent associations which were organized a few year[s] ago to urge Congress to keep the treaties which had been made with Indian tribes, are now advising the erection of a territorial government in our country and allotment of our lands in violation of our treaties and without our consent. . . . No church assembly now passes resolutions against a violation of our treaties, the abrogation of our government and an invasion of our right of property. . . . But there seems to be a sinister motive for keeping the intruders in our country. It was the contents of the wooden horse emptied inside the walls of Troy, that enabled the Greeks to take that ancient city.[35]

The death knell for the Five Civilized Tribes' sovereignty was the Curtis Act of 1898, a law disbanding their governments. Creek leaders Isparhecher and Porter recognized that resistance to allotment was futile and set about trying to mitigate the damage to the Creek people. Unlike the other Indians whose lands were subject to allotment by the Dawes Act, the Five Civilized Tribes formally surrendered to the majority will via individual tribal compacts, that is, bilateral agreements. As a last vestige of their legal rights and political power, the Five Civilized Tribes were able to participate in the negotiations over the terms of their capitulation. In 1901, the Creek signed their compact—subsequently approved by Congress— agreeing to allotment, but prohibiting the resale of individualized property for five years and exempting Creek allotted lands from taxation for twenty-one years. Each Creek would receive 160 acres. While a Creek could sell up to 120 acres five years after receiving the deed, restrictions required that forty acres be designated as a "homestead." Another important concession in the Creek Compact was that the final Dawes Commission rolls, on which allotments would be based, would be derived from 1890 and 1895 enrollments of Creek town memberships, which had been conducted, verified, corrected, and approved by the Creek National Council. This way, only those persons the Creek government deemed to be genuine citizens would receive portions of the tribal estate. The Cherokee, Choctaw, Chickasaw, and Seminole signed similar agreements. An act of Congress ended the independence of the Five Civilized Tribes and made their members citizens of the United States in 1901.[36]

Chief Porter held out hope that some measure of political self-determination for the Five Civilized Tribes could be salvaged by creating a separate state for Indians in Indian Territory. Porter and Posey played major leadership roles in the fight for a state of Sequoya in 1905–1906, but the strong grassroots effort failed. The lands of the Indians in the east and the white settlers in the west were folded into a single territory, and Oklahoma became a state in 1907. As a result, the Indian population of Oklahoma was subjected to the will of the dominant, non-Indian population.

None of this occurred without a groundswell of dismay, anger, and unrest in the Creek Nation. Beginning in the 1890s, Chitto Harjo (also known as Crazy Snake and Wilson Jones) became the leader of the Snakes, a group adamantly opposed to the pending dissolution of Creek national institutions and the imposition of alien land and political systems. "I shall never hold up my right arm and swear that I take my allotment of land in good faith—not while the water flows and the grass grows. God in yon bright firmament is my witness," he declared. In the fall of 1900, defying the Curtis Act, the Snakes formed their own government and, with their Cherokee allies, the Keetoowahs, sought a way to preserve Indian sovereignty through the White Path. They argued for a restoration of clan government and the revitalization of traditional values and spiritual ways. Chitto Harjo wanted the country to remain open for hunting and gathering, with no barriers marking off areas under private ownership. The Creek government headed by Porter nonetheless promoted Creek citizens' cooperation with the allotment process. As Crazy Snake's uprising erupted in 1900–1901, Porter's government labored to restore calm by dealing with the grievances of resisting Creeks.[37]

The Snake government tried to reassert political control over Creek lands through militant opposition to allotment. They refused to acknowledge or participate in the partition and privatization of the Creek national estate. If the town kings or others enrolled them, they refused to accept their allotment certificates. Armed with Winchesters, they whipped and arrested those accepting allotments. The Snakes continued their rebellion sporadically from 1900 to 1909. At its peak, the militant Snakes attracted a diverse group of 5,000 Creek sympathizers—about one-third of the Creek Nation—to their cause, including African-Creeks. Thousands of Creeks hoped to find an alternative to allotment. Raising money through cooperative farming, the Snakes hired attorneys to argue for the integrity of their 1832 treaty rights, but their pleas to collectively bargain for sale of their lands were rejected by Congress.[38] A decisive blow to Indian hopes that their treaties would protect them from the division of their lands and the destruction of their sovereignty came in a U.S. Supreme Court decision, *Lone Wolf v. Hitchcock*, in 1903. The decision validated "congressional plenary power," that is, the superior right of Congress to make laws governing Indian people, even if these violated existing treaty contracts.

Jackson Barnett's life from 1890 to 1912 illustrates how an ordinary Creek citizen experienced these demoralizing changes. Like many other Creeks, Barnett experienced declining security and physical displacement due to the migration of blacks and whites to Creek country, the attendant economic and environmental changes, and forced allotment. Jackson moved from the eastern border of the nation, where he had worked as a ferryman for many years, to the Barnett family settlement near the town of Bryant in Okmulgee County. Here, his father, Siah, and his siblings and their families had settled after the Civil War. Whether Jackson was pushed into the heart of Creek country by the influx of foreigners in the eastern part of the nation or was induced to come by Siah after the accidental death of his brother Tecumseh is unclear.[39] Since Jackson enjoyed traveling, it is also possible that he visited the area where his paternal kin were living in the 1880s and later decided to permanently relocate there.

Whatever the reasons for the move, the extended network of his father's family was an important resource for Jackson at midlife. He found work at the store of Siah's brother Jim Barnett, near present-day Weleetka, southwest of Bryant. Jackson stayed with a half sister, his uncle Jim, and other paternal relations. In the 1880s or early 1890s, with the help of half brother David and cousin Josh Asbury, he built a cabin or log shack a few miles from Bryant. A Creek who knew Jackson in these years recalled that Jackson was a good worker who plowed, planted, and built fences. He moved around, spending nights at his cabin or sleeping outside (not unusual for Creeks), and spending his days laboring and visiting.[40]

Coming from a family both racially and culturally hybridized, Jackson was far from a conservative Creek wedded to communal farming methods, Creek religious ceremonies, or town or clan identities. Jackson worked for wages or bartered his labor for room and board. In many respects, however, Jackson's values and behavior were conventionally "Indian." His identity was grounded in kin-based social and economic reciprocity. For Jackson, the matrilineal clan system was supplanted by his patrilineal network to provide a web of social and economic support, bending the cultural rules to his needs, as did his fellow Creeks.

Jackson's residency during the 1890s can be fixed with some accuracy because of the 1890 and 1895 township rolls ordered by the Creek National Council in anticipation of a "payroll," or disbursement of funds, to the Creeks. Town membership was not based on residency in the town. Many "Tuckabatchee" people had dispersed in the postwar era. The Tuckabatchee Town King, George Alexander, sent his agent to enumerate the people of his town in the Bryant and Senora neighborhoods where the Barnetts and others had relocated. The agent collected information for the 1890 roll at the home of Jackson's cousin Josh Asbury. Jackson is listed with half-brother, Tecumseh, in the 1890 Tuckabatchee town roll. The 1895 roll was prepared at the store of Jim Barnett, Jackson's uncle. Jackson was listed as No. 755 on this Tuckabatchee Town payroll, an entry verified by his uncle Jim. The 1895 Tuckabatchee Town tribal roll lists Siah Barnett and his family immediately followed by the Josh Asbury group. During the allotment of Creek lands, the 1890 and 1895 town rolls became important for identifying Creek citizens and awarding these individuals preemptive rights to the farms and homesteads they were occupying.[41]

The 1895 roll indicates that Jackson had lost his cabin, making him homeless. A freedman's family found the cabin vacant and claimed it during one of Jackson's periodic absences visiting and working. Illiterate and malleable, Jackson provided a thumbprint on a document that gave the freedman's family legal title. Jackson's great-niece Winey Fish Lewis recalled in a 1932 deposition: "He didn't have no place, nor no land." The Fishes thought Jackson should hire a lawyer to recover his cabin or obtain payment for it. Winey tried to persuade Jackson that he would receive some clothes and money if he would talk to the lawyer, items that would "make him look like somebody and he could buy what he wanted." Jackson found some or all of this amusing and "busted out in a laugh." When Jackson finally did agree to get legal advice, he paid no attention to the lawyer, even though he understood English, Winey recalled. The lawyer discovered that Jackson had sold the cabin—to the freedman's family and to two other buyers. Sensing an infirmity, the lawyer felt Jackson needed a guardian and told Winey, "We must keep him petted like a child to get it back." After leaving the lawyer's office, Winey Fish and Jackson "went in the store and got some thing[s] that would be good. He got a coat, a pair of boots and some blankets and he took them and walked on out of doors and wouldn't pay for them." When Jackson claimed the merchant gave him the items, Winey paid the bill and apologized, saying Barnett's mind came and went.[42]

Having lost the cabin, Barnett moved to Tiger Flats, where he lived with different families between Bryant and Henryetta in Okmulgee County while earning his keep as a farm laborer. It was not far from Hickory Ground, the Snake government's council ground and spiritual center. Displaced and homeless, Jackson was drawn into sympathy with the Snake rebellion. He owned little besides a horse and saddle. After 1900, the family of Little Fish provided Jackson with a home for several years.[43]

Jackson Barnett's condition as a landless Creek in 1900 was not atypical. For a number of reasons—ranging from political conviction, to misunderstanding of the bureaucratic process, to swindling—many Creeks failed to secure preemptive rights to lands they historically occupied. Even before the 1901 Creek Compact gave legal authorization to the allotment process, all of the desirable Creek agricultural land was taken up by speculators, squatters, and Creeks with preemptive rights. The families of Little Fish and Jackson's other paternal half siblings managed to secure their preemptive rights to their homesteads in Okmulgee County during allotment because they were willing to be enrolled and await the assignment of certificates granting them their privately owned parcels. There were no good parcels to assign to the many landless Creeks. They could only expect to obtain marginal lands unsuitable for farming far from friends and kinfolk.

Based on documentation of his familial relationship and town affiliation from the 1890 and 1895 Creek censuses, Jackson Barnett's status as a full Creek Indian was verified by the Creek government, then approved by the secretary of the Interior. The Dawes Commission understandably floundered because there were fourteen Creeks named Jackson Barnett, more than one (Jo)Siah Barnett, and many women named Thlesothle. Moreover, there were two Tuckabatchee towns and two Tuckabatchee town rolls representing upper and lower sections. Redundancy and oversight—not to mention the Snakes' refusal to cooperate—complicated the chore of allotment. Nevertheless, on January 24, 1900, Jackson Barnett was enrolled as a full-blood Creek and Tuckabatchee Indian, whose parents (both deceased) were Tuckabatchee Indians. This enrollment provided the legal basis for his allotment. Two years later, he had a land assignment made for him because he had "failed to appear and designate any land" which he "desired to have allotted."[44] Jackson, a citizen of the Muskogee (Creek) Nation, Roll No. 4524, was given an official allotment at Drumright in Creek County. The Department of the Interior approved it on October 9, 1903, and Pleasant Porter countersigned.[45] Jackson's allotment in Creek County meant nothing to him.

From the time of his displacement from his cabin until 1912, Jackson was homeless, poor, ragged, and sometimes ill. He slept outdoors throughout the year and eked out an existence as a laborer. He depended upon the kindness of his fellow Creeks for a roof over his head. Among the families he stayed with were those of Lizzie and Josh Asbury, Chief Moty Tiger, his half brothers and sisters by Siah Barnett, Sango Johnson, Roling Brown, Little Fish, William Sullivan, Boney Randall, and finally Boney Randall's son Timmie. On a month-long visit in the fall with his half sister Eliza Little Fish's family when he was ill, he lay outside with a saddle for a pillow until Little Fish ordered the family to bring him in the house.[46]

From 1904 to 1906, Posey traveled through Snake-dominated territory and along the way met many hungry, homeless, and indigent Creeks. Posey, who visited the Little Fish family, might have encountered Jackson Barnett, and Jackson surely fit Posey's general description of distressed Creeks. Like Jackson Barnett, many of these homeless Creeks had been assigned lands, but they were twenty-five to fifty miles from their friends and relatives, and they had no will to live among strangers. Posey anticipated that these full-bloods were sure to become a burden to the state. Though they possessed allotments and American citizenship, neither was of much use without a farm.[47]

One historian sums up Jackson's condition in these years accurately, if a bit too harshly, in these words: Barnett went from being a "self-sufficient, though often shiftless, laborer to a landless itinerant forced to seek employment among his friends."[48] Jackson was "around just one place and another," as one Creek recalled. As he owned horses, his radius of movement was fairly wide, extending across three counties but centering in Okmulgee County. One white farmer recalled that Jackson fed his horses on his haystack when traveling through the countryside and would never reveal where he was going or why. Jackson liked to visit his friends and relatives, enjoyed Creek hospitality, but did not overstay his welcome. Sometimes he stayed longer if there was work to do in exchange for food and lodging. Jackson was not as helpful as he should have been when he stayed for a time at the Roling Brown place around 1904, a witness recalled, but Old Lady Brown apparently felt compassion for Jackson and fussed over his clothing and overfed his horses.[49] David Fields recalled: "Well Jackson Barnett he got no home, no wife and children, just stay one place and another and work around." Though he was simple, he was not atypical: "Lot of it like him; got no education, and can't count his money. Can't make any figures, not educated."[50]

Along with his fellow Creeks, Jackson's fortunes steadily declined in the 1890s and early 1900s, but he relied upon a supportive kin network and continued to earn his keep within the Creeks' collective economic system. He also had the survival skills learned from his Creek socialization: he was a hard-working, adaptable, affable, and hardy individual with a good sense of humor. Like other Creeks, he accepted change as inevitable, but embraced the cultural ideal of harmony. He was neither an economic burden nor a troublemaker.

Jackson's resistance to allotment was a rational response given his experience and understanding. He was among those who attended councils and heard Crazy Snake's message to resist allotment. He was one of the many baffled and angry Creeks who lost control of their homelands to non-Indian settlers. They were disillusioned with the American legal process and repulsed by private property rights. Jackson played no distinctive role in the rebellion, though he imbibed its principles. William Sullivan, literate mixed-blood and former Creek legislator, testified that Jackson Barnett was a Snake and that he would not accept the deed to his allotment when it arrived. Little Fish kept the deed for Jackson. On a visit to Little Fish's home, Sullivan saw a Department of the Interior envelope stuck up under the roof of the shed. When he asked what it was doing up there, Little Fish replied, "It is Jackson's deed." Sullivan said, "Why don't you take care of it, it is valuable; that is the land of somebody; but he saw [Jackson] wouldn't have it; he would not accept it; he just stuck it up there."[51]

Jackson's experiences had ill-prepared him for private property ownership. His survival and social identity were grounded in reciprocal relationships. As a bachelor who wholly lacked entrepreneurial motives, a family farm did not suit him, and allotment was therefore meaningless. Jackson moreover lacked the many skills, managerial and otherwise, that were necessary to the operation of a family farm. Jackson was no political analyst or activist, but he did have a basic understanding that allotment was not in his self-interest. He had no curiosity about his land and made no effort to visit his Creek County allotment, much less attempt to reside or eke out a living there. He would have sold it for a pittance had the opportunity arisen and had it been legal to do so.

2

The Making of
the Incompetent Indian

During the turbulent decade of 1900–1910, Congress passed legislation with enormous consequences for the conservation and administration of the estates of Indians such as Jackson Barnett. The "amended Dawes" legislation sought to mitigate the damage the national allotment policy was doing in Oklahoma and elsewhere. Allotment created a destructive wave that crashed over the Indians of eastern Indian Territory in the first decade of the twentieth century. As it receded, little remained of the Five Civilized Tribes' treaty rights, their political and educational institutions, or their landed estate. The superintendent for the Five Civilized Tribes wrote in his annual report in 1916 that 90 percent of the Five Civilized Tribes' lands had passed into non-Indian hands. In little more than a decade, a race of landowners had become tenants.[1]

Allotment had "fallen among thieves," as Senator Dawes lamented, motivating Congress to act to prevent the total dispossession of Indians in the Indian Territory and elsewhere in the nation. Legislation such as the Burke Act and the McCumber Amendment of 1906 prevented the receding wave from carrying off the whole of the Indian estate. During the years between 1905 and 1910, Congress enacted more Indian legislation than in any earlier period. This flurry of activity was largely the product of two powerful crosscurrents: the determined efforts by some congressmen to enact legislation to stem the tide of Indian dispossession (the "protectionists/regulators") and by others to enact legislation to speed access to Indian lands and resources (the "liberationists/liberals"). Access to Indian resources was gained in a two-step political process: first, by pressuring Congress to allot Indian communal lands, and second, by pushing for the early removal of any restrictions on the sale and taxation of Indians' individualized property.[2]

Protectionists erected a federal bulwark around the allotments of Jackson Barnett and other persons of high Indian blood quantum. Without his knowledge or consent, Jackson Barnett acquired the legal status of a "restricted" Indian whose property was held in trust and managed by the federal government's Indian office. If he had not been designated a restricted, or incompetent, Indian, Barnett would most certainly have been speedily divested of his property. Because of the amended Dawes legislation, this indifferent allottee held on to the ownership of his 160 acres in Creek County even after oil was discovered there in 1912.

Members of Congress trying to protect the remaining landed estate of Indians followed a twisting path, replete with compromises and maneuverings that added great complexity and ambiguity to the administration of Indian affairs. This was especially true for the Five Civilized Tribes whose success in mirroring the ways of the Euro-Americans proved to be a legal liability in the post-allotment era. They appeared to be the best candidates for assimilation into mainstream American culture because they had high literacy rates and were economically self-supporting. A great number—men like Pleasant Porter, Robert L. Owen, and Alex Posey— were highly successful in business, politics, and the arts, and if not eager, they were ready and willing to become U.S. citizens. The turn-of-the-century tribal compacts with the Five Civilized Tribes stipulated speedier termination of restrictions than the twenty-five-year probationary period imposed by the Dawes Act. The Creek Compact of 1901, for example, specified that there were restrictions on sale of only 40 of the 160 acres of each Creek allottee. The 40 acres of "homestead" land could not be sold, nor was it subject to taxation, for twenty-one years. The 120 acres of the so-called surplus lands of each Creek allottee could be sold and taxed in five years. By act of Congress, all members of the Five Civilized Tribes became U.S. citizens in 1901.[3]

Instead of guarantees of political equality and economic autonomy as individuals, the tribal compacts and the 1901 citizenship law were the very devices that facilitated the rapid dispossession of eastern Oklahoma Indians. A majority of the Five Civilized Tribes' people opposed the division of the tribal estate; they were unprepared for the radically new economic and legal conditions foisted upon them. The Five Civilized Tribes had the most coveted resources and the largest tribal trust funds, yet they had the most fragile legal protections as they negotiated the involuntary transition from tribal citizenship and communal landholding to U.S. citizenship and individual landholding. Their collective experience of vulnerability is illustrated by the Creek citizen Jackson Barnett. Though he was resourceful, industrious, and self-reliant, the purposes that allotment was supposed to serve were totally alien to him. He had no use for the land, nor did he have—or care to have—any concept of its market value.

The dismay and disorientation of Indians like Barnett in making this transition was in stark contrast to the giddy opportunism of the white majority in Oklahoma Territory. Quite aware of the tremendous value of the Five Civilized Tribes' assets and the legal, cultural, and political advantages in obtaining them, the white majority in Oklahoma seemed to believe they had a preemptive right to the Five Civilized Tribes' property. Non-Indians anticipated the day when 75 percent of the valuable, resource-rich lands of the eastern Oklahoma tribes would enter the market economy as commodities and taxable property under the terms of the compacts. Even before statehood in 1907, Oklahoma politicians were well organized with a clear goal: to remove all of the remaining legal obstacles to Indians' ability to sell their property by promoting the necessary enabling legislation. A provision in the Indian Appropriations Act of 1904 removed the restrictions on all but the homesteads of all Five Civilized Tribes allottees "who are not of Indian blood, except minors"; it also provided for an $18,000 congressional appropriation to pay for the anticipated administrative costs associated with land transfers.[4] The lifting of restrictions on freedmen and white citizens of the Five Civilized Tribes triggered massive land speculation. Grafters—speculators "who stooped to detestable methods"—were so ubiquitous that the term "almost ceased to be a term of opprobrium." Within sixty days after the lifting of restrictions, not one adult freedman in ten had a dollar to show for land sales, reported Creek chief Moty Tiger.[5]

Chief Tiger, accompanied by Creek national attorney Marshall L. Mott, traveled to Washington, D.C., to report the "disastrous and destructive" conditions in eastern Oklahoma. They made a personal appeal to Senator Porter McCumber of North Dakota to propose corrective legislation to stop the hemorrhaging land loss in eastern Oklahoma. Alarmed by reports of graft and robbery of Indians in Oklahoma's fevered land speculation, McCumber and his allies in the Senate made a rather heroic rearguard action to protect the Five Civilized Tribes' assets. In early 1906, McCumber introduced an amendment that would protect the property of the Five Civilized Tribes' full-bloods.[6]

But it was too late to impose such restrictions. The members of the Five Civilized Tribes were already U.S. citizens. Senator Henry Teller of Colorado argued that it would be a gross and unconstitutional interference for Congress to deny the people of the Five Civilized Tribes the full and absolute control of their persons and property. Throughout March and April 1906, the McCumber Amendment sparked a heated debate. McCumber and the protectionists critiqued the allotment policy in order to persuade Congress to undo the damage it had done in Oklahoma. Allotment, they argued, was based on the unrealistic goal of making "a white man out of the Indian." Wherever an Indian had been given the right to sell his land, he had sold it, and like full-bloods elsewhere, 99 percent of the Five Civilized Tribes' people would lose their property immediately. As precedents for the federal government's moral duty in protecting the Indian from predatory local interests, McCumber cited the *Kagama* decision of 1886 and its sound principles of federal trusteeship: "From their very weakness and helplessness . . . there arises the duty of protection and with it the power." A McCumber ally in the Senate declared, "If we do not look to their interests, no one will."[7]

Liberationists argued that the vast majority of the Five Civilized Tribes' people were competent to assume the rights of private property ownership. To extend federal protection would exempt "the most wealthy of the people of the State" (the Indians) from taxation and would foist the federal government into local affairs. Citing the long-standing concept, upheld in statutes, that tribal membership and U.S. citizenship were mutually exclusive, Senator Teller stated: "Senators [should] get out of their minds the idea that these people are the wards of this Government. . . . Mr. President, there is not an Indian in the Indian Territory—not one. The 90,000 people who were Indians are not Indians today." Further, its opponents argued, the McCumber Amendment was of dubious legality as it ran counter to the terms of the individual tribal contracts, which had been ratified by Congress. If passed, the McCumber Amendment would be yet another breach of promise between the United States and the Indians.[8]

In their efforts to retroactively impose federal protections on fullbloods like Jackson Barnett, McCumber and his fellow protectionists were negotiating from a position of weakness. They could not reverse the allotment policy, even though they correctly perceived that allotment's purposes were being perverted. Senator McCumber pointed out that state politicians favoring federal legislation to remove restrictions on Indians had two vital and self-serving motives: the states wanted the lands for white settlers, and they wanted the lands made taxable. The pressure from Oklahoma in this regard, he said, "is simply terrific."[9]

The McCumber Amendment became law on April 26, 1906. One of many political compromises, the amendment was part of a package of Indian legislation passed by the 59th Congress—including the Burke Act and the Oklahoma Enabling Act—in which the protectionists were able to leverage their demand for retroactive federal control over Indians of high blood quantum against the white Oklahomans' desire for statehood over Indian Territory. While the estates of persons of high blood quantum obtained some temporary federal protections, federal oversight of persons with lower Indian blood quantum were relinquished. The Burke Act was the powerful and necessary corollary to the McCumber Amendment, for it

strengthened federal jurisdiction in Oklahoma despite the 1901 citizenship act. A seminal piece of legislation, it cast a long shadow over early
twentieth-century Indian policy—and specifically over the affairs of Jackson Barnett.[10]

The Burke Act amended section 6 of the Dawes Act to postpone the
awarding of citizenship to an Indian allottee until after he accepted a
patent in fee, which could be up to the limit of the twenty-five-year probationary (or trust) period. Until citizenship was awarded, the period of federal guardianship would be maintained. This legislation thus codified the
legal status of the "restricted Indian" as a protocitizen who was not liable
for any debts, not allowed to legally purchase liquor, and not subject to
local taxation. The Supreme Court upheld the Burke Act's amendment of
the Dawes Act in 1909, saying, "Congress in granting full rights of citizenship to Indians, believed it had been hasty." The Burke Act thus suspended
the restricted Indian in a temporary twilight zone between tribal citizenship and U.S. citizenship under the paternalistic governance of the Indian
bureau.[11]

The Burke Act established a legal point that would be pivotal in Barnett litigation, namely, that the restricted Indian would be under the "exclusive jurisdiction" of the executive branch until the Interior Department
determined that the individual had graduated from his temporary period
of tutelage, was ready to make decisions regarding property, and was able
to assume the responsibilities of U.S. citizenship. The experts in Indian affairs within the Interior Department "know best when an Indian has
reached such a stage of civilization as to be able and capable of managing
his own affairs," argued Congressman Charles Burke, who would later
serve as commissioner of Indian affairs. Moreover, Interior's decisions regarding heirship and competency were conclusive and final. Placing the
adjudication of competency within the department promised greater efficiency and shifted decision making out of the courts. Such authority appeared reasonable and necessary in view of the very real dangers of entanglement of Indian properties in litigation over clouded titles. The Burke
Act prevented selfish parties from using the courts to challenge Interior's
judgments regarding whether specific individuals had reached a state of
legal competency.

Appealing to both protectionists and liberationists, the Burke Act offered additional protection for vulnerable Indians by requiring Interior's approval for their applications for competency, while extending the promise to
liberationists that most Indians would be deemed competent by Interior before the lapse of the twenty-five-year probationary period. A program of
gradual individual-by-individual emancipation to citizenship found favor
in both prevailing racial attitudes and rational self-interests. Burke and his
fellow protectionists embraced the purportedly enlightened and realistic assessment that "childlike" Indians lagged far behind the general population
in intelligence and capabilities. Elderly persons, minors, the infirm of mind

or body, and the illiterate and monolingual full-bloods (whom Burke called "blanket Indians") were persons clearly incompetent in American business practices, and their property therefore required federal management. "Supposing you were the guardian or ward of a child eight or ten years of age," said Commissioner of Indian Affairs William Jones, "would you ask the consent of a child as to the investment of its funds? No; you would not."[12] Allowing childlike beings the power to sell their properties would quickly divest them of all means of self-support. Pauperized individuals would then be a burden to state taxpayers. Liberationists wanted valuable Indian properties shifted into the market economy and subject to state taxation as soon as possible, but they conceded the wisdom of some restrictions for a small category of incompetents.[13]

A third victory for the protectionists in the 59th Congress was the Oklahoma Enabling Act, which reinforced the concept of federal authority over Indians. While this legislation cleared the path for Oklahoma's progress toward statehood, it imposed the condition that the forthcoming Oklahoma state constitution could not limit federal authority over Indians within its boundaries. Oklahomans formally complied, but the concession appeared insignificant compared to the larger victory of statehood for local interests.

Ominously for vulnerable Indians like Jackson Barnett, Oklahoma advanced to statehood in 1907 with the full expectation that the federal role in local affairs would be temporary and minimal. Political momentum continued to build within Oklahoma for immediate removal of all restrictions on all Indian properties except for the homesteads of full-bloods. The new state was overwhelmingly Democratic, and the party's platform of 1907 railed against outsiders interfering in local matters, declaring, "We will take care of our own defectives of whatever race or color." The Oklahomans elected to the House of Representatives were committed to the emancipation of eastern Oklahoma from federal control. Oklahoma politicians and their allies introduced bill after bill in the 60th and 61st Congresses requesting the removal of restrictions on Indians.[14]

The amended Dawes legislation interjected a serious ambiguity into American Indian law over whether Indian lands or Indian persons were restricted. Attaching a condition of legal incompetency to U.S. citizens would be unconstitutional; therefore, it was the land that was restricted, not the individual. Yet, it was the characteristic of the individual—the inability to conduct business, which translated into a deficiency or incompetency in the progressive mindset—that legitimized Interior's authority over restricted lands. Oklahoma politicians and other land-hungry westerners readily exploited this legal paradox. They utilized the rhetoric of egalitarianism and assimilation to demand immediate "liberation" of Indian persons from federal control to further their hidden agenda of freeing Indian property into the local market economy. A 1910 memorial to Congress said: "These people [Indians] have long since established their right and vindicated their claim to manage their own affairs in their own way without hav[ing] thrown around them those restrictions imposed by law upon infants, idiots, and other legal incompetents." Such rhetoric appealed to those Oklahomans who feared the concentration of power in the federal government. At the same time, it served the interests of those eager to gain access to restricted Indians' resources and to shift the tax burden to Indian-held land.[15]

The final battleground in the jurisdictional war over the former Five Civilized Tribes' property and persons was the Five Civilized Tribes Closure Act, known by protectionists as the Crime of 1908. The bill "for the removal of restrictions from part of the lands of allottees of the Five Civilized Tribes" had a two-year odyssey through congressional committees before it finally became law on May 27, 1908. The power of Congress to protect Indian lands from sale, wrote Oklahoma historian Grant Foreman, was "violently agitated in Oklahoma, in Congress, and in the Department of the Interior." The Closure Act was thus the result of protracted negotiations over where to draw the line: what percentage of Indian blood quantum correlated with restricted status over how much acreage? In the final version of the bill, only the forty-acre homesteads of mixed-bloods (persons of one-half to three-fourths Indian blood quantum) and all of the acreage of full-bloods were restricted until 1931, unless the secretary of the Interior decided to lift restrictions on an individual basis before that time. Legal restrictions were lifted from enrolled whites, freedmen, and mixed-bloods of less than one-half Indian blood. As a result, nearly 13 million acres of land were released to the speculative interests in Oklahoma.[16] The flurry of real estate transactions was not confined to the unrestricted lands alone, because many believed that the McCumber Amendment would be ruled unconstitutional and even more land would be available (see appendix II).

The protectionists paid dearly in other provisions of the bill for the continued supervisory role of the federal government over the estates of Jackson Barnett and others of high blood quantum. The law made local control more prominent, thus contradicting the Enabling Act's strong assertion of ongoing exclusive federal jurisdiction over Indians in Oklahoma. The Closure Act permitted the leasing of restricted properties and declared jurisdiction over Indian minors and incompetents to be a matter of the Oklahoma probate courts. By giving county courts control over the estates of minors and incompetents of the Five Civilized Tribes, this act laid the legal foundation for local jurisdiction over Jackson Barnett's estate. The protectionist legislators fought for a concession on this point: they wanted the secretary of the Interior to hold the right to appoint local representatives to oversee the guardians appointed by the county courts and to prosecute neglect, where applicable.[17] Jackson Barnett's 160 acres in Creek County became trust property under the jurisdiction of the Interior Department, but it was subject to the Oklahoma county courts as well. Barnett's later legal complications arose from the tension between the exercise of federal power over the detribalized Indians of eastern Oklahoma and the local jurisdiction over these same Indians under state law.

Later serving as one of Jackson Barnett's lawyers, the Creek national attorney, Marshall L. Mott, became a foremost critic of the Crime of 1908 and, specifically, the Oklahoma guardianship system that legally defrauded restricted Indians of their assets. A long-time champion of federal protection, Mott fought tirelessly to protect Creek assets by contesting the procedures and the state laws expediting their transfer into white hands. During the transition to Oklahoma statehood, when Creeks' vulnerability was heightened by their unfamiliarity with the new legal and political system and by the feverish grafting by non-Indians, Mott exposed the pillaging of Indian resources and defended the Indian victims. Mott successfully conducted major suits for the Creek. The most significant one was a Supreme Court decision upholding the McCumber Amendment, which ruled that wardship was not incompatible with citizenship. Mott's legal victories brought large financial judgments to the Creek people in cases involving illegal transfers of land. Mott also lobbied for federal reform legislation, because he recognized how seriously the amended Dawes legislation had compromised legal protection for Indian property. In a state dominated by Democrats vociferously endorsing home rule, Mott was despised as a Republican carpetbagger, that is, as an outsider interfering in local matters. Political pressure ultimately forced his resignation.[18]

One of Mott's most fervent crusades was to try to close a loophole created by the Crime of 1908 by urging reform of the Oklahoma guardianship system. The Union Agency, established in 1874 at Muskogee to oversee the affairs of the Five Civilized Tribes, issued a report in July 1912 that confirmed that the nation's wealthiest wards were in Oklahoma, where 60,000 Indian minors owned $129 million in property. These minors of the Five Civilized Tribes had received privatized shares of both the trust funds and the landed estates of their respective tribes. Under the authority granted in the 1908 Closure Act, guardians were appointed for these minors by the county courts. Some guardians handled the estates of as many as 200–300 children. Guardians often sold their wards' estates to friends for below-market prices, paid scant attention to the needs of the children, and gradually dissipated the minors' estates. One guardian of a child living at the Murrow Indian Orphan Home sold the property of his ward and included in the accounting a fraudulent charge of $140 for the child's barber. In another case, two children who inherited oil land worth $250,000 died after the home in which they slept was dynamited; the guardian and his lawyer profited by handling the probate matters for this large estate.[19]

Reports of neglect, violence, and graft became so commonplace that state and federal agencies felt compelled to intervene. The Union Agency, the federal office empowered to oversee the probate activities of the county courts, attempted to dislodge and prosecute corrupt guardians. The agency, with a $90,000 budget, an agent in each of the fifteen districts (with two or three counties in each district), and a handful of federal probate attorneys, pursued suspicious guardianship transactions. While the most egregious abuses ended, the parasitical practices in Oklahoma continued. Overtly criminal methods of acquiring the assets of Indian minors were replaced by shady practices, such as investing in worthless real estate, padding guardians' accounts, and allowing excessive fees to guardians and attorneys.[20]

With the discovery of the Glenn pool in eastern Oklahoma (one of the most productive oil fields in the world at that time) in 1905, the Oklahoma guardianship system expanded its reach to bring another group of wealthy Indians under county jurisdiction by the exercise of authority over "incompetents" granted by the Closure Act. These were adult Indians, including Jackson Barnett, with newfound wealth in mineral royalties. Whenever oil, natural gas, or other valuable resources were discovered on the restricted land of a full-blood Indian, it was common practice after 1910 for the Oklahoma county courts to appoint a guardian to manage the estate. Once again, guardians collected large fees for their services, which had dubious value. As Angie Debo put it, "It was not until about 1913 that it began to be apparent that all Indians and freedmen who owned oil property were mentally defective."[21]

The notorious Oklahoma guardianship system was a veritable cottage industry, sanctioned by law, with profit sharing by numerous persons in local cliques. County judges built powerful political machines apportioning profitable guardianships among supporters. Profits and perks from guardianships were shared widely among lawyers, politicians, judges, land speculators, and retailers. To protect these profitable activities, Oklahoma politicians fought to slash the budget of the Union Agency, thereby destroying its watchdog activities. Within Oklahoma, there was widespread antipathy for the federal Indian bureau, which was seen as interfering with local jurisdiction. "If you can't abolish the office, for God's sake[,] cut off the appropriation," declared one Oklahoma county judge. With fewer agents and probate attorneys, the agency's effectiveness as the guardian for restricted Indians of Oklahoma was reduced.[22]

In the early 1910s, Marshall Mott and Charles Burke joined forces to investigate and expose the guardianship system in response to its resistance to reform, its expansion to include wealthy adults as well as minors of the Five Civilized Tribes, and the Oklahomans' attack on the appropriations for the bureau. Mott and Burke shared a belief that strong federal authority and supervision of restricted Indians' estates was the way to halt the selfish local interests from systematically pillaging the Five Civilized Tribes' remaining assets. In 1910, Congressman Burke chaired a special subcommittee of the House Committee on Indian Affairs that investigated the Oklahoma guardianship system, and what he found was reprehensible.

"The same situation exists in every state where there are Indians," declared Burke. "There are protests from the white men that the federal government stands between the Indian and the Indian's property."[23] Mott assisted Burke in saving the imperiled Union Agency from termination through budget cuts by hiring a team of fifteen men to research the guardianship system in eight Oklahoma counties. Mott's 1912 report revealed that court-appointed guardians for Indians in these counties collected extortionate fees of 20 percent compared to the national average of 2–3 percent for the services of professional guardians of white wards.[24]

Mott's findings were put to brilliant political use in 1912, when the Oklahomans in Congress launched another attack to slash the bureau's budget. During the consideration of the bill, written to eliminate all field workers at the Union Agency, Burke charged that the probate system in Oklahoma was corrupt and dishonest. An Oklahoma congressman rose to the bait and demanded proof. Burke then introduced the Mott report into the record, a move that threw the Oklahoma representatives into confusion and denial and gave Burke empirical support for his denunciation of the Oklahoma county courts and those who made careers as "professional guardians."[25]

In a move with enormous long-term consequences for Jackson Barnett and other Oklahoma Indians with oil wealth, progressives in Congress promoted an activist federal government as the counterweight and corrective to corrupt local machine politics such as the Oklahoma guardianship system. Burke's defense of federal oversight of Indian trust property in Oklahoma and elsewhere from 1906 to 1912 expressed the reformist spirit of the early twentieth-century Progressive Era. Progressives like Burke endorsed honest and efficient government by experts using up-to-date scientific methods in lieu of partisan politics corrupted by spoilsmanship and special interests. In the progressives' thinking, the important responsibility of managing the millions of acres of restricted Indian lands could only be entrusted to trained professionals with a sincere mission to serve Indian interests. To this end, Commissioner of Indian Affairs Robert Valentine established a "methods division" and took steps to organize the Indian office as a modern bureaucracy. Following the 1906 Burke Act, the federal government managed Indian trust lands like other public lands—national parks, forests, and monuments—in the spirit of conservation and the gospel of efficiency. By 1910, the "Indian problem," as Matthew Sniffen of the Indian Rights Association stated, "resolved itself into one of administration."[26] The Indian bureau had far fewer Indians and far less Indian land under its responsibility in the twentieth century than in the nineteenth. Yet it grew in size, power, and institutional complexity. The Indian office had about 225,000 "trust properties" under its care nationwide, each property with its own unique administrative issues regarding leasing and heirship. Federal authority extended over the approval of oil, gas, and mining leases and the flow of proceeds to Indians whose restricted property was being managed. The Union Agency at Muskogee handled the affairs of 36,000 restricted Indians, including by 1912, 7,500 Indians with oil royalties.[27]

Progressive federal policies of rational, efficient, and scientific management were instituted in Oklahoma and elsewhere. Although Oklahoma politicians schemed to find a way to part Indians from their newfound mineral wealth, the property rights of adults with high Indian blood quantum were legally secure under Department of the Interior management. Through trial and error, the Union Agency succeeded in devising procedures that eliminated loopholes for abuse and bridged troublesome jurisdictional issues. In exchange for leases with oil companies, Five Civilized Tribes members received fair market value at a standardized 12.5 percent royalty, and the Osage received 16.6 percent. In the 1910s and 1920s, Indians whose allotments were situated over the oil reserves enjoyed handsome and even extravagant incomes. Restricted Indians with oil wealth were wards under the protection of the federal government, but they often had guardians appointed by the county courts, too. Initially, oil royalties were paid directly to adults or to minors' guardians, but surplus funds were doled out sparingly after experience showed that Indians spent their money "too" freely and guardians were tempted to embezzle their wards' funds. After 1911, the Union Agency supervised Indian expenditures through its district agents and withheld payments from guardians suspected of mismanagement. A system developed whereby guardians were required to obtain advance approval from the agency prior to tapping the accounts of wealthy wards.[28] Thus a system of checks and balances evolved to protect the valuable property of full-bloods. This involved dual federal-county court guardianship in some instances.

One glaring defect was that a disproportionate share of Union Agency resources went into protecting the estates of a small number of rich, restricted Indians. After 1910, sensational stories—swindles by marital partners, kidnappings of minors, embezzlement by guardians, fraud, and sales of probated estates for a fraction of their true value—were frequently featured in the *Muskogee Daily Phoenix*.[29] In 1911, for example, a story appeared about a full-blood Creek woman, Lucinda Pitman, who was coerced into signing over a $1,000 monthly royalty and $500,000 in oil property to her ex-husband, a white man. Flush with funds, the paper reported, the ex-husband had run off with the couple's governess and taken the Pitmans' child hostage. As a restricted Indian, Pitman appealed to the federal Indian agency in Muskogee for an investigation and protection. After a year-long investigation by the U.S. Secret Service working for Union Agency superintendent Dana Kelsey and Creek attorney Marshall Mott, Pitman's estate was recovered.[30]

The bureau's efficient management and steadfast commitment to protect restricted Indians would have a profound impact on Jackson Barnett's affairs. So would other, less-attractive features of the institutional development of federal paternalism forged in the Progressive Era. Progressives in the Indian bureau distrusted the common people; they saw white Oklahomans as selfishly motivated and Indians as inept in business. Progressives therefore sought to remove power from the local arena and deliver it into the hands of expert federal managers. Consent and direct negotiations with restricted Indians were replaced by a vast bureaucratic apparatus and a proliferation of rules, regulations, and procedures. A hierarchical, "rule-oriented federal bureaucracy" with a staff of thousands processed paper that legitimized the bureau's activities and decisions. As historian Craig Miner observed, "Most businessmen and Indians [gave] up trying to understand what was now best left to the [bureau's] clerks."[31] A bureaucratic culture evolved within the Indian office that sometimes divorced its decision making from the preferences and even from the best interests of the Indian wards it ostensibly served. Ironically, this perversion of its original purpose was the result of a conflict of interest created by the Burke Act. The Indian office was positioned to operate the valve to release more Indian land into the general economy by declaring individual Indians competent, and it faced enormous political pressure to do so. The Department of the Interior was responsive to the majority will, and the demand for Indian land and resources was an inexorable force in national political life. Between 1890 and 1920, the non-Indian population grew 68 percent nationally, topping 113 million, while the Indian population was 250,000–500,000 in these years.

The Interior Department's conflict of interest is illustrated by the actions of Cato Sells, commissioner of Indian affairs from 1913 to 1921. On one hand, Sells unequivocally denounced Oklahoma's guardianship system for its "collusion in the sale of minors' property, excess compensation to guardians, and unreasonably large attorneys' fees," and he advocated legislative correctives to strengthen protection for restricted Indians in Oklahoma.[32] Simultaneously, in 1917 Sells enthusiastically endorsed the "New Policy" of his superior, Secretary of the Interior Franklin Lane, to liberate restricted Indians from guardianship before the end of the twenty-five-year probationary period. High crop and livestock prices during World War I drove the national demand for Indian lands to be put into productive use or to be surrendered. Sells instituted a policy of lifting restrictions on Indians whose blood quantum was below 50 percent, regardless of the Indians' preferences or capabilities. From 1906 to 1916, 10,000 Indians were "freed" from federal supervision. Between 1916 and 1921, 20,000 fee patents were issued, half of which went to Oklahoma Indians.[33] Most newly unrestricted Indians sold their allotments.

Two painful lessons were learned from the enactment of the New Policy. First, releasing Indians from restricted status resulted in wholesale land loss and Indian impoverishment. Second, the Indian office's primary indicator of competency in business affairs—blood quantum—was not reliable. That it lacked "a description of the specific attributes of competency" was candidly admitted in the 1921 *Annual Report* of the commissioner of Indian affairs: "It is doubtful if a satisfactory method has been found for determining the competency upon which to base a termination of the trust title."[34] The bureau concluded that all restricted Indians were uniformly incapable and required permanent federal management of their business affairs.

The national controversy over the Jackson Barnett estate would expose the paradoxes of Indian policy in the early twentieth century. Officially, the national goal was the speedy and full assimilation of American Indians. The Bureau of Indian Affairs had subtly shifted its emphasis from the futile and ill-conceived objective of making white people out of Indians to the institutional management of Indian property. While giving lip service to the task of harvesting competent Indians from the ranks of the incompetent, covertly the bureau's major task was maintaining Indian property under its control. "Ironically," notes historian Janet McDonnell, " a land policy initiated to 'free' the Indians from federal supervision promoted the growth of an administrative bureaucracy that worked to keep Indians dependent."[35] Were Jackson Barnett and the thousands of other restricted Indians protocitizens—whose property was being temporarily managed and protected by the Department of the Interior—or were they a permanent class of racial deficients? Ominously, one of Mott's major victories in the Creek land cases evoked this statement from the U.S. Supreme Court in 1912: "Federal representation of wards' interests on no account depends upon the Indians' acquiescence."[36] How had the Indian bureau come to acquire power that could not be checked by the courts, by the popular will, or by the Indian with restricted property? Over a little more than a decade and a half, a well-meaning paternalism had metamorphosed into an unwieldy and undemocratic bureaucracy.

3

Tar Baby
1912–1920

From the first signs of the bubbling wealth beneath his rocky allotment, Jackson Barnett's case was precedent setting. The elderly, illiterate, and inexperienced Jackson required the services of a guardian
to protect and preserve his estate, and he and his property were quickly
drawn into the system of dual guardianship defined by the Oklahoma Closure Act of 1908. This assumption of jurisdiction by the county courts potentially subjected the Barnett estate to the system of legalized robbery. To
protect Jackson's interests, federal officials sprang into action. The federal
government aggressively advanced the position in 1912 that Jackson was an
"average" full-blood, who was adequately supervised by the Department of
the Interior. This was the first, but not the last, time the Indian bureau
would defend Jackson's competency in order to defend the larger principle
of its exclusive federal jurisdiction over restricted Indians.

In early 1912, Jackson Barnett was summoned to the Okmulgee office
of Thomas Farrar, district agent for the Bureau of Indian Affairs, to approve an agricultural lease. Farrar had responsibility for approximately
2,000 restricted Creeks of Okmulgee and Okfuskee counties. The $10-a-
year lease was welcome income for Jackson, an absentee landowner, who
was then working as a wage laborer at the Randall farm outside Henryetta.[1] Jackson was driven into town by his friend and employer, Timmie

Randall, to sign the papers and collect the $10. Little did Farrar, Barnett, or Randall imagine that an oil lease on Jackson Barnett's property would soon bring Jackson a far greater income.

Oil discoveries in Creek County's Cushing field brought speculators to the Indian office to search the records for the names of owners of promising allotments from whom they could acquire oil leases. Among these speculators was H. U. Bartlett, who lived seven miles from the Randall farm and no doubt knew of absentee landholders in the vicinity. Fortunately for Jackson Barnett and others, a protocol was in place for negotiating oil leases involving restricted full-bloods. Jackson was working in Timmie Randall's cornfields when Agent Farrar requested he come to his office for an interview. This was Jackson's second meeting with Farrar in as many months. Having ascertained that Jackson spoke English and seemed to understand the proposed agreement, Farrar drew up the Bartlett oil lease on March 5, 1912. Jackson received an immediate bonus of $40. The bureau's oil inspector subsequently investigated the adequacy of the lease, and because he found the oil field promising, Bartlett was required to award Jackson $200. After approval by Dana Kelsey, superintendent of the Union Agency in Muskogee, the Bartlett lease was forwarded to the secretary of the Interior for final approval. In the interim, other lucrative oil discoveries in the Cushing field increased the speculative value of Jackson's lease dramatically.[2]

On March 17, 1912, oil was struck a mile from Jackson Barnett's allotment. Later that month, other restricted Indians with allotments in Creek County approached Superintendent Kelsey, eager to sign oil leases paying 12.5 percent royalties. Leases for allotments adjoining Jackson Barnett's holding quickly brought high prices. Samuel Richards's lease on the east sold for $8,000 ($50 per acre for the 160-acre allotment) in mid-April. Jemima Richards's lease sold for $7,000, and an oil lease on only forty acres yielded a $6,500 bonus for its owner.[3]

Production from the Cushing field far surpassed the famous Glenn pool, fifteen miles southeast of Tulsa. Again acknowledging that its earlier estimates had undervalued Jackson's lease, the oil inspector's office recommended increasing the bonus payment to $4,600. When the value of Jackson's allotment became known, his half brother David contested the Bartlett lease on the grounds that Jackson was incompetent and did not know what he was signing. In a petition to the Okmulgee County court, David Barnett asked that Carl O'Hornett, a Henryetta druggist, be appointed Jackson's guardian. This was done after a court heard testimony and ruled Jackson to be incompetent. The following day, May 1, 1912, a second oil lease was signed between Jackson's new guardian, O'Hornett, and Ira Cornelius and H. B. Gooch. When Agent Farrar heard of this, he called for an investigation. Superintendent Kelsey immediately notified his superiors in Washington, D.C., not to approve any lease until the matter was resolved and requested that the original Bartlett lease agreement be returned to him unsigned.[4]

A series of hearings and court judgments regarding the disputed Jackson Barnett oil leases in mid-1912 turned on the question of Jackson's legal competency.[5] A pattern emerged that characterized the remainder of Jackson's litigious life. Opinions of Jackson's competency—whether expressed by judges or intelligence experts, BIA employees or oil men, friends, relatives, or neighbors, Indians or non-Indians—reflected each witness's personal motives. As these changed over a span of twenty years, so did the testimony of witnesses. Whether any testimony was ever entirely truthful was difficult to determine because of the vested interests and political considerations that often influenced the opinions.

The Cornelius and Gooch partnership orchestrated the first challenge to Jackson's mental competency in order to secure control of a valuable oil lease. Cornelius claimed his actions were warranted, testifying that when he learned of Barnett's lease with Bartlett (for $40 in trade beads) from federal status reports of oil and gas leases on full-blood lands, he became immediately suspicious because he knew of Jackson Barnett's incompetence. The Creek oil speculator Joseph Bruner later testified that he had the same response. Cornelius pursued proceedings in the county court, "knowing that was the proper way to take the lease." Because Jackson had no court-appointed lawyer, Cornelius went to his relatives, first contacting Henry Bolwer, the husband of Jackson's niece. Bolwer and Cornelius convinced Jackson's closest relative, half brother David Barnett, that Jackson's best interests were served by having a court-appointed guardian. Cornelius, Gooch, Bolwer, David Barnett, and a lawyer joined forces to petition the Okmulgee County court. Gooch and Cornelius approached Carl O'Hornett to be the guardian for a "crazy Indian," which he graciously agreed to do as "a favor to them and to the incompetent." According to procedure, public notice of the guardianship proceedings was given, and Jackson was served with papers.

In the meantime, Gooch and Cornelius mustered several witnesses— many of whom had only passing acquaintance with Jackson—to testify to his weak-mindedness. Henry Bolwer testified, for example, that Jackson was occasionally tricked out of his earnings as a cotton picker; typically, Jackson was stubborn and unusually quiet, but he would become angry if teased. "I been around him long enough to see that he's weak-minded all right," Bolwer said. O'Hornett similarly interpreted Jackson's eccentric ways, such as sleeping outdoors, as evidence of his craziness. With no one testifying in defense of his competency, Jackson was declared incompetent. The judge appointed O'Hornett as guardian and approved the Gooch and Cornelius lease with the proviso that they must pay Jackson a bonus of $2,400, a sum in line with the known value of the lease. After Cornelius and Gooch filed their lease with the Department of the Interior, O'Hornett's lawyer immediately protested the original Bartlett lease. Although other oil men were in the courtroom and the judge could have solicited competitive bids, possibly yielding a higher bonus for Barnett, this was not done.[6]

While Cornelius claimed to be scrupulously following procedure, other testimony suggests underhanded methods were employed to undermine the Bartlett lease. First, there was a charge that the competency hearings were kept secret to prevent witnesses from appearing who would claim Jackson was competent. District Agent Farrar, for example, was not notified of the hearing on the new lease agreement, indicating a deliberate circumvention of his authority. Timmie Randall, Jackson's closest associate, said he first heard of the competency hearing when O'Hornett approached him with a bribe: $250 for providing Jackson room and board in exchange for Randall's cooperation in having him appointed as guardian. Randall refused the offer and denied that Jackson was incompetent.[7] Randall was further alarmed by Jackson's mysterious disappearance for three weeks in June, one in a series of kidnappings of Jackson Barnett. The kidnapper left an unsigned note saying he was carrying Jackson off for "some little piece." When the note was discovered, Randall contacted the sheriff.[8] Finally, later court testimony suggested that Cornelius and Gooch manipulated Jackson's relatives into supporting the appointment of a guardian, when they were uncertain about Jackson's mental debilitation. Jackson's niece Winey Fish Bolwer, for example, stated that her husband, Henry, was a drunk and an opportunist who had schemed with Cornelius and Gooch to overturn the Bartlett lease and that she and Bolwer expected to benefit financially by cooperating with Cornelius. In 1912, Winey testified that she "never did notice much" about Jackson's mental condition. In his 1912 testimony, David Barnett also equivocated about Jackson's competence, and in 1925, he stated he did not truly believe Jackson was incompetent. David also denied signing a petition for appointment of a guardian or having anything else to do with Cornelius and Gooch's connivances.[9]

Immediately following the declaration of Jackson's incompetency by the county judge, District Agent Farrar, Bartlett, and Randall spearheaded a movement to appeal the decision. Randall filed a motion to have the guardianship vacated on procedural grounds: properly delegated officials had failed to give the required public notice, and Jackson Barnett had not been represented at his own competency hearings. (Bartlett paid the expenses of witnesses and Randall's lawyer in the effort to set aside the guardianship.)

Within days of the first competency hearing, another was held in Okmulgee County court, but this time witnesses defending Jackson's competency were heard. District Agent Farrar played a strong role in the hearing, carefully building a case that Jackson was an average full-blood, no more or less incompetent than other restricted Indians requiring federal supervision. Cross-examining the witnesses, Farrar showed that itinerancy and sleeping outdoors were not atypical behaviors for full-blood Creeks and that the label "crazy" was derived from Jackson's early association with Crazy Snake. Randall and other Indian witnesses refuted the charges of incompetence with evidence that Jackson was a self-supporting laborer who worked hard

and handled his own money. "He working all the time for wages," said Timmie. One of Cornelius and Gooch's witnesses conceded that Jackson was the
only full-blood who sought work from him and the only one he'd engaged
as a hired hand. Another said that Jackson, as a Snake Indian, had enough
sense to oppose allotment. Bartlett's witnesses, including Jackson's nephews
William Fisher and Joe Seaborn, argued that Jackson was as competent as
any other Indian of limited education and opportunities. "I know he not
[incompetent.] I tell him he got more sense than I got; what I think all the
time," Randall testified.[10] As in the previous hearing, the testimony that
Jackson Barnett was unequipped to handle his allotment was largely from
white men. Some were O'Hornett's fellow shopkeepers in Henryetta, who
were paid by O'Hornett to travel to the hearing. Most of them called Jackson "Crazy Jack," a nickname alleged to be commonly applied to him. Jackson was described as a man who, when addressed, responded with a silly
smile or parroted the words spoken to him.[11]

The second county court hearing upheld the earlier ruling on Jackson's incompetency and did not overturn the guardianship. Farrar continued his protest of the county court's decision by appealing to the district
court. In subsequent newspaper interviews, he reiterated his assertion that
Jackson was "average," that he did not need a guardian other than the federal government, and that the original Bartlett lease, which he had negotiated, be reinstated. Two days after the second hearing, Farrar wrote to
Kelsey, his superior, emphasizing that Jackson Barnett had sufficient intelligence to sign an agricultural lease for a small sum but lacked the capability to sign an oil lease:

> Without the exercise of some supervision over the property rights
> of this allottee he would be helpless in the hands of those who
> would be disposed to take advantage of his ignorance and lack of
> business capacity. . . . The question arises, Is he sufficiently
> protected under the supervision exercised by the department? I
> took the position that the Indian, being a ward of the Govern-
> ment, is amply protected in respect to his property rights.[12]

This assessment reached Kelsey's ears at a most propitious moment. Oklahoma politicians were fighting in Congress to drastically reduce the appropriation to the Indian bureau, arguing that administrative costs were exorbitant and outside interference over Indians was unnecessary, expensive,
and unwanted. Federal agents fought to counteract the destruction of federal oversight of the restricted Indians of Oklahoma, and they perceived
control of Jackson's estate to be a challenge to federal authority. While
Jackson may indeed have been mentally incompetent to manage his rich
estate, the bureau suspiciously viewed such incompetency proceedings as a
legal maneuver used by grafters, since even those who were restricted and
therefore "adequately" protected by the federal government were declared
incompetent.

Jackson Barnett was one of a number of restricted Oklahoma Indians with a promising fortune in oil royalties in 1912. Other wealthy Indians were ensnarled in a web of graft, misrepresentation, distortion, competing interests, and legal complexities. Barnett proved fortunate in his ownership of the most productive oil leases in Indian country as well as in having friends and unbidden allies who ensured the security of his allotment and its resources. These included David Barnett, who was persuaded that the Bartlett lease undervalued the property; Timmie Randall, who refused Cornelius and Gooch's bribe and rallied other Creeks to resist the imposition of the abusive guardianship system on their fellow Creek; Burke and Mott, who were committed to federal protections for vulnerable Indians in an era of overt and unabashed grafting; and the conscientious Indian agents Dana Kelsey and Thomas Farrar. If Jackson's wealth and his vulnerability attracted those who would exploit him, they also attracted those who acted with character and principles to protect him. Finally, Jackson was fortunate in timing. The oil discovery on his land followed the enactment of the twenty-five-year trust era for restricted Indians and came after effective procedures for regulating oil leases by the Union Agency staff had been put into place. The challenge to Jackson's competency also coincided with the Indian bureau's defense of its prerogatives. By some strange quirk of destiny, Jackson's entanglement in the Oklahoma guardianship system became a test case and received the special attention of Superintendent Kelsey. Revealing key policy issues, the debate over his competence was perceived as precedent setting.

The Department of the Interior decided that the issues raised by the Jackson Barnett case were important enough to warrant an independent hearing by the Bureau of Indian Affairs. Accordingly, a hearing was held by Kelsey in Muskogee following the first Okmulgee County Court competency hearing. Federal officials, the guardian, lawyers, and lessees were present. Kelsey explained that the agency would ordinarily suspend recommendations when litigation was pending in the state courts, but he believed that it was "essential" that the independent investigation move ahead "where lack of harmony is encountered to the detriment of the restricted Indian individually, or the settlement of the questions raised concerning the interests of a large portion of Indians of certain classes." In other words, serious legal and political questions were at stake.[13]

Kelsey's most pressing objective was to resolve the contention over the disputed oil leases by further investigating Jackson's purported need for a guardian appointed by the county court. His agenda, however, was to assert federal authority as the "ultimate" guardian of restricted Indians. From the outset, Kelsey was predisposed to support District Agent Farrar's interpretation that a county court–appointed guardian was unnecessary. He also was inclined to favor the original Bartlett lease. The testimony at the Kelsey hearing was heavily weighed toward Jackson's competency. Farrar testified that Jackson was rational, spoke English, and seemed to understand the Bartlett agreement. Twenty years later, Farrar declared that Jackson Barnett impressed him as a man bordering on imbecility, but he declared under oath in this 1912 hearing, "I don't know, never heard that there was anything the matter with him. . . . I didn't see any difference whatever from the average full-blood Indian of his age." Jackson Barnett "stands in the same attitude of three-quarter and full-blood Indians of his age. . . . There should be Departmental supervision," he contended.[14]

In his testimony, O'Hornett provided little explanation for his rapid appointment as guardian and the signing of the Cornelius-Gooch lease. O'Hornett claimed he had no knowledge of the Bartlett lease. He also claimed the county court was acting responsibly by getting competitive lease offers, thus implying a local county court system could best represent an Indian ward's interests. O'Hornett even implied that Gooch and Cornelius had been overly generous: "Everybody I know said they were crazy for paying that much for it."[15]

Many Creek Indians testified through interpreters in defense of Jackson's competency. In light of subsequent investigations into his competency, this 1912 testimony constitutes an important record of how Jackson's peers evaluated his capabilities even though they were motivated to defend a fellow Creek to prevent his victimization in the state courts. Jesse McDermott, a full-blood Creek and one-time executive secretary of the Creek Nation, attested that he had known Jackson Barnett since around 1892. Though he had never had a long conversation with Jackson, McDermott drew on knowledge of other Creeks to assert that Jackson was "about as competent as any full-blood Indian of his age." David Fields, another full-blood Creek, testified through an interpreter that Jackson farmed, grew crops of his own, lived with Boney Randall (Timmie's father), Widow Brown, and others and was not crazy. Asked if Jackson knew "as much as the average full-blood Creek Indian," Fields replied, "Well he got sense enough to take care of himself." Other Creeks gave similar testimony. Full-blood Sango Johnson, fifty-seven, said he had a farm a mile and a half from the Randalls and had known Jackson well since the 1880s. Johnson said: "Yes he is [competent], just like the other full-bloods, got the same ways as the full-bloods. . . . [H]e is able to take care of himself, and he made several boats for me." Asked to compare Jackson's competence with his own, Johnson said Jackson's was "a little bit better."[16]

Timmie Randall, fifty-five, was a key witness. Speaking through an interpreter, Randall offered several proofs of Jackson's competency: home ownership before statehood, a self-supporting lifestyle, and business dealings in horses. In recent years, Jackson had lived periodically with the Randall family. At first he lived with Timmie's father, Boney, for two to three years. When Timmie married and established his own farm a mile away, Jackson moved there. A useful field hand for Randall, who had twenty-two acres in corn and five acres in oats, Jackson plowed, planted corn, and cared for the stock. Four years earlier, Randall recalled, Jackson had sold a bald-faced horse for $50 and still had $10 remaining from this transaction two years later. Randall also had personal knowledge of Jackson's interview with the county tax assessor, in which Jackson said he owned two horses worth $60 and $40, as well as a saddle. "Yes sir," Randall emphasized, "I am satisfied he can take care of his own stuff." Jackson was neither irrational nor a drinker. He behaved like an average full-blood. In the summer, he slept outside on the porch or under the trees; in the winter, he slept inside.[17]

Jackson's testimony drew a hilarious response from white observers. Bartlett's lawyer had to caution those present to maintain a proper decorum. Though he had an interpreter, Jackson answered the questions in English, initially in a faltering manner. He did not respond to questions about his name or residence, but eventually he became fairly coherent. Jackson could not say how old he was, but he had vague recollections of his past. He remembered a ferry run by an Indian; building and living in his own cabin; plowing, planting, and hoeing cotton for neighbors; building fences; and working for wages, which he spent on clothing and horse feed. He had no knowledge of the location of the land he leased to Bartlett, but he did vaguely remember signing the lease. Jackson said he did not know if he had ever married, but he did answer decisively that he had no children.[18]

Somewhat predictably, at the conclusion of the federal hearing, Superintendent Kelsey recommended that the Cornelius and Gooch lease be rejected and the Bartlett lease be approved. Bartlett had observed proper procedure in approaching Farrar, whose duty was to assess competency and administer the property of restricted Indians, while Cornelius and Gooch had not followed department channels. Bartlett was required to increase Jackson's bonus to $2,400, as a means of showing that federal government protection was as great as the county court's.[19]

Kelsey's primary objective was to make a decisive judgment to prevent an unending stream of hearings and litigation over Jackson's competency. But a second and weightier issue confronted Kelsey: the serious policy implications of the Barnett case. "If in cases of this kind a similar policy of appointing guardians is followed, 90 percent of the full-blood Indians might be adjudged incompetent."[20] Some consistent rule should be applied, Kelsey insisted. Either the federal bureau or the court-appointed guardians should serve to guard restricted Indians' estates, but not both. In Kelsey's judgment, as long as the federal government continued to support an Indian bureau whose responsibility was to transact business for Indians of this class, county court–appointed guardians were unnecessary. The fierce contest—with the inoffensive, unobtrusive Creek as its unlikely focus—involved issues that extended beyond Barnett's competency or the valuable lease. Rather, the test case involved controversies over principles and policies between state and federal politicians.

Despite the outcome of the federal hearing, Kelsey failed in the first attempt to bring the contest over the Barnett oil lease to closure. First, the lease dispute was kept in suspension when a motion for a new trial was filed after the state district court overturned the county court's judgment of Barnett's incompetency and set aside the appointment of O'Hornett. O'Hornett then vowed to take the case to the Oklahoma Supreme Court.[21] Second, the U.S. Supreme Court vindicated the county court's right to appoint guardians for incompetents in *Shelby v. Farve*.[22]

Superintendent Kelsey was concerned that oil drilling on adjacent properties to Barnett's allotment would undermine the value of the Barnett lease as the litigation worked itself slowly to the Oklahoma Supreme Court. He also suspected that the jurisdiction by Oklahoma's county court-appointed guardians would ultimately be vindicated. Seeking a speedy resolution that would serve Jackson Barnett's interests and perhaps to settle the matter of Barnett's competency in his own mind, Kelsey held another hearing on the conflicting leases in early August 1912. Again, he was skeptical of Cornelius and Gooch's testimony that Jackson had the mentality of a toddler. Kelsey knew it was not unusual for full-bloods who had received arbitrary allotments to not know anything about their properties, not as a reflection of their stupidity, but rather based on their political and cultural convictions. Jackson's behavior was fully consistent with that of disillusioned, conservative Creeks who were suspicious of any legal proceedings.[23]

As the conflicting testimony and Jackson's borderline traits seemed to preclude a final settlement on this issue, Kelsey was willing to make a compromise between the two lessees. Consequently, he told Bartlett and Cornelius and Gooch to settle, or he would disapprove both leases. The lessees agreed. Bartlett accepted control of one hundred acres and Cornelius and Gooch settled for sixty acres. As part of the compromise, the Interior Department sanctioned Carl O'Hornett as guardian. Bartlett, it was determined, had made his original lease in good faith as a speculator in "wildcat" territory before the incompetency judgment. The parties agreed that O'Hornett, as Jackson's legal guardian, would join in approving and executing the March 5, 1912, lease to Bartlett and legally invalidate the Cornelius-Gooch lease with the tacit understanding that Bartlett would immediately legally transfer sixty acres to Gooch. On September 12, 1912, Kelsey recommended approval of the Bartlett lease along with Bartlett's assignment of acreage to Gooch's newly incorporated company, Southwest Oil.[24]

Jackson Barnett was the chief beneficiary of this compromise. Painful litigation over his mental competency ended, he received a larger bonus of $4,600, and speculative drilling promised Jackson immediate royalty payments. Gooch, Cornelius, and Bartlett also enjoyed benefits. They were freed to sublease their holdings to others, which they did soon after the lease was formally approved by the Department of the Interior.[25] Although a state court was set to review the district court's ruling on Jack-

son's mental competency in September 1912, the case did not go forward
once the Bartlett-Gooch-Cornelius out-of-court settlement resolved the
dispute. By default, Jackson was legally declared mentally competent, since
the district court's reversal of the county court's judgment was not challenged. Still, the guardianship of O'Hornett had been vindicated along
with the jurisdiction of the county courts.[26] (See appendix III.)

Theoretical questions about Jackson's competency and about Indian
policy remained unresolved. Was Jackson a full-blood of average capability?
If he were average, did he require a guardian assigned by the county courts?
Was dual guardianship, as Farrar and Kelsey contended, a redundancy? Was
dual guardianship a safeguard because the Oklahoma guardianship system
was rife with corruption? Since the bureau defined all full-bloods as restricted due to culturally defined incompetency, should all full-bloods with
oil royalties require the double protection of the Indian bureau and a county
court-appointed guardian to ensure protection and to maximize bureaucratic oversight? Or was Jackson Barnett not an "average" full-blood at all?
Was he doubly incompetent—culturally as well as mentally—therefore requiring double guardianship? In Jackson's case, multiple attributes combined to suggest incompetency: his age (and perhaps the onset of senility),
illiteracy, borderline mental retardation, and culturally bred incapacity or
disinterest in business.

Though these would constitute pivotal questions in later Barnett litigation, it is doubtful that anyone worried about these technicalities in
1912, least of all Jackson Barnett. Under Kelsey's able administration, the
county courts and the Union Agency gradually worked out cooperative
arrangements for Jackson and other wealthy Indians on a case-by-case
basis. County-appointed guardians garnered a share of the incomes of
their wards and simultaneously provided services and legal protections for
wealthier Indians. There were tangible benefits to dual jurisdiction. The
appointment of a local guardian by the county court freed federal taxpayers and an overburdened Union Agency from this responsibility. Local
supervision by an honest administrator also promised greater efficiency
in attending to the minute details of rich Indians' personal financial needs
and protected their estates from the wiles of false creditors and other
predators.

Possible fraud was limited by the development of procedures of checks
and balances. All oil royalties went to the agency at Muskogee, where they
were deposited in the accounts of those with oil and gas leases. O'Hornett
and other guardians needed prior approval for all but petty expenditures.
Any request for a larger sum had to be approved by both the county court
judge and the federal Indian bureau. If approved, the agency issued a
voucher to the ward's guardian for the amount specified.

Kelsey's compromise in Barnett's case and the procedural accommodations to dual guardianship at the local level were mirrored on the national
level. Political wrangling in Congress in 1912 over appropriations for the

Indian bureau—which would have choked off funds for the Union
Agency's work—was checked by Burke's and Mott's charges of corruption
in the Oklahoma guardianship system. While major reforms did not mate-
rialize, some of the worst offenses of the Oklahoma probate system in
managing the estates of Indian minors and oil-rich adults were curbed.
Like the litigious opponents in the Barnett lease, the exhausted state and
federal contenders resigned themselves to compromise over the jurisdiction over restricted Indians' property.[27]

Carl O'Hornett's administration of Barnett's estate illustrates the bureau's modest success in curbing the abuses of the Oklahoma guardianship
system as well as the procedural accommodations of shared guardianship.
O'Hornett's tenure could be described as benign neglect. Over the next
eight years, for doing little but maintaining Jackson in shabby comfort,
O'Hornett collected a guardian fee of $200–400 per month compared to
Jackson's spending money of $40–50 per month. For this fee, O'Hornett
provided the basics for Jackson's moderate needs. Otherwise he took little
personal interest in Jackson's welfare.

The Union Agency at Muskogee took the initiative in providing a
permanent home for Jackson, using the bonus check from the Bartlett-
Gooch-Cornelius settlement for this purpose. Soon after the compromise
agreement, Superintendent Kelsey recommended buying forty acres and a
house for Jackson near Timmie Randall's homestead and fixing it up "so
that he can make a crop for himself next year." Kelsey asked Timmie to
talk it over with Jackson and Farrar, and on the same day Kelsey wrote to
Farrar with advice. "I don't want Barnett to get the monthly payment
habit. I think he is probably better able to look after small sums than many
other full-bloods. He should have enough to take care of himself and give
him a chance to see what he will do with it."[28]

After receiving a positive response from O'Hornett's attorney, Farrar
contacted the owner of thirty-five acres of timbered land near Randall's
homestead, obtained a land appraisal of $300, and made an offer. Paying
rigorous attention to procedure, the Indian bureau handled the transaction and carefully documented its actions in expending Jackson's money in
his behalf. Jackson's guardian, his lawyer, and the county court were also
involved in the legal procedure to approve the land purchase.[29]

O'Hornett later took the credit for providing a suitable home for
Jackson. Clearly, the Indian bureau had preempted him by purchasing the
property before O'Hornett received a salary for his duties. O'Hornett assumed responsibility for getting Jackson settled. He employed "negro"
boys to clear out the underbrush and fence Jackson's newly purchased
homestead. He hired workers to build a twenty-six-foot-square, four-room
house with a central stone fireplace. A barn, shed, pig pen, and chicken
shed were constructed, along with a two-room house and shed for an elderly African-American couple who served as Jackson's caretakers. O'Hornett purchased furniture, a team of ponies, and "a little red wagon and an-

other pony to ride, a milk cow and a sow pig or two," and Jackson's groceries and clothing.[30]

Since he no longer had to work, Jackson became a frequent visitor in nearby Henryetta. He rode into town on a horse or in his wagon two or three times a week. According to O'Hornett, he came as many as six times a week from 1913 to 1920. He regularly came to O'Hornett's drugstore for tobacco and malted milk, and he routinely visited his guardian's back office. O'Hornett asserted in a deposition, "He always wanted something, and he would take anything that you would buy for him."[31] This statement suggests that given the opportunity, Jackson Barnett might have developed an appreciation for more expensive consumer goods. Neither O'Hornett nor the bureau were inclined to encourage expenditures on frivolities, and the complex procedures for requesting large sums positively discouraged spending.

Jackson entered a new phase of life as a man of property and leisure. He went fishing, slept, and loafed. Always a horse lover, Jackson accumulated twelve to fifteen ponies and horses. He exercised good judgment in buying and swapping horses and treated them well. After his visits to O'Hornett's drugstore, he loitered in town, sometimes leaning against buildings and keeping to himself, before returning home at sundown. Jackson would converse about ponies but little else. Jackson "was just an ordinary Indian and attracted very little attention, and even after he had money he was as a matter of fact very hard to talk to," recalled a man who knew Jackson from these Henryetta years.[32]

In small ways, the local clerks and tradesmen liked to profit at the rich Indian's expense. Young men particularly found the reticent Indian to be a humorous oddity. W. H. Casey, a young man employed in O'Hornett's drugstore, stated that the boys would lead the compliant Barnett to the soda fountain, knowing he liked malted milk, and then charge their drinks to Barnett's account. After World War I, Casey went into the grocery business and talked O'Hornett into giving him Barnett's trade. Jackson would point at what he wanted, leaving Casey to judge the quantities he'd need. Sometimes Casey sold Jackson excessive quantities, according to O'Hornett.[33] Clerks at the drugstore and at the bank liked to shortchange Jackson just to tease him. A couple of times a week, O'Hornett would give Jackson checks for small sums—$5 or $10—and Jackson would come to cash them at the bank, endorsing with his thumbprint. One former cashier of the First National Bank, which O'Hornett directed, recalled that the "boys were always kidding with him." Jackson never said much in response but counted his money carefully. Other witnesses attested to this teasing, but only a rare witness admitted that the shortchanging ploys were successful. The bank tellers would lure Jackson to their windows with free cigars. On one occasion, while teasing Jackson, a cashier asked to whom Jackson would marry his imaginary daughter, to which Jackson, in clear English, said emphatically, "Not you!" An Indian boy would always try to get a dollar or two from Jackson, but "I do not think he ever got it, but he would try to," said one witness.[34]

At Jackson's new farm, African Americans socialized. Willie Griffin, an African American who worked on Timmie Randall's farm, became one of the frequent visitors who played music, danced, and lived off Jackson's bounty. Four "colored" people worked at Jackson's in the 1910s "getting a little wood and feeding and nothing much," said Griffin. Jackson gave them small sums of money—fifty cents or more—any time they asked. "A bunch of boys stayed around Jackson Barnett's place and ate and gambled. Jackson Barnett played 5-up for fun," George Washington, a black man, later testified. O'Hornett concurred, saying Jackson's main social contacts were his black house servants during these years. In contrast, Indian women refused to be employed by him, and other Indians kept their distance, considering Barnett "an evil spirit," said Griffin. His wealth perhaps attenuated his social contacts with fellow Creeks. As O'Hornett testified, Jackson "was just a different Indian." Jackson's own testimony was that he was friendly with his Indian neighbors.[35]

From 1913 to 1916, Jackson's unobtrusive manner, the circumspect way in which his modest needs were handled by the guardian and the bureau, and the petty grafting of those in Jackson's social orbit drew little attention. This suddenly changed in February 1916, when Gypsy Oil, which controlled one of the Barnett leases, hit an uncontrollable gusher. Soon, 14,000 barrels a day were being produced, and Jackson's royalties skyrocketed from $14,000 to almost $50,000 a month. Barnett's purchasing power also gushed: his 1917 income equaled $8.3 million in 2002 dollars. O'Hornett, too, profited, abruptly changing his career from druggist to banker after his fee rose to $600 a month.[36] Jackson's notoriety also increased. The *Muskogee Times-Democrat* featured the "deranged" Indian who roams the woods living on "herbs and bark, and what game he can kill" and who "cares nothing for money."[37] A Tulsa newspaper article under the headline "Creek Indian with Million Dollars in Bank Virtually Is Starving to Death Now" puzzled over the peculiarity that a man with such extravagant wealth lived so humbly.[38] An Interior Department memorandum romanticized Jackson as a one-time Plains nomad and freedom fighter, who lived simply on $100–200 a month, and had a reputation for integrity and sobriety.[39] Such publicity—sensationally invoking caricatures of Indians and applying them to Jackson or reporting fictitious details—created an insatiable curiosity about the inscrutable and eccentric Jackson Barnett. It also heightened awareness of Jackson's naivete about money and invited speculation about how his surplus wealth—which a "simple" Indian could not possibly spend in a lifetime—could be put to use.

An embarrassment of riches was accumulating daily in Jackson's government-controlled savings accounts. According to the *New York Times*, $115,000 had been deposited in state and private banks in Oklahoma and another $456,400 placed in nine national banks. Common

Taken about 1919–1920, this photo of Jackson Barnett, sitting in a wicker chair, shows him as a kindly and unpretentious rural American. This pose was perhaps staged by the Sells administration to portray him as a Christian philanthropist. Courtesy of the National Archives, Pacific Region, Laguna Niguel.

knowledge of this "unearned increment" was apparently a source of uneasiness for O'Hornett. During World War I, O'Hornett patriotically recommended to Oklahoma senator Robert Owen and Congressman William W. Hastings that the $800,000 surplus be invested in Liberty Loan Bonds, but there were doubts about the legality of doing so since Barnett did not initiate the request. Was the Oklahoma guardian or Jackson's federal guardian, the Department of the Interior, empowered to make such a potentially risky investment? The department hesitated as it puzzled over the limits of the guardians' authority.[40]

Meanwhile, Jackson entered the national limelight as the "World's Richest Indian" when the *New York Times* examined the proposed war bond purchase. If an Indian under guardianship was permitted to purchase Liberty Bonds, a precedent would be set, thus opening the door for purportedly voluntary (or perhaps involuntary) purchases by other restricted Indians whose assets were held in trust.[41] A *Times* editorial headlined "Why Does He Need a Guardian?" illustrated the oft-repeated public disregard for (and misunderstanding of) federal legal protection of Indian assets when overwhelming public opinion impatiently demanded the release of Indian resources into the economy. The editorial argued that public opinion was strongly in favor of the patriotic gesture. The Okmulgee County court, the Union Agency, and other agencies urged that the bonds be purchased. Patriotic fervor swept away all doubts, and Jackson's money was converted to Liberty Bonds. A photograph of Jackson Barnett, celebrating his patriotic action, was framed and proudly hung in O'Hornett's Henryetta bank.[42]

If Jackson's "idle" wealth could be used for patriotic causes, why not charitable purposes? The American Red Cross soon appealed for $50,000 of Jackson's surplus funds for its organization. Telegrams endorsing the action to further the organization's nationwide fundraising campaign flowed into bureau headquarters in the Department of the Interior. When legal advice recommended against donations without Barnett's consent, O'Hornett was informed by telegram that he had no authority to make donations to the Red Cross with Barnett's money.[43]

Though the federal government had halted the public consumption of Jackson's money for charitable purposes, within two years the campaign was renewed. The building committee of the First Baptist Church of Henryetta hatched a plan to tap Barnett's funds for construction of a new church. In March or April 1919, the building committee—which included the Reverend E. D. Cameron, chairman of the committee, and Dr. W. S. Wiley, head of the Southern Baptist Convention—made a visit to Jackson's home where, committee members recalled, they prayed and talked. Then Jackson allegedly walked to a little shelf and produced a picture of an orphans building in Oklahoma City and expressed a wish to help orphans and to also build the Baptist church. Afterward Jackson signed papers for a $25,000 donation to the building fund. In Wiley's opinion, "Jackson Barnett had as much, if not greater, intelligence than the average, uneducated Indian and fully understood the purpose and effect of his donation." Along with a letter from the committee asking for approval was a request in writing from Jackson Barnett, with his thumbprint signature.[44]

The bureau fully endorsed this charitable donation, ostensibly originated by Jackson. Both Superintendent Gabe Parker, Kelsey's successor as head of the bureau's Union Agency at Muskogee, and Commissioner of Indian Affairs Cato Sells warmly endorsed the proposal from Henryetta's philanthropically inclined Christian community leaders. After a visit to Henryetta and a meeting with the building committee and Jackson Barnett in mid-July 1919, Sells approved the donation for $25,000, and a petition was filed for approval by the county court. Having become disgusted by the continual opportunings from Henryetta churches for Jackson Barnett's money, O'Hornett opposed the planned donation and hired legal counsel to represent him. When the county judge overruled his objection, O'Hornett gave his consent but begged the court for a determination of the "legal capacity of said ward to make said gift."[45]

In examining the legality of Jackson's ability to make the large bequest, the Okmulgee County court paid scrupulous attention to due process. The building committee members testifying were unanimous in their evaluation that Jackson had the mental capacity to understand what he was doing, and the most prominent men in town vouched for his mental competence. Henryetta physician Ira Robertson attested to Jackson Barnett being "a man of average intelligence for a man in his station in life. He is at least an average full-blood Indian." Lawyer Barclay Morgan presented Barnett's bilingualism as proof of his intelligence.[46]

As a demonstration of its support for the donation, the Department of the Interior had its solicitors prepare a legal brief regarding the conditions under which a guardian could approve a charitable donation by an incompetent, based on an eminent authority on the subject. The Baptists drew upon Interior's legal brief to argue that a ward is not to be prevented from helping others if he so chooses, subject to certain conditions. Donations by persons of "unsound mind and under guardianship" could be made very cautiously to benevolent causes by a proper tribunal. The ward must have the mental capacity to understand the act, the request must be made upon his own application, and the ward must have sufficient property. Bequests could be made to immediate relatives. Moreover, it was the guardian's duty to allow reasonable comforts, and even indulge the ward in fancied enjoyments and harmless caprice, if these did not exceed the limits of income.[47]

Having duly considered the matter and finding Jackson "free of undue influence" and "considering the magnitude of the ward's estate," the court approved the donation for the church construction. All legal obstacles were surmounted once the full approval of the Department of the Interior, the county court, and the guardian had been obtained. The money was forwarded to the Reverend Cameron of the First Baptist Church of Henryetta. Jackson Barnett's name was inscribed on a memorial window in the church his money had funded.[48]

The willingness to approve the Baptist church donation from Jackson's funds opened Pandora's box for the Interior Department. There was a palpable frenzy of opportunism in the air in 1919 regarding Jackson Barnett's estate, and it was not limited to those with philanthropic or patriotic motives. Days after the approval of the church donation, Jackson's half brother David Barnett visited the Union Agency in Muskogee to ascertain the attitude of the department toward Jackson's intended bequest to him of $50,000. A man with long gray hair who eked out an existence with his daughter on a hilly farm, David apparently had his hopes raised by the news that Interior would look favorably on gifts by incompetents to immediate relatives.[49] From September 1919 to January 1920, there were requests for funding projects to rehabilitate drug addicts, for a Children's Home Finding and Welfare League, and for Nazarene, Methodist, and Catholic churches. In March 1920, there was a $75,000 request to fund a health home in South Dakota; in May 1920, funds for a memorial to the Indian Massasoit were requested. Individuals requested smaller donations to buy homes.[50]

The selfless and the selfish, the needy and the greedy found their way to Jackson's door in the following months with requests for donations. O'Hornett and the Union Agency were besieged with demands for approval of such requests. Barnett compliantly thumbprinted many documents put before him, a Henryetta resident recalled. Out of principle or discretion some Creek interpreters refused to participate in these thumbprinting schemes. Daniel Webster Watson, a Creek, testified he did not believe Jackson was competent to make bequests, "because a man could go to him and tell him just anything and he would believe you if he liked you."[51] Dealing with Jackson's thumbprinted bequests became a daily nuisance for O'Hornett.

Whetted by the success in getting the $25,000 donation, the Baptist building committee and its allies had ambitions for getting even more of Jackson's money. A document allegedly penned by Jackson Barnett in support of the church project, dated August 1, 1919, stated:

> [A]s I am an old man that I would much rather give all my money to a good cause than I would to have my money and estate fussed over after my death[.] I am thoroughly familiar that after my death that there will be many claims by supposed relatives, who no doubt will receive a portion of whatever estate I will have. Therefore, I further state that I am sorry that I can not give

all my money to a like cause of the construction of this building
or any other building or any building or donation of this
likeness.[52]

As the speculative excitement grew in the latter half of 1919, a cadre of
prominent Baptist citizens around Henryetta joined in a common goal.
Jackson purportedly pledged $226,000 to three different Baptist churches
and another $200,000 to the Southern Baptist Convention for its fund
drive. O'Hornett meanwhile went on record against any more donations,
even those supported by the Indian bureau.[53]

Commissioner Cato Sells, a Baptist, colluded with the citizens who
were trying to gain control of the bulk of the Barnett fortune for charitable
purposes. After his first meeting with Jackson in Henryetta in mid-1919,
Sells said, "I worked out in my mind the idea of his making a considerable
donation by the way of a larger sum of money for the establishment of a
hospital for sick Indians." Sells returned to Henryetta two to three months
later to discuss the project, including the location of a building site, with
local citizens. Sells claimed the plan took shape because of the persuasive
1919 county court evidence regarding Jackson's competency and the
knowledge of Jackson's "fast accumulating" wealth, estimated to be $2 mil-
lion and piling up at the rate of $10,000 per month. Sells believed that
roughly $1 million would pay for the "Jackson Barnett Hospital." Jackson
could have a home on the grounds. Sells testified that they discussed the
idea in the fall of 1919 and that Jackson Barnett gave verbal approval and
thumbprinted the documents.[54]

At Sells's request, Lafayette Walker, a bureau probate attorney who
was also a Creek, approached Barnett with the request for hospital construction funds. Walker later testified that Barnett acted like he did not
comprehend the request. George Riley Hall, a newspaper publisher and
prominent Henryetta citizen, also approached Jackson seeking $200,000
for a proposed Indian hospital. The request was made in both Creek and
English, and Jackson readily placed his thumbprint on the documents.
Hall later admitted he had been naïve and was caught up in a plan, originated by others, to mine Jackson's fortunes for philanthropic purposes.
Hall admitted he did not know who drew up the papers and that Jackson
did not know what he was signing.[55]

Was Commissioner Cato Sells engaged with Henryetta citizens in a
subterfuge to trick an incompetent Indian into donating a vast sum of
money to a pet project against the Indian's express wishes? Such a possibility appears entirely likely. Why was Jackson approached repeatedly to
sign documents if, as Sells claimed under oath, he approved the Sells plan
and willingly thumbprinted the legal documents in late 1919? Jackson later
testified that he told Sells "no" and refused to endorse the hospital plan.
When Sells testified to these events in 1926, he wept on the stand, explaining that the hospital plan "was very close to his heart." Shattered nerves

may explain his show of emotion but so too might his fear that an indictment for fraud and public humiliation was pending. Other ranking Interior officials were being indicted in the Barnett affair at that time, and Sells
had just cause to think he also might be prosecuted.[56]

At the time the donation was being solicited, Sells was troubled by the
impoverished appearance and rough clothes of the prospective hospital
benefactor. After visiting Barnett's "uninviting" home, Sells reproached
O'Hornett. The guardian defended himself by saying that Jackson never
complained, but he complied with Sells's request to make improvements.
In November 1919, the Department of the Interior approved a request for
$2,610 for a Paige Speedster car. Jackson's paltry allowance of $100–200
per month was increased to $650, and plans were approved for a $2,000
garage and other outbuildings and $1,000 for road construction.[57] Under
Sells's leadership, the bureau was shielding itself from charges of negligence
as Jackson was groomed for the role of philanthropist, and in doing so the
bureau was obliged to revise its policy of granting only minimal allowances
to incompetent Indians with oil leases. A bureau lawyer referred to Barnett
in an early 1920 legal brief as a man with "a benevolent and religious turn
of mind."[58]

The unfolding events of 1919 forged an alliance of interests among
high-ranking bureau officials at the Union Agency and in Washington,
D.C., the Southern Baptist leadership, and the "reliable and responsible"
citizens of Henryetta. As Christian organizations became the designated
repositories for the "surplus" funds of oil-rich Indians, this bureau-Baptist
alliance developed under the administrations of Cato Sells and Charles
Burke from 1913 to 1929. The federal government increasingly turned to
church institutions, and the churches in turn looked for support from the
Indian bureau in their activities. Motivating this symbiosis was the exhaus-
tion of the Five Civilized Tribes' resources. For years, Marshall Mott, Dana
Kelsey, and others had been predicting that Oklahoma Indians would become dependent upon public assistance without adequate protection by
the federal government. The Creeks and others could no longer support
their own educational institutions or assistance programs for orphans, the
ill, or the indigent from tribal funds, thereby forcing heavy responsibility
on the county and state governments and private charities. Meanwhile,
Oklahoma taxpayers were unwilling to support services for restricted Indians who were exempt from local taxation. Both the Northern and Southern Baptists sought outright gift donations from Indians with oil wealth,
and these donations made by wealthy, competent, and restricted Indians
to Baptist institutions were as a matter of course sanctioned by the Indian
bureau. Thus, Baptists and the Indian bureau joined in efforts to endow
Indian churches, hospitals, orphanages, and schools, improvements that
would undoubtedly have numerous benefits for the non-Indian community as well.

The alliance between the Baptists and the Indian bureau solidified

Jackson Barnett's home outside Henryetta, Okmulgee County, Oklahoma, from 1912 to 1921, purchased for him after oil was discovered on his Creek County Allotment. Used as an exhibit to show Jackson's impoverished lifestyle under O'Hornett's guardianship, the photo shows the $2,000 tar-paper garage commissioned by O'Hornett after Commissioner Sells chided him for neglecting Jackson Barnett. Courtesy of the National Archives, Pacific Region, Laguna Niguel.

under Baptist commissioner Cato Sells's administration (1913–1921) and remained firm during the term of his successor, Charles Burke (1921–1929). Within two short years of secretary Lane's infamous New Policy of 1917, the Indian bureau was again facilitating the transfer of Indian assets to private, non-Indian ownership, this time justifying its action with a noble, philanthropic motive.[59]

From 1912 to 1919, Jackson Barnett went through a remarkably rapid metamorphosis from a recalcitrant Snake, to an average Indian, to a village idiot, to a root-and-berry-picking savage, to a hunter-warrior with integrity, back to an average Indian, and finally to an aged Chieftain and Christian philanthropist, a man of Christian instincts.[60] These images clearly mirrored the changing desires, interests, and motives of those who advanced them.

Sells's action stripped Jackson of his legal protection. Those who coveted his money drew ever closer to devouring his estate. Even persons of high moral character fell under the temptation. It was not lust for money that seduced these respectable men, but the power to do good works, which came from control of the estate. But the best-laid plans of these men were foiled by a woman, who soon arrived and outwitted them all.

4

Anna, Adventuress
of a Most Dangerous Type
1920-1923

On Thursday, January 29, 1920, thirty-nine-year-old Anna Laura Lowe of Kansas City, an attractive and sophisticated brunette, stepped off the train at the Henryetta station. Those who looked closely may have noticed she was a bit run down at the heels. The years of using her wits and feminine charms to support herself and her young daughter had worn on her. Having placed her daughter at a Catholic boarding school in Kansas City, Lowe lived in hotel rooms and rode the trains from Kansas to Texas, working as a liaison between oil companies and lessors, always on the lookout for ways to create a life of freedom and privilege for herself. Two months earlier, while waiting to see a Texas broker about a sale, she had noticed a short article in an oil journal about the wealthy Indian in Henryetta. She decided to investigate.

After checking into a hotel, Lowe hired the Johnson livery service to take her eight miles over dirt roads to the home of Jackson Barnett. She told Johnson she was seeking a charitable donation. When she arrived, Jackson consented to a brief barnyard interview across a water trough and woodpile. The sixty-four-year-old Barnett told Lowe he could not help her with money and had no need of a housekeeper. Having failed in her entreaties for money, Anna left him with a warning about missionaries out to get his money: "[N]one of them care anything about you."[1] Anna Lowe was absorbed in thought on her return trip to Henryetta. Within hours, she again hired Johnson to drive her to Jackson's farm, telling the driver that "she was going to try another scheme. . . . If she could get him in the car she would take him and get married to him."[2]

In her second meeting with Jackson Barnett, Anna was animated and vivacious, and she soon flirtatiously suggested elopement. With her feminine charms, she enlisted the aid of taxi driver Johnson and Willie Griffin (Timmie Randall's hired man). Willie persuaded Jackson to take a ride in the taxi, and the four went to Okemah, the county seat of Okfuskee County, about twelve miles away. The other men were drinking whiskey with Anna, and she allegedly tried to pour liquor down Jackson's throat, but he was not a drinker and probably resisted her efforts. Jackson was reluctant to go to Okemah, but Willie Griffin spoke to him reassuringly in Creek while Anna pressed close to Jackson and "was trying to love him." According to Johnson's recollection, "She got right up against him and had hold of him." "What do you mean by that?" Johnson was later asked in court. "Did she have her arm around him?" Johnson testified: "No, sir, she had her hand down in his pants." Jackson "got roused up to something like young days, and after that she seemed she could handle him most any way."[3] While Johnson's graphic characterization may have been somewhat exaggerated, Anna was no innocent and undoubtedly used her sexual wiles to get Jackson to elope.

At Okemah, they went directly to the county clerk's office to apply for a marriage license. During a conversation in which the intoxicated wedding party tried to convince the clerk that Jackson Barnett wished to get married, the clerk angrily suggested that the old "nigger," Griffin, was coaching Jackson in Creek on what to say. His suspicions aroused, the clerk contacted the bureau field agent, who adamantly opposed the request for a license. The field agent in turn called the agency headquarters in Muskogee.[4] Once the authorities had been alerted, Anna was desperate to achieve her objective. She pressed the party to drive to Holdenville, the Hughes County seat, to obtain a license. They drank more whiskey and wine, but the initial exhilaration and optimism were flagging. Willie Griffin, Johnson, and Jackson had wearied of the adventure, and Johnson began to worry that Anna would not pay the taxi bill. Anna had to use all of her powers of persuasion to goad them onward. She promised Griffin "a fist full of money," and she told Johnson he would get "$1,500 if he would do the driving and she got married to Jackson Barnett." She assured him she had the means to pay, but did not say who was providing the financial backing.[5]

They arrived at Holdenville late that night, found lodging in a hotel, and went to the clerk's office the following day. There, an assistant clerk immediately recognized Jackson as that "rich Indian about Henryetta." Knowing Jackson was a restricted Indian with a guardian, the clerk refused to process the marriage application Anna had made. As in Okemah, an Indian bureau agent put in a call to his superiors in Muskogee.[6] The superintendent instructed the field agent to detain Jackson there until his guardian could be consulted. A federal probate attorney entertained the elopement party during the wait. When questioned about her motives, Anna said, "Money helps," but insisted she would marry Jackson even if he were poor. Anna also told Griffin she was marrying for love. Asked how long he had known his betrothed, Jackson responded cheerfully, "Oh, I got acquainted yesterday, and I liked her pretty well, so thought we'd get married."[7] Outside of Lowe's presence, Jackson conceded that she had solicited money from him from the start. Though Anna's motives were highly suspicious, could a marriage application be refused if Jackson were willing? Even restricted Indians married. It was a difficult call and one willingly deferred to superiors at agency headquarters.[8] After two hours of discussion, Jackson grew restless and wanted to walk around. Shortly thereafter, O'Hornett called the Holdenville field agent with instructions to hold Jackson and to withhold the license. But by then the party had left town.

Alarmed that the quartet was still at large, the superintendent at Muskogee ordered all county clerks in the vicinity not to issue a marriage license to Anna and Jackson. A day later, the abduction, the Okemah and Holdenville marriage attempts, and the efforts to prevent the issuance of the license were front page news in the *Muskogee Times-Democrat*. By then, the eastern side of the state was being combed for the elopers. When Commissioner Sells learned of the abduction of his hospital benefactor, he arranged for an immediate trip to Henryetta.

Anna conceded defeat in her first attempt to marry Jackson. Her money was exhausted, and her accomplices were discouraged. Willie Griffin explained to Anna that Jackson could not sign checks without his guardian's consent. Johnson, in fact, had to settle for a $50 voucher for the seventy-mile trip, which was some time in coming.

O'Hornett was waiting for Anna at the Elks Hotel in Henryetta when she returned. He tried to persuade her that the scheme was fruitless. In a patronizing manner, the guardian assured her she was "too smart" to fool with Jackson Barnett. As a "woman of ability," she could spend her time more beneficially on some other endeavor. Jackson's monthly allowance was meager, he explained, and she could not inherit his wealth. Lowe responded stubbornly that she intended to marry Jackson and that Superintendent Gabe Parker, Commissioner Cato Sells, and guardian O'Hornett could not stop her. During a drive to the train depot, Anna told Johnson that "they were going to run Jackson Barnett away from her." Several days later, Commissioner Sells, Superintendent Parker, and the Reverend Cameron of the Henryetta Baptist Church visited Jackson and insisted he travel to Washington, D.C. They bought him a $35 suit, a leather coat, a hat, and shoes for the trip. As Anna had predicted, Jackson was soon out of Oklahoma. Parker and O'Hornett also traveled to the capital to meet with Commissioner Sells. Jackson relaxed at the zoo while the others strategized.[9]

This meeting in early February 1920 was prompted by the need to gain speedy approval of the Henryetta consortium's applications for donations from Barnett's funds from the secretary of the Interior. The Baptists had lobbied hard in Congress for the donation, and Sells had been persuaded to make a firm political commitment in return for Baptist support for his upcoming bid for a Texas seat in the U.S. Senate. Jackson Barnett was approached by the Reverend Cameron and two allies, and Jackson on February 11, 1920, allegedly thumbprinted a document donating $1,462,000 to charity. If the deal was consummated, the three opportunists would receive shares of $105,000 for their efforts. Just two weeks after Anna's attempt to marry Jackson, front-page stories in Oklahoma newspapers announced Sells's approval of a $1.5 million bequest by Jackson Barnett. Under the distribution plan, $1 million was earmarked for the Indian hospital in Henryetta; $200,000 for the missionary, educational, and benevolent fund of the Southern Baptist Convention; $50,000 for the Oklahoma City Children's Home Finding and Welfare League; $50,000 for the Murrow Orphans home at Bacone College in Muskogee; $25,000 each for several Oklahoma churches; and lesser amounts for others. Sells leaked the story prematurely to the Associated Press, for it had not yet been approved by the new secretary of the Interior.[10]

Sells's announcement, perhaps meant to discourage Anna, backfired. As the donation had not received the requisite approval of the secretary of the Interior, Sells was compelled to issue a retraction. Moreover, a Treasury Department report on Jackson's account disclosed that his wealth had been greatly overestimated by both Sells and O'Hornett. Had someone embezzled funds?[11] As the Barnett fortune was a mere $1.1 million, the allocation of funds would need to be renegotiated among the would-be beneficiaries. Meanwhile, the National Surety Company, a New York bond company, won an injunction preventing bureau officials from disbursing large amounts from Jackson's monies. The company argued that the courts should decide the legality of any disbursement before it was made. O'Hornett probably initiated this legal action; both he and the surety firm feared criminal prosecution and financial penalties if there were any later charges of malfeasance in handling Jackson Barnett's funds.[12]

From the newspaper stories, Anna Lowe was well apprised of Sells's scheme for the immediate charitable distribution of Jackson's estate. She knew she must act swiftly and decisively if she were to secure her prize. But how? By a prior arrangement with the taxi driver Johnson, Anna resorted to coded telegrams asking, "How is mother?" If Jackson was not at his farm, Johnson would wire that mother was "not well." Responding to early inquiries on February 3 and February 12, Johnson reported, "Mother is gone" or "Mother not doing well." Explaining his motivation, Johnson said, "[Anna] said she'd give me $1,500 if they got married. . . . I got fifty later." When Jackson returned from Washington, Johnson wired: "Mom is home." Anna immediately sped to Jackson's home accompanied by some Tulsa friends, the Mooreheads, to whom she promised $1 million in return for their help in securing a legal marriage.[13]

The raiding party swept down on Jackson Barnett's farm late on the evening of February 22. Six African Americans, including Willie Griffin, were playing the graphonola and dancing. When Jackson came out, Anna and Mrs. Moorehead urged Jackson to take a ride to see his oil wells. Anna tried to induce Griffin to accompany them, but he'd been sternly warned against cooperating with her. When Jackson was induced into the car, he was shoeless, bareheaded, and without an overcoat. Anna barked orders at Jackson's caretakers to bring some clothing, and then they raced toward the Kansas state line. When O'Hornett was informed about the abduction by a black youngster about ninety minutes later, he contacted the police.[14]

In the car, Anna repeatedly told Jackson they were going to be married, and he merely grunted. They drove all night and the next morning reached Coffeyville, Kansas, which Anna mistook for the county seat. Undaunted, she took the interurban line to Independence, the Montgomery County seat, and procured a marriage license. Alvin Moorehead fronted the $10 for carfare and the marriage license. After Anna returned with the license, Moorehead arranged for a local justice of the peace, Charles Bickett, to perform the ceremony. With the Mooreheads as witnesses, the two were married at the Metropolitan rooming house in Coffeyville. Jackson recalled she did not hug or kiss him, nor did he hug or kiss her on the wedding night.[15] The press gleefully reported details of the Barnett elopement and relentlessly pursued the story as it unfolded.

Anna Lowe's swift success in establishing herself as a claimant to the Barnett fortune was as unexpected as it was devastating, derailing plans and upsetting tentative alliances. In their wildest dreams, O'Hornett, Sells, and the Reverend Cameron never expected a serious challenge would come from a woman. Opposing Anna was a powerful cast of players, foremost among them O'Hornett and his lawyers. Anna's intrusion most directly challenged their vested financial interests. They had collected service fees and shared lucrative shares of litigation costs, for example, handsome shares from income tax suits in 1917 and 1919. They also greedily anticipated large profits when his estate would be probated in Okmulgee County after Jackson Barnett's death. A second local group of players in Barnett's affairs were the Baptists and other church groups, which were aggressively bidding for a share of Jackson's estate. They took a proprietary stance that the Barnett money should be spent locally to endow local institutions and benefit the local economy. The initiative to divide the estate among local organizations enjoyed broad-based political support in Okmulgee County and in wider circles of Oklahoma and the South.

A third local player was Okmulgee County judge Hugh Murphy, who upheld the power of the county courts over Indian incompetents and believed strongly that the control of the Barnett fortune was a local prerogative. Murphy was sympathetic to O'Hornett for this reason, though he did

so in defense of the established dual guardianship system, not for any pecuniary reason. Judge Murphy and Jackson's guardian cooperated to block
Anna's access to Jackson's funds.

The fourth major stakeholder, with a strong voice in who would control and disburse Jackson's assets, was the federal Bureau of Indian Affairs,
including the commissioner of Indian affairs and his loyal political ap-
pointees at the Union Agency. With the Okmulgee County court and
guardian, the bureau shared legal guardianship and was responsible for
protecting and serving the ward. The bureau purportedly was disinterested, but in fact it had a considerable political stake in Jackson's marriage.
During Cato Sells's administration, the bureau was compelled by the con-
certed political pressure from the Southern Baptists to endorse the charitable donations. O'Hornett and his lawyers were opposed to the disbursement of the Barnett fortune to charity because they clearly wished to
preserve their lucrative incomes. But they were overwhelmed by the combined local and federal political forces arrayed against them. They adopted
a pragmatic but uneasy alliance with the bureau and the prospective charitable beneficiaries, hoping to broker a compromise in which a large portion of the Barnett estate—money in state bank accounts and the in-
coming royalties—would still be under their management. Covertly,
O'Hornett and his lawyers likely used the injunction suit by the National
Surety Company to postpone the Indian bureau's approval of the charitable disbursement until after Jackson died.

These four parties were united once Anna succeeded in marrying
Jackson. Surely their joint efforts would serve to drive off—or buy off—
this audacious female intruder. The powerful men involved were confident
that their prerogatives would be restored and their vested interests upheld.
The Indian bureau and O'Hornett went immediately into action to annul
the marriage.

Anna proved to be a more formidable foe than they anticipated.
O'Hornett's attempt to persuade Jackson to return home voluntarily was
frustrated by Anna's refusal to admit him to the hotel room. Repeated attempts were made in the next seventy-two hours to kidnap Jackson, but
Anna foiled them—on one occasion, at gunpoint. While Anna was using a
telephone on another floor and Jackson was sunning himself in a window,
men drove by holding up a fishing pole trying to entice Jackson into their
car. Before this ploy could succeed, Anna corralled Jackson in their room
and turned a pistol on the would-be kidnappers. "I'm not a gun woman
but the trespasser who crosses my threshold to assail my husband may expect to be shot," Anna told reporters.[16] "I will stop at nothing to make
this marriage stick. . . . If it's a fight [O'Hornett] wants, let him come."
Coffeyville had not seen such excitement since the days of the Dalton
boys. Jackson was probably sedated to keep him compliant and reportedly
slept during most of his Coffeyville honeymoon.[17]

Alarmed that Jackson would be stolen from her, Anna sought allies. She contacted Justice of the Peace Bickett for help. He phoned the police, who were sent to guard the hotel room. He also referred her to a Coffeyville lawyer, Harold McGugin. For the referral, Bickett wanted a 10 percent kickback of whatever McGugin and his partner, Walter Keith, made on the case. (Bickett ultimately received $1,000.) On March 1, 1920, Anna signed a contract agreeing to give McGugin and Keith 25 percent of whatever she gained from Barnett's estate if these lawyers successfully defended the legality of the marriage. In the contract, Keith and McGugin agreed to advance their own money for the legal defense; specifically mentioned was the lawyers' commitment to hire experts to attest to Jackson's competency. Anna left the Metropolitan Hotel only to confer with McGugin, and she and McGugin hovered nearby when O'Hornett was finally allowed to meet with Jackson. Under McGugin and Anna Barnett's direction, Jackson Barnett thumbprinted a document repudiating the $1.5 million donation.[18]

To their collective chagrin, O'Hornett, the Baptists, and the bureau realized that they could only annul the marriage by the argument that Jackson lacked the mental competency to understand the marriage contract since they had just verified that his church donation to the Baptists was the voluntary act of a mentally competent individual. Sells's plan for disbursement of the bulk of the estate to charity was suspended. O'Hornett immediately realized he could not underestimate his formidable opponent. He told a reporter:

> She's a mighty smart woman. She's well-backed financially and legally, and it will take a lot of hard work to defeat her. . . . And don't get the idea that she is a cheap adventuress. She had this thing figured out from every angle before she went into it. And with all her independence, she's a real lady as far as I know.[19]

Also working to Anna's advantage was the sympathetic coverage by the press. Information that she was the former wife of an Oklahoma territorial official enhanced her image of a woman of quality. While government lawyers and O'Hornett were engaged in the effort to annul the marriage, newspapers fell under the spell of romance. Flattering pictures of the couple—especially the photogenic Anna—appeared in the press daily. Anna set to grooming and clothing Jackson, and transformed his image from that of an unkempt, weak-minded Indian. With a rakish tilt to his hat and a Barney Oldfield slant to his cigar, Jackson now looked like a virile, confident, millionaire oil baron. Photographs of Anna showed a socially respectable woman, her appearance belying her hardscrabble roots and gun-toting determination. Shrewdly manipulating the media and public opinion, Anna delivered highly romanticized, fictionalized accounts of her courtship with Jackson and her past. The tangle of legal technicalities regarding Jackson's incompetency and objections to the marriage were unfathomable and uninteresting to newspaper readers; it was the romance that appealed. "I love Jackson Barnett," she told a reporter. He "is just as sane as any Indian, and has just as much sense."[20]

In her public persona, Anna presented herself as a woman in the throes of love languishing in the happy hours of her honeymoon. Behind the scenes she was feverishly and desperately creating a legal fortification for the marriage. Learning of a Kansas statute against incompetents marrying without their guardians' permission, McGugin called a fellow attorney to inquire about what law was in effect. To ensure their union was ironclad, Jackson and Anna drove to Missouri and were remarried on February 26, 1920. There, the justice of the peace joked that Oklahoma guardians had no jurisdiction in Missouri. Jackson resented the second marriage ceremony, commenting later, "I got married twice. That wasn't fair."[21]

Anna was wise to cultivate public sympathy and to fortify her marriage legally, for within a week of the elopement an attack on the marriage was being orchestrated by her many powerful adversaries. Commissioner Sells provided the leadership for the offensive and authorized the use of Jackson Barnett's money to pay for many of the expenses. Sells conferred with Superintendent Parker, O'Hornett, and the guardian's lawyers in Muskogee. Finally, Sells committed agency resources to the goal of destroying the marriage. James C. Davis, attorney for the Five Civilized Tribes, was assigned to the case. Davis filed a writ of habeas corpus in the Supreme Court of Kansas, *O'Hornett v. Lowe*, claiming that Jackson had been kidnapped and was being held against his will.[22]

Contesting the legality of the marriage was one part of the allies' strategy to get Anna to abandon her captive by making life miserable for her. O'Hornett refused all but the paltry allowance of $100 a month as long as the couple remained in Kansas. O'Hornett hinted at greater access to Jackson's money to lure Anna and Jackson back to Oklahoma. Anna refused, fearing that the courts would annul the marriage there. She later alleged she was offered a sizable sum of money to leave Jackson, which she refused. Meanwhile, the allies launched an investigation into her past in order to discredit her. An FBI investigator and a private detective agency were put on the case. By March, enough compromising information on Anna's past had been collected to enable O'Hornett to launch an appeal that Jackson be placed in his custody. O'Hornett argued that Jackson's life was endangered; he was depressed and discontented in captivity. O'Hornett now labeled Anna "an adventuress of pronounced type," who was "actuated and inspired by artful and designing motives, calculated and intended to deceive and defraud persons of their property." A "white woman of questionable reputation," she used "treacherous wiles and allurements on him, and pretends for him a love and affection . . . contrary to the laws of nature and common experience." O'Hornett's final argument for the improbable nature of the union included this observation: Jackson was "black" and old, and Anna was white, young, and pretty.[23]

Anna and her lawyers mounted a remarkably successful defense considering the powerful and well-funded opposition. McGugin and Keith attacked O'Hornett, alleging incompetence and cupidity as a guardian, among other complaints. O'Hornett kept Jackson in poverty and conspired to give vast sums to charity. Charity was a mere cover for graft, they argued. Moreover, the bureau officials were conspiring to alienate Anna's husband's affections, and O'Hornett was denying his ward the funds for legitimate expenses. Given the fact that the guardian had four attorneys working to annul the marriage, the court authorized an expenditure of $1,000 to pay for Anna's legal counsel. This was the wedge Anna needed: the right to access Jackson's abundant assets to defend a purportedly happy and consensual marriage. The court also required the guardian to pay other reasonable expenses for the couple. Jackson was in the legal custody of the sheriff and O'Hornett during the court proceedings, but these men were forbidden from interfering in the couple's marital relations.[24]

The Kansas Supreme Court refused to hear the case, but it assigned a referee to conduct a hearing, which began in early April. After several days of testimony in the hotly contested trial, the judge received permission to question Jackson in order to ascertain the rich Indian's true disposition toward the marriage. Asked how he happened to get married, Jackson replied: "Why, everybody got a wife, I thought I get one." This interview persuaded the judge that Jackson understood what he was doing, was content in his marriage, and was not being held by force. But Jackson had tired of the Metropolitan Hotel. He was anxious to return to Oklahoma. With characteristic flexibility, he told the judge, "If she is done with me I am done too. . . . If they don't want to let the woman go, I leave the woman with you."

JUDGE: Do you want the woman to come back to Oklahoma?
JACKSON: Any time she likes she can come back.[25]

The judge concluded that Jackson wished to continue the marriage in Oklahoma. Moreover, based on case law, the judge was convinced the marriage would be upheld in the courts. On April 10, 1920, Jackson returned to his farm with Anna. Along the way, they enjoyed an elaborate victory dinner at the Moorehead home in Tulsa. Afterward, they went to a local theater, where the applause for the distinguished guests lasted several minutes.[26]

The Kansas judge's compromise was reaffirmed when the court reconvened on May 31. Jackson could resume his former way of life in Oklahoma, and the guardian was not to initiate any proceedings to interfere with their marriage relations. The jurisdiction of the Kansas court over Jackson Barnett was to continue in the interim. The guardian was to furnish the couple "necessary means for their living there in keeping with his financial condition, also having in mind in a measure the life he has lived."[27] Critically, in deciding to let the marriage stand—at least on a trial basis—the court refused to allow challenges to the marriage based on evidence of Anna's checkered past. Her past was not relevant to the legal question at hand, the court ruled. The sole object of the hearing was to determine if Barnett was being held against his will and if he was competent. The judge was persuaded that Jackson understood his marriage contract. The court's decision embittered O'Hornett, who had to recognize the marriage as legal and had to provide the couple with adequate material support.[28]

With the judge unwilling to declare Jackson mentally incompetent or insane, the attempt to annul the marriage floundered. Such a determination would have been politically undesirable to Sells and to the prospective beneficiaries of Barnett charitable donations since a ruling of incompetency would prohibit Jackson's donations for the hospital and other projects. O'Hornett had no choice but to seek a dismissal, which he did in early October 1920. In total, $50,000 of Jackson's money had been expended in the failed attempt to annul the marriage.[29]

The key evidence that the Kansas court found inadmissible was a seventeen-page confidential report to Commissioner Sells based on the findings of bureau inspector W. L. Bowie and a private detective agency dated April 25, 1920. Hastily gathered in a two-month period after the marriage, this report was rife with hearsay and scurrilous innuendo. Much later, it became a crucial part of a renewed effort to annul the marriage. (The U.S. Justice Department's two-pronged attack—which Sells was unwilling to pursue in 1920—combined the charge that Anna was an adventuress with the argument that Jackson was indeed mentally incompetent. This strategy for annulling the marriage was ultimately effective fourteen years later for, according to Oklahoma statute, an incompetent person was someone "likely to be deceived or imposed upon by artful or designing persons.") The Bowie Report bombarded the reader with information that Anna was artful and designing. It covered Anna Lowe's alleged activities as a prostitute and blackmailer across Oklahoma, Texas, Arkansas, Missouri, Iowa, and Kansas. Moreover, it built a case that the kidnapping of Jackson Barnett was premeditated.[30]

The report closely detailed Anna's past. Anna Laura Randolph was born in southeast Missouri's Ozarks on October 19, 1881, to Anna Carroll and James Randolph of Virginia. She was the only girl and youngest child in the family of six children.[31] One brother ran a whiskey joint, and she associated with a whiskey runner in her youth. Her reputation for chastity was deemed "not good." Twenty-three-year-old Anna had a four-month-old daughter, Maxine, when she married Arthur Sturgis of Mt. Vernon, Missouri, in 1904. Sturgis sold whiskey at a Tulsa chili joint between 1904 and 1909. The couple divorced in 1912 on his initiative. (Anna's version of the couple's conflict was that she was very ambitious and Sturgis had "no interest in life other than his pretty self.")[32] Sturgis was "apparently very much afraid of the woman," the Bowie Report noted. Anna then took a job at the Tulsa Mutual Life Insurance Company, where she met and mar-

Jackson and Anna on their honeymoon in Coffeyville, Kansas. Anna deferentially stands behind Jackson, who manfully chews a cigar. The guardian O'Hornett, angry about the elopement, begrudgingly gave them a clothing allowance with which these matching coats were no doubt purchased. Courtesy of the Still Photo Archive, National Archives, College Park.

ried her second husband, T. J. Lowe, in 1913. The groom was fifty-seven and the bride thirty-three. Lowe, formerly the secretary of state for Oklahoma Territory, was the general agent at Mutual Life and had a reputation for indulging in alcohol. The report ascribed her motive in marrying Lowe as pecuniary. It was alleged that she tried to get deeds to his property, but Lowe's adult daughter intervened to prevent this. Within four months,

Anna was divorced again; her second husband alleged desertion and gross neglect.[33]

A shadow was cast over Anna's reputation because of the divorces and her subsequent transient lifestyle. The Lowe divorce provided her with some working capital. Though she owned her own homes, first in Tulsa and then in Kansas City, she traveled frequently. She stayed in upscale hotels in major cities from Montreal to Mexico City from 1914 to 1920. Though Anna's new profession as an oil broker may have required this constant travel, the Bowie Report intimated that her lifestyle was shady and illicit. She borrowed heavily against the homes. The report suggested that Anna had financial troubles from 1919 to 1920, borrowed small sums from friends, and narrowly avoided foreclosure on her Kansas City house.[34]

The report implicated Lowe in prostitution and bunko operations. While on the move, she frequently used aliases, such as Lucile Lowe, Ida Bartles, or Mrs. A. L. Lowe. Much of the evidence of her bad moral character was based on the suspect testimony of bellboys, who purportedly aided her in solicitation of wealthy men. Other evidence of prostitution included a Kansas City incident in 1919 in which she tried to drug and rob a male guest. Later in 1919, she was evicted from the Muskogee Hotel by the house detective. Other alleged criminal acts, based on highly circumstantial evidence, included attempts to rob an aged widow of her savings and to blackmail male acquaintances.

Anna's pattern was to form liaisons with wealthy married men. For example, she met J. B. Levy, a wealthy Tulsa oil man, on a train en route from Tulsa to Chicago around 1916 or 1917. When the pair arrived in Chicago, they had an affair at the Great Northern Hotel. Afterward, using a lawyer, she attempted to blackmail the married Levy. Beginning around 1915, Anna had a running affair across four states with Joe Bartles, a Cherokee mixed-blood with an oil fortune. Bartles drank heavily and was married. She stalked him and often asked for money but did not try to blackmail him. They might have been friends. In 1917, Anna told Bartles she intended to marry (or had married) a lieutenant in the U.S. medical corps, F. H. Gaffey. Gaffey, too, was married. After a brief affair with Anna in a Kansas City hotel, Gaffey was transferred to Chicago and decided to terminate the relationship. But Anna followed him to Chicago and then to Louisville when he was restationed. Now quite discomfited by this stalker, Gaffey tried to get rid of her with payments of money when he was approached by her lawyer. She reported Gaffey to his commanding officer, demanding that he be charged with conduct unbecoming an officer. In August 1918, Anna's agents were still approaching Gaffey for the collection claim against him.

From the investigator's report, Anna emerges as an ambitious and independent woman with a taste for the finer things in life. She was a sexually liberated woman, who had no desire to raise a daughter on a single mother's paltry income while small town gossips whispered about her divorced status across backyard fences. Anna liked the privileges and mobility that accompanied wealth and delighted in the luxury and urbanity of train travel and city life. She was solicitous of her daughter's well-being, cloistering her in a Catholic boarding school while she endeavored to support them both. While fulfilling her responsibilities as a parent, she did not sacrifice her drive for worldly pleasures.

Beyond question, she was a woman with a troubled history of relationships with men as well as women. Without taking too much liberty in interpreting the known facts, Anna's difficulties with men and her fierce independence can be traced to her childhood. Anna's father was a poor breadwinner and alcoholic; her mother's life—overburdened with work and children—provided no positive role model. They divorced when Anna was a teenager.[35] Poverty, conflict, shame, and chaos probably dominated her childhood experiences and formed her survival skills. While she traded sexual favors for material support from men on occasion, she undoubtedly genuinely sought true love. It is unclear how serious Anna's feelings were for either Bartles or Gaffey. Her perception was that men lied to her about their marital status in order to have sexual relations with her, then abandoned her. On the other hand, she seems to have deliberately set out to entrap men, as the hiring of lawyers to threaten her lovers confirms. Sex and alcohol were usually combined in her escapades. In her early as well as later life, Anna demonstrated many of the characteristics of an alcoholic: emotional instability, paranoia, rage, and obsessiveness. Frequent betrayals, disappointments, and conceivably sexual abuse early in life left her emotionally damaged and unable to trust men. She relied on her own wits for survival and that entailed becoming a predator herself. She formed no close relationships with women, having much distrust and contempt for them. She grew up with male siblings, and she was most comfortable competing in a man's world on men's terms.

When she met the fabulously wealthy Jackson Barnett, a man entirely lacking sexual aggression and constitutionally incapable of guile or betrayal, Anna instantly knew she had met her soulmate. Three weeks after her first conversation with Jackson, Anna wrote to Bartles declaring her love for Jackson and asking for a $500 loan for the elopement. Anna was more complex than the "devil in the shape of a woman" the investigators made her out to be. Anna had two faces: she could be reasonable, loyal, charming, and sexually enticing, and alternately, cunning, ferocious, and threatening. Anna's movements were so uncanny and mysterious that the army believed she either worked for the FBI or was a spy. Bartles was afraid of her, the detectives noted. The investigator concluded: "This woman is unquestionably a very dangerous character. I fear for the safety of Jackson Barnett."[36]

There is no question that Anna schemed to marry Jackson for his money and that she had few scruples about securing her goal. Soon after the marriage, McGugin and Anna purportedly conspired to find an Indian baby to be an heir. McGugin allegedly told two men: "Boys, I am in a heck of a fix. I found out [when] old Barnett dies under the Arkansas law, ratified by the State of Oklahoma . . . the widow won't get any of the money." McGugin's scheme was "to have a half-breed Indian kid baby to play like it is her's. Then she can handle that money as its legal guardian until it is twenty-one years old." McGugin, the witness said, was determined to ensure the estate's assets flowed to Anna, thereby ensuring his contractual share. "We have aired him out [in the] car and are going to air him out of some money," McGugin reputedly bragged. "We are going to be rich." Told that "those old Indians don't ever die, they live for centuries," McGugin replied, "Hell, I won't let the old son-of-a-bitch live over five years." This story, though exaggerated, is likely true; McGugin and Anna were unethical and greedy. However, some of the evidence against Anna in the infamous report to Sells was likely manufactured to defame her. It was more in keeping with McGugin and Anna's modus operandi to achieve their ends by cunningly using the law, rather than by violating it. For all of the innuendo and exaggerations about Anna's immoral character, the investigators could produce no criminal record.[37]

Bonded together in their collective pursuit, McGugin and Anna patiently held their cards and bided their time, awaiting the hour when they could pull large sums of cash from Jackson's overflowing bank accounts. Anna's cunning was evident in her politic and discreet behavior during the first year of her marriage. After Anna banished the African-American revelers, the Barnetts lived a quiet and modest life on Jackson's farm outside Henryetta. Anna could not have been content with Jackson's humble home, but the $650 allowance satisfied her for the time being. Cato Sells and his Baptist allies clung to their dream of funding the Indian hospital and local church projects. They were encouraged by Anna Barnett's promised donation of $50,000 to build a boys' dormitory at the Murrow Orphans Home. In December 1920, former bank clerk Casey (involved in the February 11, 1920, donation scheme) was again enlisted to persuade Jackson to sign papers to donate $1.5 million to local churches, hospitals, and schools. If successful, $150,000 would go to the conspirators, including $50,000 for the point man. In a secretive move, the clerk brought Jackson to the backroom of his store and managed to get Jackson's thumbprint on five documents. The papers basically reaffirmed the distribution outlined by Sells earlier in the year.[38]

To maintain pressure on Anna to accept the donations, her efforts to gain greater access to Barnett's assets were blocked. Any expenditures requested by Anna had to be approved by O'Hornett, and he refused everything except a $650 monthly allowance. The sole extravagance allowed the couple was $2,000 for a honeymoon trip to Colorado in August 1920. That continued pressure was being placed on Anna is indicated by a telegram from O'Hornett's lawyer to Commissioner Sells in early 1921:

As Anna Barnett began commanding greater access to her husband's wealth, the couple began dressing elegantly. In this studio portrait, Jackson is carefully groomed and smartly dressed. Anna wears a fox fur she loved and was often photographed wearing. Courtesy of the National Archives, Southwest Region, Fort Worth.

"Prospects of dealing successfully with Barnett settlement as per previous conference grows less encouraging. . . . Mrs. Barnett's attorneys are to insist upon awaiting change of administration in all Washington offices. O'Hornett feels prompt action essential."[39]

Anna and her lawyers were clearly powerful contenders in the negotiations over the control of the Barnett estate. Anna gradually stepped up her demands for money once the legitimacy of her eighteen-month-long marriage was on a firm footing. These incessant demands were a constant annoyance to O'Hornett, Judge Murphy, and the bureau personnel at the Union Agency in Muskogee. There was a constant stream of paperwork, county court appearances, and dickering over what expenses were legitimate. Her constant demands for a higher standard of living and her refusal to countenance a large bequest to charity until she got all that she desired created new dramatic tension in the Barnett saga. Until Anna and McGugin received satisfaction on the former, the latter was held in abeyance.

5

Dividing the Estate
1921–1923

Well they give me lot over here near Sapulpa an' they find oil well on it. Lot of money. I get plenty money long as I live an' they say no use to have 'em fight over it after I'm dead. So we fix it so there won't be none lef'.
—JACKSON BARNETT

In mid-1921, Anna and McGugin found a wedge to drive between the bureau and the guardian. The Barnetts went to O'Hornett's office almost daily asking for more money. O'Hornett and Okmulgee County judge Murphy were tightfisted and were inclined to decline these requests, but the bureau was pledged to a policy of indulging Jackson's whims during the last years of his life. The guardian hoped to conserve the estate until Jackson's death in order to garner huge fees in the probate proceedings. The bureau, on the other hand, realized that a necessary prerequisite to distributing Jackson's estate to charity was the clear demonstration that his own needs and desires had been adequately met. Anna and McGugin deliberately aggravated this difference over spending. The explosive issue was a home purchase for the Barnetts outside of Okmulgee County.

Because new appointments would be made in the Department of the Interior, the change in presidential administration provided the auspicious timing for exploiting the differences between the bureau and the guardian. During the Woodrow Wilson presidency, the Interior Department's Bureau of Indian Affairs—Sells's administration—was beholden to the Democratic and Southern Baptist interests. When Republican Warren Harding was elected in 1920, Commissioner Sells and Superintendent Parker—who Anna believed were conspiring against her—were replaced

86

by more sympathetic bureau officials: Commissioner Charles Burke and Superintendent Victor Locke, a mixed-blood Choctaw.

Under Burke's strong command, the bureau became a powerful counterpoint to local jurisdiction. Burke had a long-standing animosity toward the Oklahoma guardianship system. His partisan politics and his strong belief in the assertion of federal power over what he believed to be selfish, local interests predisposed him to be hostile to the guardian and the Okmulgee County court. Anna and Burke would find common ground to achieve their separate ambitions, hers pecuniary, his political.

Following Burke's appointment as commissioner of Indian affairs on April 1, 1921, Anna's demands for Jackson's money met with more success. The Barnetts requested an increased monthly allowance and extra sums for furniture, a luxury automobile, a new home, tuition for Anna's daughter, Maxine, and other items. Since Jackson's oil royalties were $6,000–8,000 a month, such expenditures appeared reasonable to the bureau. Burke sympathized with Anna in her struggle against the guardian's control of the Barnett purse strings. Indicative of the political shift within the bureau, Superintendent Locke in June 1921 insisted that O'Hornett approve Anna's extravagant demand of $5,000 for a summer vacation. During the Barnetts' vacation, Anna exulted in the promising change in the bureau's attitude and declared to a reporter that she would soon be enjoying $50,000 a year in allowances (instead of the current $7,800) and an elegant new $300,000 home in Muskogee.[1]

The question of a home purchase was at the top of Anna's agenda when she returned. The bureau approved the purchase of a finer home. Theoretically, this home could be anywhere Jackson chose, but as a matter of efficient administration, the Indian bureau hoped it would be in Muskogee, where the Union Agency was located. A home purchase anywhere outside Okmulgee County was absolutely unacceptable to the guardian and Judge Murphy because this would remove Jackson Barnett from their jurisdiction, and they would therefore lose their valuable ward. Southern notions of honor and masculinity may have provided subtler motives for the obstruction by Okmulgee County's political clique. As O'Hornett and others correctly maintained, the demand for a new home and other items was Anna and McGugin's idea, not Jackson's. O'Hornett, Murphy, and other prominent men of Okmulgee County cultivated a personal dislike of Anna and were determined not to be outwitted by her. O'Hornett and other locals also seemed to believe that Jackson was content where he was and that to relocate the elderly man would be a cruel violation of his preferences. One bureau official, for example, said Jackson was a "typical Snake Indian and did not have a desire for civilization or civilized people."[2] Jackson, however, was an adaptable, easy-going man. He was not weak-willed nor as dominated by his wife as most people assumed. Jackson had no close Indian friends or relatives in Henryetta; his older friends had died. He did not particularly care about moving to

Muskogee, but he wanted his wife to be satisfied—as "sane and reasonable a view as could be expected from anyone claiming to be much more intelligent," a government lawyer wryly observed.[3]

In September 1921, McGugin and Anna made a bold and calculated move. They made a direct appeal to the bureau to aid them in circumventing O'Hornett's authority. They hired a U.S. Justice Department lawyer as their legal counsel to compose a petition to the bureau complaining about O'Hornett's uncooperative and disagreeable attitude; his unwillingness to give them anything but paltry sums; his effort to discredit Anna and to destroy the marriage; his obstruction of a land purchase in Muskogee on which to build a home "commensurate with their financial condition and station in life"; and, finally, his selfish resolve "to retain control of the estate of Jackson Barnett." In this petition (thumbprinted by Jackson), the Barnetts appealed for bureau approval of $2,500 to pay for a trip to Washington, D.C., to resolve their difficulties with the guardian.[4]

Anna and McGugin cunningly raised a touchy jurisdictional issue. If they could get the bureau to approve the release of Jackson's funds for a Washington trip without going through the customary channels of first proposing the expenditure to the county court or guardian, this would set a precedent. It foreshadowed the next step, which was the bureau's exercise of power to dispense Jackson's money for any purpose independent of, and even in opposition to, the guardian and the court. The trap for Burke was baited: Anna would be open to discussing the charitable donations of the Barnett estate in return for the bureau helping her escape the guardian's jurisdiction. The donation to charity was Anna and McGugin's ace card.

This preemptive strike by Anna and McGugin was immediately recognized for what it was: a dangerous step of dubious legality, upsetting the procedures for handling restricted properties under dual guardianship. Both a bureau attorney and Judge Murphy wrote immediately to Commissioner Burke expressing their strong disapproval of the proposed trip and warning Burke to be cautious. The bureau's probate attorney for the Five Civilized Tribes characterized McGugin's bold demand for a voucher without going through proper channels as audacious. Like Murphy, he felt that Jackson had not signed the petition and did not wish to go to Washington and that it was "a scheme" to try to get Barnett's money. Feeling the political pressure from Washington, D.C., Murphy acquiesced in the spirit of cooperation and signed the voucher, but he stood firm on the principle of law. Registering a strong complaint about the way his court had been railroaded into approving the trip money, he issued a warning to Burke not to push him further. He respectfully asked the commissioner not to approve requests for donations, especially if they required subsequent approval of the county court.[5]

Taking Anna and McGugin's bait, Burke ignored these cautions. In Burke's view, the Department of the Interior was Jackson's "ultimate" guardian and would make all decisions about what was in his best interests and how to ensure the protection of his estate. He would not defer to Judge Murphy; he would act independently of the will of the guardian and the courts if he saw fit.[6] Besides this symbolic display of federal authority, Burke took another fateful step in September 1921. He decided to use his authority to give the entire donation to Bacone College and the Murrow Indian Orphans Home located outside Muskogee, institutions of the Northern Baptist Home Missionary Society (known as the American Home Missionary Society). In an earlier proposed division of Barnett's money, which had been approved by Sells, Bacone and the orphan home were slated to have a small share of the Barnett estate, but they were now the favored recipients of the entire donation. In favoring the Northern Baptist organization over the solidly Democratic Southern Baptists, the Harding administration was motivated by partisanship. Shortly after taking office, Secretary of the Interior Albert Fall rejected Cato Sells's pledge to dispense $200,000 of Jackson Barnett's money to the Southern Baptists, and this made them furious.[7]

Besides partisanship, there were additional reasons why Burke favored the donation to Bacone. Foremost among these was Burke's belief that the donation would protect the "surplus" funds of rich Indians from grafters and lawyers. Burke strongly endorsed Sells's policy of using the funds of oil-rich Indians for charitable and educational purposes. After the rejection of the pledge to the Southern Baptists, the question of the new recipient was apparently under discussion at the Union Agency. When Billy McCombs, Superintendent Victor Locke, and others proposed Bacone, Burke gave his hearty approval to a donation to this worthy, thirty-five-year-old institution, which had a strong track record of academic excellence. The college was undergoing a renaissance in 1921 as its president, B. D. Weeks, recruited Indian students nationwide, secured large donations from well-to-do Creeks, and also gained a pledge of financial support of $120,000 from the Northern Baptists. Henry Harjo, Baptist minister and alumnus of Bacone, donated money to buy land for the expansion of the Murrow Orphans Home, while Baptists Suma Burgess, her mother, Lucy Poloke, and Eastman Richards—a wealthy Creek whose son had died while attending Bacone—gave large sums for building construction. Jackson Barnett's endowment of this blossoming local institution, well equipped to carry on permanent and substantial educational work among Indians, received the enthusiastic approval of the Union Agency. For additional practical and political reasons, Bacone was a good choice for the donation. Locke and Burke anticipated that the Barnetts would soon be relocating to Muskogee, home of the Union Agency and stronghold of federal and Republican power. A mansion could be built for the Barnetts on the campus grounds, and when Jackson died, his home could be converted into a dormitory.[8]

Burke thought his altruistic and equitable plan for the donation, which included liberal allowances to the wife, Jackson's near relatives, and local institutions, would eventually be accepted in Oklahoma. Anticipating some resistance in bringing the settlement of the Barnett estate to a swift conclusion, Burke marshaled his forces for this power play against local interests. Overconfident, he calculated that his political skills and federal authority would carry the day. Contacting a special supervisor in the Indian service in Muskogee, Burke requested a full accounting of court costs, guardianship fees, attorneys' fees, and other expenses incurred in the management of the Barnett estate. Burke assigned Creek national attorney Amasa Ward as legal advisor to work with Superintendent Locke in overseeing the home purchase and protecting Jackson's assets. The bureau suspected McGugin of grafting Jackson Barnett's monies and so Ward was to keep an eye on him as well. Burke tactfully recommended that Jackson give some money to his relatives if he were so inclined.9

Burke's blunder was threefold. He assumed the whole guardianship system was rotten and inefficient; he had chosen the wrong judge to challenge; and he fatally underestimated the impact this power play would have in Okmulgee County. While the Barnetts were conferencing with Burke in Washington, D.C., on Burke's plan for the donation to Bacone—against the express wishes of Judge Murphy—news broke in the Muskogee paper of the $1 million donation for a college in Muskogee County. Worsening the situation, Superintendent Locke, a poor politician, made injudicious comments to the press that Jackson would be allowed to buy an expensive home "wherever he desires." Locke expressed the opinion that Jackson would be indulged to the point of "improvidence" in all of his wishes, adding, "He has the money and he should be allowed the right to spend it in whatever way he sees fit within the bounds of reason."10

Burke's man in the field, Amasa Ward, was seriously disturbed by Burke's high-handedness. The news stories, said Ward, had created "a turmoil of unprofitable and unnecessary agitation" in and out of the press. Ward observed that the court and the guardian could not fail to see that they had been publicly and brazenly ignored by the department. The publicity about the pending donation was a direct snub to the powerful Judge Murphy. An amicable settlement with the Oklahoma guardian and the county court would be hard to reach after this insult.11 Ward understood Burke's mistakes immediately. Unlike Burke, he did not underestimate Murphy's power, and he knew him to be a capable and conscientious judge. Ward's political instincts were correct. Serious trouble was brewing in Okmulgee County. Seduced by Anna's temptations, Burke had committed a political misstep that triggered an escalating legal confrontation national in scope.

The county court was "going to war" with the Interior Department over the Barnett estate, the *Muskogee Times-Democrat* reported. Judge Murphy, already angry about the Barnett petition of September, which had foreshadowed this circumvention of his authority, now was in a paranoid rage. "Sinister" influences were behind a plot to relocate Jackson Barnett out of Okmulgee County. Murphy declared his intention to oppose the bureau's blatant violation of the law. He would use all his power to keep Jackson Barnett from leaving Okmulgee County. The bureau was ignoring established procedure, and Murphy determined to take a stand on principle. If the department could overrule the county court's authority in one case, it could do it in all. As Murphy correctly analyzed the situation, Burke was challenging the dual guardianship system. Murphy had no objection to Jackson living in luxury in a country home within Okmulgee County, but if the bureau ignored his opposition and allowed the move to another county, he would refuse payments to guardians of restricted funds in any cases before his court.[12]

Murphy's militancy played into the hands of Commissioner Burke, who now had a reason for ignoring the county court and the guardian completely. If Murphy would deny funds to Indian wards under his jurisdiction as an act of retaliation against the federal government, the bureau would be justified in devising a new policy whereby payments from Indian funds held in trust by the Interior Department would be paid to Indians directly. This new method would replace the existing one in which the Union Agency's superintendent, the guardian, and the county court all had to approve any expenditure before money was disbursed to an incompetent Indian. If the federal government attempted to take this unprecedented action, the *Muskogee Times-Democrat* prophetically predicted, "the legal battle royal between state and federal officials will start and a test case will be made of it."[13]

Amasa Ward and others were anguished over what action to take. Ward wondered if he should yield to Judge Murphy to ensure his continued cooperation in Indian probate matters, or forfeit Murphy's good will to benefit "one Indian" and to assert the Indian bureau's ultimate and exclusive authority over the estates of wealthy Indians. What was the "greater good" in this "bad mess"? Ward wondered.[14] A number of other Indians were also trying to escape their entanglements with Oklahoma guardians and lawyers.[15] In Jackson Barnett's case, compromise might have been expedient, but the abuses perpetrated on other Creek and Osage Indians were so egregious that the bureau needed to make a stand.

Alarmed by Murphy's radicalism and the bureau's assertion of power, O'Hornett—whose guardianship fee had been temporarily suspended—agreed to cooperate with Interior Department to select a new home for the Barnetts. Within a short time, Judge Murphy, tempered by the knowledge that obstruction would only serve to justify the bureau's stripping the court of its jurisdiction, also agreed to discuss a compromise.[16]

As the chief federal negotiator, Amasa Ward presided over the discussions on the Barnett matter, and he performed his duties with determination and fairness. Meetings were held among the principals—the guardian, the bureau, the county judge, and their full contingency of lawyers—from late 1921 to early 1922. No real progress was made, though all were pledged to harmony and reason. The fundamental irreconcilable issue was the home purchase outside of Okmulgee County. O'Hornett and Murphy hoped to build a fine estate for Jackson in Okmulgee County, but Anna preferred to move to Muskogee. O'Hornett and Murphy were willing to consider large expenditures for two homes, one in Henryetta in Okmulgee County and one in Muskogee in Muskogee County and to increase the Barnetts' monthly allowances, but they would not surrender their jurisdiction.[17]

The conflict and confusion that Anna and McGugin had helped to create resulted in a marked improvement in the Barnetts' standard of living commensurate with the $2,000 per week in royalties Jackson was earning in 1921. The Barnetts enjoyed a lavish summer vacation to New York and Chicago, and later in the year traveled to Washington, D.C. In October 1921, they purchased a $9,000 Pierce Arrow automobile. A well-coiffed Anna sported a fox fur, and Jackson proudly displayed a silver buckle when they were photographed standing in front of their new luxury automobile. The Barnetts haunted Superintendent Locke's office, claiming they were broke and could not even afford gasoline. In November, the Barnetts' monthly allowance was increased from $650 to $1,000. In December, O'Hornett allowed $1,000 for Maxine's education and $2,000 for the Barnetts to go to Chicago to see shows. Anna exploited the prevailing confusion and the guardian's accommodating attitude by making purchases on credit without the prior approval of the guardian, some of which he later paid. She could look forward to elegant housing, luxury autos, vacations, and a handsome allowance as long as Jackson lived and the marriage lasted. She expressed desires for an airplane and thoroughbred race horses, and in December 1921, she entertained fantasies of becoming the editor of a Republican newspaper and Jackson becoming landed gentry as a cotton farmer.[18]

On the night of December 18, 1921, Anna preemptively moved to Muskogee, forcing a resolution on the deadlocked home purchase issue. There are indications that Superintendent Locke aided and abetted Mrs. Barnett. Household goods, chickens, dogs, and the family cat were furtively loaded on two mule-drawn moving vans under the cover of darkness. The Barnetts enjoyed a wild ride as their Pierce Arrow was piloted by "Dare Devil" Dick Canton, a former aerial stuntman. The Barnetts put on "a show of their own," a Muskogee newspaper reported admiringly. Using money authorized for Christmas expenses only two days previously, Mrs. Barnett made a $500 down payment on a seventy-three-acre hog farm with a cement block bungalow of five or six rooms and outbuildings in West Muskogee. Dressed in high-top russet boots, Jackson grinned as he unpacked, saying he was pleased with the move.[19]

Once again, Anna's shrewd and dramatic move left the others involved in the negotiations—Ward, the guardian, the county judge, and Commissioner Burke—stunned, and the public dazzled. Some Union Agency personnel were initially pleased because the move cut through some red tape. Superintendent Locke, for example, justified the unauthorized move, say-

After their flight under the cover of darkness from Okmulgee County, Anna Barnett purchased a seventy-three-acre hog farm with this cement block home in West Muskogee in Muskogee County. Upwardly mobile, the Barnetts lived here only briefly from late 1921 to early 1923. Courtesy of the National Archives, Pacific Region, Laguna Niguel.

ing negotiations had gone on too long. Public opinion, he reported, supported the Indian department taking action. Locke's indiscreet enthusiasm for the Barnetts' move to Muskogee added to Judge Murphy's paranoia; he suspected there was collusion among the federal government officials to usurp his authority. The guardian's lawyer suggested a drastic remedy: forcible removal back to Okmulgee. Instead, Burke mildly rebuked Anna for ignoring procedure, being impatient, and dictating terms.[20]

The move threw the federal and county officials into confusion about their prerogatives. Had Anna overplayed her hand? Oklahoma law provided that guardians could fix the residence of wards at any place within the state. Would O'Hornett compel the Barnetts to return? If they refused, would he block release of the money from the estate? If the county court and guardian remained obdurate, the estate could not be transferred elsewhere, and no guardian could be assigned in Muskogee. On the other hand, the Department of the Interior might ignore Oklahoma law and the guardian entirely and make payments directly to Jackson Barnett.

Anna's daring move did not break the deadlock as she had hoped. Commissioner Burke was unwilling to alienate Murphy and O'Hornett further. He refused Anna's requests for $30,000 for the Muskogee home, $3,000 for furniture, and $300 for thoroughbred horses. Burke also refused McGugin's request for travel money for the Barnetts to meet with him again in Washington. Judge Murphy and O'Hornett capitulated to the demand to approve an increase in the Barnett allowance to $2,500 in May 1922 and grudgingly made other allowances for expenses, but they held firm on jurisdictional control. Negotiations continued, and Amasa Ward doggedly sought solutions to break the impasse. He suggested, for example, that the bureau use its authorized powers to declare Jackson Barnett competent as a way of escaping the Okmulgee County's legal jurisdiction, but Burke rejected this option. An alternative was for Judge Murphy, who had no financial interest in keeping Jackson in Okmulgee County, to meet with Burke and resolve their differences.

The politics of divide and conquer appeared to be the only way out of the deadlock. Judge Murphy, O'Hornett, and his lawyer, C. B. McCrory, thought the whole matter should be settled in conference with Burke but without McGugin and Anna. McCrory endeavored to cut Anna out of the power loop that was deciding the disposition of the estate in late February 1922; he was syrupy in his pledges to cooperate with the bureau. Anna was offered $100,000–200,000 by McCrory if she would divorce Jackson. Anna and McGugin, for their part, wanted to cut the guardian, his lawyers, and Judge Murphy out of the loop and come to a resolution about the Bacone distribution with Burke separately.[21]

Though Anna's stubbornness annoyed Ward—and he knew she was motivated by greed—the selfishness and vindictiveness of the guardian and his lawyers frustrated him more. In early 1922, Ward's sympathies shifted to Anna and McGugin, apparently because Ward was continually subject to McGugin's persuasions. McGugin could not collect the 25 percent share promised him until Anna received a lump sum, so he was highly motivated to get the affair settled. McGugin realized that giving the bulk of the estate to Bacone was of the utmost importance to the bureau. To McGugin as well as the bureau, the Muskogee home purchase was secondary.

In view of Anna and her lawyer's willingness to lavishly endow Bacone in return for a cash payout and severance from O'Hornett, Commissioner Burke began researching the method by which he could circumvent the legal authority of Okmulgee County. In early 1922, he solicited opinions from a number of lawyers regarding the Department of the Interior's legal right to expend the funds of a ward directly if a guardian were guilty of obstructionism. Amasa Ward suggested that Interior Department regulations should be amended to resolve any ambiguity regarding the bureau's authority in such situations.[22]

Burke submitted the legal question to federal solicitor Edwin Booth.

To show Jackson Barnett's improved standard of living, Jackson was photographed in Muskogee in 1922, presumably on his farm there. Anna Barnett was grooming Jackson as a gentleman farmer, but this role lasted only briefly. Courtesy of the National Archives, Southwest Region, Fort Worth.

If a restricted Indian of the Five Civilized Tribes, adjudged incompetent with a county court-appointed guardian, applies to the Interior Department for permission to purchase a home suitable to his needs and station in life, but his guardian refuses to join in the application, may the Department of the Interior act independently of the probate court and the guardian? In his nineteen-page report submitted to the secretary of the Interior on August 2, 1922, Booth concluded it could: "To hold otherwise is to reach the absurd conclusion that the Secretary of the Interior in the exercise of his jurisdiction over the restricted Indian allottees . . . is subject to the control of the probate courts of the State of Oklahoma. Such a situation was never intended by Congress."[23]

Booth's opinion gave Burke the assurance he needed to proceed, and Jackson's illness provided the impetus. Jackson journeyed to the Mayo Clinic for emergency treatment (presumably for a heart condition), and there was a fear he might die suddenly. Although many lies were later told about how the donation was extemporaneously proposed on the Barnetts' trip to Washington for supposedly unrelated business in the fall, the details of the distribution of the estate were worked out in June by Ward, Burke, McGugin, and Anna Barnett. Told to keep the knowledge in strictest confidence, the indiscreet Bacone president B. D. Weeks revealed the juicy details in a letter in late June 1922. Anna would settle for a home purchase and some cash ($150,000–350,000), while most of the estate would be donated to Bacone. McGugin was in Washington for three weeks in July, conferring with Burke and Amasa Ward, and Marshall Mott was invited to participate as a consultant.[24]

When O'Hornett's lawyer caught wind of the bureau's intention, he advised Burke to put the matter before the federal court before the bureau took action to disburse the Barnett estate. Transacting business without the guardian was illegal, McCrory argued. Judge Murphy was furious about the bureau's meddling and angrily declared, "This court will refuse hereafter to recognize the Indian department at Muskogee."[25] In September 1922, the superintendent at the Union Agency was authorized to pay Jackson Barnett's allowance directly to him, and this was done. Judge Murphy saw it as yet another assault on his authority. Immediately, he attempted, without success, to call a statewide meeting of county judges to discuss the "usurpation" of their authority. The Indian bureau was prompt in clarifying that jurisdiction over the Barnett estate was the exception, warranted because his interests were being jeopardized by Murphy's intransigence. In other cases of Indian guardianship, the dual guardianship system for protecting and probating the estates of incompetent Indians remained in place.[26]

Burke enlisted the support of Secretary of the Interior Albert Fall in affirming federal authority to create the Barnett donation. In September, he wrote to Fall stating that under certain circumstances payment could legally be withheld from the guardian to serve the best interests of the ward. He further recommended an amendment to the existing Indian office regulations to permit direct payments to Indians in certain "individual cases." This was added to the Indian office regulations on October 7, 1922, and approved by Fall the same day. Such discretionary actions by the Department of the Interior were used in conjunction with acts of Congress as the law governing Indian peoples.[27]

The stage was set for the long-anticipated disbursement of the Barnett estate. Circumventing the guardian and the court for the second time, Burke authorized $2,500 in expenses from Jackson's funds for the Barnetts and their lawyers to come to a Washington, D.C., meeting. Jackson Barnett submitted a thumbmarked request to Burke, asking that his $1.1 million estate be divided equally between his wife "in consideration of love and affection in appreciation of the faithful performance of her duties" and the American Home Missionary Society of New York as a "permanent endowment fund" for Bacone College and Murrow Indian Orphans Home to promote Creek education. To guarantee Jackson Barnett an income should his oil royalties decline, a trust would be created. During his lifetime Jackson would receive $20,000 a year from the $550,000 to be deposited in the Equitable Trust Bank of New York on behalf of the Baptists. The idea was to preserve the estate from wasting litigation in probate court after Jackson's death and to protect Anna's share of the estate from those who might contest the distribution after Jackson died. Jackson's statement (authored by McGugin and Anna) declared that he had no living relatives who had any claim upon his estate. In fact, he did have relatives, whom Anna was adamant about shutting out. She insisted that she alone had taken an interest in him and lifted him up from a state of neglect, poverty, and degradation, and in the face of powerful opposition, she had taught him how to enjoy his wealth.[28]

Of her $550,000 share, Anna was contractually obligated to pay her lawyers 25 percent ($137,500) as per her agreement with McGugin and Keith. Of this, $67,000 went to Harold McGugin; $20,500 to his wife, Nell Bird McGugin; $35,000 to W. S. Keith; and $15,000 to M. L. Mott.[29] Anna received a cash payout of $212,500 in Jackson's Liberty Bonds. Of this amount, $12,500 was held by McGugin to pay off various expenses (for example, $1,000 to Justice of the Peace Bickett). The agreement stipulated that the remaining $200,000 in Anna's name be deposited in a Riggs Bank trust fund in Washington, D.C., as a second trust for Jackson. This would yield a guaranteed annual income of $8,000 if all other sources of income should fail. This provision ensured that Jackson would be the beneficiary of two trusts totaling $750,000; should Anna abandon Jackson once she had secured a large sum of money, her access to the Riggs trust could be challenged in court.

The original offer on the table for charitable purposes was $750,000. Burke was determined that the lion's share go to the Creek. However, Anna stubbornly "refused to accept less than half." Mott observed that Anna, as Jackson's legal wife, was entitled to half under state law. For discovering this legal point, McGugin rewarded Marshall Mott with $15,000. Bacone president Weeks correctly observed that the "insinuation that the gift was made to a worthy charity in order to justify the gift to Mrs. Barnett, was most unjust and without foundation. The facts are that the Indian Office wanted to give the entire estate to Bacone, but had to reckon with Mrs. Barnett, because she was the legal wife."[30]

Although greedy, Anna was realistic. She was not willing to relinquish any of the estate to charity until the bureau guaranteed her financial interests and freedom from O'Hornett. She was given proof of the bureau's good faith on December 7, 1922, when Burke authorized the disbursement of $51,000 to the Barnetts, ostensibly for a home purchase wherever Anna wished.[31]

In the final analysis, the disbursement of the Barnett estate reflected negotiations among persons with different economic and political agendas. The practical terms and details of the settlement had been exhaustively discussed among upper echelon Indian service personnel, innumerable lawyers, the good citizens of Oklahoma, and the Baptists for many months. The distribution was a feat of statesmanship, albeit of the *real politik* variety.

Commissioner Burke's challenge was to convince Congress and the American public that the donation was enlightened public policy, and he was confident that opposition could be deflected by skillful political play. As part of the public relations campaign, the Indian bureau made an official announcement about the distribution, describing Jackson—the "most advertised Indian in the United States"—as a magnet for vultures because of his great wealth. The donation served both the ward and the taxpayer, the public announcement explained. An inordinate amount of time and energy had been expended by the bureau to protect his fortune. The donation gave Jackson a guaranteed annual income of $50,000 during his lifetime and freed his estate from being subjected to false claimants' lawyers after his death.[32] For additional support, Burke asked Ward to submit a detailed report documenting the legality of the donations. Ward produced a polemic elucidating the Indian bureau's reasoning in a clear attempt to justify an agreement already forged.

Ward's report made the following principal arguments. He stated frankly that Anna married "doubtless for mercenary purposes only." Before the marriage, she had a deserved reputation as "an adventuress of a most dangerous type." The $50,000 attempt to break up the marriage had failed, however, and Anna had reformed. The marriage was harmonious and clearly beneficial to Jackson. Once "ragged, unkempt, ill-fed and slovenly," he had improved in personal habits, appearance, and living conditions. Jackson was a happier, healthier man. "[I]t is not difficult to overlook any shortcomings of the wife when one contemplates that the change has been brought about through her efforts."[33]

Second, Jackson Barnett's guardian had been negligent before Jackson's marriage, since Jackson's material conditions did not change after he accumulated vast wealth from his oil royalties. "The guardian . . . took the position that having been accustomed to a simple way of living, there was no occasion to change the situation because of a large income." Despite Anna's salutary influence, the guardian remained hostile to her and had withheld Jackson's money.

Third, Ward summarized the historical abuses of the Oklahoma guardianship of wealthy incompetent Indians, such as Jackson, and the legacy of unreasonable and unnecessary dissipation of their estates. He solicited supporting evidence for these charges from the probate attorney of the Five Civilized Tribes.[34] Ward described the typical pattern. Upon acquiring wealth, an Indian "becomes incompetent and is hauled into court and a guardian appointed over his person and estate." Thereafter, "court costs, attorneys' fees, guardian's fees and other expenses incident to the management of his estate" drained the estate. Unless Jackson Barnett's estate was settled before his death, it would be a magnet for further encroachments and dissipation by rapacious lawyers and false claimants. Inquiries regarding heirs and reports and rumors of 50 percent contingency contracts were already in the air. Persons who would claim to be heirs would join forces to keep the lawful wife, Anna, from her inheritance. Ward stated that he was not overly concerned about Anna's interest, but he did object to the needless and prolonged litigation with the likely outcome that the money would be "dissipated among a lot of people who are interesting themselves in the matter only for what they may realize out of it and who have no moral or legal claim on the estate." Too often the Indians of the Five Civilized Tribes have had their assets stolen by the unscrupulous in this manner, Ward regretfully noted.

In conclusion, Ward urged the bureau to ensure that Jackson's estate would not be dissipated in court costs. He endorsed the creation of a trust that would provide a guaranteed income for Jackson in his lifetime and an endowment "of lasting and permanent benefit to the Indian people." The report continued that, if approved, the gift to the American Home Missionary Society

> would bear the distinctive mark of the first large Indian estate in Oklahoma to be conserved for a worthy purpose for the benefit of the Indians as against a long and dubious record of Indian estates dissipated, squandered and diverted from any beneficial use whatsoever, except to those unscrupulous persons who make it their business to prey upon the helpless and improvident Indian and who unfortunately, have in the past, met with a large measure of success. In my opinion, this administration can build no greater or more lasting monument to itself than to approve this gift and thus announce to the world that it is in hearty sympathy with any worthy purpose which has for its object the uplifting of the Indian from his present unfortunate state.[35]

In January 1923, Burke sent Jackson Barnett's petition for the $1.1 million in "gifts," the Ward report, and other supporting documents with his recommendation for approval to Secretary of the Interior Albert Fall. Burke reported that $1,156,250 in Jackson's money was in government investments. Another $84,000 in accruing oil royalties were in the hands of the agency superintendent at Muskogee; $50,000 was on loan; and more oil royalties were coming in every month. Burke noted the long-standing impasse between the Indian bureau and the local guardian and court over the home purchase, implying that the local officials were unnecessarily obstructive. Though Fall's undersecretary found the size of the distribution unsettling, Fall endorsed the donation on the grounds that the ends—the educational and charitable purposes—justified the means. A day after Fall's formal approval, the Liberty Bonds were transferred to the beneficiaries: Anna Barnett and the American Home Missionary Society.[36]

Jackson as a passive, but not entirely indifferent, participant, understood the donation in a basic way and gave his assent to the transaction. He understood that his wealth far exceeded his own lifetime needs. He was generous and kind, and he genuinely desired to help his fellow Creeks and to please his wife. In a basic way, he comprehended why the donation was being made. Ward privately assured himself that Jackson understood and wanted to make the gift. After explaining matters to Jackson, Ward said: "Now, Jack, I would like to know what your understanding about this is," and Jackson replied, "My wife, [s]he get half, and the Bacone School get half."[37] Days after the distribution, a reporter found Jackson placidly rolled in blankets and napping in front of the fireplace in his Muskogee home. Maxine and Anna were absent, so the reporter interviewed Jackson about the $1.1 million gifts. Jackson said: "I get plenty money long as I live an' they say no use to have 'em fight over it after I'm dead. So we fix it so there won't be none lef'."[38]

Though the Bureau of Indian Affairs obtained Jackson's consent and carefully conformed to due process and existing statutes in creating the disbursement, the negotiations over the Barnett donation nonetheless had the air of a backroom deal made among conspirators. One reason that the suspicious odor of malfeasance clung to this transaction despite all of Burke's efforts to dissipate it was the negotiators' arrogant assumption that they had the right to paternalistically distribute Jackson's estate in light of his indifference or ineptitude. What appears strikingly unethical in retrospect is that these persons believed they could legitimately represent their individual wishes—their compromises attained in collective discussions, deal making, and negotiations—as Barnett's will, as if the bequest originated with him.

Jackson Barnett's experience was one instance in this era of a broader pattern of transferring Indian assets to non-Indian hands. Non-Indians substituted their own wishes for those of the Indian, occasionally motivated as in the Barnett distribution by a combination of self-interest and idealism. More commonly, a selfish motive was cloaked in the argument that the decision was in the best interests of the Indian. Many such persons believed their intentions were disinterested or even noble. Jackson's case was a conspicuous example of excess and hypocrisy because such a huge fortune was transferred from Indian to non-Indian hands without the Indian either initiating or actively participating in the terms of the distribution.

That half of the fortune was acquired by an adventuress also tainted the donation. Without understanding Burke's master plan to break the Oklahoma guardianship system, his complicity with Anna Barnett appears unseemly and inappropriate for a person in such a high position of public trust. His secretive backroom dealings seem conspiratorial, perverse, and motivated by self-interest even though he gained nothing materially by abetting Anna Barnett. A less confident public official might have shown more caution about how the public might misinterpret his actions in aiding a gold-digging divorcee in making off with a simple-minded Indian's estate. But to Burke, Anna Barnett was a mere pawn in a larger political game.

A man shaped by Victorian culture and the progressive ideas of his day, Charles Burke was so sure in his intellectual, moral, racial, and gender superiority that he could not imagine his actions being seriously questioned. For example, he was convinced of the superiority of Christianity and openly allied himself with Christian organizations. In his notorious pronouncements against Indian dancing—the Dance Order of 1923—he unapologetically carried out his duty to make Indians conform to appropriate standards of "civilization" by persuasion, if possible, or through coercion, if necessary. In the Jackson Barnett affair, as in his conflicts with opponents in the California Mission Indian Agency, Burke, skillfully and without compunction, used the means at his disposal to suppress critics.[39] Far from being prudish or parochial, Burke was a man who enjoyed politics. He took immense satisfaction in wielding power within the arena of Washington and beyond.

Anna Laura Barnett and Burke at first glance appear to be unlikely allies. She had a questionable moral reputation, and he had one above reproach. Yet, there was something in Burke's nature that was highly compatible with that of Anna Barnett. Whatever misgivings Burke may have had regarding Anna's character, he saw traits highly desirable in an ally: aggression, strength, intelligence, determination, and courage. What Burke loved about politics resonated in Anna's driving passions: she was a gambler who could feint, dissemble, and manipulate. She was the mistress of the bold move, the daring action fraught with risks that left her adversaries stunned. Here was a woman who could adeptly manage complex legal and political maneuvering. Anna was a mirror reflection of Burke's darker self.

While awaiting Secretary Fall's approval, Anna Barnett temporarily left Jackson in Muskogee with her brother and went to California with her daughter. Reports that she had deserted Jackson were on the front pages of the newspapers, validating, it seemed, predictions that she would leave as soon as she got Jackson's money. But Jackson joined Anna in Los Angeles in January. O'Hornett's lawyer was filing complaints of Jackson's homesickness when the news broke regarding the $1.1 million donation. The Muskogee newspapers greeted news of this large donation to local institutions approvingly and uncritically accepted the federal officials' unanimous judgment that this donation removed the estate from "grafting lawyers and fake claimants." In Indian department circles, the move was viewed as a "master stroke" avoiding "strife," "turmoil," and "litigation."[40]

In mid-February 1923, the Barnetts returned to Muskogee. Artfully articulating the bureau's justifications for the donation, Anna scorned her detractors in characteristic fashion. Sounding martyred, Anna said: "When I think of the battles I have fought over the man I love and having to fight my way at every turn against a bunch of petty grafters, I am convinced that the state judicial system is rotten to the core." Believing the fictions and foils she had designed, she seemed shocked and offended that anyone would think that she was an adventuress: "High-minded people know I married Jackson because I loved him." On February 15, Ward submitted a petition on her behalf to buy 244 acres in Kansas City for $63,000. Although the petition's well-documented nature suggested sincerity, it is likely that Anna had already determined to make the family residence in California.[41]

The affluent Barnetts made their move to California. Jackson and Anna Barnett and Maxine Sturgis took up permanent residence in Los Angeles. To all appearances, they were free at last from the legal entanglements of dual state and federal guardianship. Anna's triumph appeared complete. She was the legal wife of the World's Richest Indian, whose oil wells continued to produce a regal royalty. She had $200,000 in cash and a $200,000 trust in her own name from the $550,000 gift donation. The Barnetts owned a luxury automobile, and they reaped $2,500 in monthly allowances plus $28,000 annually on the interest from the two trust funds. In 2002 dollars, she had $2.07 million in her own name and more than $602,000 in annual income for her family. Moreover, she had the firm support of the federal government in ridding herself of Barnett's purportedly parsimonious and meddling guardian, Carl O'Hornett. Last, but not least, the Barnetts had left their past identities and difficulties behind. In the dreamscape of Los Angeles, a new beginning was possible.

All the trappings of status and glamour befitting a family of wealth and position materialized at the touch of her hand. Eyeing Los Angeles's premier neighborhoods, in May 1923 she bought a handsome Brentwood home situated on 5.59 acres for $41,260. Furniture, additional improvements, and a piano cost $19,631.35. In her early months in Los Angeles, Anna spent $59,500 of her funds on the family's moving and living expenses.[42] The sweet taste of victory was intoxicating.

6

"Poor Rich Indians" and the Turning Political Tide 1923–1925

It will all come out in the whitewash.
—ALEX POSEY'S "HOTGUN"

By late 1922, Commissioner Charles Burke's eyes were trained on the major political crusade of his public career, to which the liberation of Jackson Barnett from his Oklahoma guardian and the supervision of the Okmulgee County court was just a prelude. Burke sought a grand resolution for the "problem of riches" in Indian country. Jackson Barnett was his test case. Facilitating the Barnetts' relocation to California was an end in itself: the federal guardian's provision of the best possible security for an Indian ward. It was also a means to an end: the demonstration of the principle that the federal government's authority was superior to that of the local guardian. As the October 7, 1922, amendment to Indian bureau regulations authorized the Interior Department to circumvent the local Oklahoma guardians only in "individual cases," Burke campaigned for congressional legislation that would undermine the whole system of guardianship for restricted Indians in eastern Oklahoma.[1]

In his endeavor to promote federal legislation to secure federal control over wealthy restricted Indians, Burke's closest ally was Marshall L. Mott. They shared principles regarding federal jurisdiction over Indian wards and had worked together to rescue Oklahoma Indians from the dual guardianship system, which had gained them political enemies. They launched a well-orchestrated public relations campaign in 1923 to expose and smear the guardianship system in order to create the political climate for the major congressional reform legislation they envisioned. Simultaneously, Mott acted as the primary legal advisor and as the principal intermediary (sometimes covertly) between Anna Barnett and the Department of the Interior for more than five years.

Commencing with the gift donation, Burke and Mott were operating on two fronts. While they fought for the total surrender of Jackson Barnett's guardian, Carl O'Hornett, they also aggressively fought for reform legislation in Congress, which would gut the power of the Oklahoma county courts. Despite their initiative and early political advantages, they met with dogged resistance on both fronts. The intense power struggle over the Barnett estate was like a complex chess game. There were continual shifts in advantage as the players made their strategic moves. Anna Barnett added complexity to the game with her unpredictable and often precipitous actions. Jackson Barnett was a pawn, but on this valuable piece the success of the game pivoted. The obstruction of O'Hornett and his lawyers frustrated Burke and Mott's well-laid plans on the legislative front.

The driving force behind Burke and Mott's campaign was the urgent need to find a more expeditious and efficient way of administering the estates of the oil-rich Indians of Oklahoma, a major policy issue confronted by Commissioner Burke and his predecessor, Cato Sells. As part of its burdensome responsibility of managing the tribal as well the individual financial accounts (called "individual Indian money" or IIM accounts) of thousands of restricted Indians nationwide, the Bureau of Indian Affairs oversaw the complex financial affairs of wealthy Indians like Jackson Barnett. With most Indians, the problem was poverty, but with Jackson Barnett and other Indians with oil royalties, the "problem [was] the problem of riches," as George Vaux of the watchdog organization, the Board of Indian Commissioners, declared in 1917.[2] Bureau manpower was misallocated. The bureau personnel's time was expended investigating suspected wrongdoing and intervening to protect wealthy wards' interests against predatory attorneys, guardians, and a range of other opportunists. The Union Agency at Muskogee used more than 90 percent of its resources to oversee the financial affairs of approximately 200–300 persons (approximately 2 percent of the restricted Indian population) in its jurisdiction. Jackson Barnett's affairs alone consumed the lion's share of bureau manpower both at the Union Agency and at BIA headquarters in Washington, D.C., from 1919 to 1923. Since restricted Indians were easily persuaded to spend their money freely, bureau personnel had to continually monitor wealthy Indians' allowances and expenditures, although the bureau lacked the requisite financial management skills.

Eastman Richards's case illustrates the complexities of the bureau's quest for solutions tailored to the individual circumstances of rich Indians. A man whose business dealings plagued the Indian bureau for years, Eastman Richards was a competent Indian and made legal contracts on his own though his original allotment remained restricted. On his restricted land, Richards built the town of Richardville, which had numerous houses, a store, a cotton gin, and a bank. He bought land that was not in trust and assumed mortgages on this acquired property. From 1914 to 1924, Eastman had spent $1.3 million of his own money, which included a sizable donation to Bacone, and had acquired a debt of $117,000. The Indian bureau was reluctant to release more money to Eastman from his oil royalties because of this profligate spending. Nonetheless, the Indian agency was obligated to pay the debts he had incurred. Much agency time was consumed in continual dealings with Eastman Richards's creditors and sorting out which debts were legitimate and which were inflated or bogus.

An attempt by a Creek attorney to have Eastman Richards declared incompetent failed before a McIntosh County judge. As an expedient, Commissioner Burke and Superintendent Shade Wallen agreed to work through a Muskogee businessman and lawyer, H. G. House, to manage Eastman's money. House settled Richards's outstanding debts and then set up a trust fund for $200,000 to ensure that Richards would have a guaranteed life income. Despite these precautions, House mismanaged the estate and was later successfully sued by Richards's heirs.[3]

At the same time as the Union Agency was expending precious resources on wealthy Creek Indians Barnett and Richards, a crisis was brewing in Osage County in the early 1920s, reinforcing Burke's antagonism toward Oklahoma guardians and spurring his efforts to find legislative remedies. By special agreement, the Osage owned their oil wealth collectively and per capita oil royalty checks were delivered to the approximately 2,000 Osage headright owners (shareholders in the Osage mineral wealth). Osage oil wealth escalated in the early 1920s and their spendthrift ways alarmed Commissioner Vaux, who bewailed in 1920, "These people do not know what they are doing; they have never been trained." Accordingly, Congress passed legislation in 1921 to limit annual payments to restricted Osage adults to $4,000, conserving the remainder in federal accounts. Like the Five Civilized Tribes before them, the Osage's "surplus" funds from oil royalties were conserved by the Department of the Interior. To overcome this limitation on access to their money, many Osages applied for competency certificates. Due to flaws in the 1921 legislation, both restricted and unrestricted Osages became entangled in the county court guardian system established by the Crime of 1908. All of the worst abuses of theft and mismanagement of wards' funds that wealthy Five Civilized Tribes people experienced before the 1912 reforms were repeated in Osage country. By 1923, 439 Osage Indians were under legal guardianship and 150 minors had special guardians. Roughly 600 guardians gained control of $8 million of Osage funds by 1924. Indian wealth was siphoned off in every conceivable fashion by double-billing merchants, violent criminals, drug traffickers, bootleggers, gold diggers, con men, guardians, and so-called business managers.[4]

Compounding the bureau's administrative difficulties with the wealthy Indians were several conundrums. Though court-appointed guardians for rich Indians promised to alleviate the bureau of its administrative burden, it only complicated the bureau's work as it had to monitor the guardians' activities. Further, even Indians like Eastman Richards who were legally competent required ongoing bureau supervision if their oil lands were restricted. As the bureau learned from experience, the Indians' legal status—whether restricted or competent—could be manipulated by those wishing to exploit their wealth.[5] Rich Indians were often the targets of criminal violence. The bureau was duty bound to protect the persons and the property of such rich Indians whatever their formal legal status.

Through a trial-and-error process, the Burke administration moved toward the remedy of creating private trusts in individual cases for rich, restricted Indians as a viable alternative to public trust responsibility. In the early 1920s, a few Indian trusts at private banks were created, namely for Jackson Barnett, Eastman Richards, and a handful of others. Burke wanted congressional authorization to allow private trusts for all well-to-do Indians along with legislation to terminate the jurisdiction of the Oklahoma probate courts over the Five Civilized Tribes as defined in the Oklahoma Closure Act. Burke was confident that passage of the reform legislation he had authored would signal a larger political victory for the enlightened use of federal power.

Rational management of a ward's estate during his lifetime was only part of the "problem of the riches." What was to be done with the surplus wealth was also a compelling issue. In the late 1910s, the surplus wealth of Indians had been converted into Liberty Bonds with the federal government's holdings in accrued Indian oil assets reaching $11 million, and there was another $6 million in government accounts by 1920. Jackson's share constituted about 6 percent of the former and 15 percent of the latter. By 1927, $31 million in Osage money had accumulated in Oklahoma banks, and $18 million was in government bonds.[6]

The bureau's thinking about this surplus wealth was shaped by Henry George's idea of the "unearned increment" as developed in his influential nineteenth-century book, *Progress and Poverty*, and by Andrew Carnegie's "gospel of wealth." The rich Indians' wealth from oil profits was viewed as undeserved because they had not earned this money by their own efforts; some went even further to suggest that Indians had little claim on mineral wealth, because Indian land and resources had been "given" to Indians through federal largess. Carnegie directed that a person of wealth donate all of his accumulated income to philanthropy before his death, a philosophy in harmony with Protestant values and Social Darwinism.[7] Those inheriting such "accidental" fortunes were thus even more undeserving of the surpluses. The bureau took a proprietary interest in the surplus funds it had carefully garnered and invested, wanting to prevent the dissipation of surplus wealth in probate proceedings when rich Indians like Jackson

Barnett died. Another risk of dissipation of the surplus funds came from the fast-approaching end of the twenty-five-year probationary period, when restricted Indians' estates would be freed from federal supervision. Once unrestricted, the bureau knew, these wealthy Indians would become the prey of the unscrupulous.

From Burke's paternalistic perspective, the solution to the problem of Indian surplus wealth was to create private trusts that would provide life-time support for the wealthy Indians and ultimately transfer their assets to private institutions like Bacone College. Burke believed that Indian surplus wealth should be conserved and channeled to socially beneficial purposes, rather than dissipated by persons morally tainted by incompetence or selfishness: spendthrift Indians, corrupt guardians, fraudulent heirs, and grafters.[8]

From Burke's perspective, the disbursement of the Barnett estate must have seemed inspired: a major blow against the forces of ignorance, corruption, inefficiency, and waste. It foreshadowed a day when wealthy Indians would be secure in their estates, the U.S. taxpayer would be relieved of unnecessary administrative expense, the country would be rid of the moral stain of the corrupt Oklahoma guardianship system, and surplus funds derived from oil wealth would be used for philanthropy. In equal measure, Burke's program was progressive and regressive. It was also smugly superior and proprietary: the bureau knew better than the Indians themselves or their white neighbors what defined the "right use" of Indian wealth.

The large Jackson Barnett gift donation to the American Home Missionary Society in 1922 was not an anomaly nor even an innovation. It more or less evolved naturally as a solution to several problems that had long entangled the bureau, namely, balancing its mandate to protect and "civilize" its Indian wards with demands for economy and efficiency. Beyond the promised long-term benefit to Indian people, the primary benefit of the faith-based public-parochial alliance was to save state and federal taxpayers the burden of and responsibility for education, orphanages, and other social services for Indians. As a matter of policy, the Indian service during the Sells and Burke administrations was strongly sympathetic to plans to divert Indian wealth from channels of waste and spoliation toward the good purposes designated by Christian denominations.

Burke's reform agenda had the strong political support of the evangelical Board of Indian Commissioners, the Indian Rights Association, and the Northern Baptists. Since Bacone was Burke's favored recipient of wealthy Oklahoma Indians' funds, the Northern Baptists' support was no surprise. The Baptist-run Bacone College and the Union Agency (both in Muskogee) formed a marriage of convenience in the 1920s. In his report to his superiors, the executive officers of the AHMS, Bacone College's president, B. D. Weeks, detailed the latest pledges he'd obtained from rich Indians; the progress that older pledges were making through bureau procedures toward approval by the secretary of the Interior; the active support and encouragement he received from the Union Agency in interceding with the commissioner of Indian affairs on Bacone's behalf; and the jealousy that the Southern Baptist organization felt for the favoritism the Northern Baptists and Bacone enjoyed with the bureau.[9]

In the early 1920s, the Baptists became more aggressive in their solicitation of financial pledges from wealthy Indians. Charles White, executive secretary of the AHMS, instructed Weeks to accelerate his efforts: "We must get all we can from them in direct gifts." The donations of 1924 topped any previous year, though Weeks did some soul searching about having to pay an interpreter $100 for his assistance in getting a large donation. George Hovey, the society's secretary of education, encouraged Weeks's efforts to persuade Indians to donate "to their own needs."[10] An unnamed official strongly reaffirmed the Interior Department's commitment to Bacone in a 1927 Baptist publication:

> I will approve of the gift of every dollar any Indian has and wishes to give. This is an institution of demonstrated value. It was not organized with any expectation of getting any money. The time is coming when all restrictions upon the Indians' use of their money will be removed. The college will prepare the Indians who go through it to withstand the endeavors to rob them of their money. Many will not be so prepared and the Orphanage will care for their children when they are left penniless.

Getting all they could from the wealthy Indians was rationalized as unselfish work that served the ends of creating an educational trust for future generations of Indians. With endowments topping $1 million, Bacone ambitiously planned a campus with thirty-nine buildings. Meeting the future educational needs of Indians nationally seemed assured as Bacone grew into one of the leading institutions of higher education in the Midwest.[11]

This carefully conceived and well-meaning plan to funnel Jackson Barnett's funds to Bacone met with unexpected resistance in the months following the $1.1 million donation. The masterstroke that the Department of the Interior had struck against the guardian had not completely broken the legal hold the Okmulgee County court had over Jackson Barnett's estate. Not having been consulted about the donation, the guardian and his lawyers learned of it in the newspapers after the decision was final. This was a shock and an insult to the guardian, his lawyers, the Okmulgee County court, and Judge Hugh Murphy. Immediately after the news broke in Oklahoma in late February 1923, the *Muskogee Times-Democrat* and others following the story predicted that the case would be fought all the way to the U.S. Supreme Court. Charles Burke's display of federal power in the Jackson Barnett gift donation was "one of the most gigantic wrongs ever perpetuated," one outraged Okmulgee doctor complained to

Interior secretary Hubert Work. The rights of a helpless old man were being trampled by a band of reckless politicians and lawyers.[12]

The aggrieved parties—O'Hornett, his lawyer, C. B. McCrory, and Okmulgee County judge W. A. Barnett (Judge Murphy's successor)—went immediately into action, simultaneously launching litigation on several fronts. In March 1923, O'Hornett filed a suit in Muskogee federal court to block Union Agency superintendent Victor Locke and his cashier, Buddrus, from releasing any money to the Barnetts, including their regular monthly allowance and funds for special expenditures, for example, a home purchase in Los Angeles. After the court directed a stop payment, from November 1923 to August 1924, Barnett received no monthly allowance. Also in March 1923, O'Hornett and his counsel challenged the legality of the $1.1 million donation and sued to recover this money. Acting on behalf of Jackson Barnett as his *prochien ami,* or "best friend," the guardian brought suit against the two trust companies in which the bulk of the gift money had been deposited. This involved the $550,000 Baptist donation in the Equitable Trust Company of New York and Anna's $200,000 deposited in the Riggs Bank of Washington, D.C. These suits blocked the trust companies from issuing annuities to the Barnetts until the legality of the trusts was determined. Thus, the Barnetts were shut out of this source of income as well.[13]

The litigation to break the trusts was motivated by both political and pecuniary considerations. There was the question of whether Burke had overstepped his authority in circumventing the Oklahoma county court in negotiating the trust without the court's approval. The guardian and his lawyers also objected to the loss of the lucrative Barnett account and wanted to reclaim it, if possible. As counsel in a 1923 tax recovery case involving Barnett's assets, for example, O'Hornett's lawyers, Monk and McCrory, won $18,499.67 in legal fees.[14] Recovery of the account would mean very large commissions during Jackson's lifetime and, following his death, in the probate case. If the trusts could be broken and the Barnett money recovered for the "true" heirs among his Creek kinfolk, there was the lucrative prospect of collecting up to 30–50 percent in contingency fees from the $1.1 million. Such riches danced like sugarplums in front of the eyes of many Oklahoma lawyers familiar with the case. On June 19, 1923, for example, the firm of Cochran and Ellison of Okmulgee signed a contract with Jackson's half brother David Barnett to represent him and related heirs in challenging the trust and recovering the money for them.

Those who had an interest in challenging the trust in court labored under two very serious handicaps. The guardian, his lawyers, and the firm of Cochran and Ellison lacked the resources to conduct a protracted legal offense. And there was the formidable opposition of the Department of the Interior. Having gone to great lengths to remove the guardian's authority to prevent "wasting litigation" to the estate, the department was unsympathetic to appeals to grant legal funds to challenge its own actions and authority. For example, with Jackson Barnett's move out of Okmulgee County, the guardian's services as an intermediary were superfluous in Interior's view. When O'Hornett requested $5,000 from the Union Agency at Muskogee for lawyers in March 1923 to recover the $1.1 million donation, the superintendent refused. In April 1923, in an effort to lobby for funds directly in Washington, D.C., O'Hornett approved $500 for travel money for his attorneys to visit Secretary of the Interior Work, Fall's successor, but Work courteously denied the request for the expenditure, saying that Fall's approval of the $1.1 million gift was "doubtless beyond administrative recall." Appeals to the Department of Justice also fell on deaf ears. Cynical about the corrupt power brokers in Washington, D.C., O'Hornett became discouraged and contemplated resigning as guardian. Litigation to break the trusts might take years and ultimately prove unsuccessful, so the glittering vision of $400,000 in contingency fees lost much of its luster.[15]

Round one of the engagement was largely a crippling action. Whoever had access to Jackson Barnett's funds for legal expenses definitely held the advantage in the cases against the trust companies initiated by the guardian. Commissioner Burke fully anticipated some opposition from the guardian and the court and was prepared for the challenges ahead. Having exercised legal and political muscle in creating the Barnett trusts, he displayed a commitment to sustaining the trusts with the same focused energy.

Burke handpicked a team of loyal men to break the O'Hornett forces' opposition to the Barnett donation. The core of this team was Edwin Booth, Marshall Mott, Creek attorney Ward, and newly appointed Union Agency superintendent Shade Wallen. Ward, Booth, and Mott were capable lawyers, well versed in the Barnett case's legal complexities. O'Hornett was pressured to resign. They held many meetings with O'Hornett's lawyers regarding the procedures and terms by which O'Hornett's guardianship would be legally terminated. Facing extreme pressure, including the threat that he might be held personally liable for some malfeasance, O'Hornett agreed to resign in November 1923. Burke's forces seemed poised for a grand victory.

O'Hornett's attorneys submitted a tentative report, stipulating that once O'Hornett's final account of Jackson Barnett's estate was approved, O'Hornett would be relieved of his responsibilities and would collect a settlement of $20,000 out of Jackson Barnett's money. The agreement also imposed the condition that Okmulgee County's theoretical jurisdiction be acknowledged by requiring a successor to O'Hornett be appointed to legally manage Jackson's estate.[16] Burke agreed to find a successor since the only alternative was for the county court to determine that Jackson Barnett had become "competent" and no longer in need of supervision in his financial affairs. As a matter of political pragmatism, Burke was willing to concede that an estate guardian best served the interests of the elderly and illiterate Indian. He suggested that one of his own loyal Indian bureau employees, Orlando Swain, could fill the position as Jackson's new guardian. After prolonged negotiations, a compromise candidate, Elmer Bailey, a personal friend of Superintendent Shade Wallen, was advanced. Bailey professed to be completely ignorant of the Barnett case, and interviews indicated he would be sympathetic and cooperative with the Indian agency's objectives. Not suspecting a trick, the Burke team anticipated Bailey would "act in harmony with the department."[17]

Mott drew up the key demands that the Interior Department would present to the new guardian. These included immediate resumption of the $2,500 monthly allowances, payment of all allowances retroactive to August 1923, and dismissal of the federal suits initiated by O'Hornett challenging the donations and freezing the trust distributions. Stressing the need for harmony, Mott called for an end to O'Hornett's obstinacy, obstructiveness, and unfair treatment of his ward and the resulting deprivation for the Barnetts. All Barnett assets would be liquidated and the proceeds distributed to beneficiaries in the form of trusts prior to Jackson Barnett's demise. The new guardian and his lawyers would develop proper legal procedures to this end. Bailey was advised to "liquidate the entire estate, wipe it off the books, in the coming twelve months." With no more restricted property left to oversee, both the federal government and the Oklahoma courts would finally be relieved of guardianship responsibilities. Mott initiated negotiations to appoint a Los Angeles bank to manage Jackson Barnett's California property and pay his routine allowances. Using a carrot-and-stick approach, the bureau essentially dictated terms as a condition for Interior's approval of Bailey as guardian. Despite inducements and pleas, the expected resolution failed to materialize by mid-1924. No concessions were made on the home purchase issue, the monthly allowances, or the dismissal of court actions once Bailey was appointed.[18]

The suits launched by O'Hornett strained Anna Barnett's finances. Her ambitions brought her to the point of financial embarrassment not long after the Barnetts' arrival in Los Angeles. After purchasing a home in late 1923 out of the $200,000 she had received in cash, she coveted an even more prestigious home for her family. In February 1924, she bought a $50,000 lot in Hancock Park and commissioned a two-story, white-pillared, colonial mansion containing fifteen to eighteen rooms constructed at a cost of $35,000–40,000. This home—at 644 South Rossmore, on the corner of Wilshire Boulevard—was completed on June 30, 1926. Another $20,000 was spent to furnish this mansion. And Anna made other purchases. In March 1924, she bought 107 acres in Coldwater Canyon so Jackson would have land for his ponies. It cost $272,000. She made a $45,000 cash down payment and agreed to $20,000 semiannual payments. In addition to the Rossmore and Coldwater properties, she bought and sold other parcels in the Los Angeles boom market. Financial transactions kept her one step ahead of her various mortgage payments and obligations to Marshall Mott, her attorney.[19]

Because O'Hornett's suits had suspended the $2,500 monthly allowances as well as the annuities from the trusts, Anna appealed for help from Interior and received a swift and supportive reply. In August 1923 Interior compliantly sent its solicitor, Edwin Booth, to Los Angeles to draw up a will, which Jackson Barnett thumbprinted. It provided that Anna would inherit the entire Barnett estate except for the $550,000 donation to the Baptists, effectively ensuring that Anna Barnett was legal heir to all oil revenues accruing in government trust accounts. The same month, a formal request was made (purportedly by Jackson Barnett) that Anna be reimbursed for the purchase of the Los Angeles home from his funds held by the Department of the Interior. Subsequently, the assistant secretary of the Interior recommended approving this request; he was sympathetically inclined to dispense $51,000 to Anna Barnett as her money was tied up in the suit brought by O'Hornett challenging the Riggs trust. It appears she had an infusion of cash in the spring of 1924, but records are inconclusive as to whether she received $51,000 from the Department of the Interior to purchase the Barnetts' first Los Angeles home. Although Interior had approved this payment, the county court's injunction made this transfer legally questionable.[20]

Anna was desperate for even more cash by mid-1924 as negotiations in Oklahoma failed to end the deadlock. Thousands of dollars in back allowances and annuities from the trust funds were being withheld. Payments on the Rossmore, Coldwater, and at least five other California properties, along with the mortgages, the Muskogee home, and the Barnetts' living expenses, had exhausted her capital by 1924. Anna and Mott sought alternative ways to get the funds to her flowing again. Political pressure had not allowed Interior to bypass the authority of the Oklahoma guardian and court, so she and Mott filed countersuits to demand the interest payments due to her according to the terms of the trust agreements.[21]

In a far more dubious legal maneuver, Anna and Mott went to the Los Angeles County Superior Court in July 1924 to have Jackson Barnett declared incompetent. In her petition, Anna Barnett asserted that her husband was incompetent because he was illiterate, uneducated, and unable to understand English or conduct business. A guardian should be appointed because he was likely to be "deceived or imposed upon by artful and designing persons." Jackson Barnett was ordered to appear for a court examination. By the end of July, Security Trust Bank of Los Angeles had been named guardian of Jackson Barnett's property, and Anna had become guardian of his person. The Los Angeles judge ordered a $2,500 monthly allowance commencing with his court's jurisdiction over the estate in August. The court ordered back allowances be paid. By October, $55,000 had been deposited by Interior in Security Trust Bank for the purposes of sustaining the Barnett family.[22]

The hypocrisy of declaring Jackson Barnett legally incompetent only a few months after he had given away $1.1 million—an action that rested legally upon his competency—was glaring. The irony of the act did not escape the new guardian, Security Bank. From the beginning of negotiations, the bank was apprised of the Oklahoma litigation aimed at invalidating the trusts and had even obtained a copy of the infamous Bowie Report. Mrs. Barnett was declaring her husband incompetent, while simultaneously contending that their marriage and the trust contracts were legitimate because Jackson Barnett was competent. Sensing the legal hazards entailed in assuming legal guardianship in this complicated case, the bank agreed to assume guardianship of Jackson only with the understanding that the Interior Department intended to liquidate all of Jackson Barnett's holdings and place all of his assets under its management.[23]

Not satisfied with just the resumption of monthly allowances, Anna demanded back payments of allowances. Mott lobbied hard for this concession with the Okmulgee County court, but secured no agreement. The Interior Department told Security Bank that it did not object to retroactive payment, but left it to the bank's discretion whether to pay this sum, $25,000, to Anna. In the end, the bank adamantly refused. Bristling with indignation, Anna demanded to know how it dared disobey instructions and recommendations from the Indian bureau. To her shock, she learned that the bank intended to bring suit to recover the two trust funds in the East. As the new guardian, Security saw itself in a position to collect the 25 percent in legal fees for recovering the $1.1 million for the "true" heirs of Jackson Barnett once the trusts were broken.

In an ironic twist, Anna and Mott had reinserted Jackson into the dual guardianship system; they had placed Jackson under the guardianship of the Los Angeles County court as an incompetent, only to have the new guardian behave as stubbornly as the old. This hostile reaction from an unexpected source was a psychological and financial blow to Anna. So she appealed to an old ally, Burke, for assistance. The Interior Department soon informed the bank that, contrary to the earlier understanding, it would hold the bulk of Jackson Barnett's property in trust. Interior would retain control of Jackson Barnett's assets, thus abandoning the plan to privatize them. The bank's responsibility was simply to pay out monthly allowances from periodic infusions of money from his accounts in the Department of the Interior. Anna Barnett sued Security for the back payments but was only granted a portion of the $25,000. In February 1925, Security Bank resigned as guardian, and a replacement, Los Angeles lawyer Leslie Hewitt, was appointed. Four years later, Anna was still livid about the bank's alleged obstructionism, telling a Senate subcommittee that she counted Security Bank as a lifelong enemy.[24]

Anna's clash with Security Bank in Los Angeles in late 1924 was the first showing of blood in a legal engagement that had begun inauspiciously in Okmulgee in March 1923. Indian bureau hopes for a resolution of the Barnett estate via negotiation looked gloomy during the summer of 1924. The Oklahoma guardian, Bailey, refused to resign even though he had been replaced by the guardian appointed by the California courts. Though he received no fees, he continued the legal suits to recover the trust accounts. Failing a negotiated settlement, the Interior Department fell into a default position of continued material, legal, and political support to Anna to sustain her during the legal and political battles to come. Anna's access to funds, except for the $2,500 monthly allowance, was blocked. With her insatiable demand for money, she would not allow this state of affairs to continue.

If the situation was frustrating for the Indian bureau, Anna Barnett, and her lawyer, Marshall Mott, it looked even bleaker for the opposition. The Department of the Interior stonewalled the lawyers attacking the legitimacy of the trusts in 1924. "The task of recovering the $1.1 million thus looked almost hopeless," one lawyer reported.[25] The battle between the Oklahoma guardian's lawyers and the lawyers working on contingency for Jackson's heirs and Anna Barnett had become a war of attrition.

While Burke continued to try to dislodge Bailey as Jackson Barnett's legal guardian, he was simultaneously making a multifaceted attack on the Oklahoma dual guardianship system, with equally frustrating results. Burke's strategy was to overwhelm his opponents and force them to surrender. In his national campaign, however, as in his attack on the guardian, he made a serious miscalculation. Burke's aid to the Barnetts in their flight from the jurisdiction of the Okmulgee County court earned him the bitter enmity of a core of snubbed individuals in Okmulgee County directly involved in the negotiations of 1920–1923. His national campaign earned him more enemies.

Burke began his political offensive in 1923, encouraging Matthew Sniffen of the Indian Rights Association to begin an investigation into the corrupt practices of the Oklahoma guardianship system. Meanwhile, the Indian bureau began a separate investigation into the Oklahoma probate courts. In August 1923, Burke publicly attacked the Oklahoma courts' appointment of guardians for Indian incompetents. "Such action," said Burke, "puts the Indian in the same category with an insane man. It classifies him as *non compos mentis*. . . . This is an injustice to the Indian and also a usurpation of authority of the Secretary of the Interior."[26]

Burke's strategy was to generate public outrage about the Oklahoma probate system in order to garner public support for congressional reform legislation. This began with the disclosures of the Indian bureau report by Superintendent Wallen, submitted to Indian affairs committees of both houses of Congress on December 31, 1923. Wallen's research revealed average administrative costs of 13.7 percent. His analysis showed that when Indian property was sold, it was consistently undervalued. But when guardians wished to make loans against Indian property, the property was consistently overvalued by up to three times its worth. The former practice allowed guardians to sell devalued Indian properties to friends or cronies in return for a kickback; the latter facilitated the guardians' power over the liquid assets of their wards for investment in dubious enterprises, often leading to bankruptcy of the Indians' estates.[27]

Wallen's report was quickly followed by two other muckraking studies, which appeared in 1924 and 1925. The first of these was *Oklahoma's Poor Rich Indians: An Orgy of Graft and Exploitation of the Five Civilized Tribes—Legalized Robbery*, based on the inquiry by Gertrude Bonnin, a well-educated, full-blood Sioux political activist and representative of the General Federation of Women's Clubs and the Indian Welfare Committee, and Charles Fabens, attorney for the American Indian Defense Association. The lesser known was *The Act of May 27, 1908 Placing in the Probate Courts of Oklahoma Indian Jurisdiction: A National Blunder* authored by lawyer Marshall Mott and paid for by the American Home Missionary Society. These studies and the Wallen report reinforced each other, providing statistical evidence of exorbitant guardianship fees and describing systematic corruption. Informal networks of influential members of the eastern Oklahoma communities—county judges, politicians, guardians, attorneys, bankers, and merchants—had a vested interest in protecting the guardianship system that fleeced Indians. All three studies leveled severe criticism at the Oklahoma Closure Act of 1908 (the Crime of 1908), which had transferred jurisdiction over Indians of the Five Civilized Tribes to the county probate courts, and the studies urged immediate reform legislation. Supplementing these studies was select testimony of some Oklahomans, who hoped timely reforms would induce Barnett and the many other oil-rich Indians to return with their wealth to enrich the local economies.[28]

Oklahoma's Poor Rich Indians was a particularly powerful political weapon because it gave the statistical evidence of corruption and attendant Indian suffering a human face. The pamphlet included dozens of individual case studies and described horrific abuses, called "almost unbelievable in a civilized country" by Herbert Welsh, president of the national Indian Rights Association. This pamphlet revealed "excessive and unnecessary administrative costs" from 20 percent to 70 percent and "unconscionable fees and commissions." The heart-wrenching story of a seven-year-old Choctaw, Ledhi Stechi, who was kept in starvation while a guardian pillaged her estate, was recounted. When the child died, grafters descended upon her grieving grandmother. The authors were in evident agreement with Mott's contention: "If the machinery of the government had entered into a conspiracy to cheat, rob and defraud its Indians in Oklahoma, it could not have done it in a better way than by the laws it passed." The remedy offered in *Poor Rich Indians* to protect the property of the remaining 18,000 restricted Indians of Oklahoma lay in giving the Interior Department as much control of minors and incompetents as constitutional limitations would permit. In his pamphlet, *Act of May 27, 1908*, Mott expressed his unshakable belief that the "proud Christian government of ours will right these wrongs and right them now."[29]

Secretary of the Interior Hubert Work fully supported Charles Burke's campaign and soon joined the crusade to arouse public opinion against the guardianship system. In a May 1924 *Saturday Evening Post* article, Work described how the estates of 2,821 restricted Indians worth $14 million were costing $2 million to administer by local guardians, while the federal government administered 40,000 estates for 1 percent of their total value. Work plugged the bill pending in Congress to remedy this deplorable state of affairs.[30]

Burke was confident that his careful planning and attention to minute detail, his position of strength in the nation's capital, and a well-timed publicity campaign to pass the Burke bill would win the day. Primed by the bad publicity about the Oklahoma guardianship system, congressional approval of the Burke bill transferring the system to the federal government appeared imminent in mid-1924. A favorable, final resolution of the Barnett affair also seemed likely. Bureau lawyers in Muskogee fostered the optimism of the assistant secretary of the Interior, who wrote the U.S. attorney general that a final and equitable settlement in the "Jackson Barnett guardianship matter" was at hand.[31]

Oklahoma opposition to the bureau expanded and consolidated by mid-1924. Oklahomans were insulted by the reports and Burke's intent to deprive many Oklahoma counties of a lucrative source of revenue and political authority over Indians. While Oklahoma congressmen publicly endorsed reforms in the wake of the damaging revelations of the Wallen report and *Poor Rich Indians*, they worked covertly to defeat Burke's bill. Due in part to the political climate in Oklahoma in a congressional election year, momentum shifted dramatically between June 1924, when passage of the Burke bill appeared most auspicious, and August 1924, when the Oklahomans made an effective counterattack and carried the war into the enemy's own territory.

Burke had made a number of political mistakes. He had offended Judge Hugh Murphy; he had tried to trump local prerogative with federal power; and he had smeared the Oklahoma probate system with hyperbolic charges of corruption. In 1923, the powerful politician William B. Pine, a millionaire oilman of Okmulgee, sought to control agency spoils and put forward Judge James A. Hepburn as a candidate for superintendent of the Union Agency. Burke rejected Hepburn and instead appointed Shade Wallen as Victor Locke's successor. As insignificant as this event may seem, the appointment of Wallen was a personal rebuff to Pine, and the incident acted as a catalyst for a take-no-prisoners political war between these two powerful adversaries. Pine's power and leadership in the anti-Burke opposition increased when he was elected as a U.S. senator in 1924. In his campaign, Pine proclaimed the Barnett case to be "rotten clear through" and promised he would do what he could to get to the facts.[32]

Burke underestimated the determination and resourcefulness of his Oklahoma enemies, who had found a standard-bearer in the newly elected Senator Pine. A groundswell of political opposition was building in Oklahoma due to Mott's recent victories in a tax case, the rejection of Hepburn as superintendent of the Union Agency, the political attacks on the guardianship system, and other instances of what Oklahomans saw as federal high-handedness. The wholesale federal indictment of the systemic grafting left few Oklahoma politicians, judges, or lawyers free from its embarrassing sting.

As the collaboration of Burke and Mott became more apparent, old animosities for a man reviled in Oklahoma were rekindled. In February 1924, when it was announced that Mott was on retainer as one of Mrs. Barnett's attorneys, the *Muskogee Times-Democrat* showed unconcealed hostility toward the "unofficial minister plenipotentiary of the Department of the Interior." Rumors had long circulated that Mott had masterminded the Barnetts' escape to California and had profited handsomely from this move. Now it was suspected that he was enjoying profits as the Barnetts' attorney as well. Who were the schemers who had engineered the Barnett "gifts,"? many openly wondered. Burke's orchestrated power play to smear Oklahoma's judicial system provoked fears of a conspiracy.[33]

To Burke's surprise, political opinion shifted at the national level with regard to his proposed legislative reforms. Before his bill overhauling the Oklahoma probate system was pushed through Congress, Oklahoma congressmen demanded that a mixed committee of senators and representatives gather evidence in another investigation. A House subcommittee, chaired by Republican Homer P. Snyder, heard testimony from November 11 to December 12, 1924, at Muskogee, looking for evidence about the validity of the Wallen report and the *Poor Rich Indians* pamphlet. Matthew Sniffen, the first witness, testified that his facts were derived from agency sources, a damning admission. The investigation found errors. For example, the minor Ledhi Stechi, whose estate had been poorly managed by her guardian, had no oil on her land.

Of the many witnesses who were heard by the House subcommittee, one of the most effective was former Okmulgee County judge Hugh Murphy, who made the shocking assertion that Burke had violated the law in creating the Barnett trusts. Murphy nursed a strong personal grievance against Burke for his high-handedness in the Jackson Barnett case and for his slanders of Oklahoma's court system. Murphy indicted Burke for completely ignoring probate law under the "dual system in vogue" in the Jackson Barnett case and charged that the investigation should include Commissioner Burke. Identifying the issue at hand as simply the "idea of paternalism and bureaucracy," Murphy asserted that the probate courts of

Oklahoma were capable and honest and that a majority of judges cooperated with Washington's red tape. In Murphy's view, there was friction and
awkwardness in the dual guardianship system, which generally worked to
the Indians' financial disadvantage and which was vulnerable to "political
manipulation." Despite his own cooperation and steadfast adherence to
the rule of law in the Barnett case, Murphy said, the bureau trampled the
county court.[34]

Murphy found a national forum for his charges against Burke in Congress. On December 9, 1924, an Oklahoma congressman read a letter from
Murphy on the House floor in which he told a titillating tale of how Anna
the Adventuress seduced Jackson the Decrepit Incompetent and of the unsuccessful attempts of O'Hornett the Honest to get funds for litigation
from the federal government to redress this travesty. The story of an adventuress making off with a regal fortune intrigued and mystified congressmen. Congressman E. B. Howard of Tulsa demanded a full investigation, alleging possible criminal misconduct by federal officials. In an effort
to undo the damage, Commissioner Burke had a rebuttal printed in the
Congressional Record the next day. He claimed that Murphy dredged up the
Barnett case because of his opposition to the pending bill, which would remove restricted Indians from Oklahoma jurisdiction.[35] At Burke's insis-
tence, the Snyder committee specifically inquired into the integrity of his
own behavior in the Jackson Barnett case.

This change in the political climate enabled the guardian's lawyers to
obtain a hearing with the highest-ranking federal officials, including Secretary of the Interior Work and a representative from the Justice Department. On January 27, 1925, Secretary Work again refused their request for
money. But fearing these lawyers might meet with success with their lobbying, he made a personal plea to Attorney General Harlan Stone not to
assist the guardian's lawyers in their ambitions.[36] David Barnett's lawyer
was simultaneously lobbying officials in the Interior and Justice departments to allow funds for litigation, but he too was refused. Despite these
rejections, the lawyers persisted in demanding money so the matter could
be fairly addressed by the courts. They questioned why the Interior Department had not consulted the Dawes Rolls to see if Jackson Barnett had
any living relatives before giving away his estate.[37]

In February and March 1925, this change was signaled by the Justice
Department and members of Congress who expressed doubt about the legality of the Jackson Barnett donation and recommended that the matter
be settled in court. The first significant development was Attorney General
Harlan Stone's opinion in early February that the $1.1 million distribution
was unauthorized. He believed the federal government should recover the
money. Stone had earlier agreed with Bailey that restricted Indians lacked
the power to initiate trusts.[38] On the heels of this announcement, the Snyder House subcommittee report stated it could not determine whether Interior was within the law in creating the trusts. It saw the case as being of

"fundamental importance" and recommended that Interior spend some of Jackson Barnett's money to secure an early legal determination from the U.S. Supreme Court.

While the House subcommittee report was favorable to Burke in some respects, it opened a Pandora's box. Significantly, Burke was exonerated of any wrongdoing. Yet dissenting views were extremely damaging to Burke. Committee member S. B. Hill targeted two questions in his dissent: Did Burke exceed his authority in the dual guardianship system? This question of joint or exclusive jurisdiction required judicial review. Was Jackson Barnett competent to make a gift of $1.1 million? On this score, Hill believed, Interior had erred in its judgment. Another Oklahoma congressman, W. W. Hastings, went further, suggesting that the Interior Department was guilty of misadministration, if not conspiracy, for violating the law in not consulting the Oklahoma guardian and the Okmulgee County court. Even if Interior had such authority, it most certainly should not have disbursed Jackson's funds to the gold digger who had kidnapped Jackson Barnett. "It establishes a dangerous precedent," said Hastings. Summarizing the subcommittee report, David Barnett's lawyer said that it did not show corruption nor want of good faith by anyone in the bureau or Interior. But the fact that the guardian and the county court were not consulted raised "a legal question that can only be determined by the courts."[39]

National attention shifted radically from the misconduct of Oklahoma guardians to the misconduct of Commissioner Burke. And as the resolution of the problem shifted from the executive and legislative branches to the judiciary, the Burke reform bill faced serious opposition. According to Oklahoma critics, Burke lacked the authority to make the Barnett donation and was attempting to get statutory authority retroactively. For the Department of the Interior to make an amendment and later seek statutory authority was not uncommon, however. Oklahoman W. W. Hastings put forward a much milder reform bill. In the end, the Burke bill endorsing "exclusive" federal jurisdiction over the Five Civilized Tribes failed to pass, as did its alternative. Reform efforts ultimately led to legislation setting maximum fees for guardians and requiring that local guardians' appointments be approved by Interior. A compromise bill bringing the Osage guardians under stricter federal supervision and correcting other serious abuses passed in 1925.[40]

Burke and Mott were discouraged, but they were as steely in their resolution as Anna Barnett. They immediately began coordinating a united counteroffensive by the triple alliance: the Baptists, the bureau, and the Barnetts. Burke and Mott looked for a victory in the courts to accomplish what Congress had failed to do: vindicate the Barnett trusts and uphold the authority of the federal government as ultimate guardian over the Five Civilized Tribes. The reputation of Commissioner Burke would be redeemed in the process. Mott's legal strategy and his larger purpose is revealed in a statement he made to the American Home Missionary Society's executive secretary, Charles White, in late 1926: "above all else [I] am interested in sustaining the invulnerable reputation of officials of Interior Department who furthered the execution of the Barnett trust."[41] Though put on the defensive in early 1925, Mott and Burke were determined to overcome their adversaries. To their advantage, their purposes were clear, their campaign was coordinated and well financed, their political and legal case was strong, and their response was rapid.

7

Battle Royal:
Litigation over the
Jackson Barnett Estate
1925–1928

L itigation over the Jackson Barnett fortune—fittingly described as the "real marathon legal tangle of this century"—began in 1923 and was not resolved until the early 1940s.[1] It was national in scope with major battlegrounds in Kansas, Oklahoma, New York, Washington, D.C., and California. The legal engagement built to a crescendo of conflict from 1925 to 1928. Litigation begat litigation in the war over Jackson Barnett's money. In Angie Debo's oft-quoted summation, there were twenty-one important suits filed "in defense of this one indifferent old man, who slept through more trials, submitted to more mental examinations, and unwittingly created more personal and political enemies than any other Indian in the whole complicated history of the Five Tribes guardianships."[2]

In these decisive years, the key litigation fell into three main categories (with some overlap): prohibition suits, recovery suits, and suits to quiet title over the oil leases. The principal cases in the prohibition category were the original suits filed in 1923 by Jackson's guardian, Carl O'Hornett, to bar the Union Agency officials and the two trust companies, Equitable Trust and Riggs Bank, from disbursing funds to the Barnetts.[3] The most significant prohibition suit in these years, however, was retaliatory litigation brought by the triple alliance—the Baptists, the bureau, and the Barnetts—seeking to invalidate the legitimacy of O'Hornett's successor,

Elmer Bailey, who was continuing the recovery suits.[4] The second category involved several suits to recover the $1.1 million Jackson Barnett gift donation. This litigation was initiated by the guardian, but the Justice Department ultimately superseded him as plaintiff in these suits. Cases were filed against the Equitable Trust Company of New York, which held half the donation, and Riggs Bank of Washington, D.C., which held $200,000 in Anna Barnett's name. To recover the $350,000 remainder, separate actions were initiated against Harold McGugin, Marshall Mott, and Anna Barnett.[5] The last category of Barnett litigation, the challenge to Jackson Barnett's original 1912 oil lease, was a spin-off of the prohibition suit against the guardian.[6] *Mott v. United States* reached the U.S. Supreme Court, and *Barnett v. Barnett* reached the Oklahoma Supreme Court.

When the Justice Department threw its weight behind the guardian and against the triple alliance and contested Interior's action in approving the $1.1 million disbursement, the case became a civil war within the federal government. Two bitterly polarized camps formed. One coalesced around the Justice Department's assistant attorney general, Burt Parmenter. In this camp were all of those with a political or pecuniary motive for opposing the Department of the Interior or the Jackson Barnett trusts. In it were Justice Department lawyers led by Charles Selby (another Oklahoman), guardian Bailey and his lawyers, the counsel for David Barnett and other Creek claimants as blood kin, and Okmulgee County judge W. A. Barnett. Hoping to gain 30–50 percent fees, the guardian's team of lawyers—along with the private lawyers representing the Creek claimants—vigorously pursued the suits to recover the $1.1 million and to defend the legitimacy of the Oklahoma guardianship.[7] The other camp coalesced around Commissioner Charles Burke in the Department of the Interior. It included Marshall Mott, the American Home Missionary Society, Anna and Jackson Barnett, Anna's daughter, Maxine Sturgis, and their lawyers—all of whom were financially or politically involved in the defense of the legality of the trusts. Charles Rogers led the legal team for the triple alliance in the litigation to oppose the recovery suits and to invalidate the Oklahoma guardianship. Sharing information within the group, each camp worked on strategies to defeat the opposition.

The Barnett litigation was first and foremost a tug of war between a core of Oklahoma lawyers (and their clients) and the federal government's Department of the Interior over the Jackson Barnett fortune. It was also a political struggle between local and federal interests. The case involved principles of law regarding jurisdiction over all rich restricted Indians' estates in Oklahoma. In the convoluted and prolonged legal war over the Barnett fortune, economics, personal and political rivalries, and disagreements over principles of law were intertwined.

Who had the power to decide about the disposition of the wealth of a restricted Indian? This thorny legal question was the unpleasant legacy of the ambiguous amended Dawes legislation and its unholy compromise regarding jurisdictional authority over the Five Civilized Tribes. Carl O'Hornett, Jackson Barnett's original Oklahoma guardian, initiated the prohibition and recovery litigation on the grounds that the Interior Department's approval of the $1.1 million trust was in violation of legal precedents and procedures of the dual guardianship system. The Parmenter camp took the position that the donation was unlawful because neither the county court nor the guardian had consented to the donation.

The Interior Department Amendment of 1922 was ultimately targeted as the offending vehicle for Interior's abuse of power. The authority of the local probate courts and guardians had been violated by the illegal change in the Department of the Interior regulation of October 1922. The infamous regulation authorizing the Barnett gift was described as "an unwarranted, unlawful and arbitrary act and an abuse of the limited discretionary powers conferred upon the Secretary of the Interior by Congress."[8]

The Burke camp's counterargument was that the bureau had scrupulously adhered to procedure and the law when it circumvented the guardian and the Okmulgee County court. "Every act of the Commissioner with reference to Jackson Barnett and his affairs has been with the approval of the Secretary of the Interior or one of his assistants," Burke argued forcefully in his memorandum to Interior Secretary Hubert Work in March 1925.[9] Congress bestowed ample authority on the Interior Department as the Five Civilized Tribes' paramount guardian to amend the regulation. Interior's ultimate defense was that its decisions regarding restricted Indians were not subject to court review.

Burke had good reason to be smugly intransigent on what he deemed were the principles involved. Historical and legal precedent substantiated his position that Congress had delegated broad discretionary authority over restricted Indians to the Department of the Interior. His action was fully within the parameters of power exercised by his predecessors, and he spoke with the authority of the nation's most learned insider on Indian legal affairs.[10]

The weak argument initially advanced by those challenging Burke's action was that Interior's authority was limited to approving or disapproving a contract when it was proposed by a restricted Indian. While the Parmenter camp conceded that Interior had full authority to judge contracts involving restricted Indians' estates, it had no power to initiate a contract as it had evidently done with the Barnett donation, even though Jackson had given his assent. This key distinction between initiation and assent had brought the case to the courts to review.[11]

However, it was extremely difficult to make the Barnett case on this point because there was far more clarity in theory than in practice, as Burke well knew. Historically, the Indian bureau had rarely abided by the requirement that it merely ratify, rather than initiate, contracts. That so-called competent Indians initiated contracts for leasing land was a fiction.

Moreover, overcoming the legal technicality of "initiation" was easily contrived through perjured testimony. It is highly doubtful that Jackson Barnett initiated the gift of $25,000 to the construction fund of the Baptist
church in Henryetta, though many reputable citizens swore that he did.
Weeks, Bacone's president, aggressively solicited donations from rich Indians, which were routinely approved by Interior.

Burke's supreme self-assurance was based on his expert knowledge of
the evolution of Indian law and policy. Since the 1880s, Congress had
continually initiated policy about the disposition of Indian property, and
these actions were not decisions made by native people and quite often
violated their wishes. Since the early 1900s, when the Interior Department assumed greater responsibility for managing Indian resources, Congress had granted virtually unlimited discretionary powers to this branch
of the federal government, assuming Indian wards were childlike beings
whose consent was largely irrelevant. The courts sustained them with the
same reasoning. Indians whose lands were in trust had only a nominal
voice in management decisions. Likewise, in the first quarter of the
twentieth century, Congress, using its plenary authority, and the Department of the Interior, using its discretionary power, had lifted federal restrictions from Indians of less than half Indian blood quantum, even
though those persons did not initiate this significant change in legal status or were adamantly opposed to the change, which subjected them to
taxation.[12]

Abandoning the initiation argument, the Parmenter camp quickly
shifted its argument to state that Jackson was incapable of understanding
what he was doing in consenting to the donation because he was both
mentally and culturally incompetent. Burke's opponents declared that the
Interior Department was guilty of abuse of authority in "giving away" the
regal fortune of a feeble-minded man in defiance of his legal protectors,
the county court and guardian. Burke underestimated the power of this argument. To him, wealthy Indians had been brought under the Oklahoma
guardianship system not to protect them but to exploit them by draining
their assets in spurious court costs. The O'Hornett cases challenging the
Barnett trusts were seen as cases in point. Indians had endured legalized
robbery for years. Burke passionately believed he was saving these estates,
long ensnarled in this imbroglio of dual jurisdiction, from dissipation at
the hands of opportunistic lawyers by using Jackson Barnett as his test
case. To the charge that he had overstepped his authority, Burke strongly
countered that the ends justified the means. The possible dissipation of
this rich Indian's funds in probate justified the bold action by Interior to
conserve the estate as a permanent educational endowment.[13] To Burke,
the abuses of the Oklahoma guardianship system were far more compelling than Jackson's alleged mental weakness.

There were two primary reasons that the litigation became so complex
and convoluted. First, the colonial form of governing Indian people under

the amended Dawes legislation gave an enormous amount of flexibility in the discretionary authority of a few empowered individuals in the Interior Department. Second, there was a great deal of murkiness around the specific criteria regarding the definition of competent versus incompetent Indians. Poorly defined boundaries regarding legal status blurred even more when lawyers tried to make fine distinctions between incompetent restricted and competent restricted Indians.

Burke's intellectual approach to the Barnett trust, steeped in paternalism and myopically fixed on his righteous crusade to triumph over the Oklahoma guardians and probate courts, failed to calculate how perplexing his case would be to those less schooled in Indian history and policy. Burke overprepared some aspects of his case while he was also fatally unprepared to deal with the seminal issue of Jackson Barnett's alleged mental weakness. Rather than fighting the case on the turf that Burke had chosen, Bailey's lawyers anchored their assault to Jackson's deficiencies. The mind-numbing perplexities of the means and ends of dual guardianship retreated to the background, where they could be safely ignored. The sensational and lurid aspects of this case were foregrounded, and these captured the public's attention.

Recovery Suits

To recover Barnett's money, Bailey's lawyers made the comprehensible and highly persuasive argument that Jackson Barnett was seriously mentally impaired and that Anna Barnett was a shameless gold digger, who had taken advantage of his mental state. This argument was advanced in early 1925 in the first of the recovery suits to be litigated—the guardian's suit to recover the $550,000 held by the Equitable Trust Bank of New York and the American Home Missionary Society (hereafter, *Equitable*)—and was used by the other recovery suits as well.[14] In the presentation of their case in the spring of 1925, the private lawyers argued:

> Jackson Barnett is approximately 75 and at all times he was an imbecile, ignorant, uneducated, and unable to read or write, and wholly incapable of understanding and comprehending the value, condition, character, nature and extent of his estate . . . incapable of caring for himself and managing his property, and incapable of discerning or appreciating the motives and designs of any person or persons with whom he came in contact, and wholly incapable of comprehending or understanding any of the written instruments, purported trusts, requests and agreements hereinafter mentioned.[15]

The briefs emphasized Anna's alleged prostitution, her pecuniary motives, and her plots to kidnap the "imbecile." The Bowie Report of 1920 created a shockingly persuasive picture of Anna's dissolute character and her greedy motives. Anna, "a designing and unscrupulous adventuress, of bad moral character" took advantage of Jackson's weak mentality by using "seductive smiles, petting, and persuasions."[16]

Having asserted Jackson's imbecility and Anna's immorality, the guardian's lawyers claimed that the Interior Department aided her scheme by fraud or abuse of authority, either by individuals or by a larger conspiracy. Early court papers alleged that Anna's attorney's, McGugin and Keith, Union Agency lawyer Amasa Ward, "and probably others" had aided her nefarious scheme to kidnap and defraud Barnett. The Indian bureau had willfully ignored evidence available in the definitive Dawes Rolls that Jackson had a living half brother. It was alleged that Secretary of the Interior Albert Fall (forced to resign in 1923 because of his misdeeds in the corrupt Harding administration) lacked authority to approve or pay out Jackson's funds, making him party to the deception or abusing his discretion. His approval of the $1.1 million gift, they said, was procured by "fraud, imposition, deceit, and misrepresentation" by persons in the conspiracy. Bailey's counsel argued that the Interior Department was guilty of either "cupidity or stupidity."[17]

When these allegations were made by the guardian's lawyers in the initial pleadings in the *Riggs* and *Equitable* cases, the Interior Department was shocked that its actions would be questioned and embarrassed that it had gotten dragged into this tawdry public scandal as a criminal suspect. Secretary Work and Charles Burke were named as defendants in the *Equitable* and *Riggs* cases. The Department of Justice was alerted and began monitoring these suits to recover the trust money. In April 1925, Justice filed an answer to the plaintiff's petition, which said that it "believed the action taken by the officials of the Department of the Interior was within the scope of their authority."[18]

The Prohibition Suit

As he prepared to defend Anna Barnett in the *Riggs* recovery suit, Marshall Mott devised a strategy that would short-circuit all of the Barnett litigation and therefore make a complicated defense in the recovery suits unnecessary. He sought a court order to vacate O'Hornett's appointment and all of the guardian's acts. The tangled events of the 1912 competency hearings provided a loophole that could result in the guardian's dismissal. If the guardianship were thus invalidated, O'Hornett (and his successor, Bailey) had no legal right to bring the recovery or the prohibition suits blocking Anna's access to Jackson Barnett's funds. All of the suits filed by the guardian as "incompetent" Jackson's *prochien ami* would fall by the wayside, and the trusts would stand. In addition, successfully invalidating the guardianship "would set up matters involving Federal questions" (presumably Interior's position as paramount guardian), Mott assured Burke.[19]

At Mott's instigation, R. B. Drake, a Union Agency probate lawyer, filed suit in Okmulgee County court as Jackson's *prochien ami* to set aside the Oklahoma guardianship. In his petition, Drake asked that the Oklahoma state court uphold the exclusive power of Interior to adjudicate and administer the funds involved. Bringing this prohibition litigation had an additional benefit to the Burke camp: the limited resources of the private lawyers would be spread thin, as they tried to litigate in the recovery and prohibition suits simultaneously. Meanwhile, Interior steadfastly denied the guardian's lawyers access to Barnett's funds for their litigation.[20]

While striving to weaken the opposition, Mott and Burke consolidated their own forces. They insisted that both the Baptists and Anna Barnett join with the Interior Department in the action to vacate Bailey's appointment on the basis of their shared interests in protecting the trusts. In late March, the Baptists joined in the action challenging the legitimacy of the Oklahoma guardianship. Mott would represent Anna Barnett only on the condition that she materially aid the *Equitable* litigation to sustain the gift to the Baptists. To maintain a coordinated effort, Mott and Burke pressured the hesitant Baptists and Anna Barnett to hire Charles Rogers to conduct the litigation in both the prohibition and recovery suits. Burke and Mott had a decided advantage over their opponents in terms of financing, strategy, and coordination.[21]

If it were not for the rebellious, albeit self-interested, forces fomenting in the Justice Department to challenge Interior's action, no doubt Burke and the triple alliance would have reigned victorious. In 1925, the Department of Justice was still on the fence, uncertain whether to side with Interior or the guardian. Opinion at Justice was never unanimous between the summer of 1925 and 1928, the prime years of intensive Barnett litigation and political controversy. While Attorney General Stone tended to doubt the legality of the trusts, his successor, John Sargent, vacillated over the question. On the one hand, Justice was reluctant to lock horns with Interior over an action that Interior maintained was legal and proper, and Work and Burke busily lobbied to sustain that opinion in the Justice Department. Also, Justice knew that the private lawyers challenging the trusts were primarily motivated by hopes of financial rewards. How could the Justice Department justify abetting self-interested private lawyers to destroy an endowment to an Indian university? The initial response of Justice in April 1925 suggested a united front with Interior. Meanwhile, the private Oklahoma lawyers trying to crack the trusts maintained daily contact with Justice as they attempted to persuade the department of the rightness of their cause. Many conferences were held to discuss various theories and complicated questions of law and procedure. It was "only after diligent, persistent, and prolonged efforts" that the private attorneys were successful in inducing the Department of Justice to intervene, said one of Bailey's lawyers.[22]

An important reason that Justice ultimately decided to use its prestige and legal resources against the Interior Department was that a highly partisan faction within the Justice Department dominated the Barnett litigation after mid-1925. Oklahomans made up the core of this vigorously anti-Burke/anti-Mott faction within Justice, and their political sympathies were with their fellow Oklahomans, the private lawyers trying to destroy the trusts. Leading the anti-Burke faction in the Justice Department was B. M. (Burt) Parmenter of Lawton, Oklahoma, appointed to the Justice Department on July 1, 1925. He hired his former law partner, Charles Selby of Oklahoma City, as a chief counsel in the Barnett case. Both were protégés of Okmulgee County politician and U.S. senator William Pine.[23]

Heavily reliant on the private lawyers to brief them on the Barnett case, the Justice Department gradually came to understand that if Mott's skilled legal team successfully overturned Bailey's guardianship in the prohibition case in the Oklahoma state courts—and it looked like they would—then the recovery suits would be dismissed. If that happened, the federal courts would not be able to examine the difficult legal issues of dual guardianship involved in the Barnett case as the House subcommittee had recommended.

A strong reason for the Department of Justice's decision to intervene was to allow the federal courts to review the principles involved in the Barnett case. Along with some members of the Justice Department, Interior Secretary Work took the high ground that the merits of the case should be determined in the courts: "My opinion is that every effort should be made to sustain the [action] of the Department, frankly placing the whole case before the courts whose ultimate decision should either sanction what has been done or, undoing what has been done, restore the status existing prior to the transaction."[24]

Burke also publicly stated that he wanted the issues of law involved in the Barnett trusts fully reviewed in the courts, but he secretly worked toward having the guardian's legitimacy quashed via the prohibition suit masterminded by his ally Mott.

Parmenter saw through Burke's duplicity. Burke claimed the Oklahoma prohibition case did not involve the Department of the Interior, although a bureau probate attorney had filed the suit. As Parmenter rightly observed, the federal government was hamstrung by a conflict of interest in the prohibition case. The Justice Department could not intervene to defend the guardianship in Oklahoma if the United States (that is, the Interior Department) was vitally involved on the opposing side of the case. If Justice did not intervene to defend the guardianship, the merits of the case might not be heard. Parmenter insisted that Drake withdraw.[25]

Burke was dismayed by the growing hostility of the Justice Department. He prepared an elaborate memorandum to attorney general Sargent in September 1925 in defense of his action in creating the Barnett trusts.[26]

The attorney general found Parmenter's argument more persuasive than Burke's, and he put pressure on Secretary Work to withdraw Drake, the bureau probate lawyer, from the prohibition case. An alarmed Mott telegrammed Burke, convinced that this would mean disaster for their legal strategy to protect the trusts. Burke had heated words with Parmenter. He requested help from the other members of the triple alliance in trying to persuade Justice to act in harmony with Interior. Immediately after Drake was withdrawn from the prohibition case in November 1925, the Justice Department entered the case on the opposing side to defend the guardianship. In an even more foreboding action, the U.S. attorney general filed motions the following month to intervene in *Equitable* on the guardian's side and against Interior. Justice requested, however, that the money be returned to the Interior Department, not to the guardian Bailey, if the trusts were held to be invalid.[27]

The Justice Department's entrance into these cases signaled its openly adversarial relationship with Interior over Jackson Barnett's $1.1 million donation. The Interior Department fought unsuccessfully to block Justice's intervention in *Equitable*. In January 1926, the judge ruled:

> When the Attorney General appears in a court of justice to assert the rights of the United States, questioning the action of a Cabinet officer (in this case the Secretary of the Interior [Fall]) as unauthorized by law, he appears for and represents the sovereign, and it is not the function of the court to look beyond the statutes authorizing him to do so.

As the judge granted the motion to intervene, the Justice Department joined the guardian Bailey as plaintiffs challenging the legality of the $550,000 donation to the Baptists.[28]

This unexpected intervention in the *Equitable* suit was a great blow to the triple alliance, particularly Burke. In testimony before a Senate subcommittee in 1929, Burke represented Justice's actions as tricky and duplicitous, contending that Justice had implied it would intervene on Interior's side once Drake was withdrawn. More critically, Burke's sense of injustice was based on Justice's reversal; in 1925, Justice defended Interior's action, but then made specific charges of fraud against Burke in early 1926 after joining the case.[29]

Driven by political vendettas against Burke, the Oklahomans, who had found key allies in the Justice Department, were not content to simply recover the money nor to vindicate the dual guardianship system. They wanted to politically destroy Burke by bringing criminal indictments. The core of opposition came from those Oklahomans bruised by Burke's political and legal challenges to the Oklahoma guardianship system or those with a financial interest in breaking the $1.1 million gift donation. They were convinced that the Barnett trusts involved "sinister" forces and were determined to ferret out the dastardly deeds of the conspirators. In Ok-mulgee County, the news that Burke was being shaken from his "throne" had the sweet taste of revenge.[30]

The Justice Department's team of lawyers and the private Oklahoma attorneys conducted an aggressive and tireless legal challenge after November 1925 in Oklahoma on the prohibition case and in New York on the *Equitable* case. Eventually, the Justice Department dominated the litigation as the widening war required more coordination, strategy, and resources. New legal suits were filed to recover McGugin's, Mott's, and Anna Barnett's shares of the $1.1 million.[31]

Belatedly discovering that their enemy within the Justice Department was Parmenter, the Burke forces struck back. A member of Burke's legal phalanx urged the Baptists to formally protest Parmenter's pending appointment as assistant attorney general, which they did, to no avail. Parmenter was confirmed.[32]

Tension was running high in Oklahoma in 1926 as the hour of reckoning approached. Momentum was building for charging Burke and other Interior officials with criminal activity in the Barnett affair. Federal obstructionism, cover-ups, and conspiracies were at the root of the Barnett affair, many Oklahomans believed. Their native son Jackson Barnett had been kidnapped and was being held against his will. Demands for a full investigation of federal corruption were loud and shrill. Indictments against McGugin, Burke, Fall, and others were anticipated.

A federal grand jury was impaneled in Muskogee to hear the case against Interior Department officials and others for criminal actions in the Barnett donation. Jackson Barnett was subpoenaed to appear on July 8, 1926. When he failed to appear, Oklahomans concluded that his captor, Anna Barnett, had prevented it. Judge Robert L. Williams ordered that Jackson Barnett be seized and brought before the court. A federal marshal arrived in Los Angeles on August 19, 1926, to serve the writ, accompanied by police officers and men from the U.S. Secret Service.[33]

Anna Barnett had anticipated such a move to separate her from her husband and was vigilant in her watch over him. Anticipating her opposition, the marshal and Secret Service agents took up a vigil across the street from the Barnett home, awaiting their opportunity to abduct Jackson Barnett. When they were finally able to seize Jackson and escort him to the waiting car, Anna Barnett emerged from the house, calling the officers bandits and kidnappers, and threatened to shoot them.[34]

Once in custody, the compliant Jackson behaved in a manner suggesting that he was happy to be liberated from his wife. A man whom Commissioner Burke enlisted to spy on Selby and ascertain his next moves substantiated what others who interviewed Jackson during this time asserted: Jackson was happy to be home in Oklahoma and wanted to live his last days among his friends. "Undoubtedly, the poor old man is very discontented in the fashionable surroundings in which his home is located and the crowded city life of Los Angeles, where he has no one of his own with whom to talk."[35]

Anna stormed the gates of the Muskogee hotel where Jackson was being held in custody and was abrasive in her condemnation of those who kept Jackson from her. Jackson referred to the excited Anna as "she bad woman." Selby reported to Parmenter: "[O]ld Jackson has been combed from the start. . . . [His wife] will abduct him in a holy minute if she gets her hands on him" and would hire agents to do it if necessary.[36] Anna and Justice faulted each other for using strong-arm tactics, yet both used the same techniques of plotting, kidnapping, and coercion to acquire "the body" of Jackson Barnett.

Because she was refused access to Jackson by his guards, Anna contacted the national wire service to get her message out to the press: Jackson had been kidnapped in a gross abuse of power by the Department of Justice. She received some favorable publicity in the press as well as sympathy from Bacone College's students and staff in Muskogee. She presented herself as a long-suffering, harried victim of government persecution, whose simple goal was to get her aged spouse home. When an Indian student from Bacone recognized Jackson on the trolley, the student went after Jackson's guards "hammer and tongs."[37]

Anna Barnett also enlisted the aid of Harold McGugin to recover her husband. The two lobbied President Calvin Coolidge. Anna wrote to the president, denigrating the federal grand jury as a kangaroo court. Its purpose, she said, was to poison public opinion against Commissioner Burke because "I dared spoil their little party of robbing Indian estates." Anna imperiously made demands, gave orders, invoked the sacrosanct values of church and patriotism, and ultimately resorted to threats. She warned Coolidge that she would turn the women's vote against him. "Mr. President, is this Russia, or free America?" McGugin also wrote to Coolidge to protest the interference into the Barnetts' lives and Jackson's "imprisonment" in a hotel. Since McGugin's fees were being contested by Justice, he also demanded the resignation of Parmenter, levying nine charges of fraud against "a defrauder, a prevaricator and a betrayer of public trust."[38]

Burke and his allies within the Interior Department also strenuously objected to the federal grand jury and were busy lobbying Attorney General Sargent to call off the dogs in the Justice Department. Although Selby became more and more convinced that Burke and other Interior Department officials were guilty of criminal offenses, he lacked conclusive proof. Many of his colleagues in Justice remained ambivalent about the legality of Interior's action. The grand jury was cancelled, and Jackson was released to his wife on a $2,500 bond. The Barnetts could not go home, however. Jackson Barnett was ordered to appear to testify in New York in the *Equitable* trial. Again, federal officials planned a cloak-and-dagger operation to recapture Jackson Barnett. This time, at Selby's insistence, a "daylight kidnapping from Muskogee's principal street was executed."[39] For a second time in one year, Jackson was carried into captivity. Anna followed, and again he was released into her custody. The two settled in to await the beginning of the *Equitable* trial.

The publicity over the case and Anna and Burke's lobbying efforts had the desired effect of bringing the case to the attention of President Coolidge, who became concerned about the potential political fallout. Coolidge was advised that discretion and a show of unity between Justice and Interior were advisable. There might be political damage to his administration if the trusts were overturned. Coolidge sent an intermediary to talk to Attorney General Sargent about the case, presumably to get the Justice Department to moderate its prosecution of the Interior officials.[40]

On October 20, 1926, just days before the *Equitable* trial, Sargent issued an opinion extremely favorable to Burke. The discretionary power placed in the hands of Interior, Sargent said, was clear under the law, and the secretary of the Interior's actions could not be questioned "unless there is an abuse or arbitrary exercise of that discretion." Selby was furious when his superiors in Justice forced him to moderate his stance against Interior. He and the guardian's lawyers were scouring the thousands of documents Parmenter had subpoenaed and were assiduously building a case of malfeasance, usurpation of authority, and deliberate fraud by Burke and other Interior officials in the *Equitable* case. Selby saw Sargent's pronouncement as yet another example of Burke's power plays to keep himself above the law. Selby became more determined to expose the conspirators in the Barnett cover-up.[41]

For his part, Burke saw a conspiracy behind the Justice Department's obsession with finding criminal actions. Burke became convinced he was being hounded. Therefore, any attempt to defend himself or the trusts—including surreptitious actions and power plays—were justified, in his view. The Justice Department left him "no other recourse," Burke later testified; he was "forced to counsel with and advise and assist in every legitimate way the defense of the validity of the amended regulation and of the Barnett donation through the attorneys representing these defendants." Because it became politically damaging for Burke to appear to be openly involved in defense of the trusts, he could only act covertly after 1925 to orchestrate the defense and maintain morale. His principles, ego, and reputation were at stake.[42]

Selby's suspicions that a conspiracy existed to defraud Jackson Barnett—and that Burke was its mastermind—were confirmed by Burke's aggressive, secretive, and collusional defense of the trusts. He unquestionably exercised a great deal of power, and he continued to orchestrate the defense of the trusts. Selby was right in some respects about Burke. He was the mastermind, often covertly pulling the strings. But Burke was not concealing criminal conspiracy.

The *Equitable* Trial

The *Equitable* case opened with a strong and lucid statement made by the
guardian's lawyer for invalidating the Equitable trust on the grounds that
Jackson Barnett was doubly incompetent. He was a restricted Indian
under the jurisdiction of the Department of the Interior and he was seriously mentally impaired, a condition that placed him under the jurisdiction of an Oklahoma county court. The plaintiffs held the strong advantage in that they did not have to engage the difficult task of distinguishing
between a competent and an incompetent restricted Indian. The plaintiffs
only had to cast doubt on Barnett's mental competency in a social climate
that was predisposed to see Indians as mentally inferior. The "facts" of
Jackson's life supported this proposition: the plaintiff claimed he was
homeless, never did "anything," and had no education or occupation. Carroll Walter argued for the plaintiffs that the case involved "if not fraud a
gross abuse of discretion which the court can review."[43]

The plaintiffs' easily comprehensible argument that Jackson was doubly incompetent was effective before John Knox, a federal judge who had
little familiarity with either the historical abuses of the Oklahoma guardianship system or the historical use of Interior's broad discretionary powers, on which the arguments of the defense relied. Having decided the trials of Germans accused of unpatriotic activities and Mann Act violations
during World War I, Knox was sensitive to moral offenses against the weak
and defenseless. When the triple alliance's lawyer, Charles Rogers, rose to
make the reasonable protest that the question of the legitimacy of the trust
must follow an adjudication of the rule of law regarding the foundations
and limitations of Interior's discretionary power, Judge Knox snapped that
he would hear the testimony, then decide the law. Acknowledging his severe limitations regarding the "rule of law" as it applied to restricted Indians, Knox chose to decide the merits of the case on the question of Jackson
Barnett's mental competency, which he felt qualified and empowered to
judge.[44]

The Baptists' lawyer, Charles Fettretch, with the strong support of
Commissioner Burke and his crack legal team, made a multifaceted defense of the Equitable trust. In their brief, they attacked the two main
premises on which the opposition built their case. Fettretch and Rogers
denied Jackson was a mental incompetent, declaring that he was "above
average" in intelligence and understood what he was doing when he chose
to marry Anna Laura Lowe. They also argued that lurid reports about
Anna's character were distorted. The various allegations against Anna derived from the Bowie Report should be stricken, they argued, because they
were "scandalous, impertinent, uncertain, indefinite, vague, and insufficient . . . immaterial and irrelevant."[45]

Additional arguments included the point of law on which Burke believed the case rested. Authority vested in the Oklahoma courts had not been violated because the federal government was the paramount guardian. No laws or procedures had been violated. The transfer of gifts was within the secretary of the Interior's jurisdiction under acts of Congress and "were merely the exercise by him of an official discretion." In the absence of fraud, such actions were not subject to the jurisdiction of any court to review, vacate, or set aside. Another argument was that the guardianship was invalid. The 1912 court proceedings revealed faulty procedure and the 1912 judgment rendered Jackson Barnett competent. Moreover, the case that had been brought by the guardian was not in Jackson's "best interests" and should be dismissed.[46]

Rogers delivered a poorly organized, rambling opening statement, which did not identify or focus upon the critical issues. The complexity of the case overwhelmed him, as did his divided loyalties to Burke, Anna Barnett, and the Baptists. He highlighted seemingly disconnected incidents and details that only confused. Burke later said that Rogers became sidetracked in "insignificant details," some serving to underscore, rather than dispel, suspicions of Interior wrongdoing. Rogers repeatedly insisted that competence was not the central issue and asked the court not to rule on that subject.[47]

Fettretch realized that Jackson's competency would be the pivotal issue in the *Equitable* case and produced a brief that presented a systematic and thorough defense of Jackson's competency. Fettretch pointed out that those who claimed Jackson was incompetent barely knew him and exaggerated his limitations. Those who knew Jackson personally, as Dana Kelsey did, testified he was "about like the ordinary uneducated full-blood Indian." Fettretch quoted various case studies and precedents to argue that a person of subintelligence can make a valid bargain and can comprehend the nature of a will.[48]

Neither side called Jackson Barnett to the stand despite his being under a writ to attend the New York trial. The guardian's camp feared Jackson would appear more intelligent than their case was making him out to be, while the defense team feared he would appear less intelligent than it claimed. Toward the end of the trial, Judge Knox called Jackson to testify. Jackson's answers regarding his activities and preferences were brief and direct. He had no clear understanding of the court proceedings nor why he had been summoned there. When asked about his charitable contributions, he averred that his money would benefit the school when he died, but he added quickly, "I ain't dead yet." For now, "I am going to keep it and eat off it." After his testimony, Jackson warmly shook the hand of Judge Knox. Anna tenderly helped Jackson on with his coat, and he grinned. The trial testimony in *Equitable* had concluded.[49]

The major weakness in the defense of the Equitable trust was that the attorneys, Fettretch and Rogers, could not agree on the fundamental issues in the case. To Fettretch, there were many facts unfavorable to the defendant's interests, such as Anna Barnett's moral character, the payoffs, and Jackson Barnett's vague understanding of the contract. As their loyalties were primarily to Commissioner Burke, Mott and Rogers disagreed, saying these facts were irrelevant, and the single question involved was the right of the courts to review Interior's judgment absent any charge of fraud. No matter how much he was urged to dismiss these "unsettling" details as trivial and unimportant, Fettretch remained unconvinced. Lamenting the serious handicap of an ineffectual legal team, Burke placed the blame on the Baptist counsel, Fettretch. Burke repeatedly urged the Baptists to hire Charles Evans Hughes as counsel. A Baptist and a man of enormous public stature, Hughes was formerly the Progressive governor of New York, a presidential candidate, and secretary of State in the Harding administration. Burke hoped a person of such prestige would add moral weight to the Baptist cause in *Equitable*.[50]

The coordinated effort to defend the Equitable trust was hampered further by distrust, doubts, and resentments within the Baptist organization. The Baptists had willingly entered the triple alliance with the Barnetts and the bureau because the organization felt loyalty and gratitude to the bureau for its generous assistance in helping them obtain rich Indians' "surplus" funds to build Bacone into a leading institution of learning. They were also overawed by the bureau's assurance of ultimate success in the *Equitable* suit. The Baptists had dared not risk incurring Burke's displeasure by refusing to hire Charles Rogers as their attorney as Burke and Mott had insisted. To reject Rogers, President Weeks said, is to "lose a hundred thousand" from other sources.[51]

When the Justice Department intervened in the case and greater expenditures of money were required with less certainty of success, the Baptists grew increasingly resentful. In June 1925, the AHMS treasurer informed Burke that it could not afford to incur further expenses to defend the Barnett donation to Bacone. After they learned that Rogers was also working for Anna Barnett, the Baptists suspected Rogers was exaggerating expenses and prolonging litigation only to get every cent he "can get out of it." Rogers continually made demands for more money, because of the "unusual and extraordinary display of official vindictiveness by the Department of Justice officials." To strengthen the resolve of the AHMS in the long and expensive litigation ahead, Rogers told them that not only was Jackson Barnett's trust fund jeopardized but so were all of the donations the Baptists had obtained from Indians. Rogers had the audacity to ask the Baptists to pay for Anna Barnett's travel expenses to New York as she was a very important witness. Fettretch was also called upon to support Anna in her Riggs Bank trust defense and to authorize Rogers to represent the Baptists in that litigation. Fettretch flatly refused both requests.[52] The AHMS increasingly suspected it was being used to fight other people's battles.

Anna and Jackson Barnett in 1926, at the peak of the couple's affluence, perhaps on a trip to Washington, D.C., to confer with Burke during the New York Equitable *trial. Courtesy of the National Archives, Pacific Region, Laguna Niguel.*

The moral righteousness of the Baptist organization added respectability to Anna Barnett, but the Baptists felt dragged down by their association with her. Newspapers questioned the Christian organization's affiliation with Anna, a woman of ill repute. From the pulpit of the First Baptist Church in Henryetta, built with Jackson Barnett's money, the Reverend Cornelius Bowls delivered a scathing sermon entirely devoted to Jackson

Anna Barnett, Jackson Barnett, and Commissioner Charles Burke, 1926. An Underwood and Underwood Photo. Courtesy of Los Angeles Herald Examiner Collection, Los Angeles Public Library.

Barnett in which he referred to Anna as "devilish" and a "woman of the underworld." The Baptists' resentment of their alliance with morally corrupt persons intensified over time.[53]

As the Baptists' commitment noticeably faltered, Burke and Mott repeatedly found cause to criticize Fettretch's lack of aggression and incisiveness in the case. Fettretch bluntly told Mott that his sideline coaching was not appreciated. The Baptists blamed Rogers for the weaknesses in the defense and resented Mott's interference. Squabbles over money and strategy, personality conflicts, moral misgivings, and blaming fractured the triple alliance.[54]

Oklahoma Supreme Court

Four days after the testimony in *Equitable* ended and Knox went into chambers to contemplate his decision, the Oklahoma Supreme Court nullified the Oklahoma guardianship. This quick reversal of Judge Hepburn's upholding of the guardianship was a grand victory for the Burke camp. In part, the invalidation of the guardianship was based on the technical grounds that the 1912 district court ruling that Jackson was competent was never formally rescinded.[55] Secondly, the court's argument was that the litigation initiated by the guardian to block the trusts was not in Jackson's interests. Wisely, the Oklahoma court sidestepped the question of mental competency, making the pragmatic argument that Jackson Barnett

> is in a more or less enfeebled mental state, if not actually mentally incompetent. . . . What may be the actual state of his bodily health or mental powers at present is beyond the scope of the instant inquiry. . . . He has left but few remaining years of his already prolonged and too much troubled life.

Remanding this case to the district court would engage Jackson in litigation outlasting his lifetime and would dissipate Jackson's estate, the court concluded. The duty of guardian E. S. Bailey was to serve the ward, and he could not initiate litigation with "adverse or selfish purpose or interests." Therefore, the court reversed the district court ruling and voided Bailey's guardianship.[56]

This ruling meant that Bailey had no jurisdiction to bring suit against the trusts or McGugin, Mott, and Anna Barnett to recover the $1.1 million. One Oklahoma Supreme Court justice told a reporter that the decision would automatically strike down the other suits. An ecstatic Charles Burke fully anticipated that lawyers would seek dismissals of cases pending in the federal courts in Washington, D.C., New York, Kansas, and Oklahoma. Most observers believed that the Oklahoma Supreme Court decision had brought the contest to a close. In its 1927 annual report, for example, the Indian Rights Association (IRA) stated that the decision

> is to the effect that supreme authority is vested in the Secretary of the Interior by Congress to act as guardian for the Government's Indian wards and that local courts of the State of Oklahoma are without jurisdiction over them. The decision is expected to have a far-reaching effect on litigation now pending in the Federal Courts over Jackson Barnett's property.

Anna Barnett was quoted in the IRA report saying that the decision was a landmark in the long-awaited destruction of the vicious guardianship system in Oklahoma. Jackson's philanthropic intentions were highlighted. Those who knew him best said he was "unusually good natured. He won't fight over his money."[57]

Parmenter's faction in the Justice Department reeled from this decision. It immediately issued denials that the Oklahoma decision had any bearing on the *Equitable* case in New York despite Bailey's apparent lack of authority as a plaintiff. The case would continue because the United States had intervened and because Interior was in conflict with *its* paternalistic duty to Jackson Barnett and was without authority of law when it had authorized the gift donation.[58] In euphoria, Burke expressed the wish that the *Equitable* case would continue in order to deliver the *coup de grace* to the Oklahoma probate court. He was confident that Judge Knox would uphold the trust and thereby vindicate the lawful and noble actions of Interior, for they had benefited Jackson Barnett and conserved his estate for philanthropic purposes. The principle that supreme authority was vested in the Interior Department as guardian, Burke predicted, would be upheld. Calling Selby and his other enemies in Justice "incompetent," he further charged them with "deliberately aiding the Oklahoma syndicate that has promoted the litigation for the sole purpose only of keeping the funds of Jackson Barnett intact until his death in order that they might be divided among the members of the syndicate to a large extent."[59]

Quieting Title to the Oil Lease

To Burke's dismay, the Oklahoma Supreme Court's decision was not the final word. The decision invalidating Bailey's guardianship opened another can of worms. Anna had Jackson declared incompetent by a Los Angeles court, but his guardian there had narrowly defined responsibility. Since Bailey's guardianship had been invalidated, this meant that Jackson had no guardian to protect his interests in his property in Oklahoma, including the valuable oil property in Creek County. Several persons eagerly stepped forward to act as Jackson's legal representative. The Interior Department unsuccessfully tried to block these guardian appointments in Muskogee and Creek counties, arguing that it added unnecessary expense.[60]

Ominously, the guardian approved by the Creek County court in early 1927, Fred T. Hildt, immediately initiated more wasting litigation. The Oklahoma Supreme Court decision ruled that Carl O'Hornett, who had signed the original 1912 Bartlett lease, was not the legal guardian, thereby invalidating the original lease and the rights of current subcontractors. Hildt, representing Jackson Barnett, sued the sublessees, including Gypsy Oil, in federal court for $15 million.[61] This action threatened to wreak havoc with those with vested interests in the lucrative Cushing oil field. Anna Barnett, the Gypsy Oil Company, and the Interior Department rose to defend the original Bartlett lease. In response to the threat to its property rights, Gypsy Oil brought an action to resolve the ownership of the lease. Since unsettled title would throw the subcontractors into chaos, Burke urged the Justice Department to defend the original lease, upholding Interior's exclusive jurisdiction over such matters.[62]

In the *Gypsy* case, the validity of the original lease rested on the issue of Jackson Barnett's competency. Only if Jackson were competent to sign a contract on his own would the 1912 lease stand and the interests of Gypsy Oil and other subcontractors be upheld. To protect its interests, Gypsy Oil sought experts to examine Barnett and attest to his competency. One of these was Dr. Smith Ely Jelliffe, a professor at Fordham University who had specialized in nervous and mental disease for forty years, was a consultant and neurologist at Manhattan State Hospital, and was a well-published expert on mental disease, including a two-volume work on the treatment of mental disorders.

At Anna Barnett's expense, Jelliffe did a four-hour mental examination of Jackson Barnett in May 1927 and administered several state-of-the-art intelligence tests. Jelliffe concluded that, "according to his cultural level, that is a full-blood Indian, without having been to school, without having learned to read and write, I would say he was a man of excellent intelligence, and one that was mentally healthy in every respect."[63]

After Jelliffe's examination, Burke and Rogers wanted this new, authoritative evidence introduced in the *Equitable* trust case, but Fettretch was uncooperative. The Baptists' lawyer, Fettretch had already concluded that the case rested on whether Barnett had sufficient capacity to understand the value of his estate and the terms, conditions, and provisions for the donation and trust agreement. Pessimistically, Fettretch felt the Equitable trust would be invalidated, and if he were right, every other gift donation to Bacone by wealthy Indians could be challenged. Already, the Interior Department was refusing to approve any more donations to the Baptists from wealthy Indians, pending the outcome of the Barnett litigation.[64]

Cases multiplied because of the imbroglio over Jackson Barnett's competency. The Oklahoma Supreme Court decision proved anticlimactic and inconclusive. The record contained reams of testimony that supported opposing positions, most of it tainted by the self-interests or cultural biases of the witnesses. Was there anyone free of personal motives or cultural bias who could objectively judge Jackson's competency? Who was qualified and who was empowered to make the determination? Whose opinion would be definitive and final? Would the litigation ever come to an end?

Burke believed that the testimony of Dr. Jelliffe would be persuasive when joined with the broad discretionary authority granted by Congress to Interior over determinations of Indian competency. With the Burke Act of 1906, Congress had conferred ultimate authority on Interior to determine when Indians were ready to assume rights as citizens. Litigation would swamp the courts if the judicial branch had the power to review whether an individual Indian had been freed prematurely from federal guardianship. Burke found encouragement for his interpretation that Interior had ultimate and unreviewable power to judge competency in Oklahoma Supreme Court judge V. Branson's opinion of July 1926. Branson validated Interior's discretionary authority in making the gift, but more important, he declared Interior to be the final arbiter of Jackson's competence to make donations to his wife and to charity.[65]

When Fettretch remained unconvinced and refused to file a motion to reopen the case to admit Jelliffe's testimony, Rogers and Burke plotted to go over his head to get the consent of the Baptist leadership. In their closing statements to Judge Knox, Rogers and Fettretch worked at cross-purposes, each blaming the other for the weaknesses in the defense. If the trust were ruled invalid, the money could potentially be recovered by Anna Barnett, suggesting to the Baptists that Rogers, who was also Anna's counsel, had sabotaged the case. Burke became resigned to losing the *Equitable* case, blaming the Baptists.[66]

On August 10, 1927, Judge John C. Knox delivered his opinion, striking down the trust. Judge Knox said that from the time oil was found on his allotment and Jackson Barnett became wealthy

> until the present he has been the shuttledore in a game of battlecock, in which the stakes were high. Solicited and importuned for donations, to which he readily affixed his thumbprint for most anyone who asked it; kidnapped and married by an adventuress and annoyed by her attorneys and their allies, who enlisted the support of officials of the Government—and who were probably convinced of the justification of their subsequent action—he was finally induced to assent to part with Liberty bonds in the vast sum of $1,100,000. . . . [Admitting that the trust agreements provided a lifetime income] and that the object of the trust created for Bacone University is a worthy one, and that Mrs. Barnett, so far as is known, has been a good wife to the Indian, the provisions for his support . . . will not suffice to lend countenance to the ravishment of property rights that here occurred nor warrant officials of the Government in substituting their judgment for that which Barnett was unable to exercise.

Knox understood the Department of the Interior's rationale in creating a trust but said that this did not justify Interior's redistribution of his property. To Knox, there was no serious doubt about Jackson Barnett's mental competence. "While he is not insane and is not an idiot, his intelligence is so stunted and undeveloped that he lacked the capacity to know what he was doing." He had no ability to make a contract, thus the "gift" he had made to the American Home Missionary Society for educational efforts among the Creek was invalid.[67]

The *New York Tribune* was so taken with Judge Knox's rendition of the Jackson Barnett melodrama of kidnapping, sexual promiscuity, bribery, and victimization that it published the Knox opinion as a serial.[68]

Arrogant and headstrong, Burke refused to surrender and began rallying the troops for his appeal. He insisted that Knox had no knowledge of Indians' general incompetence and mistook Barnett's cultural difference for mental disability. B. D. Weeks, Bacone's president, concurred with Burke that Knox erred because he had "no understanding, whatever, of Indians."[69] Nothing less than a U.S. Supreme Court ruling would satisfy Burke. He enlisted the aid of Malcolm McDowell, secretary of the Board of Indian Commissioners, to bolster the Baptists' morale with the assurance that they would win. Burke outlined the appeal argument. Knox had not addressed the "rule of law." Instead, Knox had "merely expressed his opinion regarding the competency of Jackson Barnett." Knox's ignorance of Indian culture and government policy regarding restricted Indians had led him to erroneous conclusions, Burke believed. Jackson was an average restricted Indian because he had an average Indian's cultural and educational disadvantages and needed federal guardianship. Jackson Barnett was a mentally competent restricted Indian, not a mentally incompetent restricted Indian, Burke argued.[70]

The Baptists' confidence in Burke had been shaken by the Knox decision, and the leadership equivocated about pursuing the appeal. They wanted the endowment for Bacone but harbored doubts the appeal would succeed. They were tired of being used to vindicate Burke's policies and of being tainted by their association with immoral persons. Weeks, after talking to Burke's agents, urged the Baptist leadership to go forward with the appeal, predicting airily, "[W]e will never lose the money."[71] Commenting on Weeks's passionate urgings, one of the Baptists' chief legal consultants, George Allin, wrote bitterly, "He simply brings to us the great desire of the Department of the Interior and the Indian Bureau that we continue to pull their chestnuts out of the fire and take an appeal in the Barnett case."[72]

Burke's anxiety intensified as two precious months elapsed, and the Baptists remained uncommitted to appealing Judge Knox's decision. Burke arranged a conference between the AHMS leadership and ranking Interior Department officials. If the Knox decision were not appealed, Burke warned, graft could overtake the estates of other Indians who had given donations. From the beginning, Burke said, he considered it "a crowning achievement of his administration" to have money flowing to Indians by the "accident of oil put to some good use" by placing it in the "right hands"— churches and philanthropic societies—rather than having it "stolen by the unscrupulous." He also told the Baptists that if they did not challenge the decision, the Department of the Interior would have no choice but to play it safe legally and reject all gifts by rich Indians to Baptist institutions. The Baptists questioned why they had to carry the burden of this fight, instead of letting the *Riggs* case decide the issue. Playing a final card, Burke assured the society that he could put it into contact with eastern people with money to finance the appeal, including John D. Rockefeller, who was enlisted to pay the anticipated $28,000 in expenses.[73]

Rather than having their concerns assuaged, the Baptists were more circumspect after this interview. As a policy, they decided to distance themselves henceforth from the federal government, Anna Barnett, and the unscrupulous lawyers who had been foisted upon them. Rogers's contract was terminated. "It is from every viewpoint most unfortunate that our society must carry the burden of disproving all these noisesome [*sic*] allegations," a Baptist lawyer wrote.[74]

The Baptists referred the matter to fellow Baptist and eminent jurist Charles Evans Hughes for final arbitration. For Hughes, the central point was whether Jackson Barnett wanted to make the gift or whether well-meaning persons concocted the plan. Hughes saw no hope of sustaining the legal action and declined to take on the appeal, a great blow to Burke, who had hoped Hughes would take the case to the Supreme Court. Burke eventually muscled the Baptists into appealing the case, but they did so halfheartedly.[75] Because the Baptists determined to act independently of Anna Barnett and Charles Rogers, the Equitable trust and the AHMS failed to perfect an appeal. In 1928, the U.S. Supreme Court upheld the Knox decision. The grand question of law—whether the courts had jurisdiction to modify or abrogate a decision of the secretary of the Interior—was not addressed by the Supreme Court as Burke had fervently wished; the Court rejected the appeal on procedural grounds, a crushing disappointment to Burke. (See appendix III.)

The final matter to be determined was the awarding of legal fees. The guardian's lawyers, who had worked five years on the Barnett suits, exulted in their 40 percent share of the amount recovered; the $550,000 trust account had grown to $657,843.27 between February 1, 1923, and November 2, 1927. Hypocritically, the Justice Department opposed this large fee to its former comrades. Feeling betrayed, the private lawyers fought the case to the U.S. Supreme Court. In 1931, Supreme Court justice Willis Van Devanter reduced the fees to $50,000, saying that the Justice Department had done much of the legal work in the *Equitable* case and the "facts were few and easily demonstrable."[76]

The McGugin and Mott Recovery Suits

Though its appeal of the Knox decision was floundering in mid-1928, the Burke camp's confidence was restored by federal district court decisions, which affirmed the principles of law that Burke believed were binding in the Barnett donations. In Kansas district court on July 5, 1928, federal judge John C. Pollock dismissed the Justice Department's suit in *United States v. McGugin*, which sought to recover the fees his legal firm had collected as Anna Barnett's representative. Pollock criticized the lengthy, prolix, tedious brief of the Department of Justice, which, Pollock said, violated every rule of pleading known to federal practice. The suit was premised on a theory of the existence of a conspiracy by Anna. "[T]he fact is," wrote Pollock, "she had the right to go out and get him if she could . . . [and they are] lawfully married. Nothing can be done about that in this litigation, in this court." Because Interior approved of the transfer, it was not the government's business how and what she paid McGugin, unless there were allegations of fraud, collusion, imposition, or deception in the plaintiff's bill, which there wasn't. Pollock cited U.S. Supreme Court precedents *Lone Wolf v. Hitchcock* and *United States v. Kagama* and the amended regulation of October 7, 1922 (as confirmed by the attorney general's opinion of October 20, 1926) to affirm Burke's legal exercise of authority.[77]

This strong vindication of Interior's authority was reinforced shortly afterward in the Oklahoma federal district court. Judge Franklin Kennamer dismissed the Justice Department's case against Marshall Mott, which had also aimed to recover legal fees he had collected from Anna Barnett. The judge announced he would follow Pollock's precedent unless Justice clearly charged that Burke and Fall's action to transfer the funds to Anna Barnett was willfully corrupt and fraudulent. In May 1929, Judge Pollock dismissed an amended petition by the Justice Department in *United States v. Mott.* The issue came down to the Department of the Interior's exercise of power over its Indian wards, which it has always exercised, said Pollock.[78]

The course of the Barnett litigation in the 1920s was a wild roller coaster ride with exhilarating triumphs and crushing disappointments. In mid-1928, the Burke camp's hopes were rising. With the two favorable federal court rulings of 1928 and the Oklahoma Supreme Court's ruling of 1926 as victories, the score was three to one in favor of the Burke camp in 1928. At the very least, the Pollock and Kennamer rulings were a counterweight to the Knox decision. At best, Burke's camp could hope that these decisions would scuttle the Justice Department's suit against Anna Barnett in Los Angeles and sway the *Equitable* appeal (still pending in 1928) to the U.S. Supreme Court in its favor. Burke, moreover, took considerable satisfaction in Justice's decision to join in the defense of the Gypsy Oil contract. Ironically, Justice was intervening to defend Interior's guardianship decisions for a restricted Indian against opportunistic persons, who had claimed to represent the interests of a government ward, bringing costly and unnecessary litigation to enrich themselves. In Burke's eyes, Justice hypocritically had aided such opportunists in the *Equitable* case, lining the pockets of Bailey's lawyers and depriving Bacone College of its endowment.[79]

The Parmenter camp was thrown into utter turmoil by the Pollock and Kennamer rulings in *McGugin* and *Mott* in 1928. Desperate attempts were made to sabotage the *Equitable* appeal by shattering the triple alliance. Bacone president Weeks was assured that if the Baptists severed their case from Anna Barnett, they would "easily win the case before the Supreme Court." Most frustrating for Parmenter and Selby was that their strategy for prosecuting the remaining recovery cases was dashed. If they did not make charges of criminal misconduct, there was no case to recover the money from McGugin, Mott, or Anna Barnett. Attorney General Sargent had barred them from making such allegations against Interior officials in October 1926.[80]

In early 1928, the embattled foes in the Barnett litigation were bruised and weary, and victory was far from certain. For four contentious years, the legal battle had consumed the time and energy of scores of public servants within the Department of the Interior and the Department of Justice—secretaries, clerks, lawyers, officials, and agency superintendents—as well as the staffs of dozens of private law firms. Over the course of the engagement, there were secret strategies, covert alliances, abrupt reversals, ambiguous developments, counterattacks, omens, and auspicious turns. With satisfactory resolution of the matter in the courts proving elusive, Congress decided it must act to address the issues raised in the Jackson Barnett litigation.

8

Who Will Guard the Guardians?
Indian Policy on Trial
1924–1928

In passing I will say for the information of this committee and anybody else that is interested, that in my opinion an incompetent Indian is incompetent and there is no such thing as a competent, incompetent Indian.

—COMMISSIONER OF INDIAN AFFAIRS CHARLES BURKE

The American public had long held a schizophrenic view of Indians—as both protocitizens and inferior human beings. The construction of Jackson Barnett made by the Parmenter camp—all those with a political or pecuniary interest in challenging the $1.1 million donation—played upon both images simultaneously without perhaps consciously being aware of the contradiction. As a stupid, irredeemable Indian buffoon, but also a protocitizen and property owner, Jackson's rights had been egregiously violated. The Indian bureau had continuously labored to create practical Indian policies for protecting and managing Indian persons and property by bringing the two views into one image with mixed success: the Indian wards under its care were protocitizens but their property was restricted. With full authority vested in them by the U.S. Supreme Court and Congress, the bureau managed Indian lands and resources—selling or leasing as the national will demanded. The Indian owners neither actively participated in or controlled the proceeds of these transactions. That these long-standing practices appeared autocratic to outsiders did not deprive them of their full validity under the rule of law.[1]

As the Barnett litigation worked its way through the courts with Interior and Justice taking opposing sides, the Barnett scandal seriously damaged Commissioner Charles Burke's credibility and raised doubts about bureau policies. The persistent allegations of wrongdoing and the titillating details of the Bowie Report scandalized, intrigued, and confused members of Congress. Seemingly caught red-handed in the act of parting a wealthy Indian from his property, Burke audaciously denied that the courts had any power to review his decisions. The more Burke repeated that what he was doing fit legal and procedural standards for incompetent Indians—the more he relied upon the "exclusive" and "unreviewable" nature of the commissioner's decisions—the more disturbed Congress and the general public became. Something must be seriously wrong with Indian policy if such an enormous sum of money of an incompetent Indian could be transferred to the hands of an immoral woman and a private institution.[2]

The Barnett case drew the attention of Congress and Indian rights activists and became the lightning rod for a national reform movement. For Progressive congressmen like Robert La Follette of Wisconsin and a behind-the-scenes agitator, John Collier, the Barnett scandal was a useful instrument to trumpet calls for reform. The Barnett case came into the national spotlight in the mid-1920s as a notorious case of bureau mismanagement, the symptom and symbol of a diseased Indian policy. The Barnett case delivered a crippling blow to Burke and became the catalyst for Congress's reexamination of the fundamental premises of the Indian administration. During the crucial years from 1925 to 1928, when the outcome of the Barnett litigation was far from certain, Congress increasingly felt compelled to act to provide legislative remedies should the courts confirm Burke's position. The bureau's mishandling of Barnett's estate became the reformers' flagship issue in their drive for a full congressional investigation surveying the condition of Indians in the United States. Such an investigation was necessary in order to identify the ills and abuses suffered by Indians and to assess their needs preparatory to a new legislative program. Aiding New Deal architect John Collier as he formulated his ideas and ascended to power, the Barnett case was certainly a driving force behind the reformulation of policy that led to the Indian New Deal of the 1930s in which the ill-conceived allotment policy was ended, bureau power was checked, and Indian sovereign rights were in some measure restored.

The Jackson Barnett case brought focus, mass, and unity to the Burke administration's critics. The Barnett scandal brought four groups into a coordinated political movement: Oklahomans, Progressives, Indian political activists, and non-Indian reformers, like Collier, from the proliferating Indian rights organizations. Each of these groups arose independently, but they all shared the desire to dislodge Burke from power. Leading the assault on Burke's credibility in Congress were the Oklahomans. In early 1924, Oklahoma congressman E. B. Howard alleged before Congress that the Bureau of Indian Affairs had mismanaged more Indians' estates and lost more money in the previous three years than all the guardianships combined. Howard called for a full investigation whose goal was "the pro-

tection of the Indians from the Bureau of Indian Affairs."[3] Following up
on Howard's charges were the dissenting views of Congressman W. W.
Hastings in the Snyder report and the heavily damaging charges of Judge
Hugh Murphy later that year. Yet, various investigations and executive
branch pronouncements exonerated Burke of any misdoing in his handling of the Barnett estate. These were condemned as whitewashes by
Oklahomans and a few other skeptical members of Congress. Oklahoma
Republican senator John Harreld gained the powerful position as chair of
the Committee Affairs in 1926, and he joined Congressman Hastings to
introduce legislation authorizing the Justice Department to pursue its litigation in the Barnett cases.[4]

Progressives like Senator La Follette and Congressman James Frear,
also of Wisconsin, and Senator Burton Wheeler of Montana represented
the second group of Indian policy critics, whose principal concern was the
constitutional liberties of Indians. Seeking to free the Indian from federal
control, they pushed the Indian Citizenship Act through Congress in 1924.
This conferred U.S. citizenship on all Indian wards nationwide, even if
they lived on reservations with communally held property or if their individual allotments were restricted. This group was appalled by the undemocratic aspects of bureau practices and its inefficiency and dishonesty about
its failings. In 1919, the Inter-Church World Movement had published a
report exposing conditions of poverty and disease on reservations. The
Red Cross did a follow-up study, but Burke refused to release the results.
Like the states' rights advocates in Oklahoma, many progressives believed
that the Indian "problem" would be improved if health and education services were transferred to the states.[5]

The third group of critics—and the most vociferous—were the ones
suffering under the bureau's yoke: the Indians. Nonnegotiable demands
that the bureau be abolished had begun in the 1910s by the Society of
American Indians under the leadership of Carlos Montezuma, a Yavapai.
Heavily influenced by Montezuma's critique of the crippling impact of the
bureau's paternalistic policies, southern California's Indians formed an organization called the Mission Indian Federation that was engaged in a regional ground war against the bureau throughout the 1920s. Oklahoma
Indians mobilized in the mid-1920s to protest bureau misadministration
of their property, racial prejudice, and discriminatory hiring practices in
the wake of the publication of *Poor Rich Indians*. The National Council
of American Indians, established in 1926 under the leadership of Gertrude
Bonnin and her husband, Raymond, was another Indian organization
fighting for Indian rights and protection of Indian properties. In contrast
to the progressives and Oklahomans, Indian activists and the white-domi-
nated Indian rights organizations had greater concern about protecting Indian resources.[6]

Indian rights organizations with non-Indian memberships comprised
a fourth group. Older organizations of this kind, such as the Board of In-

dian Commissioners and the Indian Rights Association, had a Christian humanitarian perspective, and they tended to support the bureau's actions. But dozens of newer organizations had come into being in the 1920s. Many of the newer reformers embraced concepts of cultural relativism, and they pursued a fresh approach to the varied, complex, and serious problems within the nation's many reservation communities that stemmed from fifty years of erosion of Indians' land base, racist policies, and the bureau's paradoxical role of protecting and liberating Indian resources. They publicized conditions of poverty and disease and lobbied against bills that would further reduce Indian resources or violate Indian civil rights. Collier, secretary of the Northern California American Indian Defense Association (and its national counterpart, the AIDA) formed an alliance with Stella Atwood, head of the Indian division of the National Federation of Women's Clubs. In the early 1920s, the two had become convinced of the bankruptcy of Indian policy during their fight to defeat the Bursum bill, which would have divested the Pueblo peoples of the Southwest of their crucial resources. Thereafter, Indian affairs became Collier's life work.

Collier became the intellectual leader for the national Indian reform movement, focusing and coordinating the energies of these various groups. He wrote scathing articles denouncing the bureau in national magazines and newspapers and became one of Washington's major lobbyists. With Stella Atwood's help, he agitated against bills unfavorable to Indian interests and shaped and supported the progressives' Indian bills targeting the Burke administration. The American Indian Defense Association demanded major and radical reforms, including a return to tribal corporate land holding, self-government, religious freedom, and the reorganization of education, health, and irrigation services. What Collier found most intolerable was that the Interior Department had so much discretionary power over managing Indian persons and property. Decision making was removed from Indian people as well as from Congress.[7]

The Jackson Barnett affair appeared to be no more than a footnote in Collier's busy lobbying career and Congress's slate of Indian bills in the 1920s, but it assumed a place of centrality as a propaganda device to mobilize opposition to Burke. Collier did not fail to note the cause of the changing mood in Congress regarding Burke and the bureau during the 1925 watershed year in the Barnett litigation. Burke's judgment was openly questioned. The attorney general and the Snyder committee recommended court review, the Department of Justice shifted its weight against Interior, and Burke's bill to ratify his decision in the Barnett case was scuttled by a suspicious Congress. Collier began grooming Congressman Frear to be Burke's chief critic in Congress. Frear, who emerged abruptly in this role, persistently referred to the Barnett scandal as his banner issue. At Collier's instigation, no doubt, Atwood made a visit to Frear's office and persuaded him to become the spokesperson for the work to reform—in Frear's words—the "responsible arrogant Bureaucracy." In early February

1926, Collier invited Frear to meet with the Bonnins and other reform-minded persons to discuss a plan "now in the minds of all of us," by which he meant a strategy to dislodge Burke by inaugurating a muckraking congressional investigation into all of the bureau's misdeeds. A willing vessel for Collier's ideas and agendas, Frear nonetheless wanted to understand the reasons that certain bills were to be supported or opposed. Collier offered lengthy explanations, referring to Indians' current status as "chattel . . . inside a virtual slavery" under bureau paternalism.[8]

Frear, by calling for an investigation into the Indian bureau on the floor of Congress on March 4, 1926, declared war against Burke. Already engaged in war with the Justice Department, this assault was another political blow to Burke. Condemning the bureau's "75 years of Spanish inquisition guardianship," Frear alleged that the bureau with its "notorious scandals, robbery of its wards, and systematic oppressions has outlived any usefulness it was supposed to have when it was first organized." Only recently appointed to the House committee on Indian Affairs, Frear was overawed by the enormous amount of power the bureau wielded over restricted Indian property—$1.6 billion in land and resources and $90 million in money. There were disturbing indications that the property of roughly 225,000 restricted Indians was declining and the condition of the Indians steadily deteriorating. A current bill before Congress authorizing funding for the Indian Court of Offenses particularly baffled him. Why were restricted Indians, though citizens, denied due process of law and instead ruled autocratically by the Indian bureau's institutions and rules?[9] Collier had several thousand copies of the "illuminating" speech printed and mailed, many to Stella Atwood for distribution within her network of women's clubs.[10]

Burke appeared before the House Subcommittee on Indian Affairs to answer Frear's "misinformed," "misleading," and "untrue" charges in April 1926. He condescendingly forgave Frear for his ignorance, saying he had been naively misled by misinformation supplied by Collier, the American Indian Defense Association's chief propagandist and Washington lobbyist. He proceeded to lecture Frear about Indian law, procedures, Supreme Court decisions, and history. He claimed that history had shown that Indians lost up to 90 percent of their fee patent property when restrictions were lifted.[11]

If Collier were a usurper, Burke was old guard. A capable, knowledgeable administrator, he could not see beyond the institutional bureaucratic culture he had done so much to create during fourteen years as a congressional representative, a member of the House committee for Indian Affairs (for a time as its chairman), and several years as commissioner of Indian affairs. He had set as his goal the destruction of the corrupt Oklahoma guardianship system, and he would not be deterred from his objective, especially by congressmen with a very superficial understanding of Indian policy. These congressmen, in his view, seldom saw behind the veil: the Byzantine jungle of federal laws, Interior Department regulations,

Supreme Court rulings, precedents, principles, procedures, power structures, and the customary ways of thinking about Indians that made up the bureaucratic culture of the Indian bureau.[12]

Burke's inflexibility was his downfall. He had little but contempt for those, whether Indian or non-Indian, who criticized his policies or the high-handed way he enforced them. The ignorant rabble, represented by Congressman Frear and Stella Atwood, were not unlike the childlike, misbehaving Indians over whose lives he presided with broad discretionary power. As its head, the Bureau of Indian Affairs was an extension of himself. Collier thought a BIA radio release describing the commissioner as the father of the largest family in the world quite ludicrous, but the description is not entirely faulty. Burke saw himself as a benign patriarch. The louder his critics became in the 1920s, the more stubbornly he defended himself, refusing to admit any flaw or failing and dismissing all criticism as politically motivated. For example, he responded to Stella Atwood's criticisms of specific bills by charging her with malfeasance and dishonesty. He alleged that her misguided views resulted from her affiliation with the AIDA, a "dangerous" organization. Patronizing, adversarial, and autocratic, Burke failed to recognize the shift in public opinion. As Jackson Barnett's first biographer, Benay Blend, wrote, Burke "staunchly defended the government's Indian policy even when no longer politically feasible."[13]

Frear's attack on Burke was timely. Congress was considering a number of hotly contested Indian bills, among them the Hayden-Bratton oil bill, which Collier described as a "surrender of Congress to invisible bureaucratic and special interests."[14] As opposition to bureau hegemony mounted by reformers, Harreld and Hastings marshaled enough votes to pass a bill in April authorizing the Justice Department to aggressively seek recovery of the disbursed $1.1 million Barnett donation. The Harreld-Hastings Act had a two-year statute of limitations. Burke attempted damage control by having his assistant, E. B. Meritt, tour the West Coast to speak out in defense of administrative policies, particularly in the Barnett matter. In response, an agitated Collier persuaded an ailing Frear to follow Meritt's trail and rebut his comments.[15]

An awareness that "something is radically wrong with the management of Indian affairs" had been awakened in Congress. Few besides Collier had the energy, commitment, or mental capacity to undertake a trenchant analysis of the contradictory statutes and unconventional court rulings that imprisoned, infantilized, and pauperized Indians while at the same time educating and protecting them. What Congress could grasp was the Indian bureau's abuse of authority in the Barnett case and the economic decline of the Indians. The juxtaposition of the two developments—the accumulating evidence of Indian poverty and the national prominence of the Barnett scandal—was Burke's undoing.

Alluding to whitewashes and cover-ups, Frear again attacked Burke and his policies on the House floor in late 1926. Fueled with information about the Barnett litigation from Charles Selby, the Justice Department's chief litigator, Frear declared the Indian bureau's approval and management of "a scandalous settlement of over $1,000,000 of the property of Jackson Barnett, a half-witted Indian," to be one of Burke's most reprehensible actions. Frear questioned what "actuated the Commissioner" to acquiesce to payoffs totaling $200,000 to McGugin and to Burke's "close friend," Marshall Mott. What could explain the anomaly of giving away "practically all of the property" of a "feeble-minded" Indian while keeping Indians of all "standards of intelligence in subjection" without control over their property? Frear was dismayed and disturbed by the Interior Department's unreviewable power to determine an Indian's competency. Using the Barnett scandal, Collier and Frear renewed their call for an independent congressional investigation of Indian affairs.[16]

To quell critics, Burke approached Interior Secretary Hubert Work, suggesting a full report be made on conditions in Indian country. Work commissioned an independent firm, the Institute of Government Research, to do the inquiry. (This investigation was popularly known as the Meriam Report.) Distrusting the Interior Department, Frear decried Work's authorization of a private study as inadequate. Any committee authorized by Interior would be "steered past neglect and mistreatment" by bureau minions, said Frear. "Only a congressional investigation committee can adequately diagnose the existing disease and prescribe a constructive remedy," he said in January 1927. As the *Equitable* case in New York was uncertain and might turn on other issues, only a real investigation could get to the key issues of malfeasance.[17]

Collier, who had described the Barnett case as simple in 1926, became so engrossed in its suspenseful developments and the political damage it was doing to Burke that he was criticized by the AIDA for getting sidetracked. By 1927, Collier realized that the Barnett case involved pivotal questions of law, and he no longer underestimated its value as political propaganda. When Judge Knox made his decision in August 1927, Collier expressed delight at the outcome and had several hundred copies printed for national distribution.[18] More clearly than any of his contemporaries, Collier appreciated the import of the Knox decision and its pending appeal to the Supreme Court. During a Senate hearing in early 1928, Collier identified the questions of law at stake. If Burke successfully appealed the *Equitable* case to the U.S. Supreme Court and the court upheld the $550,000 to the Baptists as a lawful exercise of Interior's authority, reasoned Collier, then the law granting such sweeping power to Interior is wrong and must be changed by Congress.[19]

The Barnett case shed light on the excessively broad discretionary power of Interior as well as the highly compromised federal trust relationship. It also raised awareness about the failure of allotment and the need for ongoing federal protection for Indian property. In the early 1920s,

Congress complacently relied on the simplistic argument that Indian wards were failing to become economically self-sufficient because they were not free to manage their own property. After the testimony of Assistant Interior Secretary Meritt, Congress understood that freeing Indians from restrictions was not necessarily in their best interests. Meritt loyally defended Burke's actions in the Barnett donation throughout the hearings of 1927 and 1928, denouncing the policy of Commissioner Franklin Lane, who had succumbed to the clamors to "turn the Indian loose." Such rhetoric had led to the "greatest fraud" of all at White Earth in 1906, when 99 percent of those liberated by Secretary Lane's "competency commissioners" lost their land and homes. If restrictions on Indian lands were removed, Meritt testified repeatedly, "90 [percent] of the Indians of this county would have no land" within ninety days. Meritt educated the committee members about the context in which the bureau's absolute authority in determinations of Indians' competency and the disposition of their property via leasing and inheritance had developed. Experience had shown that rounds of review by courts permitted opportunistic lawyers to waste Indians' estates in protracted litigation. Though conceding that Jackson Barnett did not initiate the donation and that he lacked the "competency that an ordinary white man would have," Meritt endeavored to convince the committee that Burke was "actuated by the highest motives" in preventing the estate's dissipation.[20]

Such testimony could not defuse the partisan momentum to have the Barnett case tried by the political branch of the government. When Senator William King of Utah submitted a resolution calling for a general survey of the condition of Indians and the bureau, Burke objected, calling the Senate investigation unnecessary since the Meriam Report on reservation conditions was already under way. Burke correctly feared that his enemies were seeking another venue for indicting him for alleged abuses in the Barnett case. Though "getting Burke" was on many people's agendas, proponents of the resolution claimed the proposed survey was not about blame, but rather about unearthing the reasons for Indians' accelerating impoverishment and lack of civil rights.[21] But as savvy political insiders knew, the centerpiece of this proposed Senate investigation was the Barnett case as symptom and symbol of a diseased Indian policy. Frear identified the Jackson Barnett case—"the most miserable thing I have ever seen in public life"—as the catalyst for his insistent demand for a full investigation of the bureau. A single case was sufficient to indicate the "general trend of the work of the department" in its fraudulent mishandling of incompetent Indians' assets. Frear pushed for an inquiry and recommendations on how to change this system of legalized robbery, arguing that it raised troubling questions of mismanagement and autocratic government control.[22]

Nudged along by the Barnett scandal, Congress gradually came to understand some of the most serious defects in Burke's Indian policy. They realized that Indians' well-being and consent were being disregarded; that freeing Indians from restrictions meant further impoverishment; that continued Interior management of Indian property on an individual basis was unwieldy, inefficient, and arbitrary; and that Interior's exclusive, unchecked authority was not in keeping with America's democratic traditions. Congress also realized that having previously given unlimited discretionary power over Indian property to the Interior Department, it must now act to correct the perceived wrongs. The National Council of the American Indians strongly concurred that addressing Indians' complaints and resolving problems lay with Congress since the *Lone Wolf* decision had placed Indian policy in the "political branch" of the government.

Lynn Frazier, chairman of the Senate Committee on Indian Affairs, posed thoughtful questions: Was the Indian trust estate rapidly melting away? And if so, what kind of laws should be adopted to alleviate the administrative guardian of the impossible task of pitting his own unlimited discretion against innumerable local and vested interests? "The whole allotment law needs reconsideration," said Frazier. "Individualizing Indian property may have been thought a good thing but it has been proven beyond a doubt to be bad for them," testified Gertrude Bonnin.[23] Clearly, the current administration of Indian affairs was failing to accomplish the ends of Indian economic self-sufficiency.

The influential Meriam Report, submitted to Secretary Work in February 1928, found rampant disease and poverty at reservations and "dictatorial" bureau methods. As bureau judgment had been found to be fallible, the investigators recommended court reviews of its decisions. While the Meriam Report is held up as a path-breaking, radical critique of the bureau, in most respects the study was conservative, endorsing most of the Burke administration's policies. Apologetically excusing itself for passing judgment on the bureau since the Indian service needed twice the appropriations to carry on the duties the Meriam committee recommended, the report advocated the same measured policy of assimilation that Burke and the bureau had endorsed since 1921 and straddled the same contradiction between liberation and protection. Believing that a scientific way could be found for measuring progress toward competency, the report condemned Indian dependency, approved the overarching goal of assimilation, and yet simultaneously declared the bureau's conservative policy of withholding Indians fee patents as fundamentally sound. Many Indians "are still children," the report stated; the rights of wards should be more carefully guarded than at present. The report assessed the missionary activities among Indians and cooperation between the federal government and the Christian organizations as benign. Significantly, the report overwhelmingly endorsed Burke's policies for rich Indians in Oklahoma, arguing that Indians required additional federal protections, not fewer. While the investigators did not think the creation of private trusts for rich Indians was a wise policy, they were very critical of the Closure Act of 1908, which gave Oklahoma county courts jurisdiction over Indian incompetents. The report proposed even stronger federal controls over Indian property in Oklahoma. The Oklahoma guardian system should be abolished, and "thoroughly competent national government officers" should take the responsibility for administering Indian property and income with the Indians being reasonably taxed for the service. The Meriam Report also recommended that Congress extend federal restrictions for Oklahoma Indians beyond the twenty-five-year probationary period due to expire in 1931.[24]

Most tellingly, the Meriam Report supported Burke's view that the bureau had a duty to channel the surplus funds of rich Indians to "productive objects" under the direction of "trained industrial and social instructors" rather than permit rich Indians to continue their "natural inclination to laziness." Rich Indians are benefiting in an unseemly way from an "unearned increment" from leasing, the report said, and they wantonly squander their money if allowed to do so. Indian money should only be used to advance Indians in ways the dominant culture delegated. The Meriam Report unequivocally endorsed the same theory that Burke used to justify his action in transferring Jackson Barnett's surplus wealth to Bacone, declaring that the functions of trusteeship of property and the training of Indians should not be divided. In strongly paternalistic language, the report said:

> It should be made clear to the Indians that they can do as they please with what they themselves earn by their own efforts, but that the government as guardian has a distinct responsibility over what comes to them through the property the government has secured them. . . . The restricted property of the Indians and their tribal property are materials to be used in promoting their economic and social betterment.[25]

In other words, income from leasing was not the Indian allottee's private property, but something to be used for the ward's education and development. Choices made by the federal guardian in this capacity did not require the ward's active participation in decision-making. The presumption was that child-like beings could not participate wisely, hence the necessity for expert and disinterested management as the ideal. The Meriam Report advocated court review of Interior decision-making as an appropriate check on administrative autocracy.

While the Meriam Report of 1928, which documented the impoverished condition of restricted Indians under the bureau's supervision, has been seen as the trigger for the abrupt loss of credibility of Burke's paternalistic policies, its role in catalyzing policy changes has been much overrated. The report in fact sustained much of Burke's approach to Indian policy, particularly in Oklahoma.[26]

Fortified rather than demoralized by the report's findings, Burke persisted in his legislative agenda. Shortly after the Meriam Report was made public, Burke testified at hearings over his bill to get statutory authority for creating private trusts for Oklahoma Indians with oil wealth. The bill was in equal measure progressive legislation and a desperate attempt to get congressional support for handling the Barnett estate. The proposed legislation would settle the questions of bureau authority raised in the Barnett litigation and take away any incentive to challenge such trusts in the future.[27] On the progressive side, Commissioner Burke advanced an argument that was appealing to Congress. Passage of the trust bill would free the bureau from fiscal responsibilities far beyond its expertise, promote greater efficiency and economy in government, and protect rich Indians from predators. The wealth under discussion was considerable. The Five Civilized Tribes' oil and gas royalties during the fiscal year ending in June 1927 was $4.8 million. The Osage received $3.9 million in bonuses and royalties of $10.5 million that year. Given the pressures to separate these Indians from their money, Congress should give the Department of the Interior statutory authority to create individual trust estates to conserve and protect the wealth of rich Indians. Because Indians continually changed their minds about agreements made, Interior needed to initiate these trusts. By turning over the management of Indian financial affairs to private trust companies, the Indian bureau would be freed from the responsibility of managing, protecting, and conserving the funds of a minority of rich Indians and could instead devote its energies and efforts to helping the uneducated and indigent Indian majority. Simultaneously, Burke urged Congress to pass legislation to extend the period of restrictions beyond the twenty-five-year probationary period defined by the Closure Act for Oklahoma Indians. Also in 1928 the Interior Department approved regulations for Individual Indian Money (IMM) Accounts.[28]

As Burke recommended, Congress did enact legislation to extend the twenty-five-year trust period for persons of one-half or more Indian blood of the Five Civilized Tribes in 1928 and of the Osage in 1929, thus keeping the restricted property of richer Indians in public trust. But his bill to create private trusts for wealthy Indians did not pass. A long-time foe of Burke and McGugin, Congressman W. H. Sproul of Kansas, disagreed with Burke's view that Interior's judgment should be substituted for the ward's will. Why put such excessive power into the hands of the Interior Department, given the serious malfeasance and misadministration within the Indian bureau? Should the Department of the Interior have the power to affect a ward's status and property without his wishes or understanding?[29]

Burke's justification for Interior's exclusive and absolute control over Indians' property past, present, and future was founded on the unstated but firmly entrenched conviction that restricted Indians, such as Jackson Barnett, were deficient beings by definition. What made Interior's guardianship exclusive was Jackson's legal status as an "ignorant full-blood" restricted Indian. Burke was doing exactly what the law allowed and required him to do in making decisions for such incompetents. What made Burke's apparently tortured argument coherent was racism. Quoting a distinguished source, Burked offered his best definition of an incompetent Indian: "the average full-blood Indian is about the equal intelligently and morally, of a white child of ten."[30]

Burke's construction of Jackson Barnett as an incompetent but average Indian was supported by others who shared his views on Indians' genetic racial inferiority, such as Judge Branson and the expert Dr. Smith Ely Jelliffe. Putting the issue into the historical frame of reference that Burke endorsed, Branson vindicated Interior's long-exercised authority over Indians such as Jackson. His incompetency was not "due to mental deficiency, however, but to racial weakness, lack of education, and business training."[31] In Jelliffe's opinion, Jackson Barnett was not an imbecile, but ranked near the educated Anglo-Saxon child of thirteen or fourteen. He had an IQ comparable to the average intelligence of U.S. Army recruits and on a par with the average, unschooled Indian. Though Jackson had no formal education, he was "an intelligent high grade Indian." Giving cultural explanations for Jackson's terse testimony before Judge Knox, Jelliffe explained that it was characteristic of "primitive man" to give assent, or to be silent, or to state in reply to questions that he "doesn't know." Jelliffe claimed to have penetrated Jackson's frame of reference and conducted a practical and comprehensive interview. Jackson made

> a whimsical and rather intelligent and extremely expressive indication in response as to whether he still enjoyed sexual activities; he had stated previously he had had them and had enjoyed them. . . . [He] said, "when the tree begins to die, expect it to fall."

Jelliffe took Jackson's sense of humor as a sign of his intelligence. Jelliffe pointedly testified that he had not observed the slightest indications of Jackson Barnett being a drooling idiot and declared him a "man of excellent intelligence . . . mentally healthy in every respect."[32]

Burke's Herculean efforts to explain himself proved futile. Instead of vindicating his principles, policies, and personal integrity, the Jackson Barnett trust was a millstone around his neck. As often as Burke appeared to clear himself of culpability, his enemies would find another way of renewing the political attack. Any victory for Burke on the legal or political front was denounced as a whitewash or cover-up and only redoubled the commitment of his opponents. In April 1928, the two-year statute of limitations expired on the Harreld-Hastings Act, offering Burke some hope that the Justice Department's litigation would finally abate. But within days of the expiration of its authority, the Justice Department doggedly filed lawsuits in three district courts against McGugin, Mott, and Anna Barnett to recover their portions of the $1.1 million donation, though chances of recovery were nil.[33] Adding insult to injury to the Oklahomans, Senator Pine's candidate for superintendent of the Union Agency, Judge James Hepburn, was rejected again. In his testimony regarding the appointment, McGugin enjoyed pointing out that Judge Hepburn was treasurer of the

Baptist church in Henryetta in 1919 and had sworn under oath to the competency of Jackson Barnett when Jackson's gift of $25,000 to the church building fund was under review.[34]

Motivated by frustration over the indecisive Barnett litigation, a desire for revenge for Hepburn's rejection, and partisan politics, the Parmenter faction in Justice called for yet another grand jury hearing in Muskogee to bring indictments against Burke and others, repeating what Oklahomans in the Justice Department had attempted in 1926. A grand jury investigation was scheduled for July 9 before federal judge Robert L. Williams, a Burke foe. Charles Selby, who had formed the unshakable opinion that Burke was indictable for fraud, believed he now had the proof he had lacked two years before and busily prepared to present his case. Nearly one hundred witnesses were to be called.

Greatly aggrieved and alarmed at these developments, Burke assailed the proceedings in a letter to Secretary Work. Though Attorney General Sargent had earlier reined in the Justice Department zealots, Parmenter and Selby were again making allegations that should be stricken. Sargent, wrote Burke, should be informed that his underlings were acting to "gratify a personal and political grudge" in ways contrary to his directives. Burke asked that the pending grand jury proceedings be brought to the urgent attention of Sargent and asked that the matter be referred to a lawyer besides Parmenter and Selby "who has an open mind and with no previously formed opinion."[35] Two days later, Work sent the following telegram to Sargent, then on vacation in Ludlow, Vermont: "Indictment of Commissioner Burke in Oklahoma threatened. Please have it stayed. Mrs. Burke is critically ill." Selby was subsequently informed that his superiors had ordered a postponement. At Burke's request, Sargent authorized an impartial Justice Department investigation by Pierce Butler Jr., the son of a Supreme Court justice.[36]

Selby, the prosecutor, and Pine, the politician, were angry at these latest rebuffs. Selby suspected that the postponement was a partisan move to protect the Republicans from scandal in an election year.[37] Selby expected the Butler investigation to whitewash alleged federal wrongdoing yet again. Senator Pine said he would do what he could to get to the facts, by Justice action or by a Senate committee investigation.[38]

Once again, Burke briefly had saved himself through skillful maneuvering. But the last confrontation in the war over Jackson Barnett approached.

9

Witch Hunts:
The Senate Subcommittee
Investigation
1928–1929

Congress authorized the Senate "Survey of Conditions of the Indians" in February 1928. The heightened congressional interest in the Jackson Barnett case drew prominent senators to the issue of Indian policy reform, some for partisan reasons. The Senate subcommittee's goal was to make a general investigation into nationwide conditions. Beginning its fact-finding tour in 1928 in the Pacific Northwest, it did not complete its work until 1944. Lynn Frazier of North Dakota chaired the subcommittee. Also serving on the survey were Burton Wheeler of Montana, Robert La Follette, Jr., of Wisconsin, and W. B. Pine and Elmer Thomas of Oklahoma. The preamble of the "Survey of Conditions" clearly proclaimed its view that American Indian policy needed to be completely overhauled. The preamble indicted the bureau for denying Indians "free and independent use of [their] property," for controlling Indian property but with no accountability to civil courts or Congress, and for failure to develop Indians' "self-reliant citizenship."[1]

The driving force for creating the hearings was the Parmenter camp's determined effort to bring Burke's alleged mishandling of the Barnett estate to the court of public opinion. Just as Mott and Burke had sought to achieve through the courts what they could not achieve in Congress in 1926, Selby and his fellow Oklahomans used the Senate investigation to gain what they could not win decisively in court. There was an unsettling feeling that Burke was escaping accountability. Senator Wheeler quoted a newspaper article on the Senate floor in early January 1929, "An uncomfortable public feeling has been produced by the apparent ease with which two Cabinet Officers, behind the scenes, can manipulate legal proceedings."[2]

Most of the testimony in the first three sections of the "Survey of Conditions"—a full two-thirds of the first 2,000 pages—was on the Barnett case. Included in the survey's record was prosecutor Charles Selby's amassed evidence, including a chronology of documents (dating from 1921 to 1929) introduced as evidence by the Justice Department in the Barnett litigation—916 documents relating to Commissioner Burke, 913 referring to the Baptist society, and hundreds of other miscellaneous documents, mainly correspondence. Both Jackson Barnett and his wife, Anna, were subpoenaed to testify at the first hearing in November 1928 in Riverside, California. Asked if he wanted to make the donation of $1.1 million, Jackson responded succinctly: "Yeh; said when I died they could have it; that is all."[3]

If some members of the Senate subcommittee hoped to air the critical issues in the Barnett affair and bring Burke's malfeasance to light, they were soon disabused of this naïve expectation. Rather than finding wrongdoers to publicly excoriate or clear-cut legislative solutions, the Senate survey was a foray into the heart of darkness. The record of the survey investigation into the Barnett case reveals much about the senators' political motives, racial and gender biases, and fundamental ignorance of Indian policy's paternalistic underpinnings.

On January 9, 1929, the Senate subcommittee on Indian Affairs met in Washington, D.C., to hear more testimony on the Bureau of Indian Affairs' alleged mishandling of the Jackson Barnett estate. Wheeler—a blustery, partisan Democrat who had led an inquiry into Attorney General Harry Daugherty's actions in the corrupt Harding administration and forced his resignation—spearheaded the attack on the Burke administration by questioning Charles Selby, the Justice Department's chief prosecutor in the Barnett litigation. Wheeler, a man described as having more guts than brains, was posturing theatrically for the American public. Selby, a man of single-minded purpose, had spent the better part of his life since November 1925 combing thousands of documents for evidence of Interior Department wrongdoing in handling the Barnett estate.[4]

In what was undoubtedly a prearranged dialogue, Wheeler asked for a briefing. Selby launched into a discussion about the most recent developments in the Barnett litigation and patiently summarized the key aspects of the case: Jackson Barnett was "generally known" as a "mental incompetent" with a mentality of a five- or six-year-old. Selby described the marriage of Jackson and Anna in 1920 and Interior's approval of a donation of Jackson's money without the knowledge of Jackson's guardian. Incredulously, Wheeler asked, "[Anna Barnett] is merely an adventuress?" Though he feigned amazement at this sudden revelation, Wheeler was familiar with the 1920 Bowie Report into Anna Barnett's checkered past before her marriage to Jackson and had already formed a unshakable opinion about her character.[5]

The subcommittee asked Selby to share information not already known about the case. After some fidgeting, Selby said that many details were not presented in the *Equitable* case in New York. After the *Equitable* case went to trial, he explained, the Justice Department received copies of correspondence and other documents exchanged among the trust company, the American Home Missionary Society, the commissioner of Indian affairs, and their attorneys. Senator Wheeler, feigning ignorance of the particulars in the Barnett saga, begged Selby to tell the whole story. Selby obliged, tracing the unfolding of events, the characters, and their motives.

The dignity of the well-heeled U.S. senators, lawyers, and ranking public federal officials and the gravity and formality of the proceedings could not conceal the rising tensions in the room as Selby spoke on this winter day. He unraveled the threads of tangled lies and transparent cover-ups and spun a tale of a conspiracy, in whose web he had long been held an outraged and frustrated captive. At last, he could condemn the criminals and tell the world of the heinous crimes which had become so clear to him: the scheme of Anna and McGugin, Jackson's virtual imprisonment, the payoffs, the crossing of state lines, the guardian's habeas corpus action to retrieve Jackson, Burke's complicity, and the manipulation of the law. Interior had "invented" a regulation—it had changed the rules—just so it could bring the cover of legality to a reprehensible transfer of money from the hands of a helpless Indian.

Senator Thomas, sympathetic to Commissioner Burke and Anna Barnett, interrupted Selby's tight narrative to ask if there were possible alternate interpretations of these events. But Wheeler, fascinated by the intrigue, pressed Selby to continue. With obvious indignation, Selby recalled the events of mid-November 1926, when someone "higher up" ordered him to quash the charges of fraud made by Justice against the Department of the Interior officials. Playing his part, Wheeler quoted Judge Knox's opinion regarding the sordid aspects of the case. Then, Wheeler applauded the Justice Department for its valiant role in the *Equitable* trust case in unmasking the Interior Department's mismanagement of Jackson Barnett's estate. If left unchallenged, the precedent would have allowed the arbitrary dissipation of a ward's property.[6]

After accepting this tribute to his worthy contribution in the pursuit of justice, Selby returned to his story. Long convinced that the co-conspirators in the Barnett affair should be prosecuted, Selby had brought the criminal features to the attention of federal judge Robert L. Williams in eastern Oklahoma. Williams had called for a grand jury on July 9, 1928. Selby had diligently prepared for this event, but a few days before the jury was to meet, there were mysterious orders again from his superiors to postpone the proceedings. The excuse was that Justice was not prepared to make its case, but Selby believed otherwise. Commissioner Burke, Selby implied, had engineered the cancellation of the grand jury both in 1926 and in 1928. After reviewing the evidence for three years, Selby concluded that "a conspiracy existed that grew out of the early plan of this woman to acquire the estate and fortune of Jackson Barnett, that had for its objective the . . . interference with the Government's proper handling of the restricted funds of Jackson Barnett."[7] Asked by Wheeler who likely would have been indicted had the grand jury proceeded, Selby named Anna Barnett, Harold McGugin, Amasa Ward (as he had "clear knowledge" of Anna's original plan), Marshall Mott (having knowledge and participation), along with the top officials in the Department of the Interior, Burke and Secretary of the Interior Albert Fall. Selby concluded, it "is a notorious, typical case embodying probably the worst that could be conceived in Indian management" in terms of publicity and attendant notoriety.[8]

Senator Thomas again challenged Selby. What were Jackson Barnett's living conditions before his marriage? Selby and Wheeler shrugged off this point and shifted the focus to what to them was foundational: their moral outrage at Jackson Barnett's entrapment by a woman of notoriously bad character. Thomas took another tack. Why did the Justice Department assail a trust to endow an Indian school and orphans' home and pay private lawyers $180,000 to destroy this philanthropic donation? Weakly, Selby said that both Justice and Interior opposed these exhorbitant legal fees.

Evidently, the Department of Justice and the Department of the Interior were working at cross-purposes in the recent *Equitable* case. Senator Thomas ventured: "I think the record will show who was protecting the Indian." The reply from Senator Pine was: "Let us make a complete record, then." Following these steps in the partisan dance, the Senate subcommittee investigation of the Jackson Barnett case formally began.[9]

The proud Charles Burke had no patience with these niceties. Much incensed by Selby's testimony impugning his character, Burke interrupted the planned performance in the afternoon session, demanding to be heard. With disregard for decorum, Burke punctured the illusion that the committee was impartially seeking justice. Commissioner Burke angrily and impetuously pointed an accusatory finger at those who portrayed him as a co-conspirator. Just the opposite was true, Burke contended. He charged that Senator Pine, for political reasons, was out to destroy him because of a trivial slight: Pine's candidate, James Hepburn, had not been appointed superintendent of the Five Civilized Tribes. Pine was using his political lackeys in the Department of Justice, Selby and Parmenter, to accomplish his aim. Conspiring with Pine, Burke declared, was "John Collier, a notorious Indian agitator, who is actively engaged in a campaign trying to destroy me and the Indian Service." Those present were stunned by this unexpected outburst. No one commented on Burke's statement. Lynn Frazier, the chairperson, turned to the next witness.[10]

Burke's impulsive accusation was political suicide. Pine adamantly denied charges of a conspiracy, criminal or otherwise, against Burke. The senators demanded that Burke immediately present evidence for the charges or retract them. Collier also challenged Burke to present evidence that his organization advocated destruction of the bureau. Burke hastily assembled his evidence, a summary largely premised on the alleged evils of the Oklahoma guardianship system that he had been fighting since 1910, and he summoned witnesses. But his presentation was a humiliating failure. What seemed so clear to him about the righteousness of his cause and the persecution he had suffered at the hands of his enemies failed to convince the Senate subcommittee of a conspiracy against him. Burke could not substantiate his claim that Pine was directing the attacks against him, and he could not prove the implausible claim that Hepburn's rejection was the cause of the persecution. Under questioning, Burke retreated from his earlier charge of conspiracy. Yet Burke continued to claim he was the victim of a coordinated "campaign of propaganda and misrepresentation." His arguments appeared to be the imaginings of an unbalanced, paranoid, defensive individual. Senators Frazier, La Follette, and Wheeler found his evidence baseless. In early February 1929, they announced there was not "a scintilla of evidence" to support Burke's charge of a Pine-orchestrated conspiracy.[11]

Most historians agree that the Senate subcommittee hearings were, at the outset, politically contrived to discredit Burke. Angie Debo, an expert on Oklahoma history, situates Pine as a central figure in a web of Okmulgee County lawyers and judges who had pecuniary and political motives for wanting Burke removed as the commissioner of Indian affairs. Pine, a millionaire oil man from Okmulgee, was elected to the Senate in 1924, having made a campaign promise to return the Barnett estate to local supervision. He had helped promote Parmenter to his permanent position as assistant attorney general. The two often discussed the developments in the Barnett litigation. There was substance to Burke's general argument that Oklahoma lawyers from Pine's home county had economic motives and much to gain by preserving the lucrative guardianship system, which Burke was using all of his powers to destroy after 1923. Pine's lawyer, Almond Cochran, was active in the Republican party in Oklahoma, signed contingency contracts with Barnett heirs in 1923, campaigned for Pine's election, and advocated for Judge Hepburn to be named superintendent. Moreover, Collier was capitalizing on the Barnett scandal to promote his own career as well as much-needed reform in Indian policy.[12]

As Burke emphasized, Selby's presentation cloaked the complex and varied motives of those who joined in the witch-hunt. There were pecuniary motives (the lawyers for the guardian and the Creek heirs); personal vendettas against Anna Barnett, Charles Burke, Marshall Mott, and others involved in the creation or defense of the gift; and political ploys as Democrats hoped to embarrass Republicans or as states' rights advocates opposed federal abuses of power. Those with political motives also sought to oust Burke from his entrenched position of power.

Burke's outburst was a blunder, but it was somewhat understandable. Selby's representation of the facts was one-sided. For five years, Burke had withstood a constant barrage of charges of criminal wrongdoing, which he had deflected time and again with political skill and an enormous strength of will. Embattled for his faulty policies and his well-meaning role in the Jackson Barnett affair, Burke finally reached the point where he could endure the criticisms no longer. The fresh sallies into his conduct, ripe with innuendos of willful wrongdoing, distortions, and the half-truths voiced by his chief adversary, Selby, in a hearing dominated by another enemy, Pine, brought him to the breaking point.[13]

The more one knew about the issues and details of the Barnett case, the more the elements seemed to be able to recombine in an infinite number of patterns. Casting Jackson as a helpless victim meant the "blame" must fall on the woman and the Indian bureau. For Wheeler and those motivated to unseat the trusts and to damage Burke's credibility, both Anna Barnett and Jackson Barnett were aberrations—she as an empowered, and therefore dangerous, unnatural woman and he as a powerless "idiot." Wheeler vociferously condemned Anna as an unspeakably disreputable "type" of woman. Wheeler asserted that the bold "facts" about her character—when combined with Jackson's uncontestable status as a "mental imbecile"[14]—were the pivotal questions on which the Barnett case rested. He wanted the facts as presented in the Bowie Report placed in the record. In Wheeler's view, undermining any defense of the trust agreements was the irrefutable argument that Anna was an adventuress and therefore any pact Interior made with this "witch" was unholy. Such an empowered woman represented a threat to the moral and legal order regarding Indian relations.

Once Anna's immorality, her assault on male power prerogatives, and Jackson's imbecility were established, the conclusion was clear and inescapable: the Indian bureau's action in approving the gift was incomprehensible except as some outrageously secretive and conspiratorial plot, undeniably self-serving and nefariously motivated. Therefore, the bureau was guilty of shameful, if not criminal, malfeasance (symptomatic of its general mismanagement) and a political whitewash. In January 1929, beginning with Parmenter and Selby, the Senate heard witness after witness who constructed the case in this manner. Parmenter agreed with Selby that the grand jury should have been allowed to bring in indictments. "Amazed that a situation of this kind could exist under the shadow of the dome of the National Capitol," Parmenter melodramatically declared, adding, "The cold shivers run up my back, when I had to see these conditions prevailing."[15]

After anti-Burke witnesses made their case that Interior's act in the $1.1 million donation was a presumptuous and illegal assault on Oklahoma's authority, Senator Thomas became exasperated with the unrelenting cries of mismanagement. A fair-minded politician working toward protections for Oklahoma's Indian population, Thomas had a more comprehensive and objective view than most of the other senators at the hearing. Because of the historical abuses in the Oklahoma guardianship system, he understood what the Indian bureau was trying to accomplish. "I would like to have some constructive suggestion for the management of the great estates in Oklahoma belonging to what might be termed incompetent Indians."[16]

Elmer Thomas and the witnesses who defended Burke and the trust agreements challenged the characterization of Anna. Marrying someone for money was not illegal if the compact were consensual.[17] The Indian bureau did try to annul the marriage in 1920, but was unable to do so. As Jackson's legal wife, Anna Barnett was entitled under state law to half of his estate. The trusts preserved half "for some good cause in the State, rather than be fought over by attorneys."[18] Thomas assailed the infamous Bowie Report as being conducted by a subcontractor—a private detective firm—not the FBI. It was based largely on hearsay, which was inadmissible as legal evidence. Basing the case for Burke's mismanagement on Anna's purported reputation was a weak reed. Since the marriage, Anna had behaved as a "good wife" and had improved Jackson's quality of life dramatically. Neither Anna nor Jackson were distorted caricatures, but rather two human beings who enjoyed a consensual union that brought benefits to both. Of all of the people who claimed to represent Jackson's interests, Senator Thomas believed, Anna had her husband's well-being at heart. She raised him from a hog's shack, said Thomas, to a level befitting a millionaire.

Pine and Wheeler were not moved by these arguments in defense of Anna Barnett's entitlement. Anybody who knew Indians, Wheeler contended, understood they are happier with their own kind than in "some gilded cage" down in California. Convinced by the Bowie Report of Anna's lurid reputation, Wheeler hammered on the issue of her sexual promiscuity in his questions to other witnesses. When Secretary of the Interior Hubert Work testified, Wheeler opined caustically that it would be better if the bureau protected Indians' money from floozies. Work conceded that Burke exercised some poor judgment in the case but did nothing criminal. He questioned the guardian's motives in bringing a lawsuit. Guardians were interested in serving rich, not poor, Indians, while the bureau was in a constant "struggle" to protect Indian funds from the vultures.[19] Work tried with little success to broaden Wheeler's vision to see that the bureau made decisions in a context in which rich Indians were subject to predation from any number of sources. Given the years of interminable acrimony over the case, Wheeler's fawning approbation for the Justice Department's actions elicited a dry comment from Secretary Work: "I think it is a good thing for all of us to have had this talk and arrived at an understanding."[20]

On the question of Jackson's competency, several witnesses tried to
dislodge the stereotypic notion that Jackson Barnett was an imbecile.
Commissioner Burke had the testimony of Jelliffe and several others entered into the record to show Jackson as more or less average.[21] Work
stated: "I have seen Jackson Barnett a time or two and he talked very little,
but he had the expression and the appearance of a man that was quite intelligent, considering his race, his education, and his opportunities. . . .
He, fortunately, seemed to know what not to say." Wheeler countered
with an example of Jackson Barnett's faltering testimony, saying that it
demonstrated that Jackson was mentally incompetent. Work equivocated:
"That is a matter that is difficult to prove, because you know the habits of
the Indian. They protect themselves. They are always brighter than they
appear to be."[22] Burke doggedly reiterated that Barnett possessed "the
mentality of the average illiterate, uneducated Creek Indian of his age."
The idea that Jackson was "crazy" stemmed from a misunderstanding due
to his association with the Crazy Snake movement. If Jackson were terse in
his responses in court, it was because he was a Snake. Jackson Barnett was
not an imbecile, and no judge had ever declared him incompetent by reason of imbecility.[23] Nat M. Lacy, a special assistant to the attorney general
who had worked alongside Selby on the case from its inception, stated,
"There is a great deal of discussion and argument as to what the understanding of his incompetency is." Wheeler bullied and badgered Lacy
to agree that Jackson was "an ignorant old Indian," but Lacy stood his
ground.[24]

When Wheeler interrogated another Justice lawyer, the two men
slipped easily into their smug assumptions about Jackson Barnett and his
wife. The attorney insisted that Jackson was delighted to be rid of his wife
when the Justice Department seized him in 1926 and took him to Oklahoma and that Jackson was happy to see his Indian friends, his shack, and
his dogs. Asked if Jackson were anxious to get out of the "gilded palace,"
the witness said, "Oh, yes. They revert to type." There was no doubt of
Jackson's imbecility in this witness's mind.[25]

Given the characterization of Jackson as an imbecile, Jackson's testimony before the Senate subcommittee was very embarrassing to the anti-
Burke forces. Well groomed, Maxine, Anna, and Jackson made a dignified
entrance into the Senate Office Building in Washington on February 4,
1929. The seventy-five-year-old Jackson smiled broadly and reported details of events in his life guilelessly. Under questioning, Jackson stated he
did not know how old he was or in what state the towns Muskogee or
Henryetta were located, except "Indian." Compared to testimony on other
occasions in which he had showed only the vaguest notions of Los Angeles
geography, he clarified that he did not live in Hollywood, but a couple of
miles west of the main part of the city or about three miles from Hollywood. While he candidly admitted to being ignorant of or forgetting
many aspects of the management of his money and the principles involved

in the litigation, the elderly Jackson was quick and responsive to the battery of questions. He had a good recall of dates, places, and names and displayed a simple understanding of money values.

Jackson Barnett was unfailingly honest. He remembered the details of the courtship, for example, Johnson driving the jitney after he met Anna. On her second visit, he recalled, Anna asked him to marry her. He recounted getting in the car after dark and going to Okemah beyond Holdenville, spending the night, and coming back. Frankly, he did not understand why he was held in Coffeyville, but he denied being locked up in a Kansas hotel room: "I never did learn what it was all about." He resented having to be married twice, that is, having to repeat the marriage ceremony in Missouri after he and Anna were married in Kansas.[26]

While many aspects of his experiences since becoming wealthy were a great mystery to him, he was anything but passive, feeble-minded, or idiotic. Wheeler and Pine subjected him to a grueling two-hour interrogation. These senators made a fatal miscalculation by thinking aggressive questioning would make Jackson look stupid. During questioning, Wheeler patronizingly corrected Jackson's grammar and heckled Jackson when he hesitated to answer a question, suggesting that he would withhold the truth because he was afraid of Anna Barnett. Wheeler tried to lead Jackson to say he really wanted to return to Oklahoma. After describing Jackson's seizure in Los Angeles by U.S. marshals and his removal to Oklahoma in 1926, Wheeler asked: "You wanted to stay there, did you not?" Jackson answered, "No, not in Muskogee." Wheeler contradicted this answer by quoting a report sent to the Indian bureau that suggested Jackson wished to live in Oklahoma. "Have you been as happy down there with the white folks in Los Angeles as you were with the Indians down on the reservation?" asked Wheeler patronizingly. Jackson Barnett replied: "Yes," then qualified his answer by saying he liked living both in Oklahoma and in California. Wheeler continued to badger him, hoping to establish that Jackson was unhappy in California or to reveal him as a confused old man. Jackson clarified that there was not a great deal of difference to him about residency since most of his friends in Oklahoma had died long ago. He'd go back to Oklahoma when he was ready, but until then: "I want to see some more; I want to hear some more before I go back." When questioned by Senator Thomas, Jackson expressed his appreciation of his lifestyle in California. He liked his nice home and automobiles and his liberty of movement; he enjoyed spending money; and he had a good time in Los Angeles.

Jackson's attitude toward Anna could be described as cautious, circumspect, or distant, but not deferential or fearful. He referred to Anna as "that woman" or "the woman." He was unclear about how Anna got some of his money, but understood that a check routinely came from Muskogee out of which he received money. "She never tells me anything. She wants the money; that was all. She never tells me anything."

Regarding money issues, Jackson candidly admitted the limitations of his understanding. He did not know what a will was and did not recall signing one. There was a note of fatalism regarding his inability or disinclination to oppose the strong opinions of others regarding his "surplus" funds. He gave money to McGugin because "the woman" wanted it. He did not remember giving $550,000 to Bacone. The commissioner had arranged it; he was told about it after the fact. Astutely, he said: "They knowed I got the money, and they wanted it, and they would get it." He understood that after he died, Bacone would get his money, but he was not sure how much.[27]

Most embarrassing to Pine and Wheeler was Jackson's utter guilelessness and his uncorruptible character. His testimony demonstrated that he could not be badgered or manipulated though he lacked a sophisticated understanding of financial transactions. Jackson repeatedly denied that he had been coached by his wife, her attorneys, or Burke. Jackson then finally admitted he had been coached, but guilelessly added that he "didn't know what they meant." Jackson alluded to Wheeler as one of those who attempted (without success) to coach him. Wheeler, caught in his own trap, stammered: "No, I mean—I did, of course."[28]

Senator Pine was among the last to question Jackson Barnett, whose testimony was not proceeding as Wheeler and Pine had planned. Jackson's enjoyment of the interrogation seemed to increase and he laughed out loud at some of the questions. Perhaps to amuse himself, his answers became flippant, and he enjoyed playing a joke on the bald Senator Pine:

> PINE: How do you get the money on that check, Jackson?
> JACKSON: What?
> PINE: How do you get the money?
> BARNETT: I just make a check out after I get the check.
> PINE: You say you make it out after you get the check?
> BARNETT: [the witness laughing]
> PINE: What do you do with it then?
> BARNETT: I spend it.[29]

When Barnett candidly admitted his illiteracy, Pine thought he could use a ruse to expose Barnett's ignorance of money matters:

> PINE: Do you know the difference between a $20 bill and a $5 bill?
> BARNETT: Yes; I have one in my pocket here—a twenty.
> PINE: You have a twenty?
> BARNETT: Yes [taking bills from his pocket]. Do you know?

Laughter rippled through the courtroom. Pine then asked Jackson to identify a $10 gold piece, and Jackson called it a silver quarter. Rogers objected to this as trickery as the coin was held at some distance from the witness. Pine began to sweat with anxiety, which was more embarrassing when Barnett called attention to it.[30]

As the testimony before the Senate subcommittee progressed, the partisan assault was blunted by Jackson Barnett's self-possessed testimony. For those who were open-minded, the introduced evidence provided a legal and moral context for Interior's action in creating the trust. When Selby's premise that Anna and Jackson were aberrant human beings faltered, the witch-hunt against Burke lost momentum. Burke insisted the donation was "legal" and had been made according to bureau procedure; the donation had gone through seven steps of approval from Superintendent Victor Locke to Secretary of the Interior Albert Fall.[31]

When Wheeler, grandstanding, stated he wanted to get to the bottom of the corruption in the Indian bureau and let "the facts" speak for themselves, he was reminded by more than one witness that the facts could be interpreted in different ways. He was told there was no consensus that fraud had been committed. The Justice Department's lawyer, Nat M. Lacy, testified that he did not think the fraud charges were justified, though he did find some minor financial transactions (specifically, loans made by Anna's attorneys, which appeared to be payoffs) suspicious. While questioning Lacy, Wheeler reverted to his refrain of letting "the facts" speak for themselves, but when Lacy asked which facts he meant, Wheeler refused to go beyond his simplistic statement.

Despite his earlier humiliation, the indefatigable Burke bombarded the subcommittee with information until the senators finally asked him to desist, claiming they lacked funding to continue the investigation into the Barnett matter. Exhausted by the effort to assimilate the voluminous evidence in the Barnett case, the senators conceded they could find no resolution to the case that had long burdened the courts. With the Barnett case at an impasse, Burke once again had successfully fought his foe Selby to a draw.[32]

The high-profile Senate investigation provoked national press coverage and produced a range of responses. Most of the coverage was sensationalistic, superficial, and transparently partisan. But some of it displayed thoughtful analysis. One newspaper stated that the "dynamite" evidence of conspiracy by which government wards were defrauded had been heard by a grand jury, that indictments were probable, and that the unfolding scandal would eclipse "the oil grabs of Fall and Sinclair and Doheny." It added that the forces of the Department of the Interior arrayed against the Department of Justice was "one of the most unusual circumstances in the history of the American government!"[33] *Time* reported the story with many factual errors and much hostility toward Burke, Anna Barnett, and the American Home Missionary Society. Referring to Jackson's testimony, *Time* said: "Mrs Barnett pinned [Jackson] under a beady stare until he wriggled and giggled uncomfortably and professed great lapses of memory." The Baptist society was excoriated for the "attempted stripping of an aged and mentally helpless victim" in what were construed as backroom deals by the Interior Department.[34]

On the other hand, *Latta's Fortnightly Review* published a sympathetic analysis by Alexander Vogelsang, a former assistant secretary of the Interior, entitled "Case of Jackson Barnett," in response to a previous article, "The Indian Commissioner in Hot Water." The paltry sum of $250 a month doled out to the multimillionaire before his marriage was described as "ample and even far beyond his simple needs." Anna and Jackson's marriage had been thoroughly investigated; she was no more guilty of conspiracy than others of her gender in snaring rich husbands. An "entirely unreasonable clamor has been raised over this man's affairs." What better use of the money than to fund Bacone and the orphans' home? This was a wise policy for surplus funds, far better than the shameful expenditure of $250,000 since the marriage in legal and guardian fees for needless litigation.[35]

The *Tulsa World* had a better grasp than most of the tabloids on the higher purposes for the old Indian's fortune. The newspaper hoped that a definition of policy would emerge from the controversy. The big question was Jackson's right to use his money—to donate to a reputable Indian school—versus the right of lawyers and government agents arbitrarily to take charge:

> Who was about to be hurt by that donation? The heroic efforts by the Justice Department to save the old man from his good intentions has been tremendously costly to him—and to the benefit of whom . . . ? Vulturous lawyers have hounded this old man for many years. . . . He has no known vicious intentions and can be guarded from professional beggars. The government should not set up a lot of one-sided safeguards for an incompetent Indian and then allow blood-sucking, egg-sucking, conscienceless predatory lawyers and schemers to waylay his every step.[36]

Indian Truth, an Indian Rights Association magazine, quoted a *Tulsa World* editorial, "Results All that Count":

> Nobody has contributed as much towards his comfort and care as the woman who inveigled, if she did inveigle him into marriage. She found him in a hovel, living in filth and dirt and without proper food or raiment, and she dressed him up and elevated and improved his standard of living. The old Indian says he never has been so happy."[37]

The money donated to charity was well spent, the article concluded. The Department of the Interior acted wisely and directly for Jackson's welfare and his interests. These widely divergent interpretations in the court of public opinion mirrored the deep ambivalence in American thinking about Indians and the ambiguities in Indian law and policy during the 1920s.

With no consensus emerging in either the legislative or judicial branches of the government, the executive branch stepped forward to try to resolve the intractable Barnett case. After the foiled grand jury hearing of 1928, the matter had been referred to the Justice Department's special investigator, Pierce Butler, Jr., who submitted his report on March 4, 1929, just as the Senate subcommittee became deadlocked on the matter. Butler found much that was "reprehensible" in the donation but insufficient evidence to warrant prosecutions of the public officers who had administered Jackson's property. Butler said there was no fraud, conspiracy, or intent to deceive. Interior thought it had the authority to make choices for incompetent Indians. "Indeed the whole transaction was predicated upon the assumption [Jackson Barnett] was incompetent." Attorney General John Mitchell said that he would follow Butler's recommendation and "make no indictments against any one connected with the matter."[38]

The Butler report voiced the legal opinion that Interior had no power to make gifts of Barnett's restricted funds. The abuse of authority, in Butler's view, was the 1922 amended regulation from which Burke derived his authority to circumvent the Oklahoma guardian and courts in his decision regarding the disposal of $1.1 million of the Barnett fortune. This amendment, generated internally by the Interior Department and lacking congressional approval, could not be construed as granting legal authority for the commissioner of Indian affairs to make such a large bequest, concluded Butler. Congress could not empower Interior to give away the proceeds of a lease save by the valid act of the Indian. Significantly for Anna and Jackson, Butler considered their nine-year marriage as legally dubious. In the course of the litigation begun by the guardian to recover the $400,000 that Anna had gained in the donation, Parmenter and Selby had begun litigation in Los Angeles District Court to annul the Barnett marriage on the grounds that Jackson was mentally incompetent and had been victimized. Butler recommended that the Department of Justice vigorously pursue this suit. Copies of the Butler report were sent to Interior and to the Senate Indian Affairs Subcommittee. In his remarks to Senate, "Is It the End of the Road?" Wheeler gloated over Burke's defeat.[39]

Burke escaped prosecution but resigned as commissioner of Indian affairs shortly after Butler's report became public. He left public office under a cloud, saying he was "very glad indeed to get out." His health and his reputation had suffered in the 1920s in the arduous political struggle. Disillusioned, he destroyed his personal papers.[40] A Baptist society official viewed the implications of the Butler report as "very bad for us." The implications of the report were even more severe than the Knox decision. Large gifts from restricted Indians would no longer be possible. The society might be sued for the recovery of all past gifts from restricted Indian donors. Thereafter, the only way to get legal donations from rich Indians would be if all restrictions were lifted from them.[41]

The other fatal blow to the $1.1 million Barnett donation came with the U.S. Supreme Court's decision in *Mott v. United States* in June 1931. Sitting judges on the Supreme Court at this time included former Attorney General Harlan Stone and Charles Evans Hughes, both of whom had been involved in the Barnett case earlier. (In the same session as *Mott v. United States* was delivered, the court made the final determination of lawyer's fees in *United States v. Equitable Trust*.) In the *Mott* decision, the Supreme Court reversed Judge Pollock's 1929 federal district court ruling, saying the $15,000 fee Mott had received as part of Barnett distrubution was unlawfully obtained. In his opinion in *Mott*, Justice Willis Van Devanter relied heavily on Judge Knox's 1927 judgment in the *Barnett v. Equitable* case and Pierce Butler's 1929 Department of Justice report. The distinctions between initiation and consent and between "competent" restricted Indian and "incompetent" restricted Indians were the pivots on which the legality of a donation rested according to Van Devanter. He doubted Jackson was the competent agent Interior claimed him to be.

The decision is significant in that the Court took a position dramatically in variance with the interpretation of restricted Indians' property rights held by judges Pollock, Branson, attorneys Booth and Davis, Commissioner Burke, and the esteemed authors of the Meriam Report, namely that Interior's discretionary power was an instrumentality and Indians' unearned and surplus wealth the "materials" to achieve the end of instilling proper dominant culture behaviors and values. Rather than constructing restricted Indians as "child-citizens" or a more-or-less permanent class of mental deficients, the Supreme Court viewed restricted Indians as persons of normal rights and abilities for whom common-sense notions of participation in decision-making about property transfers applied.

At one level, Van Devanter's opinion in *Mott* appears to sidestep rather than engage some of the knottier issues in the Barnett litigation far less clear in practice than in theory. It nonetheless marks a significant watershed in the checks and balances system regarding federal trust responsibility. Van Devanter upheld federal protective responsibilities to conserve a "restricted" Indian's estate, but declared Interior had violated its mandate in presuming to dissipate the estate on its own initiative. Most important, Van Devanter affirmed the judiciary's right to review the judgments made by Interior. Van Devanter resoundingly condemned Interior for abuse of authority in the Barnett donation and thus strongly condemned administrative autocracy.

> The suggestion that his approval supplied the necessary intent on the part of Barnett is but another way of saying that the Secretary could make the gift merely of his own volition. The further suggestion that he must be presumed to have found Barnett free from disability and that this determination cannot be questioned in the courts is without merit.[42]

Thus, the issues of the volition of the guardian (as a substitute for the ward), abuse of power, and dissipation of Indian estates were joined in the Barnett litigation as morally unacceptable correlates. In calling for court review in such cases, Van Devanter set higher standards of accountability of federal officials. This was an important signpost in the evolution of federal trust doctrine. Historically, the distinction between initiation and consent, competent and incompetent restricted Indian, and benevolent and malevolent paternalism had been blurred: Interior's role had been as a broker between Indian and non-Indian interests as much as a protector of Indian lands and resources. The culmination of the Barnett litigation in the U.S. Supreme Court decision in *Mott v. United States* in 1931 marked a shift from a facile acceptance of historic practices that worked to the Indians' disadvantage.[43]

Justice had been served by Van Devanter's ruling in *Mott v. United States* as he rejected the virtually unlimited discretionary authority the Interior Department exercised over the property of restricted Indians. It took a $1.1 million donation and an odd trio—a simple and good-natured Creek millionaire, his termagant wife, and an arrogant commissioner of Indian affairs—to bring the sweeping powers of the Interior Department to the attention of the court.

It was Burke's misfortune to have been confronted with the practical realities of Indian administration in an era where no clear theoretical guidelines existed to guide Indian policy. In administering Jackson Barnett's estate, Burke sincerely believed he was pursuing enlightened public policy. In fashioning the donation, Burke was motivated by the desire to secure at least a part of the vast Barnett estate as an endowment for Indian people and keep the estate from being wasted in litigation. He wanted to curb an exploitative Oklahoma guardianship system that was sorely in need of reform through corrective legislation by Congress. Although the means of accomplishing these aims were of questionable legality, Interior had acted in the best interests of Jackson Barnett: to improve his health, quality of life, and long-term security. The Parmenter camp dismissed Burke's higher purposes and demonstrated scant regard for Jackson Barnett in pursuing its own agenda in protest of the arrogant exercise of federal power. Most unconscionable was the Parmenter camp's construction of Jackson as a drooling imbecile.[44]

The resolution of the Barnett case was not a clear watershed in how Americans in the dominant culture viewed their relationship with Indians, but it did provide some clarity and direction in Indian affairs after nearly three decades of ambivalence, conflict, and confusion. Out of the turmoil came a public attitude that Indians needed protection and that the Department of the Interior's virtually unlimited discretionary authority should be checked. Also, the long-standing practice of controlling Indian "surpluses" was condemned as a "ravishment of property rights," in Judge

Knox's words. What had served as Burke's standard for enlightened public policy—a mixture of Christian paternalism and Social Darwinism—was becoming less palatable to the American public. Less attached to Victorian values, Americans in the 1920s and 1930s were developing some curiosity about and appreciation for the native cultures they had almost succeeded in destroying.[45]

Letting Indians speak for themselves was the best defense against an ethnocentric legal system that presumed Indians to be incapable of making valid choices. "Give the poor Indians, who have been so completely controlled and managed all these years, a chance to be heard," Sioux activist Gertrude Bonnin had passionately urged. The Senate survey, despite its impetus by politicians wishing to destroy Burke, gave Indians this chance. The Barnett case was a catalyst for Congress to become more educated about conditions in Indian country. Following the hearings on the Barnett case, Congress authorized additional funding for the Senate subcommittee to travel throughout the nation for the next fifteen years, interviewing hundreds of Indians. In allowing Jackson Barnett and others to be heard and thereby give witness to their full humanity, the Senate subcommittee performed a credible service.[46]

10

The Gilded Cage
1926–1938

The government is suing an old "injun" from Oklahoma. They claim he was "out of his head" because he gave his wife money, and they want her to give it back, not to the Indian, but to the government. . . .

[I]f the government wins this, the next case you hear of will be: "The U.S. Government vs. Mrs. Will Rogers," in behalf of another Indian ward of the government, Will Rogers, who has been out of his head at various times since November, 1908. . . .

If the government gets anything back from her, I am willing to split with 'em on the usual government basis, U.S. taking 80 percent, citizen 20 percent.
—WILL ROGERS

B ounteous wealth from Oklahoma oil royalties carried the Barnetts to Los Angeles, where they embraced the luxurious lifestyle of multimillionaires. But the wife of the World's Richest Indian was not entirely free from anxiety. The $2,500 monthly allowance—which in 2002 dollars would be comparable to $25,000 each month—purchased the symbols of status and fortune; it did not furnish permanent security. As major legal battles were lost on the East Coast and political support from Washington eroded, Anna Barnett's spendthrift habits, combined with speculation in Los Angeles real estate and escalating legal expenses, ushered in financial difficulties within three short years of the Barnetts' arrival in Los Angeles in 1923. Once buoyed by the sympathetic support of Charles Burke, after 1928–1929, Anna was bereft of powerful allies in the federal government and lacked the deep pockets to hire lawyers to defend her interests. Alone, Anna faced the wrath of the Justice Department.

In 1926 the Barnetts had moved into their opulent, eighteen-room, colonial mansion in the prestigious Hancock Park neighborhood. Though initially homesick for Oklahoma, Jackson soon came to enjoy the material

*The Barnetts' eighteen-room mansion at the corner of Wilshire and Rossmore in Los
Angeles. Jackson can be seen to the left of the driveway. A culmination of Anna
Barnett's ambitions for wealth and status, this home was completed in 1926 in the
prestigious Hancock Park neighborhood, where Lillian Gish and other wealthy
celebrities lived in the 1920s. Jackson lived here until his death in 1934. Anna and her
daughter, Maxine, lived here until they were evicted in 1938. The home was destroyed
in the 1960s. Courtesy of the Carl Albert Center, Congressional Archives, University of
Oklahoma.*

comforts and pleasures of Los Angeles life. The Barnetts went to the race
track, the beach, the movies, and seaside amusement parks. Jackson fished
and kept ponies at his 107-acre ranch in Coldwater Canyon. A chauffeur
awaited his command to drive him to his stables. Jackson enjoyed an entire wing of his colonial mansion for his personal use. Spending money
jingled in his pocket. He liked the diet in California, which included mel-
ons and oranges, and the simple daily pleasure of fixing snacks in the well-
stocked kitchen. Anna kept him immaculately groomed. To the world, he
looked every bit the confident, contented millionaire, an image enforced
by his passion for smoking cigars and his habit of smiling broadly. Anna
described Jackson's routine in Los Angeles: "He went to the beach on Saturday as a rule and he played on the concessions and he was very lucky.

. . . Sometimes he would come home with bushel baskets of groceries and things he had won. He was such a perfect pitcher and shot; he attracted large crowds and they were glad to see him come."[1]

The Barnetts became prominent as well as wealthy Angelenos. Jackson Barnett was a popular tourist attraction in the mid-1920s. He enjoyed directing traffic on Wilshire Boulevard in front of his home, which he frequently did for three to four hours a day. Jackson's harmless eccentricity and affable charm made him a beloved local icon. For eight years, the well-groomed millionaire Creek Indian from Oklahoma, dressed smartly in expensive three-piece suits and white gloves, was Los Angeles's version of Eiler Larsen, Laguna Beach's colorful "greeter." The World's Richest Indian was featured in Los Angeles guide books and was even part of the itinerary for a mid-1920s bus tour through the city. Tourists could admire Jackson Barnett's palatial home and those of his Hancock Park neighbors, such as Hollywood stars Harold Lloyd and the Gish sisters and producer Sam Warner. Particularly lucky tourists had an opportunity to observe Jackson Barnett directing traffic.[2]

The judge who performed the Barnett marriage ceremony in Kansas was among the many who witnessed Jackson performing his public service as citizen traffic controller. The judge reported that, as he drove past Rossmore, Jackson "flagged me down, and after the other fellow passed then he motioned for me to go on."[3] Anna said that the first thing Jackson would do in the morning was cross the street to direct some traffic. Afterward, he would go to the ranch in Coldwater Canyon to take care of his horses. He enjoyed taking the bus and often went to the movies or ate lunch downtown, took a nap, then directed some more traffic. He crossed Wilshire Boulevard a dozen times a day. Asked in court, "How long would he stay out directing traffic?" Anna replied, "In the afternoon sometimes until seven o'clock. He would come in and have supper."

> Q: And it got to be one of the sights of Los Angeles seeing a crazy man directing traffic?
> A: Everyone loved his kindly gesture, and his pleasing smile was a grand sight for tourists who appreciated his undertaking.
> Q: He was helping out the police officers?
> A: He certainly was.[4]

Whether Jackson was doing anything useful is debatable, but the police indulged his whimsical behavior. One person who recalled seeing Jackson in the early 1930s said his traffic-control activities were largely ceremonial. Jackson stood on the curb on the northwest corner of the intersection, which was opposite his mansion. He gestured with his arms to guide traffic on Wilshire or Rossmore. There might have been a signal there, "which meant that traffic was obeying the signal and not Barnett, but he seemed blissfully unaware of the fact. My family had heard, Heaven knows from where, that his wife pushed him out of the house every morn-

Jackson Barnett at one of his favorite hobbies, directing traffic on Wilshire Boulevard across the street from his home, in the early 1930s, shortly before his death. Courtesy of the Los Angeles Herald Examiner *Collection, Los Angeles Public Library.*

ing and his traffic direction was all he had to do. People smiled at him as they drove by and often waved."[5]

Anna's enemies argued that Jackson—kidnapped and coerced into marriage—was being held captive in a "gilded cage." Anna's rejoinder was much more plausible. When she eloped with Jackson, he was living in a three-room, dirt-floor shack, a gross and incomprehensible condition given his fortune. She had lifted him up to his true station in life. As a de-

voted wife, she had liberated Jackson from a life of neglect and from an exploitative Oklahoma guardian and had given the aging Indian the happiest
days of his life. "I gave my husband the first shave he ever had and bought
him the first good suit he ever wore," Anna reported.[6] Anna told a *San
Francisco Chronicle* reporter in 1934: "I have used his money to make him
comfortable. . . . I taught him to enjoy his millions. He went horseback
riding by day and got to know all the big movie stars by sight. . . . And
they call me an adventuress because I married him and made him happy
and healthy. What's the use of being a good faithful wife?"[7] To her way of
thinking, any right-minded person could see that the gilded cage analogy
was patently preposterous.

Truly, the idea of someone being kidnapped into a life of luxury was a
hard sell. Secretary of the Interior Hubert Work made light of Senator
Wheeler's characterization of the situation, saying, "We all know that men
of almost any color sometimes stand around waiting to be kidnapped."[8]
Jackson repeatedly testified that he was quite content with his life in Los
Angeles. He was proud of his home with its electric lights, bathtub, radio,
piano, phonograph, and oil painting of himself over the mantle. Harold
McGugin—then being sued for the $67,000 he had received of Anna's
$550,000 "gift" from her husband—audaciously claimed partial credit for
raising Jackson's standard of living. It is, he said, "with personal pride that
I look upon my services which took [Jackson Barnett] from squalor and
penury to luxury and comfort."[9] Anna went even further, taking credit for
the long-sought solution of raising Indians from poverty: "If I kidnapped
him, the government ought to hire other women like me to go out and
kidnap the rest of the Indians."[10]

Though the gilded cage metaphor falters in describing Jackson Barnett's life in Los Angeles, it is an apt description of the legal structure that
Anna temporarily used to hold captive the wealth of the World's Richest
Indian. Despite her bravado and unflagging legal maneuvers to prevent it,
the door to the gilded cage was slowly wedged open, and the bird of fortune threatened to fly. The fairy-tale life of the Barnetts—for all its apparent security, grace, ease, and luxury—was ephemeral.

Anna Barnett began having money problems in 1925. Between 1923
and 1925, she had acquired eight tracts of land in Los Angeles and claimed
"from two years' active trading in Los Angeles real estate, I have two million dollars worth of property." Though she may have been rich on paper,
she could not meet her mortgage payments because the guardian's litigation blocked her access to money from the trusts.[11]

Mounting legal expenses drained Anna's resources. For the quarter of
a century after her marriage to Jackson Barnett, she was continuously engaged in litigation, usually with multiple contests in different jurisdictions
going on simultaneously. Anna was compelled to hire legal firms in each
venue to monitor suits across the country. She had no fewer than fourteen
legal firms working for her during the intensely litigious period from 1920

to 1938; the number of individual lawyers she hired and fired probably reached two dozen or more. Marshall Mott and Charles Rogers conducted the multisuit defense of the trusts. She contracted to pay them $50,000 if her suits were successful.[12]

As the prospects for favorable resolutions for Anna Barnett diminished, lawyers became less willing to work on contingency. They demanded retainers or wrote to the Interior Department asking for direct payments for their services from Jackson Barnett's assets. Anna Barnett and her lawyers, in Jackson's name, made urgent requests for funds for legal costs in 1926 and 1927. When she faced a $10,000 demand from her Washington, D.C., lawyers in the spring of 1927, she became very upset. Anna demanded results, and when she did not get what she wanted, she blamed the failures on the lawyers and sometimes refused to pay them. Nor did she have qualms about resorting to subterfuge: she tried to get money from Jackson's assets to pay a "debt" (which in fact was a retainer to a lawyer), insisting Interior was obliged to pay Jackson's legitimate debts out of his restricted funds.[13]

Burke and the Interior Department initially heard Anna Laura Barnett's financial appeals with sympathy. When the Barnett allowances were blocked, Commissioner Burke arranged for direct payments of the disputed funds to the Barnetts by Interior, thus bypassing the appointed guardian. Burke believed that the Interior Department had the discretionary authority to dispense Barnett's funds for reasonable needs, including legal fees, using Jackson Barnett's surplus funds deposited in federal bank accounts. When Rogers appealed for $5,000 of Jackson's money in late 1927, Burke approved the expenditure, but Interior would only allow $1,500.[14]

Anna Barnett obtained much of the money she needed for litigation from special allowances. From 1926 to 1929, Burke routinely approved periodic expenditures from Jackson's oil royalties for vacations, luxury automobiles, and furniture. For their Christmas holidays in 1927 and 1928, for example, the Barnetts were allocated $4,000.[15] Burke probably knew Anna used some of this money for legal costs, and Selby and other members of the Justice defense team angrily suspected it. That Burke surreptitiously channeled money out of the account is suggested in a memorandum requesting a $2,000 disbursement. "No publicity," Burke instructed the acting superintendent of the Union Agency. The Justice Department's persecutions and bad faith, Burke later testified, gave him "no other choice" but to engage in such secretive methods to support the Barnetts' defense of the trusts. Paradoxically, the Interior Department was funneling money to Anna Barnett from funds impounded within the federal government to defeat the suits brought against her by the Justice Department.[16]

The Justice Department gradually tightened the noose around Anna's access to Jackson's funds, but it could not cut her off completely. All financial transfers were carefully scrutinized by the Justice Department, especially those suspected of funding opposition to its lawsuits against Anna. In late 1928, Senator Pine even objected to the Barnetts' receiving their $2,500 monthly allowances. After Burke's resignation and the accession of new Interior appointees in the Hoover and Roosevelt administrations, the monthly allowances continued, as did periodic supplemental awards for vacations and other expenses. The merits of each request for extra funds were weighed individually.[17]

After 1926, the Interior Department approved several expenditures from Jackson's federal bank accounts to pay for overdue mortgages and taxes on Anna and Jackson Barnett's many properties. If the federal government did not pay, the Barnett assets would be lost via default, opening the department to the charge of failing to conserve the restricted Indian's property. One four-acre tract off Beverly Boulevard was foreclosed, and Anna lost her $8,000 initial investment. From 1926 to 1928, the Muskogee farm, the Coldwater Canyon property, and the home in Hancock Park were threatened with foreclosure. Interior was continually engaged in rescue operations, stepping in to pay the balances due from Jackson's impounded funds. When the Muskogee farm went into default in late 1926, for example, Jackson Barnett made a personal request that his funds held by Interior be used to pay the balance of $11,042.26. The property was in Anna Barnett's name; she had $26,600 invested in it. Interior paid the note, but required Anna to sign a promissory note to her husband at 8 percent interest.[18]

Because some of this property was in Anna Barnett's name—or because Anna was trying to put it in her name to maintain control should the marriage be annulled—these financial operations were handled circumspectly by Interior and were studied closely by Justice. In 1928 Anna Barnett requested $142,244.46 to pay off the Coldwater Canyon property, which she claimed was worth $259,710.[19] Skeptical about her exaggerations and her methods, Burke requested a report on the value of the California property: "I want to know whether there is any real equity in it. No one can depend on anything that Mrs. Barnett represents."[20] When the bailouts occurred on the Coldwater Canyon acreage, the title was carefully transferred to Interior as trustee for Jackson Barnett.[21]

Anna's propensity to lie, the real estate imbroglios, the close oversight by Justice, and the worsening political situation combined to tighten Interior's grip on the Barnett purse strings. Burke demanded to see copies of bills for attorneys' fees and refused to pay Mott's or Rogers's fees in the unsuccessful *Equitable* case. Anna's subsequent evasions and lies under oath before the Senate subcommittee regarding her legal expenses bolstered opinions of her bad character already established in the minds of committee members. Burke's diversion of funds to Anna Barnett to defend the trusts was under intense scrutiny. Anna tactfully concealed information about her legal contracts, except when she saw a personal advantage not to do so.[22]

Justice Department investigator Pierce Butler's recommendation in March 1929 gave the green light for Justice to proceed in the federal district court against Anna Barnett. *United States v. Anna Laura Barnett, Leslie R. Hewitt, and Bank of Italy, National Trust and Savings Institute* sought to annul her marriage and to recover the $200,000 she had obtained in Liberty Bonds via the gift donation. This suit sought the return of any property acquired with this money and to block Anna's inheritance of any part of Jackson's estate. Butler averred that the gifts from Barnett's funds were not "for the benefit and use of Barnett." Although payments to the wife for reasonable maintenance and support might be construed as such, the payment, Butler said, had been taken from him and given to her "free of him;" therefore, "It is good policy to set aside the marriage and permit inheritance of Barnett's wealth by whatever Indians may establish themselves as his heirs." The same month the Butler report appeared, Interior denied Anna's request for money for a new Cadillac and a $50,000 trip abroad. The U.S. attorney in Los Angeles recommended that passports for the Barnetts be withheld; the attorney general and secretary of state agreed. Anna Barnett had become a flight risk.[23]

From 1930 to 1932 the legal picture grew grimmer for Anna. Her strongest argument for sustaining the gift from Jackson—the Interior Department's discretionary power to make the donation—was weakened by the 1931 U.S. Supreme Court decision in *Mott v. United States.* Her financial straits prevented her from paying retainers to top legal talent. Prospects for hiring lawyers on contingency dimmed. As the Great Depression reduced real estate values, the potential income via sales or mortgages on properties she held in her name in Los Angeles also declined. Most devastating, however, was the loss of her alliance with the Interior Department. Indian bureau officials, having come perilously close to being indicted for fraud, were no doubt anxious to distance themselves from Anna's cause. Selby meanwhile spent eight years relentlessly building a case against her, which consisted of hundreds of depositions and a massive volume of government documents and correspondence.

Anna's relationship with the Interior Department steadily worsened as the trial to defend her marriage, her inheritance, and her Los Angeles real estate holdings approached. Her desperation brought out the worst in her character, leaving her further estranged from officials in the federal government. In January 1932, when she requested $5,000 for a new automobile, the department insisted on supervising the purchase. Anna refused the terms they specified for the expenditure, and an ugly confrontation with the local federal official sent to supervise the transaction ensued. Several months later, the Interior secretary and Anna Barnett were still haggling over the car purchase.[24]

By the early 1930s, the Justice and Interior departments were speaking with one voice. They now shared the view that Anna's attempts to get additional funds for legal fees and to obtain free and clear legal property titles had to be blocked. Payment for $50,000 for her attorneys was refused. When she demanded an investigation into how Selby and Lacy, counsel in the Los Angeles case, were being paid, she was informed they were government officials whose salaries were paid by taxpayers.[25]

Her incessant demands to Interior for money denied and her maneuverings thwarted, Anna became abusive. In the spring of 1932, Interior Secretary Lyman Wilbur received several complaints, allegedly written by Jackson Barnett but composed by Anna, containing intemperate comments with scurrilous asides. Wilbur sought advice on how to respond. Attorney general Mitchell told him to ignore all of Anna's telegrams and correspondence. Frustrated at the lack of response, Anna wrote a belligerent note to Wilbur, telling him she would not tolerate any interference with her real estate.[26]

When the Hancock Park home went into default in 1932, Interior had to come to the rescue. Wary of Anna, the federal government would only pay off the note on the condition that Jackson's ultimate guardian, the Interior Department, hold the title in trust, pending the outcome of the government's lawsuit against Anna. This would ensure that the property after Jackson's death would go to his legitimate heirs, who were yet to be determined. Anna refused. A 1932 telegram to Interior, signed by Jackson Barnett, requested $25,000 to pay off the Hancock Park mortgage to prevent foreclosure. "We deserve only the cash. We will not consider for a moment a mortgage or transfer of the title of the property," she telegrammed. Eventually, the department agreed to pay off the outstanding taxes and debts on the Barnetts' mansion, probably negotiating a promissory note between Anna and her husband, as it had with the Muskogee property.[27] These precautions proved ineffective. Anna surreptitiously borrowed $25,000 against the Hancock Park home and engaged in other maneuvers to preserve title in her name. In February 1933, the Justice Department ordered the property title delivered to Interior for safekeeping. Infuriated, Anna threatened to sue Secretary Wilbur. "The attempted theft of the Barnett estate, is the greatest attempted theft ever attempted," Anna charged.[28]

In early 1933, the Justice Department was ready to try its case against Anna Barnett in federal district court in Los Angeles. On this litigation hinged Anna's right to any of the Barnetts' real property, including the Coldwater Canyon acreage and the Hancock Park home. The government's case rested on two main arguments. The first was that Jackson Barnett was mentally incompetent. The second was that Anna had engaged in multiple illegal acts—bribery, seduction of a mental incompetent, payoffs, kidnapping, misrepresentation—in a well-planned conspiracy to abscond with Jackson Barnett's money. From the former flowed the argument that the marriage was not legal. From the latter, the government held that Anna had no right to inherit any of Jackson's assets. Anna Barnett and codefendant Leslie Hewitt, Jackson's guardian appointed by the Los Angeles County court, made several counterarguments. The Interior Department had legal authority to approve the donations and create the trusts; Interior's action was not reviewable by the courts (this argument was subsequently discarded when the Pollock and Kennamer district court rulings were reversed); and Jackson Barnett was competent (at least until July 1924, when the Los Angeles Superior Court had declared him incompetent). Further, they argued, the federal government lacked jurisdiction over the marriage relationship. Anna had acted continually in Jackson's best interests and bettered his material condition; Jackson wished to continue in their happy marriage; and the contested assets belonged to her as they had been purchased with the profits from her real estate investments.[29]

Angelenos followed the newspaper coverage of the sensational story during the depositions phase in 1932 and the trial, which began in February 1933. Anna became progressively more shrill and desperate. Understandably, she was humiliated by some of the testimony publicly aired in the Los Angeles courtroom, which painted her as a shameless gold digger and delved into the intimate details of her courtship with Jackson. "She worked him over plenty," testified Johnson, the taxi driver whom Anna had bribed for his help in getting Jackson to a justice of the peace.[30] To the delight of onlookers and the press, numerous outbursts punctuated the proceedings as Anna interrupted testimony with angry disclaimers. After graphic descriptions by witnesses of Anna's ardent wooing of Jackson Barnett in the back seat of the getaway car, a trembling Anna leaped to her feet and screamed: "I appeal to Your Honor to halt this farce . . . [,] a conspiracy on the part of bankers and politicians to get control of the Chief's estate. They are fighting us with our own money and have defrauded us."[31] Anna and her lawyer stressed that the legal attack on her was politically motivated. "We have been persecuted and prosecuted for thirteen years," Anna told a reporter, choking back tears. Her lawyer argued, "Jackson Barnett has been but the pawn in a long political game."[32]

Angelenos found the federal government's determination to annul the Barnetts' long-term marriage hard to fathom. Theirs was a classic Creek union: a marriage of opposites. While she was as contentious as he was compliant, their marriage worked to the betterment of both lives. To the public, this litigation was unnecessarily cruel and unfair to a woman who faithfully cared for her elderly and quite possibly senile husband. Hazel White, a neighbor and member of the local Indian Welfare Committee and the Federated Women's Clubs, supported Anna in a 1932 letter to Commissioner of Indian Affairs Charles Rhoads. The Barnetts, White maintained, "are quiet inoffensive residents in my own neighborhood and have come to be well-known figures to all Los Angeles." Rhoads replied with a lengthy explanation of why the federal government opposed Anna Barnett, but Los Angeles residents remained perplexed by the intricate Barnett scandal.[33]

The Los Angeles trial took a heavy toll on Anna. A photograph taken in 1933 shows a woman frayed and depressed by the relentless downward

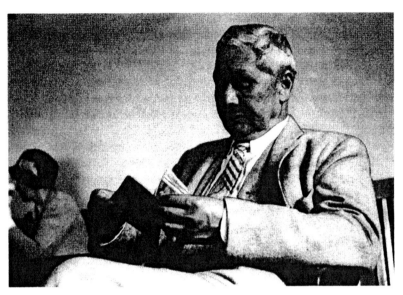

In court in 1932, as he had many times before, Jackson Barnett was required to count money as a test of his competency to handle his fortune. Asked by an attorney to produce the money he had with him, Jackson hesitated until Anna said it was all right and then counted correctly two $50 bills and five $20 bills, a large sum of pocket money in the years of the Great Depression. Jackson Barnett grew bored with this routine and would play tricks on his interrogators. Courtesy of the Los Angeles Herald Examiner *Collection, Los Angeles Public Library.*

spiral of events. Jackson, a veteran of the legal system, endured the proceedings with grace and even seemed to enjoy his celebrity, often waving grandly to the courtroom audience. His wealth had come unbidden and effortlessly, and he enjoyed it with matter-of-fact simplicity and innocence. A man of simple integrity, he had made a decision to marry and did not swerve from his commitment, nor did Anna. "I'm glad she got my money. She's a good wife. She gets me shaved and keeps my hair cut," Jackson Barnett told a government attorney. "Indians get married like other people. Why don't you let us alone?"[34]

As he had done during his testimony before the Senate subcommittee, Jackson revealed his sense of humor and reversed the tables on those who wished to portray him as a simpleton. He periodically made wry observations and played tricks in the courtroom. While giving testimony regarding his financial competency, Jackson was given money to count. Tired of the same routine, he began improvising. On one occasion, after the exercise was completed, Jackson pocketed the bank notes, flustering the lawyer: "Hey, that's mine, not yours. You're to count it." On another occasion, he said, "Now I ask one," and he drew a fifty-cent piece from his pocket and asked the Justice lawyers to identify it. Suspecting a trick, they warily examined it before venturing that it looked like a half dollar. Jackson gaily laughed and said, "Sure!"[35]

Anna Barnett's case was not without merit, and she audaciously continued to make demands on Interior for money. In a hopeful mood, Anna traveled to Washington, D.C., in early 1933 to persuade the new Democratic administration of the justness of her cause and to get money for her defense. She was denied access to top officials, but gained an audience with an administrative assistant in Interior from whom she demanded $35,000: $5,000 for a Cadillac, $10,000 for the balance on a mortgage, $5,000 for interior and exterior repairs on the Hancock Park home, and $15,000 for construction and improvements at the Coldwater Canyon ranch.[36] During the visit, Mrs. Barnett also appeared at the court where the *Riggs* suit was being tried. The Justice Department was seeking to recover the $200,000 she had placed in a Riggs trust fund. Her former lawyer would not proceed with the case without a retainer of $5,000 and, lacking legal representation, she obtained a continuance. After considering this conundrum, the new Secretary of the Interior, Harold Ickes, refused to authorize any expenditure from Jackson's funds to pay for Anna's legal expenses. If Anna Barnett wanted to preserve the trust, she must use her own money. Thousands of dollars of Jackson Barnett's restricted funds had already been paid out to Mrs. Barnett for extra expenditures, said Ickes. It was not in Jackson Barnett's interests to "defeat the action pending here."[37]

This refusal for money in her time of dire need by the new Democratic administration fueled Anna Barnett's rage and paranoia. In March 1933, Anna, likely drunk, wrote a rambling and raving letter to Ickes. She and her husband, Anna said, were perfectly capable of spending their funds as they saw fit. Ickes should know she was not an "Indian hag" but the "wife of the wealthiest Indian [and] the best one of the Indians." This intemperate outburst infuriated Secretary Ickes, who immediately refused all payments of money—including travel expenses already authorized—although there was $832,000 impounded in Jackson's government accounts in 1933. He was later compelled to make some extra allowances to the Barnetts and backed down from his earlier reaction.[38]

Anna's nasty letters, filled with vicious anti-Semitic remarks, curses, and threats, earned her Harold Ickes's permanent enmity. In July 1933, based on what he superficially understood about the incredibly complex case, Ickes concluded that Interior officials probably were involved in a conspiracy to defraud Barnett. Moreover, in a letter to attorney general Cummings, Ickes asked that Mrs. Barnett be indicted for criminal conspiracy. He wanted Selby—suffering from cancer—kept on the case as the great bulk of the litigation was still pending: the *Riggs*, *McGugin*, and *Anna Barnett* cases.[39] Ickes provoked Anna's most venomous responses. In one of a series of vituperative letters, some in her name and others signed

"Jackson Barnett," she vowed she would revel in the time when all political gangsters were "dragged out by the neck" and given all that they had coming to them.[40] Such immoderate language accompanied irrational demands for money for trips, automobiles, furniture, an airplane, and Christmas expenses. Ickes refused these requests and renewed his call for Anna Barnett's criminal prosecution. But by early 1934, the statute of limitations had expired.[41]

During the 1920s, Anna had presented herself as a proud and sophisticated millionaire's wife, but by the early 1930s she repeatedly made wild statements to reporters. She threatened and even physically confronted persons she described as "gangsters," "thugs," and "hags," who were conspiring to destroy her. Politicians, bankers, and lawyers were looting the Barnett estate, she claimed.[42] From 1934 to 1938, her accusations were angry and paranoid.

In December 1933, a representative of Jackson's Creek relatives approached Anna with a settlement proposal. Each of fourteen claimants, descendants of Siah Barnett, would accept $10,000 from Anna in return for dropping their claims against the estate. Senator Thomas, one of her most stalwart political supporters, urged her to work out a compromise with the Indian bureau. Anna refused, denying these "imposters" would ever get a penny of Jackson's fortune.[43]

In March 1934, federal Judge William P. James annulled the Barnetts' marriage. James based his decision on the mountain of detailed evidence Selby had amassed regarding the alleged kidnapping, Jackson Barnett's incapacity to make sound choices, Anna's bad moral character, her schemes to defraud the estate in collusion with others, and the important precedents set by the 1927 Knox decision and the 1931 *Mott* decision. He held that the secretary of the Interior had no power to make donations of an incompetent Indian's property. Like many before him, he was captivated by the sensationalist stories of Anna's seduction of Jackson Barnett, calling the entire situation a "comedy-tragedy."[44] He wrote:

> Mrs. Lowe [Anna Barnett] is a woman of great determination of character, and possessed of considerable business and executive ability. Unfortunate it is that she could not have turned her attention to some more legitimate enterprise, having an object not directly in conflict with the government's duty with respect to its Indian subjects. . . . The fact alone that she married Barnett because of his wealth, would not entitle her to great condemnation, for we know that such a motive is of considerable influence in actuating many women when they embark upon marital ventures. Where the man is sane and capable of exercising reasonable judgment, such bargains are at his own discretion and risk. . . . That Mrs. Lowe ever entertained real affection for the husband is not to be believed. She at no time during the trial affirmed any

such feeling. Besides it is not reasonable that she should have had such sentiment. At the time of the alleged marriage ceremonies she was a woman in her thirties; Barnett was already an aging man, a black Indian. Mrs. Lowe, as photographs show, was at the time an attractive-looking woman, one who would likely encounter many a prepossessing man of the white race who would become interested in her.[45]

James found no basis for any of Anna's arguments. In his view, Jackson was a below-average Creek, and no witness from the local neighborhood rebutted the testimony regarding Jackson Barnett's substandard intelligence. During the trial, Barnett "appeared to be a simple old Indian of gentle disposition, unconcerned with what was going on about him," James stated. "The chief fault that may be found in the handling of him by Mrs. Lowe, is that she brought him far away from his own country and people and established him in a mansion." The judge found it hard to believe Barnett would want to live in a mansion, ride in a chauffeured limousine, or direct traffic "in a childish way."[46] That Jackson was content in his marriage was not a salient issue for James.

James ordered all property acquired by Anna since the marriage to be returned to the Interior Department to be held in trust for Jackson's heirs. According to the order, Jackson Barnett's $200,000 gift to his wife (that is, the portion of the original $550,000 gift to Anna not placed in the Riggs trust nor paid to McGugin, Keith, or Mott for legal services) was null and void and must be returned to Interior. This meant the Hancock Park home, Coldwater Canyon acreage, and all furniture, fixtures, autos, horses, and personal property was forfeit. Anna's marriage to Jackson, the will of 1923 naming her as beneficiary, and Hewitt's guardianship were voided. In a patronizing concession to Jackson Barnett's wishes and to Mrs. Barnett, James said that it would be "without the slightest reproach of moral impropriety" for Anna to continue to act as the aging Jackson's caretaker and to enjoy his monthly allowances—although the couple were no longer legally married. Her nursing and housekeeping would be strictly supervised by the local federal Indian superintendent. With predictable outrage, Anna vowed to appeal and snorted: "Our marriage illegal— h[arr]umph for that!" The "chief" is "good for another fifty years yet."[47]

An Interior Department lawyer analyzing the decision doubted the James opinion would be the final word. Anna would most certainly appeal, and the James decision very likely could be overturned. He wrote that there was no general rule for measuring with precision the degree of mental imbecility necessary to vitiate a marriage contract. "It is safe to say, however, that comprehension of the marriage relations and its duties and responsibility does not require a particularly strong mentality and it is not beyond the realm of possibility that the appellate court may disagree with the findings of the trial court on this point." Because the strong possibility for a reversal existed, said the attorney, the department could not proceed safely with any action to disturb the marriage relations. Using euphemistic language that anticipated yet another kidnapping of Jackson Barnett, the lawyer coldly advised Interior to lay plans to separate the couple and take possession of Jackson Barnett should James's decision be affirmed by the higher courts.[48] Despite these cautions and Judge James's recommendation to continue the $2,500 monthly allowances, Ickes gave orders to immediately suspend payment of the allowances.

Senator Thomas interceded in Anna's behalf, requesting the Indian bureau continue liberal allowances to benefit Jackson in his last years. Perhaps unknowingly, Thomas was proposing to do in 1934 what Burke had been repudiated for doing: creating a charitable trust to prevent the dissipation of the estate in heirship proceedings. As everyone familiar with Jackson Barnett's case had understood since 1919, Thomas wrote to Commissioner of Indian Affairs John Collier, Jackson's estate upon his death would become "a juicy plum for the lawyers and others who are now conspiring to divide the estate." Thomas wrote:

> It also occurs to me that if Barnett could be induced to place all or a large portion of his funds in trust for the benefit of Indian hospitals or Indian education, that this would be in harmony with good public policy. Otherwise, the estate will, in my opinion, be divided up among unscrupulous firms of attorneys who are now eagerly awaiting the passing of Barnett.[49]

II

The Battle of Wilshire Boulevard

On May 29, 1934, seventy-eight-year-old Jackson Barnett died in his
sleep from heart disease. Front-page news accounts across the nation wove hyperbole, ignorance, romanticism, agism, sexism, and
racism into a story for popular consumption. The *New York Times* reported that Jackson was born a half-wit in a miserable hogan (Navajo
housing). He was referred to as a "Copper-skinned Croesus" who directed
traffic, "a perpetually grinning moron [who] . . . acquired new clothes,
false teeth, had been forced by his wife into taking occasional baths." The
Muskogee Daily Phoenix's assessment of Jackson Barnett's life story and his
character was closer to the mark: "Jackson Barnett's Indian fortune is one
that has rocked national administrations, brought on senatorial investigations and demands for cabinet resignations. Jackson alone of the principals
concerned in the million dollar litigations has remained calm and undis-
turbed as the drama of human greed broke about his aged head. . . . He
sipped of that which he approved and ignored that which disturbed the
tranquility of his childlike mind."[1]

In death as in life, the body of Jackson Barnett was contested. The last
person to want to see Jackson Barnett dead—Anna—was preposterously
accused of poisoning her husband. In an anticlimax, the autopsy confirmed that Jackson died of natural causes. After an alleged 500 Creeks met

at the Old Council House at Okmulgee, a Creek resolution demanded the return of Jackson's body to Oklahoma. On behalf of Jimmy Barnett and other Creek heir-apparents, Jackson's Okmulgee County guardian George Riley Hall also protested the burial in Los Angeles: "He should not be buried on what to him is foreign soil." Anna's plans to bury Jackson at Forest Lawn Cemetery in Glendale on June 1 were interrupted by telegraphed instructions from John Collier, commissioner of Indian affairs, to stay the interment. Superintendent John W. Dady and Jack Meyers of the Mission Indian Agency rushed to Los Angeles to secure the postponement. Over Anna Barnett's vociferous protests, Pierce Brothers Mortuary put the body of Jackson Barnett in cold storage.[2]

Collier decided to have Jackson buried in the Barnett family cemetery at Bryant, telegraphing, "Ship the Barnett body at once by express." Anna Barnett ignored her attorney and Collier's orders. She obtained a temporary restraining order in Los Angeles Superior Court, claiming it would cause her "great mental anguish" if Jackson's body were removed to Oklahoma. Her success in controlling Jackson's corpse was viewed as a victory in establishing herself as his legal widow. Meanwhile, the mortuary refused to release the body to anyone without a court order. Faced with the iron determination of Anna Laura Barnett, the federal government wavered. After a conference between the Indian bureau and Justice Department representatives, the U.S. attorney's office in Los Angeles won a reversal of the restraining order. Superintendent Dady authorized the funeral services to proceed.[3]

On June 7, 1934, the "sachem of Wilshire Boulevard," as a Los Angeles paper referred to him, was laid to rest at Hollywood Memorial Cemetery alongside Tyrone Power, Rudolf Valentino, and other Hollywood celebrities. Like other vanishing Indians, Jackson Barnett had made his way to "the happy hunting grounds." The Episcopalian minister who conducted the ceremony intoned: "We commend his soul to the Great Spirit." A number of Creeks who were hostile to Anna, as well as some curious onlookers, attended the funeral. The Indian bureau allowed Jackson's body to be buried at a location selected by Anna Barnett, although it attached the concession that "in the event she is determined not to have been the wife of said Jackson Barnett, the body will be disinterred and removed to Oklahoma" to a place selected by Barnett's lawful heirs. Anna's reasonable request for a $1,475 marble memorial headstone to mark Jackson Barnett's grave was refused, presumably on the theory that the body would ultimately be moved. Even in death, the Creek Indian was not safe from removal. Only $41 for a humble bronze memorial tablet was authorized for the World's Richest Indian, a suitably unpretentious plaque for the grave of the modest Jackson Barnett.[4]

The annulment of the Barnett marriage and Jackson Barnett's death in 1934 immediately severed Anna's access to funds from his estate. Despite bleak odds for her inheritance, Anna nonetheless fought for her widow's rights. Just as she fought pugnaciously for Jackson's body, she pressed for the continuation of the $2,500 monthly allowances in the face of Ickes's opposition. With "a will of her own" (dated August 24, 1923), she sought control of the fortune as legal heir. When her May 1934 check was cut to a mere $50, she invoked revolutionary rhetoric: "Give me liberty or give me death." She insisted she was and would always be Mrs. Jackson Barnett, a loyal wife of fourteen years and a victim of state interference into the private family affairs of U.S. citizens. At the very least she had rights as a common-law wife.[5]

Anna's fight evoked the sympathy of the Los Angeles courts and the community at large. The Los Angeles Artists' Foundation publicly supported Anna, and several women's clubs took her cause to heart. Even after her most crushing legal defeat and her husband's death, Anna could hold on to the silver lining of a legal loophole: because Jackson's death occurred between the time of the decision and the formal decree, Jackson had died before the marriage was formally annulled. Anna's hopes soared after a spirited 1934 hearing in Los Angeles probate court. Judge Charles Crail responded favorably to her plea to administer the estate as the couple's joint property was under the jurisdiction of California law. He was persuaded that Anna had a large personal investment in the Los Angeles real estate at issue. Its value was wildly inflated to $24 million, and Anna claimed that her share, due to her investments, was approximately $2 million. Crail thought that taking money from a woman who had cared for a man for fourteen years in order to "give it to Indians that Barnett never saw before" was "odd." Judge Crail also supported Anna's lawsuit against John Dady, the federal Indian bureau superintendent of southern California's Mission Indian Agency assigned to oversee the Barnett estate. Anna demanded payment of $3,668.85 in withheld allowances and threatened to have Dady jailed if he didn't comply. In early July, Crail ordered the $2,500 allowance be resumed for three months. Anna found refuge in the state courts with the argument that the federal court had no jurisdiction to nullify marriages between U.S. citizens. Ironically, in her appeal she cited *In the Matter of Heff*, the Supreme Court ruling that Burke had labored against in order to protect Indians from the state courts.[6]

In early July, the federal government reasserted its authority. A federal court nullified the will filed in Crail's probate court, which had given Anna authority to administer the estate. It ordered that Anna surrender all real property and legal claims to being the wife of Jackson Barnett. But, in typical style, Anna was back in Crail's court a week later to demand back allowances. Judge Crail challenged the federal decision: "Everybody knows that [Barnett] was kept clean, well fed, well dressed and happy."[7] Justice Department lawyers appeared in appellate court to block Crail from insisting on the payment of $3,668.85 to Anna. The Ninth District Court of Appeals issued an order restraining Judge Crail from proceeding further in the matter. All allowances due Jackson Barnett were suspended indefinitely. Muskogee judge O. Brewer bent to federal authority and surrendered probate of the estate to the federal courts.

When federal district judge James issued his formal decision annulling the marriage, Anna vowed to continue to fight: "I know there is justice in this world and I shall keep what belongs to me." She brought a motion for a new trial, based on purportedly new and authoritative evidence of Jackson's competency. Anna received encouragement from federal judge Robert Williams, who said he would not be bound by Judge James's court ruling and would give a fair hearing to Anna Barnett's claim to inheritance of the Jackson Barnett estate in his federal court in Oklahoma, where the heirship case would be decided.[8]

There were occasional, encouraging signs that Anna might be able to reverse the James decision, maintain her allowances, and inherit Jackson's estate. Soon after Judge James's decision, Congressman McGugin tried to make an out-of-court settlement, offering to surrender $20,000 of the $67,000 he had received. By late 1934, having gained some clarity about the disadvantageous situation she was in, Anna Barnett also entertained the idea of a compromise. Her lawyer suggested a settlement to Interior: she would turn over 20 percent of the funds in the Riggs trust in return for the retention of the remainder by herself. Though her cause was lost, she could still create nuisance litigation. Secretary Ickes refused to consider either settlement. He wanted to prosecute. Stonewalled, she made a personal appearance in Washington to demand money in late 1934, but went away empty-handed. "They are just passing the buck back and forth," she complained.[9]

In February 1935, Anna suffered a severe setback when the Riggs trust case was decided against her. She lost all claim to the $200,000 (plus interest) she had deposited in the Washington, D.C., bank.[10] Moreover, she was critically weakened by the cessation of the allowances. She could not afford the routine upkeep on the Hancock Park home, much less pay her debts to lawyers, and panicked that she would lose the home through foreclosure. Not knowing where else to turn, she again approached the Interior Department, where she received a cool reception. As her financial situation became more desperate, she vented her frustration on Secretary Ickes, suing him for prejudices against her family to the tune of $20,000. In May 1935, she demanded $50,000 from Ickes (with assurances that this would be her last request for a while): "You unprincipled, evil Jew beast, I wish we had a Hitler running America to place you Jews in your place, which is down In Hell." In a letter to President Franklin D. Roosevelt the same month, she blamed Ickes for Barnett's death and demanded the secretary's dismissal.[11]

Deprived of Jackson's calm presence and income, Anna's desperation and alcoholic behavior carried her to the brink of insanity. Her letters, replete with anti-Semitism and libelous accusations, were mailed without the knowledge or approval of her lawyer. During this period of derangement, the volatile Anna Barnett turned on her staunchest ally, Senator Thomas. She cursed Thomas, his "gang," all the Barnett "conspirators," and their families to suffer "heart aches, disappointments, dire poverty, filth, degradation, tortures for a hundred years." "[T]he most despised thing," she spat, "is the one who poses as a friend."[12] Anna's continued demands for money from Harold Ickes appeared to be the acts of an insane woman.

Anna's need for money was so acute that she composed a pamphlet, *Truth*, and sold it for fifty cents. The cover showed Jesus and the Devil and was emblazoned with the slogan "Evil is ruling—and the Lord will not Permit Evil to Rule." She challenged her readers with the question: Which do you choose: Good or Evil? She told them to use their own minds rather than be led to false conclusions by her detractors and persecutors. A populist defense of family privacy from governmental interference, the pamphlet also contained vituperative attacks on nearly everyone—Amado Peter Giannini, the Baptists, the Rockefellers, the women's clubs, Harold McGugin, and Judge Crail—all of whom she believed conspired to steal her estate. *Truth* was a figment of Anna's distorted, paranoid view of reality, laced with self-justifications, contradictions, and self-deceptions. The federal government considered prosecuting Anna for sending libelous material through the mail.

Among those questioning Anna Barnett's mental competency was Harold McGugin. Anna included in *Truth* a letter that McGugin wrote to her lawyer, Paul Hutchinson, in 1934, advising that Anna Barnett ought to be declared incompetent and have a guardian appointed:

> All that she can do is to abuse some one and that is not a competent defense. . . . Her conduct of charging every one of every administration of being corrupt, going around to see judges in the absence of her attorneys, and demanding orders and decisions which are out of all sense of reason is complete proof that the woman is unbalanced and incapable of defending herself.

McGugin observed a marked change in her conduct from 1931 to 1934. Anna characterized McGugin's letter as "the most vile thing" she had ever read and called him an "ungrateful monster."[13]

In view of Anna's irrationality, a government official recommended that a receiver be appointed to take care of the Hancock Park mansion, but Anna Barnett refused this as an incursion on her rights. She called it "just another move to oust me from the house the big chief built for our home."[14] Her threats to Secretary Ickes continued as only small allowances for water bills were allowed toward upkeep of the property. In one 1936 telegram, she wrote: "Send me my allowance or I shall come to Washington and settle with you!"[15]

In early 1936, Anna's appeal in the James decision was denied by the Ninth U.S. Circuit Court of Appeals in San Francisco, and the U.S. Supreme Court declined to hear the case. In the supporting brief, Anna and her lawyer Hutchinson followed McGugin's advice and stressed two main arguments: Jackson Barnett was competent, and the federal court lacked jurisdiction. Anna made the belligerent and gratuitous interjection: "*There is no Jackson Barnett Estate. The Estate passed to me, his widow, upon his death. There are no heirs other than myself.*" As legal wife and heir, she had been unlawfully denied money from "my vast funds held by the Secretary of the Interior Ickes." The brief claimed that Anna was the true owner of the Hancock Park home because she paid for it with her real estate profits and had met tax obligations until 1935.[16]

Still nursing the futile hope of winning a share of the Barnett estate in the Oklahoma equity case, Anna made a determined stand to preserve her only remaining asset, the Hancock Park mansion. Attempting to bluff her way into obtaining title to this family home, she sued the Bank of America for the title. She acted as her own counsel because her former lawyer, Hutchinson, had sued her for $25,000 in unpaid legal fees.[17]

By 1938, as the result of unrelenting financial strain, Anna faced incarceration for debt. As her bank accounts drained, "monster bankers" (as she called them) cut off her credit. A furniture company sued her for $7,652 for furniture, rugs, and tapestries. She was arrested when she failed to appear to face a contempt of court charge for her unpaid debts in June 1938. Unvanquished, Anna told a reporter at the time, "I'm not through fighting by any means. Racketeers and gangsters in the garb of judges and politicians and government agents have persecuted me for eighteen years but they haven't beaten me down yet." She called the arrest "part of the whole frame-up against me to get my estate" and related it to "the conspiracy" to prevent her appearance in Oklahoma federal court in the equity case, which she unrealistically believed would be decided in her favor. While jailed, she desperately tried to escape by breaking away from a matron and racing for the elevator. Incarcerated in county jail for violation of state law, she screamed, "I'm a ward of the federal courts and you can't hold me here any longer." Her behavior finally landed Anna in solitary confinement. After two weeks in jail, she agreed to surrender $6,500 in furnishings to secure her release, then rushed to Oklahoma.[18]

Spurred by widespread sentiment that action was needed to protect a widow from being evicted from her home, the Pleiades Club—led by Mrs. Burton Fitts, wife of the Los Angeles district attorney—took up Anna's defense in June 1938. The Los Angeles Breakfast Club also unequivocally condemned the eviction. On July 1, 1938, fifteen hundred persons attended a mass meeting at the First Unitarian Church, where they raised money to pay Anna's legal fees. Headquarters were established to coordinate citywide efforts with other women's clubs. Viewing the threat to Anna as a challenge to the property rights of women, the women insisted that, at the

Crowds surrounded the Barnetts' Hancock Park home for many weeks in mid-1938. A carnival atmosphere, including food vendors, prevailed. A newsreel camera was even set up in hopes of filming the dramatic eviction that was anticipated. Courtesy of the Los Angeles Herald Examiner *Collection, Los Angeles Public Library.*

very least, Anna was a common-law wife and was entitled to a portion of the estate. A Pleiades clubwoman was quoted as saying: "I don't care if she had a temper like Satan—she should be looked after!" In one editorial, a woman passionately defended Anna, saying there was no law against an Indian marrying a white; oil was the issue. "If he hadn't been rich, the government wouldn't care!"[19]

On July 11, 1938, Anna's final legal appeal was refused, Judge James ordered her to leave her home within thirty days. "I won't get out—now or never," she raged. She felled a woman sympathizer with her fist as she dove for an elevator at the courthouse. "These women are just trying to make political capital out of me. A lot of politicians are trying to get a ride on my coat tails."[20] Even while women's groups triumphed her cause, Anna persistently insulted and spurned other women. As she explained in one interview, "With six [five] brothers, I was a tomboy as a girl. Perhaps that's why women never really understand me."[21]

Public interest in Anna's plight reached a fevered pitch in Los Angeles. People rang the city newspapers to protest the eviction. The *Los Angeles Evening News* reported the rumor that a whole tribe of Oklahoma Indians had "slunk like shadows into the house," "to do or die" for Mrs. Barnett. Curious observers had seen feathers and speculated that Indians had taken a "blood oath" to defend the "chief's" interests against all "white invaders" and had come to defend the home. It turned out to be the feathers of Anna's two hens.[22]

Undaunted by Anna's disparaging remarks, the clubwomen completed their project of collecting signatures and forwarded a petition for a stay of execution signed by 200,000 residents to U.S. attorney general Homer Cummings. They appealed to the governor of California, state and federal representatives, and even Eleanor Roosevelt "as a foremost defender of

During the eviction proceedings, Anna Barnett was harassed by newspapermen wanting to photograph the famous widow of the World's Richest Indian. Ever sensitive to persecution, Anna's temper flared when she and Maxine were intercepted by this photographer when returning home one evening in April 1938. Courtesy of the Los Angeles Herald Examiner *Collection, Los Angeles Public Library.*

Los Angeles women vigorously protested the ruling that Anna Barnett was not Jackson's legal wife after fourteen years of marriage. To prevent the widow's eviction, 200,000 signatures were collected on petitions and sent to Attorney General Homer S. Cummings. Shown here packing the petitions for mailing are (left to right) Mrs. Bernice Johnson, Mrs. Burton Fitts, Mrs. L. R. Wharton, and Mrs. Shirley Hall. Courtesy of the Los Angeles Herald Examiner *Collection, Los Angeles Public Library.*

women's rights." Senator William McAdoo replied with a telegram, acknowledging the general sentiment that a "grave injustice" was being done. Furious letters were written to congressmen, demanding the introduction of legislation to prevent the eviction. Moved by the thousands of his constituents vitally interested in Anna's case, a California congressman declared his intention to introduce a bill to protect the estates of white women married to Indians. He tried to obtain another delay in the eviction. Senator Thomas introduced a bill to create a trust fund for Anna from money earned from sale of the Barnett real estate, but it did not pass.[23]

At Interior, Secretary Harold Ickes responded to a clubwoman's letter in condescending tones. Given the previous court decisions, the government had no recourse but to evict Anna from the Hancock Park home. Ickes volunteered that "even had Mrs. Lowe been a wholly different type of woman, it still . . . would have been the government's duty to resist the kidnapping of Jackson Barnett. . . . [H]er enterprise was a cold and entirely cynical business adventure."[24]

Commissioner of Indian Affairs Collier responded to the political pressure by providing a detailed justification for the eviction. Collier's figures showed that Anna had been compensated handsomely for her services as caretaker to the elderly Barnett. He estimated that $379,500 in regular allowances had been issued to the Barnetts between 1920 and 1934, along with $65,000 in special allowances for purchases, including luxury cars, Christmas presents, and vacations. Collier repeated Ickes's contention that Anna had ample opportunity to save some of the money paid over the years.[25] The implication was that she was an adventuress who calculatingly married an elderly, mentally enfeebled man for his money and was not to be pitied. The federal government was therefore exonerated from any wrongdoing in sustaining the eviction. The clubwomen took issue with the overpowering sexism of the government's position. They made great sport of the fact that Ickes had married a woman forty years younger, implying that love could not possibly explain the relationship. Perhaps the government should look into the matter of preventing older gentlemen from making such unions, said one clubwoman.[26]

In a bizarre reversal, employees in the Justice Department became sympathetic to Anna Barnett, claiming there was some merit to the public outcry that Anna was being unjustly persecuted. Justice officials argued that Secretary Ickes's dislike for Anna had shaped his unfair treatment of her. In hindsight, the annulment of a consensual union and the eviction of a widow seemed to be an unwarranted intrusion into citizens' private lives. The attorney general's Los Angeles office, unsettled by the agitation over the eviction, appealed to Attorney General Cummings, who granted a stay on the eviction until mid-October.[27] Amid the flood of appeals, Anna won a temporary, sixty-day reprieve on August 13, 1938. The right-wing Creeks of the American Indian Federation urged the federal government to resist the pressure being brought to bear on public officials by women's clubs.[28]

Scores of individuals expressed intuitive explanations for the injustice they felt was being done to Anna Barnett. Many of the letters of protest had merit and insight, though these individuals had only a limited understanding of the complex case. Among the many eleventh-hour appeals was a letter from one highly literate male critic, who with acid invective denounced the federal government's treatment of women, specifically an elderly widow. Indicting the federal government for its complicity in "whatever crime there may have been," he said, the core was "just a dirty, odorous Frame-Up, my dear sir, a tyrannical use of power and legal technicalities, a modern exhibit, a New Deal." One woman, speaking for the women's clubs of Los Angeles, made an appeal based on a more mundane analysis. Anna had been considerate of Jackson's condition, tireless in looking after his grooming, and "made a man of him." She closed with the rallying cry: "Set free Annie [sic] Laura Barnett, Oct. 1938."[29]

Even Frank Merriam, governor of California, made a personal appeal by telegram to President Roosevelt to consider the petitions of thousands of southern Californians in a "spirit of human understanding."[30] But the attorney general would delay no longer. There was no further avenue of appeal or negotiation. Anna had said repeatedly, "You will have to kill me to get my house."[31] Judge James as a precaution insisted that the Barnett mansion have fire insurance.

As all of the last-minute appeals to prevent the eviction had failed, Los Angeles residents anticipated a confrontation. Crowds of curious onlookers came to gawk at the home of the World's Richest Indian. Supporters, curiosity seekers, and newspaper reporters milled around the Hancock Park home, hoping to witness the moment of attack. Hot dog, popcorn, and ice cream vendors sold their wares, leaving litter on the yellowing lawn. To protect her privacy, Anna drew her shades and remained in seclusion. She bitterly resented the media attention, while simultaneously feeding the public spectacle with her gritty defiance, intemperate outbursts, and verbal volleys. Anna shoved aggressive reporters and even vocal supporters. "Spies hanging around early and late," Anna had written in her diary on October 10.[32] Rumors circulated that she had fortified herself with supplies of food and ammunition for a long siege. On August 10, a *Los Angeles News* story had been headlined "LA Widow Threatens to Blow Up Mansion." The *Riverside Press* reported Anna's threats to kill anyone who tried to evict her: "I'll use a gun and a knife." The *Los Angeles Herald* reported, "Everybody anticipates . . . a show . . . that will go down as unique in the annals of the federal government."[33]

The battle of Wilshire Boulevard, as it was dubbed by the press, began as a wary federal marshal, Robert Clark, and his deputies served Anna with notice of a thirty-day eviction on the evening of October 18, 1938. The officers feared the volatile crowd and Anna. After "stalking the teepee," Clark—who wore a cowboy hat while performing his duties—approached Anna and Maxine's car as they entered the driveway of the Hancock Park home. An attempt was made to hand the notice to Anna, who stiff-armed the marshal and bolted for the house. Maxine reluctantly accepted the eviction papers, and the cameras started to flash. This infuriated Anna, who began throwing rocks, sticks, and flashbulbs as the crowd of "several hundred" cheered her on. As some newsmen retreated behind the five-foot picket fence, the two women started hurling the items from their grocery bags at the deputies and reporters. The crowd was gleeful as Mrs. Barnett menaced a photographer with a broken flashbulb, as if she might scalp him. "I hope she kills him," someone yelled. Another shouted, "Imagine them trying to cheat her out of her home! Hasn't she been tortured enough already?" In her diary, Anna wrote that as she arrived home that evening, newspaper "gangsters" and a marshal with an eviction order greeted her: "We finally chased the army away. Lovely day." The events confirmed the federal officials' suspicion that Anna would not go peacefully.[34]

In view of Mrs. Barnett's numerous threats to blow up the mansion with dynamite or to "scalp" anyone who tried to eject her, the marshals proceeded cautiously. They secured a writ of assistance, which allowed them to use force if necessary. "I am instructing the officers to place under arrest anyone who interferes," warned one federal official.[35] Protests continued to pour in to the federal building. Excited crowds numbering in the hundreds milled around the home. On October 20, as last-ditch efforts were being made by clubwomen in appeals to Washington, forty policemen patrolled a crowd of one thousand camp followers. The next day, a newsreel camera was set up to record the dramatic spectacle of eviction for posterity. Onlookers were sometimes ignored or run off by Mrs. Barnett. When a sympathetic local radio philosopher and a high school student attempted to offer their aid, Anna hurled rocks at them. A small American flag was pinned on the front gate with a note that read: "To put this poor woman out of her home is a disgrace to this flag. Is this America? God help us!"[36]

Marshal Clark and other federal officers discreetly mapped out a strategy reminiscent of Custer's attack on the Washita. They decided to advance on the house in a decisive and swift action in the early morning hours of Sunday, October 30. Around 7 A.M., five carloads of deputies roared up to the Hancock Park mansion. Anna, who was outside, rushed into the home, bolting the door behind her. Armed with crowbars, eight deputies (including two women, Betty Smith and Ester Walling) rapidly smashed two doors on the north side and beat in a heavy door and French windows facing Wilshire. The crash of glass and the shrieks from the women woke the neighborhood. A frightened group of spectators, fearing Anna would deliver on her oft-repeated promise to "blast the house to bits" with dynamite, was poised to flee for safety. Anna stood at the top of the grand stairway with a hand axe. As the two female deputies, accompanied by two men, resolutely mounted the stairs, Anna warned them to leave her house "and you keep you old fish hags out of here too." After she made a menacing gesture with the hatchet and threatened to "hack" their heads off, a deputy launched a tear gas cartridge against the wall behind Anna. She simultaneously released the hatchet. It flew wildly down the staircase without hitting anyone. As the tear gas took effect, Anna was dragged from her home, screeching "like a Comanche and clawing and biting." She was hustled into a car and held there by a husky deputy. Maxine, weeping and gasping from tear gas, was taken into custody in her pajamas without a struggle.[37]

Anna, characteristically, fought to the bitter end. Marshal Clark offered her a choice of destinations: "We'll take you anywhere you say or we'll take you to jail." Anna shrieked, "To jail!" and on the ride loudly threatened her captors. When a reporter asked her for a statement, she obliged with the "full eloquence of her right foot." She hurled a pitcher of water at the matrons at the county jail for patronizing her with "fake sym-

*On October 30, 1938, using tear gas, the U.S. marshal evicted
Anna and Maxine from their Hancock Park home. Anna
behaved more like a "caged tigress than a woman," said one
commentator. In this photo, Anna shields her face with a silk
scarf as she signs a promise not to trespass on the mansion in
order to secure her release from custody. Her daughter, Maxine,
stands behind her. Courtesy of the* Los Angeles Herald
Examiner *Collection, Los Angeles Public Library.*

pathy." The widow of the World's Richest Indian paced back and forth in
her Los Angeles County jail cell, "her feathered bedroom mules beating a
slithering tattoo on the floor."[38]

The dramatic eviction on October 30, 1938, was front-page news. Angelenos voraciously consumed every detail in the climactic episode ending
the bizarre drama that had been building for weeks. In her desperate attempts to preserve "her" property, Anna sued, cursed, shoved, and threw
things. Her resistance was punctuated by courtroom outbursts and wild
denunciations of those conspiring to ruin her as well as of her would-be
friends.

At the arraignment before U.S. commissioner David Head, Anna Lowe Barnett and her daughter, Maxine, were charged with "forcibly resisting, interfering and intimidating Federal officers with the use of a dangerous weapon, to wit, a hatchet" and were held on $1,000 bail. The women angrily complained of excessive and unnecessary force. Anna ranted against "Uncle Sam's minions and his courts." Anna claimed she had been on her way to repair the front gate with the hatchet when the officers surprised her. The very idea that she would brandish a weapon against anyone was "ridiculous," she said. Commissioner Head suggested that Anna ask some of her wealthy women friends to post bail, and in fact one did offer her a rustic refuge. Anna replied: "Friends—I have no friends. Those ladies you talk about wanting to help me—they're just a bunch of old hags. They're just trying to cash in on me."[39]

Maxine, a woman quite different in temperament from her combative mother, was ready to concede. In the newspaper's hackneyed puns, Maxine "buried the hatchet" and "smoked the peace pipe" with the authorities after the arrest. She was allowed to return to their home for a change of clothing. She then attired herself in a wine-colored jacket and shirt and a black hat, while Anna insisted upon wearing her wrinkled leopardskin coat with a bandana draped over her face. Her red silk dress, like her coat, had seen better days, a reporter cattily noted.[40] The federal government had no desire to prosecute Anna for the alleged assault with the hatchet and quietly let the case drop. Maxine negotiated for their release with a promise of good behavior and lectured her mother to keep her mouth shut, so they could move to their new residence, a one-room apartment. The irrepressible Anna, however, was soon back in court, making numerous allegations and demands. To her dying day, Anna Barnett vowed to continue the fight to regain "her property."[41]

12

Speculative and Protracted Litigation

One of the strangest and most sordidly romantic stories in the history of the rich Creek Nation came abruptly to an end with Barnett's death—and another began, as the *Muskogee Daily Phoenix* astutely observed. The number of Oklahoma claimants to his wealth and their lawyers multiplied exponentially. A "miniature convention of the Barnett family" converged upon the federal building at Muskogee in the days after Jackson's death. The Oklahoma papers identified the heirs from both sides of Jackson's family and printed photos and genealogical charts. However, contentions arose immediately, as some claimed to have more right to the fortune than others.[1]

When the Department of the Interior made a formal announcement for claimants to the estate to appear, 700–800 persons from fifty different groups came forward, all alleging to be closest to Barnett in kinship. Swelling the number of legitimate claimants were an army of false ones and their opportunistic lawyers. With the country in a depression, many desperate people made a bid for the fortune. Just as the Burke administration had predicted, needless, prolonged litigation and dissipation of the estate occurred since the money was not secured in a trust prior to Jackson's death. The lawyers for the strongest claimants to the Barnett estate—Jackson's half siblings by Siah Barnett of Bryant and their descendants—had to refute the claims by these adversarial groups point by point to maintain their advantageous position.

The equity case proceedings in *In the Matter of the Estate of Jackson Barnett* (Equity 4556) to determine Jackson's true heirs began in 1934 when lawyers began taking depositions. It took more than five years to establish Jackson Barnett's heirs. At 8,832 pages, the record fills twenty-five bound volumes.[2]

The massive evidence presented a significant challenge for federal judge Robert Williams, a veteran of Barnett litigation. Because documentary evidence for Jackson Barnett's life before 1912 was scarce, the case rested on oral testimony of memories of long-ago events. There were fourteen Jackson Barnetts—eleven on the Creek tribal rolls and three on the Creek freedmen rolls—and multiple Thlesothles and Siah Barnetts in the Creek Nation at the time of the Civil War. Descendants of persons with one of these three names brought forth their family histories; even sincere testimony was tainted by mistaken identities and wishful thinking.[3] Widely different interpretations could be drawn from this copious oral testimony, which detailed events and relationships in Jackson Barnett's life. Testimony lacing true historical details with falsehoods is difficult to evaluate. The record in the equity suit is a dense mass of information with "sharp inconsistencies and irreconcilable conflicts," as one federal judge described it.[4] Many claimants contended they were related to Jackson as wives, children, and siblings. "Four different women claimed to have married him, and two or three of them to have had issue by him, and four sets of adverse claimants founded their claims upon those alleged marriages."[5] To further complicate the matter, suggestive testimony was presented that Siah Barnett of Bryant was not Jackson's true father. Siah's half brother Jim Barnett was alleged to be the real father, as was Andrew Sullivan, an African-American slave of William Sullivan,[6] perhaps the father of Jackson's brother, Tecumseh.

One improbable (and fraudulent) claim came from Bennie Scott, a man who alleged he was the son of an eccentric prospector, Walter Scott, who built Scotty's Castle in Death Valley, California, and Jackson Barnett's sister Thlesothle. They lived in the desert castle until the day when Jackson, Anna, and two gangsters came to Death Valley, kidnapped his mother, and threw Bennie in the cactus, "which sure hurt."[7] Needless to say, Bennie was not one of the successful litigants. Another person claiming a close kinship relation was Wesley Barnett, a former member of an outlaw gang, who had served prison time. Wesley stated that his grandfather was Yarda Barnett (or Josiah Barnett) of Quarsartee Town, who had a relationship with Thlesothle of Tuckabatchee town.[8] With con men like Bennie Scott and ex-convicts like Wesley Barnett as claimants, a lawyer for a rival group of claimants was prompted to comment:

During the long trial of the case, the court room scene, so far as claimants were concerned, looked like a convention of criminals. Thieves and ex-convicts were conspicuous. It appeared that a large percent of the worst element of the Creek Nation regarded Jackson Barnett as a common ancestor whose vast estate could be acquired by ingenious perjury without limit.[9]

To make a determination of the true heirs, Judge Williams was faced with a daunting task, which may in some measure explain his eccentric behavior. In the trial testimony, for example, he gratuitously interjected that "trained dogs and ponies and insane people shake hands, and that only children like spotted ponies" to refute one of Anna Barnett's witnesses' contention that Jackson Barnett was happy in California. Williams delivered long monologues on feudalism in the Middle Ages, journalism, and other topics. Given the confusing mass of testimony, much of it perjured, Williams's growing impatience and cynicism can explain his digressions and occasional flippant and rude remarks. But Williams also had deep-seated biases, which shaped his perceptions of the proceedings. Williams—whose earlier activities included convening the grand juries in 1926 and 1928 and ordering Jackson to be seized and brought to testify in Muskogee in 1926—had formed an opinion about Jackson Barnett's mental incapacity prior to the equity case, which blocked his willingness to seriously consider the claims of the different women who said they were Jackson's wife.[10]

The judge's Anglocentric notions of patrilineal kinship, rather than the Creek's matrilineal forms, shaped his ideas of the legitimate heirs. But the most glaring problem of Williams's thinking was his racism. As a former governor of Oklahoma who promoted literacy tests to prevent African-American voting after the grandfather clauses of the Oklahoma constitution were ruled in violation of the Fifteenth Amendment by the Supreme Court in 1915, Williams's thinking was steeped in the notions of racial segregation. He seemed to find it impossible to imagine that Creeks and African Americans or whites intermarried in the past: interracial relationships apparently violated his sensibilties.

Williams's biases were apparent from the opening oral arguments in *In the Matter of the Estate* in Muskogee in March 1937. Confronting him were twenty-eight lawyers representing twenty-eight groups. The erstwhile widow of Jackson Barnett, Anna Laura Lowe, represented herself. When Anna testified, she was at her sociopathic best, confidently spinning a fictional and melodramatic tale of her first meeting with Jackson in the 1880s. But even when she was truthful, she lacked credibility. Williams, convinced Jackson was a man of "weak will and incompetent mind," was not moved by Anna's accurate observation that Jackson was a man of honesty and independence. "What he said was his own. He wasn't mimicking anyone. . . . He lived his life in his own way," testified Anna. Williams ridiculed Jackson Barnett's behavior as a volunteer Los Angeles traffic cop and chided Anna for giving a feeble-minded man excessive freedom in such unsupervised street-corner activity. Referring to the other claimants in the courtroom, some of whom were African Americans, Williams challenged her: "Would you leave him in this room with this crowd of nigger men?"[11]

Williams's racial prejudices were evident in other aspects of the trial, for example, his treatment of the testimony of Bertha Barnett, an African-American woman. She claimed to be Jackson Barnett's wife and mother of his two children. By far the most voluminous aspect of the equity suit, Bertha's claim involved ninety-three witnesses and 3,700 pages of testimony. (In late 1936, William Fisher, son of Jackson's half-sister Hannah, was told the "government" had done a great deal of work investigating the claim of the "Negro Bertha" in hopes of securing the inheritance for

Some of the Creek claimants and their lawyers in Henryetta, Oklahoma, giving depositions in the Equity case to determine Jackson Barnett's heirs. William Fisher, one successful Creek claimant, sits in the rear of the room to the right of the door behind the balding man. Courtesy of the Lance Hall Collection, Fort Worth.

the "full-blood Indians." His patience strained to the breaking point by the false testimony, at one point Fisher brought a gun to court and intimidated some of the witnesses.[12])

Bertha Barnett testified in Williams's court in April 1937. She made the plausible argument that she married Jackson about 1890, when he was working as a ferryman for Uncle Leecher. The thirty-nine-year-old Jackson had married her according to the Indian custom during a three-week feast at a Creek stomp dance, she said. She claimed that two children were born to this union, Mayetta and Henry. Then, Jackson, who was purportedly drinking and bootlegging in those lawless days along the Arkansas River, deserted the family.

Defying protocol, Anna Barnett leaped to her feet to cross-examine the startled witness, asking her pointed questions about Jackson's build and eye color. Bertha—if she had known Jackson Barnett—had not seen him for more than forty years and was unable to answer. Anna charged that Bertha Barnett was involved in a Jewish conspiracy led by Secretary of the Interior Harold Ickes, an outrageous claim that the bewildered Bertha denied. Anna's confidence soared in response to what she mistakenly viewed as Judge Williams's sympathy toward her maneuver. Williams had allowed Anna, the white woman, to browbeat the presumptuous black woman. Williams evidently relished witnessing the collapse of Bertha Barnett's claim. The alleged daughter of Bertha and Jackson, Mayetta, was revealed as an imposter; her real identity was Rosella Sims. Bertha and her co-conspirators attempted to flee but were brought back to court and charged with perjury. Several grand jury investigations into alleged perjury, forgery, and fraud grew out of the case. Though the weight of the evidence suggests otherwise, Benay Blend, Barnett's first biographer, believed that Bertha Barnett and her children were the legitimate heirs.[13]

In the battle over the fortune, one of the contentious questions was whether Jackson's father, Siah, was African American or Indian. Several witnesses testified that Siah Barnett of Bryant was part "Negro." It was well established that Jim Barnett was African American and that he was the half brother of Siah Barnett of Bryant, the man generally accepted to be Jackson's father. Knowing Williams's prejudices, lawyers for competing groups were willing to play the race card to discredit their opponents' claims. For example, Wesley Barnett said that his Creek grandfather Siah (or Yarda) Barnett was Jackson's father. Yarda, a Confederate army veteran, did not call himself Josiah (or Siah) Barnett, because he did not want to be named like that "Negro" at Henryetta, explained Wesley.[14]

There were several African-Creek Barnetts who had fought in the Civil War as Loyal Creeks and who were on the Dawes Roll. A number of African-Creek claimants made a very strong case that Siah Barnett was their kinsman.[15] Solid documentary evidence that Siah was black came from his Loyal Creek claim of December 1869. Captain F. A. Field and Major General Hazen examined Siah Barnett, reduced his statement to writing, and made an award. They described Siah as half-Creek, probably Creek and black. The award was not paid until Congress finally appropriated the money in 1905, and by that time Siah was dead. Siah's widow, Mary Beams, appeared before the U.S. inspector to collect Siah Barnett's family's share of this award. Providing a loophole that other claimants exploited in advancing their claims, Mary Beams Barnett did not list Jackson Barnett among Siah's descendants.[16]

Those claiming closest kinship to Jackson via their descent from Siah Barnett of Bryant faced a formidable challenge from these African-Creeks —for example, the Tiger and Curns-Gentry claimants—and from Creeks claiming a relationship on the maternal side. According to Creek matrilineal kinship forms, Jackson's maternal relatives, not his biological father's relatives, were his kin. Moreover, so the maternal kin claimed, Siah had made little or no effort to claim Jackson as his son, and this constituted proof that he was not the true father. Even if he had fathered Jackson, this argument stressed, Siah abandoned Jackson at birth and never acknowledged him as his biological son. Further, it was argued that Siah's children by Mary Beams egregiously spurned and neglected Jackson, then backtracked when he became wealthy. Family relations between Jackson and his father's side of the family were distant, they argued. In contrast, there was a close relationship between Jackson and his maternal half brother Tecumseh, with whom he worked at Leecher's ferry, as a number of witnesses attested. The names of Tecumseh (aka Cumsey Antrew) and Jackson appear together in census documents in 1857, 1859, 1882, and 1890.[17] These claimants played upon Judge Williams's prejudices, drawing a picture of a strong connection to the maternal Creek kin and an attenuated relationship between Jackson and his biological, part-black father.

To counter these arguments, lawyers for Siah Barnett's descendants blamed the estrangement on Jackson's mental incompetency. John Jacobs testified that because Jackson was "idiotic" and couldn't conduct an intelligent conversation while young, "he was of the type which was quite naturally somewhat neglected by other members of the family," but Jackson ultimately returned to Siah's fireside. The Barnetts acknowledged him, they argued, even though he was poor and slow.[18] The historical evidence from the late 1880s onward shows an undeniable relationship between Jackson Barnett and Siah Barnett's family in Bryant. Jackson was a frequent visitor at the homes of his Barnett relatives, and Jackson Barnett himself acknowledged that he knew these people with some intimacy. Moreover, David Barnett, as Jackson's half brother, participated in court proceedings in 1912 and was quoted in a 1919 newspaper as Jackson's half brother.

To neutralize Judge Williams's biases against blacks, the Barnett claimants advanced testimony that Siah of Bryant was viewed as a Creek, not as an African American, by his contemporaries. Caroline Henry, a white schoolteacher who moved to Indian Territory in late 1889 and later taught at an Indian school near Bryant, testified that the school was called the Barnett schoolhouse as only Barnetts attended at first. According to her, Siah was recognized in the community as an Indian; she never heard anything otherwise of Siah's family. Siah and his offspring "always attended white schools," she said.[19]

The overwhelming evidence that Siah was part African American seemed to make the paternal Barnett kin vulnerable to other claimants. One of the strongest groups of claimants on the maternal side were the Conners. Allegedly, the Conners were pure Indians, Creek and Seminole. One of their advantages was that they had taken the initiative in 1934 to print genealogical charts showing their connection to Jackson Barnett in Oklahoma newspapers. Important testimony linking Jackson Barnett's mother to the Conners came from Baptist minister William McCombs, who situated the Conner family at Fort Gibson in the war years and claimed that Jackson's aunt Jennie Conner briefly cared for Jackson after his mother's death.

A claim with a much stronger evidentiary base, however, came from those who asserted that Uncle Leecher was Thlesothle's brother. Jackson testified on numerous occasions about his years working on the ferry, whereas he did not recall any association with any member of the Conner family. The Conners lived in the southwestern part of the Creek Nation, while Jackson was probably born on the eastern edge of the Creek Nation. Unquestionably, Jackson spent the first quarter of his life along the Arkansas River, probably in close association with one or more of his maternal half brothers.[20] The Conners, the Leecher group, and many others claimed exclusive relations to Tecumseh and Haryaryeche, Jackson's half brothers, but no evidence was conclusive.

The strongest groups of claimants decided to merge their interests by forming a family compact. In 1936, they agreed to unite their claims and defend them against the dozens of other groups. Group I, the litigants who claimed kinship via Jackson's paternal side, included Jackson's half siblings: David Barnett, Mariah (or Sissy, who married John Davis and Willy West), Ellen (who married James Grayson, John Walker, Sebor, and William McQueen), Hannah (who married James Fisher), and Eliza (Elizabeth or Lizzie, who married Little Fish). As most of these siblings had died, the fourteen Group I claimants consisted of the descendants of these half siblings, including William Fisher, the son of Hannah and James Fisher. All were listed on the Creek roll.[21] They had contracted to pay lawyers 30–40 percent if successful in their suits as claimants to the Barnett fortune.

Group II and Group III claimed close kinship through Jackson's mother. Group II was composed of sixteen claimants from the Conner family, who were Jackson's cousins: the children of Jackson's maternal uncles and aunt. The four people in Group III were the children and grandchildren of Jackson's half brother Haryaryeche (or Jim Lowe). Jackson's other half brother on the maternal side, Tecumseh, died without issue.[22]

Groups II and III promised their attorneys fees ranging from 33–50 percent of any award they might receive. In the settlement contract, these three groups agreed to a division: Group I members would share 50 percent of the estate, and Group II and III members would receive 25 percent shares.

In December 1939, Judge Williams made his ruling. He favored descendants over wives, real or imagined, and Indian descendants over African-Creeks. The losers included Bertha and Anna Barnett, along with another seven hundred claimants, represented by one hundred lawyers. The court accepted the premise that Jackson was a mental incompetent, thus disallowing claims of the women, like Anna, who said they had valid marriages to Jackson. Williams asserted that Jackson from his youth was not only ignorant and illiterate, but mentally impaired as well; he was known as "Crazy Jack." Williams described Jackson as a man of a retiring and reticent disposition, who shrank from contact with other people.[23] Thus, a chorus of judges—Knox, James, and Williams—reached the same conclusion about Jackson's incompetency.

The winners were the people in the family compact. What was ultimately the most persuasive evidence were documents from the Dawes Roll and other Creek payments and censuses, combined with key testimony from white and mixed-blood witnesses. Despite the overwhelming evidence that Siah was part African American, all of the heirs were described as "full-bloods," with the exception of one woman, who was a mixed-blood. The claims of people with obvious or admitted African-American ancestry were denied. Though the Creek descendants on his mother's side were successful litigants, Jackson's relations descended from his dark-skinned uncle Jim Barnett or aunt Lizzie Asbury on his father's side—whose relationship to Siah was well documented—were not considered legitimate heirs. Williams displayed an inability at this time to see the Creeks as a highly genetically complex people. If they were living before the Civil War, they were considered full-bloods.[24]

Williams's decision was contested by 350 unsuccessful claimants, who appealed the judgment. The family settlement contract was attacked as collusion in the Williams court, the appellate court, and the U.S. Supreme Court. Some asserted that Judge Williams was hostile and prejudiced. All appeals failed.[25] After eighteen years, the litigation over Jackson Barnett's estate finally approached closure in the early 1940s. In 1943, Judge Williams's judgment was affirmed with finality.

Judge Pollock's 1929 decision upholding the legal fees to McGugin and Keith was reversed in 1940. The federal judge in the case described Jackson Barnett as a "befuddled, bewildered performer" in an all-star cast of "fine ability," including the "keen and vigorous" Anna Lowe and the "brilliant" McGugin. McGugin's defenses, among them that the Harreld-Hastings Act had expired, were dismissed. Though Jackson Barnett had died, the Department of Justice was justified in pursuing the suit not only for Barnett's benefit, but "for the protection of every dependent Indian under the guardianship of the United States," the judge ruled. McGugin lost, and he was required to return the money. The following year, the appeals court also ruled against J. B. Walker, who alleged that Jackson Barnett had thumbprinted a document giving him $1 million.[26]

Unlike Judge Van Devanter, who scaled down the lawyers' fees in the eight-year *Equitable* case to less than 10 percent, Judge Williams regarded a 25 percent fee, plus expenses, as reasonable compensation to the lawyers in the difficult and risky equity case, which had taken nine years to litigate. Williams viewed the family compact claimants as by and large illiterate and indigent full-bloods, who were unable to refute the claims of the seven hundred other litigants on their own.[27]

An accounting of the Jackson Barnett estate in 1943 estimated its value at $1,714,097 or $17 million in 2002 dollars. This included $1.1 million in bonds, rental income, a pending federal tax refund of $70,764.93, real estate valued at $138,400, and personal property worth $28,500. The $1,235,724.72 million estate was the total estimated to be divided among the heirs after disbursements for state, federal, estate, and inheritance taxes, administrative costs, and the lawyers' fees of $329,110.[28] On July 14, 1943, the first payment of $517,042.40 was made, and the payment of the remainder awaited the liquidation of Jackson's bonds and the assets in California and Oklahoma. As per the agreement, half of the inheritance went to the members of Group I and quarter shares each to Group II and Group III heirs. With adjustments, the amount distributed among the heirs was $1.012 million. Some received shares of $1/20$, $1/28$, $1/36$, or $1/216$ with the largest shares totaling between $36,000 and $50,000. Many received smaller fractional shares as heirs of claimants who had died before the fortune was ultimately disbursed.[29]

Some heirs had waited twenty years for this inheritance. While hopeful of inheriting a king's fortune, many were perilously close to starvation during the depression years in Oklahoma. Some of the family pact lawyers, confident of eventual victory in the case, arranged for local grocery stores to extend credit to Jackson's paternal relatives. Tunney Graff, whose mother was Katie Fish Litsey (daughter of Jackson Barnett's half sister Eliza, born 1867, who married Little Fish), recalled that it took so long to get the settlement that two grocery stores that provided food and supplies on credit went bankrupt before the successful litigants were paid. When the money finally arrived, she recalled that her mother insisted the grocery store be paid first. Tunney was a teenager, and she said her family purchased nice clothes for her. Within four years, all of the Litsey family inheritance was gone.[30] Tunney's son Bill Graff recalled this family anecdote:

> This is a story told to me by my cousin, Paul Litsey, Jr., and it basically relates to what the family did with all of the money that they did receive. When the court case was settled, and the family

started getting money, my cousin must have been a small child, around the age of four or five.

Back then, a Packard was considered one of the most prestigious cars to own. The most successful businessman in the neighborhood usually drove a Packard. And every year, my Aunt Winey would buy a brand new Packard, too.

But what would she do with the previous year's car? She would abandon it in the front yard, never to be driven again. Each year, she would park the latest one right next to the previous year's model—they were all lined up nice and neat.

The family often had get-togethers at Aunt Winey's house. After a few years, she had quite a few Packards in her front yard. I don't know what the grand total was, but I know it was a lot. All of the kids used to play in them, like they were jungle gyms, or monkey bars. My cousin was always excited about going over to Aunt Winey's, because he couldn't wait to play in the Packards. It's amazing to think that such a prestigious automobile, in perfect running order, could be used as a child's plaything.

My dad [a non-Indian] was always amazed that the family spent every dime of the money that they were awarded. He couldn't fathom that someone could go through such a considerable amount, especially for back then, in such a short time. But after hearing that story, I understand where it all went. And I definitely know what Aunt Winey did with a lot of her money—it rusted away in her front yard.[31]

William Fisher, another beneficiary, received $12,485, and gambled away some of it.[32]

The final payment to the heirs awaited the liquidation of Jackson Barnett's remaining assets, including the Hancock Park mansion from which Anna Barnett had been evicted. The California real estate was held up in litigation and required congressional hearing and an Act of Congress to resolve in 1944. This mansion was temporarily occupied by a former Mission Indian major league baseball player, Jack Meyers, and eventually was leased. The Hancock Park home was sold for $62,550, and the 107 acres in Coldwater Canyon near Beverly Hills sold for $183,908, a fraction of what Anna said they were worth. Into the 1940s and 1950s, despite the act of Congress, the chain of title was unsettled as Anna still claimed ownership. The state of California was still trying to collect inheritance taxes on the Barnett estate in the 1950s. The Hancock Park mansion deteriorated and was torn down to make way for an insurance company's headquarters in 1962.[33]

Anna Lowe Barnett lived in a small frame home in Los Angeles with her daughter, Maxine, who remained unmarried and was her mother's only means of support. Penniless, Anna could not afford the operation to remove a malignant tumor, and on August 7, 1952, she died of cancer. An Oklahoma Indian relief organization paid for her cremation.[34] Her ashes were buried next to Jackson Barnett, as she wished, but the plots were in a predominantly Jewish section, a final indignity to the viciously anti-Semitic Anna Barnett. The issue of removing Jackson Barnett's remains had not been raised during the heirship case.

For a man whose money was scrupulously and repeatedly examined by auditors during the course of his lifetime, many questions remain about Jackson Barnett's estate, eventually valued at approximately $3.5 million. As closely as can be estimated, Jackson Barnett with Anna Barnett's assistance probably spent 15 percent of it. Had he not married Anna, his expenditures would have been far, far lower. Approximately 25 percent was distributed among the approximately three dozen distant Creek heirs, who spent most of the money very rapidly. Another 30 percent was paid to lawyers. Another $100,000–150,000 was paid for guardian fees. The remainder, 25–30 percent, if not grafted, appears to have been expended in miscellaneous court costs, taxes, administrative fees, and other managerial processes to defend and protect the estate.[35]

None of the money was used as a living trust for the Creek people.

Epilogue:
A Matter of Trust

Those people who undertake to steal the Indians' money—I would not say "steal," but I would say get, acquire, or abstract, maybe in a legal way—are apparently numerous.
—INTERIOR SECRETARY HUBERT WORK

The seminal U.S. Supreme Court decisions of 1831 and 1832—*Cherokee v. Georgia* and *Worcester v. Georgia*—defined as a principle of law the federal government's duty to protect Indian people and to honor its treaty promises. Among the federal government's responsibilities are protecting Indian legal rights as sovereign but dependent nations, guarding Indian persons from attack and their resources from theft, and providing guidance in adjustment to the dominant culture. As Indian nations signed treaties selling large tracts of land to the U.S. government, tribal funds were placed in federal trust accounts, adding to the list of responsibilities. Linking partners of unequal strength, Justice John Marshall described the federal trust relationship as analogous to the relation between a guardian and his ward. This relationship has frequently been marred by the abuse of power. Authority was delegated to protect the weak, but the law served the interests of the strong.

The federal trust relationship underwent a radical redefinition in 1887 with passage of the Dawes Act. To fulfill its mandate to democracy, Congress determined to bring the Indians' state of inequality, or "pupilage," to a close by the individuation of all collectively owned lands and trust funds. Indians attained the status of U.S. citizens by sacrificing their collective identities and rights as members of "domestic dependent nations." How-

ever, sober second thoughts about how to guard vulnerable, unaccultur-
ated Indians during the twenty-five-year transitional period prompted
Congress to pass the Burke Act of 1906. A new relationship of trust was established, one between the federal government and *individual* Indians
who had accepted their private allotments of partitioned reservation land.
These persons had restricted allotments that were not yet free from federal
supervision. Neither members of their own nations, nor fully citizens of
the United States, so-called incompetent Indians occupied a twilight zone.
They lacked full control over their property and were suspended in an in-
determinate status with ill-defined rights. The imbroglio over the Jackson
Barnett fortune resulted from the ambiguities inherent in this redefined
relationship.

The Jackson Barnett scandal generated a lengthy debate about the
proper limits of the federal trust relationship. On the low end of the scale,
the liberationists in Oklahoma and elsewhere clamored for a fast and firm
end to restrictions, so that Indian lands would be taxable and alienable.
Ultimate termination of the trust relationship was the policy goal defined
by the Dawes and Burke acts, and this solution seemed most in keeping
with America's democratic ideals. However, historical experience showed
repeatedly that Indians' loss of resources came in the wake of the removal
of federal trust protection. Moving up the scale, there were more moderate
federal efforts for various types of controlled transitions. Finally, there were
the New Dealers who wanted to reorganize the trust relationship and restore the original relationship of the federal government to corporate Indian communities.

At the grandest level of analysis, the Barnett drama was a power struggle between the federal government and Oklahoma over who could best
fulfill the legal trust responsibility of protecting Indian property. The
volatile issue of the overlapping jurisdictions of the Department of the
Interior and the Oklahoma courts was made even more problematic by
its intersection with other axes of tension, for example, the bifurcation of
paternalism into its malevolent and benevolent manifestations and the
bifurcation of opinion on Jackson Barnett's competency. Both the probate
courts and the federal government were legally bound to serve their dependent wards' needs; their empowerment with managerial control was
predicated on fulfilling this trust to incompetents. Yet both were guilty of
betraying the trust and siphoning off Barnett's resources.

Commissioner Burke repeated endlessly that the Oklahomans were on
the malevolent end and the federal government was on the benevolent end
of the paternalism axis. Relatively speaking, Burke was correct. The federal
government was actuated by higher motives of disinterested public service
to a disadvantaged minority. The Burke Act unquestionably preserved and
protected Indians' allotted property at a critical time in history. The selfish
motives embedded in the Oklahoma guardianship system are obvious.

Plundering Indians, argued Angie Debo, was a patriotic act in Oklahoma: "personal greed and public spirit were almost inextricably joined."[1]

Yet, the purity of the federal government's motives was tainted by a conflict of interest between its trust relationship to Indians and its mandate to do the will of the American majority. Authority that Congress delegated to the Interior Department to manage Indian resources implicitly contained unwritten strictures: an economic mandate not to burden the taxpayers with expenses for Indians' economic uplift and a regulated but steady release of "surplus" Indian property for taxation and consumption by the non-Indian majority. The federal government placed a check on local greed, but it could not resist the powerful political and economic forces driving to assimilate the Indian minority's property into the market economy. The Burke Act slowed and regulated the process, but the Indian estate steadily drained away. The federal government's role in the attempted transfer of $1.5 million of Jackson Barnett's assets to non-Indian institutions in the Sells administration—and Commissioner Burke's illegal transfer of $1.1 million of assets to Barnett's wife and to a Baptist institution—was emblematic of a larger historical process of controlled release. Most revealingly, there was a consensus among non-Indians that channeling Indian surplus wealth to more capable hands was appropriate.

Jackson Barnett had an undeniably large surplus, and its alleged mismanagement attracted national attention. The magnitude of the Barnett gift to Bacone was what drew suspicion, not the principle of donating Indian surpluses to charity. Other Oklahoma Indians gave comparable shares of their fortunes to Bacone, but their gifts were ruled legitimate.[2] Conserving Jackson Barnett's funds for the greatest good for the greatest number was a laudable ambition. Had the gift to Bacone not been flawed by the slight to Jackson Barnett's Indian relatives, Indian education might have received a precious endowment.

One of the most striking and ultimately the most tragic aspect of the Barnett saga was that Jackson Barnett's choices regarding the disposition of his estate were deemed irrelevant in the courts. The grand controversy over the Barnett fortune had less to do with Indian consent or the lack thereof—or who was serving Jackson Barnett's best interests for security, health, or happiness—than with the question of who was legally entitled to mine the huge fortune. Jackson Barnett's case stands as a towering monument to the mockery of "trust."

Barnett's story illuminates many of the power structures and cultural paradigms that disempowered restricted Indians in the twentieth century. It is a window through which the underlying politics of economic self-interest and racial control are exposed beneath the rhetoric of liberation and protection. So-called incompetent Indians were held captive in a legal status that silenced their voices and rendered them powerless. It was not an uncommon practice for Indian surplus funds to be diverted to pay the administrative costs of federally imposed programs, often without Indian consent and without giving the Indian owners a proper accounting. Tribal funds were eyed as the means of supporting missionary schools, for instance, but in the early twentieth century, the U.S. Supreme Court denied missionaries the use of Indian trust funds for their educational work among the tribes.[3]

A number of restricted Indians of Jackson Barnett's day had money impounded in federal accounts for lease transactions on their allotments. Though the accounts of Jackson Barnett and the oil-rich Osage were overflowing and the accounts of poorer Indians were insignificant comparatively, rich and poor shared a federal guardian in the Indian bureau. The bureau had definite beliefs about what were legitimate expenditures, and in the early twentieth century it routinely blocked individuals' access to their own funds based on convictions that income from inheritance or leasing was undeserved or that Indians should be forced to work rather than live on "unearned" income.[4] In this lopsided system of racial control, the collection of Indian monies in individual accounts posed a great temptation. The loss of restricted land was slowed by the Burke Act, but the Individual Indian Money (IIM) accounts were insufficiently protected. And as the Jackson Barnett case revealed, the greatest danger of pilfering may not have been the dishonest bureau employee bent on embezzlement, but rather the well-meaning bureau employee wielding too much power over impounded Indian funds. A system designed to promote agency discretion and flexibility lacked the precision and accountability of a record system designed to make payouts to account holders.

The legacy of the Jackson Barnett scandal was that it forced a reexamination of the federal trust relationship. With the passage of the Dawes and amended Dawes legislation, Congress had unknowingly created a self-perpetuating bureaucracy within the Department of the Interior with virtually unlimited powers over individual Indians' legal status and the disposition of their property and its proceeds. Other flaws were exposed, namely, that the bureau lacked a meaningful definition of incompetency to undergird its exercise of broad power.

The Barnett scandal in the 1920s heightened congressional awareness regarding the unwieldy bureaucratic problem of federal trust administration of restricted Indians' individual accounts. The Bureau of Indian Affairs had little expertise in financial accounting or investment. The Interior Department became the middleman in a miasma of transactions: negotiating and approving leases for grazing, logging, and minerals on Indian lands, then collecting, banking, investing, and distributing the proceeds. A host of unanticipated difficulties arose regarding recordkeeping on more than two hundred thousand individual Indian trust properties. When the accounting system was established in the early twentieth century, no one anticipated the complexities of dealing with the estates of very wealthy Indians like Jackson Barnett nor the problems of managing Indian properties over the course of several generations. Accounting problems multiplied as the original allottees of 160-acre parcels died and the properties were divided among their heirs and then divided again by succeeding generations of heirs. The General Accounting Office reported problems from the 1880s, and Commissioner Burke sounded the alarm loudly in the late 1920s during hearings on the Indian trust bill. In an effort to more efficiently manage and protect Indian resources, Burke believed, the management of the small percentage of wealthy Indians should be turned over to private trust companies, leaving the bureau to focus upon the remaining Indian trust property.

The leading edge of congressional reform in the wake of the Barnett scandal was redefining the administrative practices for the rich Indians in Oklahoma. Disabused of any naïve notion that Indians with oil property would retain their mineral properties or accumulated money if federal protection were lifted, Congress inched reluctantly toward the decision to extend federal protection over the Osage and the Five Civilized Tribes for another twenty-five years beyond 1931. A benchmark reversal of the official public policy of speedily bringing public responsibility to an end, Congress decided to take the tack of "controlled transition" in the late 1920s. While this was unquestionably a significant indicator of the direction of congressional movement in the New Deal, this hallmark legislation represented less a conscious shift in national policy than yet another round of compromise legislation between the state of Oklahoma and the federal government over whose jurisdiction controlled Oklahoma Indians' valuable property.

For Burke and his successors, Commissioner Charles Rhoads and Interior Secretary Lyman Wilbur, finding a legislative solution for the minority of rich Indians was compelling. Although Congress had refused to pass Burke's legislation to sustain his action in creating private trusts for Jackson Barnett and a handful of other rich Indians, his successors followed this plan for privatization, lacking an alternative. After the Barnett trust was broken, the Department of the Interior used its well-defined authority to remove the restrictions on some wealthy Indians; as their first act, these competent Indians contracted private trust agreements. Commissioner Rhoads, a former banker and trust executive, liked this approach. A 1933 law gave statutory authority to the creation of these private trusts. Another 1933 law conserved the large accounts of rich Indians with oil royalties under federal supervision; Congress refused the Oklahoma guardians' demand that $28 million in Indian oil royalties held in federal government accounts be turned over to them to manage. During Franklin D. Roosevelt's presidency, Commissioner John Collier and Interior Secretary Harold Ickes moved carefully to create more private trusts and to break up questionable ones.[5]

The search for new ways to improve the bureaucratic system for managing the estates and individual accounts of the vast majority of Indians was not seriously engaged until John Collier became commissioner of Indian affairs during the New Deal. Collier's legislation, the Indian Reorganization Act of 1934, tried to strike at the heart of the problem: first, acknowledge the wrongs done by allotment, individuation, and paternalism and then institute a new paternal system for Indians reorganized into collectives. It attempted to realign the trust relationship with the Indian nations according to the rule of law defined in the *Worcester* decision and to restore the federal trust relationship on a government-to-government basis. To accomplish this, Indian communities were encouraged to reorganize politically and economically, to write constitutions, and to incorporate. At least in theory, self-determination, due process, and civil rights returned to Indian communities. The unworkable legal category of incompetent Indian based on blood quantum, was permanently jettisoned. In the extraordinary circumstances of widespread suffering in the Great Depression years, Congress was persuaded that all Indians—poor and rich, above-average in intelligence and slow-witted, old and young, full-bloods and mixed-bloods—should have an opportunity to regroup as tribal entities to promote economic recovery. Exempted from the Indian Reorganization Act, Oklahoma Indians were ultimately offered the option to reorganize under the new trust relationship by the Oklahoma Indian Welfare Act of 1935. A few Creek towns subsequently regrouped as tribal communities.[6]

Although Collier provided a framework for reorientation that would eliminate the worst abuses of the allotment era, the Indian Reorganization Act could not reverse the past and reabsorb individualized Indian property back into collective tribal ownership. Tribal incorporation and collective resource management lacked a public mandate. Congress provided very little money to repurchase land lost through allotment. Many Indians had come to believe that assimilation into the dominant society was the best course and fully embraced the concept of private property ownership. They were unwilling to risk their lands in an untried experiment in collective tribal ownership and management. To many educated and Christianized Indians, it appeared as if the bureau was trying to throw them back to the "blanket," that is, to antiquated systems of "primitive" people. Some, like the successful Creek oil man Joseph Bruner, repudiated Collier's New Deal as communistic. As a result of such opposition, a majority of Indians who had been allotted lands earlier in the century continued to hold individual trust properties; as in the past, the federal government managed their lease agreements for grazing, logging, and minerals.

After World War II, the national policy pendulum swung dramatically back toward assimilation, individualization of Indian property, and termination of the federal trust relationship. Once again, termination proved to be an economic fiasco for Indians and was quickly reversed. During President Lyndon Johnson's War on Poverty in the 1960s and the era of self-determination that followed during Richard Nixon's presidency, there was a return to Collier's policies of government-to-government relations as the honorable course. In the last seventy-five years, the federal trust relationship has become permanent. The federal government continues to play a key role in resource management on Indian lands into the present day, more by default than by conscious design.

Critics like Ward Churchill and Winona LaDuke are highly skeptical that the 1934 Indian Reorganization Act and the reaffirmation of government-to-government relations in the 1960s and 1970s did much to reorient the federal trust relationship in a positive way. The federal government's relationship to the nation's "internal colonies" has not changed significantly from the Burke era, they argue. Indian choice and Indian benefits are illusory, even though Indians in the nation's reservations are the lawful owners of one-third of the nation's low-sulphur coal, 20 percent of known U.S. reserves of oil and natural gas, and more than one-half of uranium and other mineral deposits. There is a strong impetus to pull these vital resources into the service of majority interests as need demands. U.S. corporations and the federal government collaborate to exploit Indian resources, LaDuke and Churchill maintain. Royalties from minerals provide only small per capita incomes for reservation members, and their mining causes irreversible environmental damage.[7]

Giving substance to this interpretation that change is illusory were the conditions in Oklahoma as the Jackson Barnett case passed from memory and the flurry of reform activity subsided. The Oklahoma probate system remained impervious to reform, and the dynamics of Indian politics in Oklahoma remained much the same, brokered between the federal and the state guardians. In the 1960s, Clyde Warrior, a Ponca Indian of Oklahoma, wrote:

> The local white power elites who protest the loudest against federal control are the very ones who would keep us poor in spirit and worldly goods in order to enhance their own personal and economic station in the world. Nor have those of us on reservations fared any better under the paternalistic control of the federal administration.[8]

From 1934 to 1999, 17 million acres of trust land nationwide were lost to Indian owners. Creek lawyer Marcella Giles asserts that 90 percent of oil-rich trust land in eastern Oklahoma has fallen out of Indian hands in the last fifty years. Moses and Frances Bruno's oil property, for example, was sold in the 1960s to satisfy a $97 grocery debt. The Bruno descendants have spent thirty years trying to understand why the family's oil property was sold. "In Oklahoma, it's the fox guarding the henhouse," says Giles. "There is a simple reason why: oil."[9] Though some Indians are fortunate to have income from royalties for mineral resources or other leases, the checks received from the bureau do not raise them from poverty.

More troubling still, a majority of the approximately 300,000 Indians in Oklahoma and across the nation with IIM accounts in the Department of the Treasury today cannot get an accounting of their own assets from the trustee. "There's no question the trust system collapsed years ago," says Kevin Gover, a Pawnee, who headed the Bureau of Indian Affairs during the Clinton administration. But neither the executive nor legislative branches have the political will to fix it.[10] Lacking political clout, Indians' complaints about the malfunctioning trust system are ignored. A quick summary of the trust relationship in Indian country, quips Cheyenne-Muskogee artist and commentator Suzan Shown Harjo, is "They don't trust us and we don't trust them."[11]

After many years of sweeping the problem under the table, the national crisis over the malfunctioning trust system has exploded and plagues the George W. Bush administration. Elouise Cobell, a member of the Blackfeet tribe of Montana, filed a class-action lawsuit in 1996—*Elouise Peion Cobell et al. v. Bruce Babbitt et al.*—against the secretary of the Interior because of the repeated failures of the bureau to accurately account for Indian money and to distribute it to its rightful owners. It is the largest case ever brought by Indians against the U.S. government. The projected sum owed Indians has ballooned from $2.2 billion in 2001 to $137.2 billion in early 2003. Suzan Harjo says the case isn't about money: "It is a matter of trust." Keith Harper, a Washington-based attorney for the Native American Rights Fund, which is conducting the case for the plaintiffs, concurs: the trust fund case is "about redefining that relationship."[12]

Cobell provides a personal view of the poignant consequences of the mismanagement of Indian trust funds over the last half century. She recalls as a child in the 1950s, that elders came to her father's house to ask where their money was. People who desperately needed cash were given excuses and delays. They were intimidated into passivity and powerlessness. They didn't know who to ask for information about tribal trust accounts or individual accounts containing income from leasing. They were not informed who had leased their land or for what purpose, how much the lease yielded, or how long the lease was to run. Checks for a pittance were mailed to Indian recipients without an accounting or an explanation.[13]

Cobell has been a moving force behind exposing the misadministration of the Indian trust accounts. After obtaining some training in business and accounting, she became the treasurer for the Blackfeet tribe and endeavored to find out about her people's money. Where was it and how much? What interest was it earning? Shocked to discover there was negative interest, she persisted in demanding an explanation, only to learn that the Indian bureau had loaned her tribe's money to another tribe and had forgotten to replace it. When she failed to get accounting information locally or at regional bureau offices, Cobell went to the Department of the Interior. The spreadsheets she prepared showed huge gaps where oil and gas companies had leased out land. To her immense surprise, Cobell discovered that Interior and the Treasury had no accounts receivable systems in place.

In 1989, Cobell attended a meeting in the White House arranged by Oklahoma Democratic congressman Mike Synar. In 1992, a House committee issued a scathing report titled "Misplaced Trust," and two years later Congress passed the Indian Trust Fund Mismanagement Reform Act. Paul Homan, a banking executive, was appointed as trustee to make a full accounting of the money owed to the Blackfeet and several other tribes west of the Mississippi.[14] Homan reported that the bureau's accounting system was the worst operating system he had ever seen.[15] When no reforms were forthcoming and Cobell failed to get satisfactory answers in a meeting with Attorney General Janet Reno's staff in February 1996, she decided litigation was the only remaining option.

The class-action suit filed by Cobell has three objectives. First, the suit asks for an accurate annual accounting for about 300,000 Indians with IIM accounts involving 11 million acres of Indian land and for 280 tribal trust accounts involving another 45 million acres. A late 1990s audit revealed that tribal trust transactions made between 1973 and 1992 could not be traced through documents. The second goal is to get compensation for unpaid royalties.[16] Third, the suit aims to get Congress to fix the system and redefine the trust relationship to be more accountable to Indians. Only the threat of litigation, plaintiffs and their counsel argue, will force Congress to make real reforms. "The trust is a shambles and in need of top-to-bottom reconstruction," Secretary of the Interior Gale A. Norton said in November 2001 as the Interior Department struggled to extricate itself from the lawsuit.[17]

Like the Jackson Barnett case in the 1920s and 1930s, the current trust fund mess is scandalous and shocking in its proportions. The hyperbolic rhetoric of the plaintiffs regarding the Bureau of Indian Affairs' "egregious misconduct" and "reckless disregard for Indian assets" seems justified.[18] What makes the case truly scandalous are the highly disturbing revelations about the arrogance of power and the gross negligence. Cobell faced denials and inaction from the federal government even though she had unearthed evidence of serious flaws in the accounting system. Keith Harper, Native American Rights Fund attorney, comments that no other group of people could have its funds taken and mismanaged over the years and then have the government say, "'We're not going to provide you an accounting or fix the problem.' It's a blatant manifestation of the Indian/non-Indian relationship."[19] After the court case began, the court ordered the Interior and Treasury departments to produce all records for the accounts of the plaintiffs going back to the beginning of allotment. The process revealed financial disarray; documents had been lost, damaged, and destroyed. The records are in an utterly chaotic state. Records for only 50,000 accounts (about 17 percent of the 300,000 plaintiffs) can be tracked, government officials admit. The federal government's closest estimates as of 1999 are that 61 percent of the IIM trust accounts had less than $25 in them; 22 percent had up to $1,000; 14 percent had up to $100,000; and less than 1 percent had more than $100,000. "We've been trying to undo more than eight decades of problems," said Thomas Thompson, acting trust manager.[20] Kevin Gover puts the problem in perspective. He has a 1/27 share in a forty-acre allotment in Oklahoma. His 1995 accounting was for seven cents. The millions of dollars it would cost the U.S. taxpayer to recover documents far exceeds the value of the majority of these IIM accounts.[21]

Though the plaintiffs were willing to settle out of court initially, the Justice Department put the kibosh on this, figuring it could win the case on appeal. Most abhorrent is the recent revelation in the case that the defendant (the U.S. government) repeatedly violated court orders and shredded documents, including destroying between 1998 and 1999 162 boxes of Indian financial records that had been stored in a Maryland warehouse. After Interior issued statements that the problem was being fixed, the court discovered that the federal government was taking no action. The exasperated federal judge slapped a contempt of court charge on Secretary of the Interior Gale Norton and ordered court supervision of the defendant's progress in repairing the system. Cobell and her coplaintiffs are seeking jail time and fines for Norton and her predecessor, Bruce Babbitt, along with thirty-seven other high-ranking federal government officials for "malfeasance, lying to the court, destruction of evidence, refusing to comply with court orders and covering up gross mismanagement."[22] Critics like Senator John McCain called the tribal trust fund mess a "national disgrace."[23]

The course of the current trust fund scandal invites comparison to the Jackson Barnett case. Representing manifold historic failures in accountability and due process, both pivot on the arrogance of power and the mismanagement of Indian resources. In each case, the Department of the Interior stonewalled, denying there was any problem and attempting to squelch litigation; federal power was used to insulate the government itself from criticism, which would challenge the status quo. Only when Congress demanded action did the plaintiffs get the break they needed. Once the situation was exposed to public scrutiny, questions were raised about the relationship of the federal mismanagement of Indian trust funds to persistent Indian poverty. Suspicions arise that somehow the Indians' fair share of the proceeds from valuable resources is being siphoned off illegally. As in the Jackson Barnett case, the initial expectation that overt corruption in the form of graft or embezzlement would be exposed through investigation has eventually given way to more complex explanations. Many of the Indian's purported losses are the result of bureaucratic malfunctioning, expedient compromises, and legal processes that funnel monies from leasing contracts to non-Indian hands. For example, private corporations, such as oil companies, have the legal expertise to work the laws in their favor whereas Indians are often poor and powerless. Lacking mechanisms of accountability, those Indian funds carefully conserved in trust accounts continue to be diverted to serve non-Indian interests, without the Indian account holders' knowledge or consent. For example, Indian money from a general fund was used to bail out New York City during its 1975 fiscal crisis and to save Chrysler Corporation from bankruptcy.[24]

As in the Barnett scandal, the trust fund suits promise to have long and tortuous tours through the federal courts, causing considerable political damage to the moral credibility of the Department of the Interior and to the Bureau of Indian Affairs. High-ranking public figures are being held culpable for the inactions and failings of their predecessors. Humiliating publicity enlarges the possibility that the need for a major reorganization in resource management will prompt Congress to take action. Without the threat of litigation and the attendant national scandal animating Congress, no reform of this antiquated trust system would be likely.

Unlike the Jackson Barnett litigation, in the current case, Indians are the plaintiffs. The Justice Department (at least so far) has maintained solidarity with Interior. The Justice Department has deep pockets for litigation and has a legion of lawyers working on the case. The fees for the Native American Rights Fund lawyers have to be raised from private sources. In the Jackson Barnett case, payment for much of the litigation ultimately came from Barnett's own funds. In the current mess, taxpayers will fund the federal government's defense of the class-action suit. Thus far, there have been more than $600,000 in fines, and the litigation and efforts to fix the system have cost $614 million. $110 million was devoted to trust management reform in 2002. Secretary Gale Norton has removed the trust accounts to a newly created agency within the bureau, the Bureau of Indian Trust Management, and has asked for an additional $84 million in the budget. The House Appropriations Committee has expressed concern for the endless expenses, which thus far have yielded so few results.[25] The results of a study by a private firm made public in early 2003 reveal that the plaintiffs' claims of $137 billion due them are wildly overstated. As the study tracked only the accounts of four individuals, Dennis Gingold, the lawyer for the plaintiffs, discounted the results, as did some members of Congress. Nonetheless, as the $20 million survey of the four individuals' accounts over ninety years entailed the examination of 162,000 documents and yielded such insignificant discrepancies, Congress will probably refuse to fund further studies as fiscally irresponsible, and an out-of-court settlement for far less than the plaintiffs' claim appears likely.[26]

The current trust fund fiasco underscores a great irony: a system based on the premise of native people's incompetency in business has been unmasked for its abject failure in sound business procedures. Jackson Barnett's case poignantly attests to the earlier manifestations of the poisoned fruits of the individuation of property for Indian people in an era when racism was more blatant. Barnett's mental debilitation was exaggerated proportionately to the size of his wealth by the Oklahomans and defined as a deficiency typical of Indians by the bureau. The individuation of Indian communal property was foisted on unwilling Indians, purportedly to bestow the sacred right of private property upon them, yet what belonged to Indians was actually made more vulnerable to exploitation, thus throwing the onus on Indian people for their own victimization. As Chitto Harjo once said, he "would not mind so much playing the white man's game if only the white man would not make all the rules."[27]

In its historical trust relationship with Indian people as collectivities and as individuals, the federal government has shown itself to be a fickle trustee. At times, the Indian bureau has valiantly and heroically championed Indian interests and defended Indian property rights in the face of monumental forces waged against it. On the darker side, Congress and the Department of the Interior have been complicit agents in the transfer of Indian resources to the non-Indian majority. Untangling the twisted strands of benevolent and malevolent paternalism is a seemingly insuperable task, but what is abundantly clear is twofold. Power over Indian lands and resources has been a corrupting force, and greater accountability to native people is urgently needed. In a moving speech commemorating the 175th anniversary of the Indian bureau in 2000, Kevin Gover pointed toward a mode of redress to the historic inequities and injustices in the federal trust relationship. Gover called for an end to a policy that proceeds from the "assumption that Indians possess less human genius than other races" and that made the bureau "complicit in the theft of Indian property." To heal the wounds, Gover offered a heartfelt apology.[28]

The great crimes exposed in the Barnett scandal ultimately do not lie in violations to Jackson Barnett personally—except insofar as his wishes for the disposition of his fortune were ignored—but in the legacy of shame and pain for Indian people that continues today as destructive forces in Indian communities. Jackson Barnett symbolized the wedding of well-meaning paternalism with the abuse of power in one moment in history.

Appendices

Appendix I:
Assets of the Five Civilized Tribes in 1894

	Trust funds (dollars)	Acreage	Final Dawes Roll (number of persons)
Cherokee	2,716,979.98	4,420,068	41,824
Choctaw	975,258.91	6,953,048	25,168
Mississippi Choctaw			1,660
Chickasaw	1,206,695.66	4,707,903	10,966
Creek	2,275,168	3,079,095	18,761
Seminole	2,070,000	365,852	3,127
Totals	9,244,102.40	19,525,966	101,506

From Debo, *And Still,* 6, 7, 47.

Appendix II:
Final Rolls of the Dawes Commission
Breakdown by Ethnicity

	Full-Blood	Mixed-Blood	Subtotal	White	Freedmen	Total
Cherokee	8,703	27,916	36,619	286	4,919	41,824
Choctaw	7,087	10,401	17,488	1,651	6,029	25,168
Mississippi Choctaw	1,357	303	1,660			1,600
Chickasaw	1,515	4,144	5,659	645	4,662	10,966
Creek	6,858	5,094	11,952		6,809	18,761
Seminole	1,254	887	2,141		986	3,127
Totals	26,774	48,745	75,519	2,582	23,405	101,506
	(26.4%)	(48%)	(74.4%)	(2.5%)	(23.1%)	

From Debo, *And Still,* 47.

Appendix III:
The *Equitable* Case and
the Oklahoma Prohibition Suit

United States v. Equitable Trust Co., 283 US 738 (1931)

This case was begun by O'Hornett and refiled by Bailey—*Jackson Barnett, a Mental Incompetent, by Elmer S. Bailey v. American Baptist Home Missionary Society and Equitable Trust Company of New York*—Equity 31–91 in the U.S. District Court for the Southern District of New York on January 22, 1925, to cancel the AHMS's trust at Equitable Trust Company. The United States joined the plaintiff on January 20, 1926.

   Barnett v. Equitable Trust was decided by Judge Knox in August 1927 (21 F. 2d 325), invalidating the gift of $550,000 to the AHMS (donee), which was held in a trust account by Equitable (trustee). Voiding the gift and trust, the court ordered the money to be returned to the secretary of the Interior, disallowing Bailey's request that the money be returned to the guardian. The case was appealed to the Second Circuit Court of Appeals on February 15, 1928, by the AHMS. As the AHMS and Equitable held money in "joint decree" and only AHMS filed the appeal within the deadline (which expired February 22, 1928), there was a motion to dismiss for nonjoinder of necessary party. The Baptist counsel Fettretch made an unsuccessful motion to separate the Baptists from the Equitable defendants, and subsequently a motion was made to join Equitable to appeal the Knox decision to the Supreme Court. However, Charles Rogers missed the date for filing. The appeal was thus rejected on procedural grounds. In the Appeal and Error, the appeals court granted the plaintiff's motion to dismiss on May 7, 1928 (26 F. 2d 350). In October 1928, the U.S. Supreme Court heard No. 320, *ABHMS v. Jackson Barnett*, 278 US 626, declined the petition for writ of certiorari, and thus refused to hear the case.

When the guardian's lawyers applied for legal fees for their five years of work in breaking the trusts, working side by side with the Justice Department lawyers, Justice opposed the awarding of the sum requested. Commissioner Burke also opposed the granting of attorneys' fees in the *Equitable* case, fearing the money in the guardian's hands would strengthen his litigation in other cases pending in the Barnett estate. On December 20, 1928, the Justice Department filed a motion to oppose allowances, arguing that its lawyers had done the lion's share of the work from 1926 to 1929. Moreover, since Jackson Barnett's money was restricted, the court had no authority over allowances, and Bailey's counsel was instructed to apply to Interior for payment.[1] The lawyers for the guardian felt betrayed and argued for their 40 percent share of the recovered funds in the Equitable account, which had grown from $550,000 to $657,843.27 from February 1, 1923, to November 2, 1927. Hummer and Foster and their subsidiaries, the firms of Cochran and Ellison and McCrory and Monk, had worked on the Barnett case for six years, from 1923 to 1929, and Patterson, Eagle, Greenough and Day, which handled the *Equitable* case in New York for Hummer and Foster, had labored without pay for four years. (Carroll Walter was the trial lawyer for this firm.)

In a supplemental decree on January 9, 1929, *United States v. Equitable et al.* (34 F. 2d 916), Judge Knox ruled regarding the division among the lawyers: one-third of the total was to go to Patterson, Eagle, Greenough and Day and two-thirds to Hummer and Foster, Cochran and Ellison, and McCrory and Monk.[2] Knox refused to give them the 40 percent they demanded, deeming 25 percent plus $10,000 in expenses to be fair and adequate remuneration. The total for the lawyers was $184,881.08, which included $4,282.93 for expenses, $7,500 for the guardian Bailey, and $500 for his expenses. That it had cost the Barnett estate this large sum to set aside the charitable donation to Bacone University and the Murrow Orphans Home was appalling to many, including Justice, which contested the 25 percent award.[3]

A petition for writ of certiorari to the Circuit Court of Appeals for the Second Circuit was granted. Judge Learned Hand reduced Bailey's attorneys' fees to $100,000, because Justice did not require Bailey's withdrawal once it had intervened, and Bailey's lawyers did much of the work; the case was complicated, and the hazard was real because the outcome was uncertain, and they might have remained uncompensated (280 US 550).

Justice appealed the decision to the Supreme Court, arguing on December 1–2, 1930, that the fees were in conflict with the existing restrictions on the disposal of the trust fund and were excessive. *United States v. Equitable Trust Company of New York* was decided on June 1, 1931 (283 US 738, 746); Justice Van Devanter reduced the attorneys' fees to $50,000.

Supreme Court of Oklahoma Prohibition Suit

Contrived by M. L. Mott, this suit was designed to overturn the guardianship of Bailey. The key issues were Jackson Barnett's competency, federal authority in making such determinations, and questions based on a mishandling of the incompetency preceedings in 1912.

In 1912, the Okmulgee County court's finding that Jackson was legally incompetent and in need of a guardian was appealed to the district court, and Judge Wade Stanfield overturned the lower court's ruling, finding Jackson mentally competent on June 24, 1912. When county judge George A. Johns refused to enter orders after the filing in the county court of the judgment of the district court, on July 8, 1912, he was required to do so by a peremptory writ of mandamus. The district court (22d Judicial District) was not reconvened in Sapula until September 3, 1912. This order was not recalled. On September 5, 1912, the judge of the district court of Okmulgee County attempted to make an order setting aside its said judgment of June 24. But from August 7 to September 5, the journal of the district court shows orders entered "in vacation." The court thus never formally rescinded the June 24, 1912, Stanfield decision, yet O'Hornett and Bailey acted as Barnett's guardians. (This case was exceptionally carelessly and indifferently handled, according to the Oklahoma Supreme Court decision in *Barnett v. Barnett*, 252 Pac 414.)

The U.S. probate attorney R. B. Drake filed suit in the Okmulgee County court in Jackson's name to set aside the guardianship in 1925 in *Jackson Barnett by His Prochien Ami R. B. Drake et al. v. W. A. Barnett, County Judge of Okmulgee County, and Elmer Bailey, aka Barnett v. Barnett.* Simultaneously, Mott's partner Lytle filed in U.S. District Court for the Eastern District to carry the case forward as Elmer Bailey was successful in his motion to remove Drake as plaintiff; an appeal was taken to the Oklahoma appeals court, which sustained Bailey's motion to dismiss the case (40 Okla. 541). Thus, the appeals court judged Barnett to be incompetent. Judge James Hepburn heard the case at the appellate level and made the decision on July 16, 1926.[4]

Judge Branson's Dissent in *Barnett et al. Plaintiffs in Error v. W. A. Barnett, County Judge of Okmulgee County et al.* (247 Pac 1115, July 13, 1926, Defendants in Error, No. 1678).

Branson criticized the court for failing to write an opinion, saying the county court attempted to exercise jurisdiction that violated an act of Congress (act of May 27, 1908), which did not give the county court jurisdiction over adult allottees of the restricted class. Congress reserved these exclusive rights via the act of 1908 and the Enabling Act. Barnett's incompetency was not "due to mental deficiency, however, but to racial weakness, lack of education, and business training." The secretary of the Interior's paramount guardianship, conferred by Congress, was in keeping with the public trust and humanitarian justice. Interior Department regulations made in pursuance of the statue have the force and effect of law. The actions of the purported guardian were against the ward's will. The Hepburn decision construed the gifts to Anna Barnett and the AHMS as "loots."

> Can it be said that a gift by a man to his wife is a loot? Can it be said that a gift for the benefit of an educational institution, whose efforts are confined to Indians, among whom the donor has spent his life, and of whom he is one, can properly be referred to as a loot when the Indian who makes the gift recites in the written document the purposes thereof and the reason therefore? Can it be said that he loots his own estate by the donation to his wife of what apparently is much less than the succession laws of Oklahoma give a wife on the death of her husband? (1116)

Cherokee Nation v. Georgia cited the duty of Interior to protect Indian rights in the absence of specific provisions of law. *Heckman v. United States* (224 US 413) says:

> There can be no more complete representation than that on the part of the United States in acting on behalf of these dependents, whom Congress, with respect to the lands, has not yet released from tutelage. Its efficacy does not depend upon the Indians' acquiescence. (quoted p. 1116)

Branson traced the source of the Barnett trust's legitimacy to the Interior regulations bestowed by the plenary control of Congress, which recognizes no "limitations that are inconsistent with the discharge of the national duty." Conferring citizenship is not inconsistent with the continuation of federal guardianship:

> A practical knowledge of the action of any one of the great departments of the government must convince every person that the head of a department in the distribution of its duties and responsibilities, is often compelled to exercise his discretion. He is limited

in the exercise of his powers by the law; but it does not follow that
he must show statutory provision for everything he does. (1117)

Interior's authority to deal with restricted property is superior to the sources
of authority of county courts and guardians, who cannot substitute their
guardianship for the federal guardianship. "If this were possible in one case,
the county courts, if they saw fit, might appoint guardians for each and
every restricted Indian," thus logically constraining the secretary from carrying out the laws of Congress by dealing with a person (i.e., a guardian)

> whose desires, whims, and caprices he could be compelled to re-
> spect. . . . If the mental competency of this ward to initiate the
> donation was questioned, it was within the quasi-judicial power of
> the Secretary of the Interior to pass on the same, and ascertain
> whether he was of disposing mind; this is a power necessarily given
> him in performing the duties as to Indians, imposed by Congress.

A guardian appointed by a court has authority to protect the person but
not the property of a restricted Indian, which is reserved in the secretary of
the Interior or conferred on such by the courts (1117).

Supreme Court of Oklahoma Decision: *Barnett v. Barnett,* 121 Okla 142 (1926)

Both of the appeals in the *Barnett v. Barnett* case—No. 17061 and No.
17062—were perfected to the Supreme Court of Oklahoma. In the appeal
of Jackson Barnett No. 17061 (252 Pac 410), on Nov. 30, 1926, the Oklahoma Supreme Court reversed the Oklahoma appeals court decision of
judge Hepburn regarding Jackson's mental incompetency and nullified the
guardianship. The Oklahoma Supreme Court ordered E. S. Bailey's appointment as guardian vacated, ruling that "the actual state of his bodily
mental powers" of Jackson Barnett is "beyond the scope of the instant inquiry," (415–416). The court said that the guardian is to serve the ward and
cannot have "adverse or selfish purpose or interest to subserve" in bringing
litigation. In other words, the guardian was self-serving rather than serving
the interests of his ward in bringing the obstructive legislation to block the
trusts. Charles Mason delivered the opinion. Nicholson, Branson, Phelps,
Lester, Hunt and Riley concur red. Judge Harrison agreed that Bailey's
guardianship should be vacated, but made a dissent as he viewed the federal government as having exclusive jurisdiction over restricted full-bloods
as a "federal instrumentality," thus he believed that the Oklahoma Supreme Court had no jurisdiction in the case. *Barnett v. Barnett,* No. 17062,
Supreme Court of Oklahoma, Dec. 7, 1926 (252 Pac 418) resolved the com-
panion case in the proceedings instituted in the county court of Okmulgee
by R. B. Drake. The identical cases were argued and briefed together, and
the decisions were the same.

Notes

Abbreviations
         AB   Anna Laura Lowe Barnett
      ABHSA   American Baptist Historical Society Archives, Valley Forge, PA
       AHMS   American (Baptist) Home Missionary Society
   And Still   Angie Debo, *And Still the Waters Run*
         AR   *Annual Report*
    Att. Gen.   Attorney General
     Bancroft   Bancroft Library, University of California, Berkeley
     BIA Circ   Records of the Bureau of Indian Affairs, procedural issuances,
               orders, and circulars, 1854–1955
       Blend   Benay Blend, "Jackson Barnett and the Oklahoma Indian Probate
               System"
   Chronology   Department of the Interior chronological file on Jackson Barnett,
               1907–1936, Box 11445-1, RG48, National Archives II, College
               Park, MD
         CIA   Commissioner of Indian Affairs
          CO   *Chronicles of Oklahoma*
 Collier Papers John Collier Papers, Yale University, New Haven, CT
          CR   *Congressional Record*
         CSB   William C. Sturtevant, ed., *Creek Source Book*
        dep.   deposition
         D/I   Department of the Interior

D/J	Department of Justice
DO	*Daily Oklahoman*
Eq-N67	*United States v. Anna Laura Barnett*, Case in Equity, N-67, Boxes 314–318, RG21, Records of the District Court of the United States for the Southern District of California, NARA, Pacific Region, Laguna Niguel, CA
ET	Elmer Thomas Collection, Carl Albert Center, Congressional Archives, University of Oklahoma, Norman
Exh.	exhibit
f.	file or folder
FW-Micro	Selected Records relating to Jackson Barnett, 7RA-99, RG75, NARA, Southwest Region, Fort Worth, TX
HH	House Hearing
HRep	House Report
IRA	Indian Rights Association
JB	Jackson Barnett
Kappler	Charles Kappler, ed., *Indian Affairs: Laws and Treaties*
LAH	*Los Angeles Herald*
LAPL	Los Angeles Public Library
LAT	*Los Angeles Times*
MDP	*Muskogee Daily Phoenix*
MIA-LN	Mission Indian Agency Records, RG75, NARA, Pacific Region, Laguna Niguel, CA
MTD	*Muskogee Times-Democrat*
NAI	National Archives I, Washington D.C.
NALC	National American Legal Collection, Equity 4556, "Depositions Taken in a Suit to Determine the Heirs of Jackson Barnett [1934–1936]"
NARA	National Archives and Records Administration
NYT	*New York Times*
OCHS	Okmulgee County Historical Society, Okmulgee, OK
ODT	*Okmulgee Daily Times*
O'H	Carl O'Hornett
OHS	Oklahoma Historical Society, Oklahoma City
RG	Record Group in National Archives
RG21-FW	Records of the District Court of the United States for the Eastern District of Oklahoma, Equity 4556; "In the Matter of the Estate of Jackson Barnett," NARA, Fort Worth, TX
RG21-NY	Records of the District Court, *Equitable* Case, NARA, Northeast Region, New York
RG48-CP	Department of the Interior, Office of the Secretary, NARA, College Park, MD (aka National Archives II)
RG60-CP	Records of Department of Justice, NARA, College Park, MD
RG75	Records of Office of Indian Affairs
RG118-FW	Records of the U.S. Attorneys and Marshalls, Equity 4556: "In the Matter of the Estate of Jackson Barnett," NARA, Fort Worth, TX
SH	Senate Hearing
SRep	Senate Report
Survey	U.S. Congress, Senate Committee on Indian Affairs, Survey of

Introduction

1. Kenny Franks, *Oklahoma Petroleum Industry*, 68–77; Kenny Franks, Paul Lambert, and Carl N. Tyson, *Early Oklahoma Oil*, 82.

2. Cato Sells to Mr. Bradley, May 22, 1917, in Chronology; "History of Drumright Public Schools," downloaded Aug. 28, 2002, http://www.drumright.k12.ok.us/history.htm.

3. Franks et al., *Early Oklahoma Oil*, 82.

4. Laurence F. Schmeckebier, *Office of Indian Affairs: Its History, Activities and Organization*, 114; Edwin Slosson, "Lo, the Rich Indian," 337–338; W. G. Shepherd, "Lo, the Rich Indian!" 723–734; "Lo the Rich Indian, How He Blows His Coin," 62; and William Draper, "Depression in the Osage," 113–114.

5. Joel Martin, "Rebalancing the World in the Contradictions of History: Creek/Muskogee," 102.

6. Morris Opler, "Report on the History and Contemporary State of Aspects of Creek Social Organization and Government," 36–40.

7. Unmarked newspaper clipping, Box 200, RG75-LN, MIA, f. 23 3/3.

8. "Richest Indians," 14. When they sold their land in Kansas in 1872, the Osage bought land in Oklahoma from the Cherokee. Because the land was theirs by purchase rather than treaty, they had significantly greater legal control over it. In the Osage Allotment Act of 1906 (after oil had been discovered), they leveraged better terms for themselves. See Lewis Meriam et al., *The Problem of Indian Administration*, 174–175, 446, 450; and Wilson, *The Underground Reservation: Osage Oil*, 93, 97, 136. The Osage experiences are recounted in many books and novels, including Edna Ferber's *Cimarron*, which was made into an Academy Award-winning motion picture in 1930, John Joseph Mathews's *Sundown*, and Linda Hogan's *Mean Spirit*.

9. Mathews, *Sundown*, 91, 243.

10. U.S. Board of Indian Commissioners, *Annual Report* (1917), 17.

11. *Jackson Barnett by Elmer Bailey v. American Baptist Home Missionary Society and Equitable Trust Company of New York*, 21 Fed 2d 325 (1927).

12. Quoted in Sharon O'Brien, *American Indian Tribal Governments*, 73.

13. Quoted in John Williams and Howard L. Meredith, *Bacone Indian University*, 50.

14. O'Brien, *American Indian Tribal Governments*, chap. 5: Thomas Holm, "Indians and Progressives: From Vanishing Policy to the Indian New Deal"; Chap. 6: "'The Great Confusion in Indian Policies': 1900–1924." Lane quoted in *Annual Report of the Secretary of the Interior*, 1914, 3.

15. Congress granted extensive powers to the Department of the Interior to act as an instrument—in other words, as a means to the end—to form Indians into self-sufficient farmers and U.S. citizens. *Barnett v. Barnett*, 247 Pac 1115 (1926).

16. Holm, "Indians and Progressives." iv; Francis Paul Prucha, *The Indians in American Society*, 56.

17. Mathews, *Sundown*, 243

18. C. B. Glassock, *Then Came Oil*, 156.

19. Ibid., chap. 12; *And Still*, 58, 86–87.

Chapter 1

1. Hitchcock, *A Traveler in Indian Territory*, 152–153.

2. Thomas Woodward, *Woodward's Reminiscences of the Creek, or Muscogee Indians*, 95; Benjamin Hawkins, *A Sketch of Creek Country*, 66; Jackson Barnett genealogical information, 1996 genealogical sheet, Lance Hall Papers. The birthdate of 1842, recorded on JB's Los Angeles gravestone, is often quoted, but more persuasive evidence places the date in the mid-1850s. Sources include the testimony of David Barnett, Jackson's paternal half brother, who saw the young Jackson after the Civil War north of Muskogee; Billy McCombs, who said Jackson was between six and eight years old in the mid-1860s; and the 1882 Tuckabatchee payroll, which listed Jackson as twenty-seven years old and David as 28 years old. Other evidence is drawn from photographs and verbal descriptions of Jackson's health and level of activity. David Barnett dep., Apr. 14, 1925, N67, f. 13; McCombs is quoted in an unmarked newspaper clipping, Jan. 9, 1927, Box 53, ABHSA, f. 1. Lance Hall places Jackson's birth earlier in the 1850s. Hall to author, Oct. 23, 2002, e-mail correspondence. See also Donald Fixico, *Invasion of Indian Country*, 13; Blend, 19–25.

3. Siah appears in a separate household with his maternal relatives in Tuckabatchee Town on the 1857 Creek payroll. Source of the 1857 and 1859 Creek Payrolls is Microfilm 7RA-23, and 7RA-43, RG75-FW, Lance Hall to author, March 6, 2003, e-mail correspondence. See Answer Brief of *Tiger et al. v. Sussie Conner et al.*, Equity 4556, 10th U.S. Circuit Court of Appeals, No. 2174-78, 100, 108–109, Box 3, RG118-FW.

4. Old Man Conner is identified as the "Irish Tuskegee Micco"; he traded with the Seminole (and possibly the Osage) and lived on Shell Creek before the Civil War. For the Kinnairds, see Kathryn Braund, *Deerskins and Duffles*, 174, 182; Daniel F. Littlefield, Jr., *Africans and Creeks*, 99; Grant Foreman, *History of Oklahoma*, 92; W. David Baird, ed., *A Creek Warrior for the Confederacy*, 27–28, 48, 135–136; Winnie and Willie Conner deps., 1934–1936, NACL; and William McCombs dep., Apr. 14, 1925, Eq.-N67, f. 13.

5. D. C. Gideon, *Indian Territory*, 16. The testimony of several witnesses in Equity 4556 supported the Leecher kin relationship: Martha Jane Walker, her niece Pauline Stanfield, John Cat, Eliza Sterling, Josephine Spaulding, and Lucy Curns. Lance Hall to author, Oct. 25, 2002, e-mail correspondence. See also "Some Miscellaneous Testimony Taken 1935–1937," downloaded Oct. 28, 2002, http://freepages.genealogy.rootsweb.com/~texlance/jackson/testimony.htm, and J. Leitch Wright, Jr., *Creeks and Seminoles*, 74–80; *Survey*, 1573.

6. Hitchcock, *Traveler in Indian Territory*, 112, 144. A staple food, sofkey was beaten corn cooked with lye and water to form a gruel thin enough to drink; it was left to sour for two or three days.

7. Daniel F. Littlefield, Jr., *Alex Posey*, 243; Wright, *Creeks and Seminoles*, 14–18; Carolyn Thomas Foreman, "The Yuchi: Children of the Sun," 480–485; and Wright, *Creeks and Seminoles*, 9, 44, 61, 113, 169.

8. Hitchcock, *Traveler in Indian Territory*, 113–128; and Morris Opler, "Report

on the History and Contemporary State of Aspects of Creek Social Organization and Government," 30–41; see also articles in *CSB* by Albert Gatchet, John D. Swanton, Mary Haas, and Alexanger Spoehr.

9. Hawkins, *Sketch of Creek Country*, 66, 68; Wright, *Creeks and Seminoles*, 68, 169; Muriel Wright, *A Guide to Indian Tribes of Oklahoma*, 133; and Littlefield, *Africans and Creeks*, 37, 45, 71, 66. One of Timothy Barnard's sons, Billy, married Peggy Sullivan, the mixed-blood daughter of James Sullivan, a trader at New Yorker town. From this union came Tom, Siah's father. Peggy is listed as the head of household with ten slaves in the 1832 Tuckabatchee town census. Lance Hall, "Barnard Family Genealogy: Descendants of Thomas Barnett," downloaded Oct. 4, 2002, http://freepages.genealogy.rootsweb.com/~texlance/my/barnett/pafg03.htm.

10. Hawkins, *Sketch of Creek Country*, 66.

11. Anthony F. C. Wallace, *Long and Bitter Trail*, 6–7.

12. Opler, "Report," 44.

13. Wright, *Guide to Indian Tribes*, 130, 133–135; Wallace, *Long and Bitter Trail*, 85–88; Foreman, *History of Oklahoma*, 23–24; Wright, *Creeks and Seminoles*, 245–309; and Hitchcock, *Traveler in Indian Territory*, 116, 157.

14. Wright, *Guide to Indian Tribes*, 136–137.

15. Ibid.; Martin, "Rebalancing the World," 102; Littlefield, *Alex Posey*, 260; Littlefield, *Africans and Creeks*, 181; and Hitchcock, *Traveler*, 45.

16. Foreman, *History of Oklahoma*, 100.

17. Ibid., 105–123; Wright, *Guide*, 137–138; Jess Epple, *Honey Spring Depot*, 11–13; and Jonathan Greenberg, *Staking a Claim*, 20–23.

18. Jackson Barnett deposition, Oct. 4, 1932, Eq-N67, f. 1. Answer Brief of Appellees Seaborn Fisher et al., Equity 4556, Box 3, RG118-FW; *Survey*, 1573, 1674–1675.

19. "Youth Stolen at Fort Gibson in Early Days," unmarked newspaper clipping, Jan. 9, 1927, Box 53, ABHSA, f. 1; McCombs dep., Apr. 14, 1925, Eq-N67, f. 13.

20. "Youth Stolen;" JB's residency with McCombs is not corroborated in other sources and was later rejected by federal judge Williams. Foreman, *History of Oklahoma*, 149; *Survey*, 1674–1675.

21. Angie Debo, *Road to Disappearance*, 252. JB provided sketchy autobiographical information on several occasions, including in 1912 competency hearings, for example, 1018 Probate, Eq-N67, f. 11, and in 1928–1929, *Survey*, 882–888, 1542–1575, 1643–1645. There were four ferries across the Arkansas near Muskogee: Drew, Simon Brown, Leecher, and Nivens.

22. Debo, *Road*, 272; William Sullivan dep., RG118-FW, Box 13; JB testimony under cross examination, Oct. 4, 1932, Eq-N67, f. 1.

23. Mary Fields dep., Sept. 7, 1932, Vol. 2, Eq-N67, f. 17; and Dunsey dep., Eq-N67, f. 17; David Barnett testified to the head injury in 1912; M. C. Hickman said the accident occurred when JB was twelve. Eq-N67, ff. 11–12.

24. *Survey*, N15, 1568.

25. Littlefield, *Alex Posey*, 240; Katja May, *African Americans and Native Americans in the Creek and Cherokee Nations*, 97–98.

26. Quoted in *And Still*, 13–14.

27. John Williams and Howard L. Meredith, *Bacone Indian University*, 11, 46, 57–59.

28. Foreman, *History of Oklahoma*, quoted on p. 183; 179–182.

29. Quoted in *And Still*, 13–14; Foreman, *History of Oklahoma*, 183–212.

30. Quoted in Littlefield, *Alex Posey*, 244; May, *African Americans*, 104; Debo, *Road*, 285–287.

31. Debo, *Road*, 326.

32. Opler, "Report, 42–44; John B. Merserve, "Chief Pleasant Porter"; and Merserve, "Chief Isparhecher."

33. Debo, *Road*, 345; Craig Miner, *Corporation and the Indian*, 143–163.

34. Baird, *Creek Warrior*, 163.

35. Quoted in *And Still*, 27–29.

36. Ibid., 53–54; Creek Agreement, 31 Stat. 869, No. 28, in Kappler I:730–731. Each of the Five Tribes' compacts had different terms; the Cherokees' homestead land would not be alienable for twenty-five years. Kappler I:718.

37. Quoted in Littlefield, *Alex Posey*, 197; May, *African Americans*, 145–153; and Mace Davis, "Chitto Harjo."

38. Littlefield, *Alex Posey*, 197; Opler, "Report," 50; May, *African Americans*, 153–158, 260.

39. Jackson is listed with brother "Cumsee Antrew" (or Tecumseh) in the Leecher family group in the 1882 and 1890 Creek censuses. Lance Hall to author, March 6, 2003, e-mail correspondence. Lizzie Wynn testimony, Box 27, Equity 4556, RG118-FW; Answer Brief of Appellees Seaborn Fisher et al. Lance Hall, "Jackson Barnett, the 'Richest' Indian," 20, downloaded Aug. 23, 2002, http:\\freepages.genealogy.rootsweb.com/~texlance/jackson/jackson.htm.

40. Sullivan dep., 1912, Eq-N67, f. 12. Debo, *Road*, 302. Jackson's cabin had a Senora post office address according to the Old Creek Census card #2613, family 184. "Synopsis in opposition to Wesley Barnett claim," Box 677, FG21-FW, file Sept.–Oct. 1938.

41. Answer Brief of Appellees Seaborn Fisher et al., 16–17, 20–21, RG118-FW.

42. Winey Fish (Lewis) dep., Sept. 1932, Vol. 10, 55, 58, Eq-N67, f. 24. Creek witness Adam Grayson said Jackson lived in his cabin "up until people got to taking up their allotment, and sombody filed on his allotment and he got contrary and left there." NALC.

43. Sullivan dep.; Debo, *Road*, 302. Little Fish married the daughter of Jackson's paternal half sister Elizabeth (b. 1864–1867), daughter of Siah Barnett and Mary Beams.

44. Acting chairman of the Dawes Commission to JB, Sept. 26, 1902. Papers of the Approved Creek Roll, RG75-FW, Roll 2; Synopsis in Opposition to Wesley Barnett Claim, Sept. 7, 1938, Equity 4556, Box 677, RG21-FW, f. Sept.–Oct. 1938.

45. A photocopy of JB's allotment deeds (one for 120 acres and one for 40 homestead acres in Sec. 5 T 17N, R7E) is in Book 16, Box 677, 262, RG21-FW, f. Aug. 2, 1938; Porter signed on Aug. 28, 1903, and Acting Secretary of the Interior Thomas Ryan signed on Oct. 9, 1903.

46. J. O. Hamilton dep., 25, Eq-N67, f. 23.

47. Littlefield, *Alex Posey*, 240, 242.

48. Blend, vii.

49. Samuel J. Checotah dep., Eq-N67, f. 21.

50. Fields dep., 1912, 39, Eq-N67, f. 12.

51. Sullivan dep., 1912, Eq-N67, f. 12; Hamilton dep., Eq-N67, f. 23; Daniel

Starr testimony, NALC. Asked if Jackson was a "Snake," Starr replied, "No sir he didn't know anything."

Chapter 2

1. *AR* (1916).

2. Schmeckebier, *Office of Indian Affairs,* 87; Melissa Meyer, *White Earth Tragedy,* 142–156; Lawrence Kelly, *Assault on Assimilation,* 149.

3. Act of March 1, 1901 (31 Stat. 861), negotiated Mar. 8, 1900, Kappler I:729. The Act of March 3, 1901 (31 Stat. L. 1447) extended citizenship to the Five Tribes people by amending sec. 6 of the Dawes Act of Feb. 8, 1887 (24 Stat. L. 388). *And Still,* 90; Opler, "Report," 44.

4. 33 Stat. 189. Subsequent appropriation acts contained financial allowances to expedite land transfers. In 1906 (34 Stat. 137), $18,000 was allocated and $25,000 each year from 1907 to 1909. Schmeckebier, *Office of Indian Affairs,* 87; Carl C. Magee, "Removal of the Restrictions," 10–11.

5. Foreman, *History of Oklahoma,* 355.

6. William Dudley Foulke, "Despoiling a Nation," 40–44; Kappler III:176–177; *CR* (1906): 3273–3275.

7. *CR* (1906), 4650–4655; Senators Spooner (quoted), Beveridge, and Hale supported McCumber; Senators Moses Clapp, Stone, and Clark were opposed. *United States v. Kagama,* 118 US 375 (1886); Kappler IV:1154; Angie Debo, *History of the Indians of the United States,* 287.

8. *CR* (Apr. 3, 1906), 4654–4656. For the committee's hostile report to McCumber's amendment, see SRep 5013. "Affairs in Indian Territory with Hearings" (1906). In late June 1906, following this debate, the Senate authorized a select committee to travel to the Five Tribes' territory to investigate public sentiment regarding the restrictions. Chief Tiger and Mott tried to organize a referendum to demonstrate that McCumber's amendment did not violate the Creek will. *And Still,* ii, v, 126–151, 168–180. For the famous "Plea of Crazy Snake [Chitto Harjo]" before the committee, see Edward Spicer, *A Short History of Indians of the United States,* 165–170.

9. *CR* (Apr. 3, 1906), 4652–4653.

10. The McCumber Amendment is sec. 19 of the act of April 26, 1906 (34 Stat. 137), designed "to provide for the final disposition of the Affairs of the Five Civilized Tribes." The Burke Act passed on May 8, 1906 (34 Stat. L. 182); it amended sec. 6 of the Dawes Act to extend federal guardianship in Oklahoma. The Oklahoma Enabling Act of June 16, 1906 (34 Stat. 267) appropriated money to settle the Five Tribes' financial and legal affairs (e.g., 33 Stat. 189). Kappler III:169, 181; Schmeckebier, *Office of Indian Affairs,* 87.

11. *United States v. Celestine,* 215 US 278, 291 (1909) upheld the Burke Act. Petra Shattuck and Jill Norgren, *Partial Justice,* 100. A U.S. Supreme Court decision in *In the Matter of Heff* (1905) removed federal authority over liquor trafficking among restricted Indians. It generated support for creating a "perpetual legal and political limbo" for restricted Indians; see David Wilkins, *American Indian Sovereignty and the U.S. Supreme Court,* 25, 122–125.

12. Quoted in Frederick E. Hoxie, *A Final Promise,* 155, 215, chap. 4.

13. *CR* (Mar. 9, 1906), 3598, 3601; Committee on Indian Affairs SRep 1998, "To Amend the Act Providing for Allotment of Lands to Indians," (1906), 3.

14. *And Still*, 168; Gertrude Bonnin et al., *Oklahoma's Poor Rich Indians*, 9–11; SRep 575, "Removal of Restrictions from Part of the Lands of the Five Civilized Tribes" (1907–1908), and Senate documents 511 and 514. Bills introduced in the Senate in 1907–1908 are 3814, 4644, 5586, 6720, 6721, 6794; in the House, 15641, 15831, 16495, 16962.

15. *CR* (Dec. 13, 1912) 607; *And Still*, 221, ix; in 1972, Debo lamented she had unconsciously perpetuated this confusion by using the term "restricted Indian" in earlier writing.

16. 35 Stat. 312; Foremen, *History of Oklahoma*, 355–357; Mary Jane Warde, *George Washington Grayson and the Creek Nation*, 212–216.

17. SRep 575; *CR* (Jan. 14, 1908), 673, (Apr. 26, 1908) 5425, (May 20, 1908) 6598.

18. *And Still*, 137–138, 204–212, 242. Mott's victory for the McCumber Amendment was the Marchie Tiger case, *Tiger v. Western Investment Co.*, 221 US 286 (1911); identical wording is found in *United States v. Nice*, 21 US 286 (1916). Wilkins, *American Indian Sovereignty*, 24, 124, 127–128. In May 1912, Mott and Grant Foreman won a suit requiring the return of about $100,000 collected in taxes since 1909 in violation of the 1901 Creek Compact and prohibited further taxation until 1927. Mott also was successful in his litigation on town lot frauds, a complex and far-reaching suit called the Thirty Thousand Land Suits. *Heckman v. United States*, 224 US 413 (1912); *And Still*, 131, 145, 205–209, 250–252.

19. *And Still*, 183–190; *Frontier Missionary Problems*, 44–47, in Box 163, ABHSA; Warren K. Moorehead, *Our National Problem*, 16–21.

20. Kate Barnard, Oklahoma's commissioner of charities and corrections, committed herself to ending the exploitation of Indian children throughout the 1910s. Barnard file, John Collier Papers, Box 2, CCF, RG75, NA I; *And Still*, 222–234, 312–314; and Schmeckebier, *Office of Indian Affairs*, 81, 135–136.

21. *And Still*, 305.

22. Ibid., 231; *Survey*, 6624; Schmeckebier, *Office of Indian Affairs*, 173–175; and Lawrence Kelly, "Cato Sells," 245.

23. *Survey*, 1318; "Protecting the Indian," *New York Independent*, Jan. 2, 1913, pp. 39–42; SRep 575 (1907–1908).

24. *And Still*, 232–234.

25. *Survey*, 1318; Samuel Adams to Att. Gen., July 14, 1911, Box 134, RG48-CP, Guardianships file; *CR* (Dec. 12–13, 1912), 597–609.

26 Quoted in Hoxie, *Final Promise*, 174, 175–178; Robert Wiebe, *Search for Order*, 160–170. Commissioner Francis Leupp said virtually the same thing in 1919. William Hagan, *American Indians*, 147.

27. *MTD*, May 29, 1912, p. 2, and July 6, 1912, p. 2; *And Still*, 287; Holm, "Indians and Progressives," 165.

28. Oklahoma politicians endeavored to lift restrictions on oil-rich properties of full-bloods via amendments tucked into congressional appropriations bills. Proposals for another "Indian Removal," this time to Mexico, were made. The Standard Oil Company was reported to have made an $8 million bid for Osage mineral rights. *MDP*, Jan 1, 1911; *And Still*, 195–196, 287.

29. *MDP*, Mar. 7, 1912 (re: minor Marcus Covey kidnapping); Mar. 15, 1912 p. 3 (re: sensational Indian probate case of Hilly Bear, née Hayes); Aug. 15, 1912 p. 8 (re: guardian jailed for embezzlement of funds); Mar. 26, 1912 (re: Carrie Cochran, Cherokee heiress worth $0.5 million, kidnapped); Apr. 12, 1912 (re: sixty-two-year-old restricted Indian woman, Mrs. George Scott, victimized); May 7,

1912 (re: mixed-blood Cherokee girl kidnapped); May 9, 1912 (re: Peggy Sanders, Cherokee oil heiress, kidnapped); May 10, 1912 (re: full-blood Creek woman Lina Lowe's land sold under value); May 16, 1912 (re: sixty-two-year-old Cherokee Mrs. Scott finally left alone by grafters); May 28, 1912 (re: guardian fraud case); June 6. 1912 (re: embezzlement by guardian); Sept. 20, 1912 (re: conviction of guardian for embezzlement); and Moorehead, *Our National Problem*, 4–42.

30. *Survey*, 1314; *MDP*, Oct. 20, 1911, 1–2.

31. Miner, *The Corporation and the Indian*, 191, 208; Janet McDonnell, *The Dispossession of the American Indian*, 5; and Hoxie, *Final Promise*, 184. Francis Paul Prucha defines malevolent guardianship as "lands, resources, political rights as commodities to be unilaterally and forcefully taken or abrogated." Quoted in Wilkins, *American Indian Sovereignty*, 14; Francis Paul Prucha, *The Indians in American society*, 11, 23.

32. CIA, *AR* (1914), 50–51, quoted in Kelly, "Cato Sells," 245; CIA Sells to Charles Burke, Dec. 6, 1918, Chronology; Prucha, *Indians in American Society*, 26.

33. Kelly, "Cato Sells," 244, 248; McDonnell, *Dispossession*, 4–5, 88–105; Schmeckebier, *Office of Indian Affairs*, 152–156; CIA, *AR* (1917), 3–4; and *And Still*, 281–282.

34. David L Beaulieu, "Curly Hair and Big Feet," 290; CIA, *AR* (1921); and *And Still*, 163–170. See Superintendent of Indian Affairs, *AR* (1916), 282: "Time and developments have demonstrated that quantum of blood does not indicate business capacity." Estimates of the land lost by Indians declared competent range from 60–80 percent to 90–99 percent. See McDonnell, *Dispossession*, 89; Meriam et al., *Problems of Indian Administration*, 174; Assistant CIA E. B. Meritt's testimony, "Survey," Jan. 10, 1928, 23, 27, 32, 34, 38; and Lawrence Kelly, "Charles Henry Burke," 256.

35. McDonnell, *Dispossession*, 122.

36. *Heckman v. United States* 224 U.S. 413 (1912).

Chapter 3

1. Farrar and Randall testimony, Apr. 29, 1912, *In the Matter of Guardianship of Jackson Barnett, Incompetent*, No. 1018 Probate (hereafter 1018 Probate), Probate Minutes, Book 10, Okmulgee County Court. Certified copies of transcript in Eq-N67, f. 11.

2. Copy of original lease in *Survey*, 1670–1673, and Eq-N67, f. 24; Kelsey Report to CIA (hereafter, "Statement of Facts and Findings"), Sept. 7, 1912, Eq-N67, f. 12.

3. *MDP*, Mar. 22, 1912; C. Morrison testimony, Apr. 29, 1912; and Bartlett testimony, June 7, 1912, No. 1018 Probate, Eq-N67, f. 12.

4. *And Still*, 87, 286, 338; "Statement of Facts and Findings."

5. The Apr. 29, 1912, and May 8, 1912, hearings testimony is in a 222-page report in a May 25, 1912, Union Agency document, Eq-N67, f. 11. Hearings were held in Superintendent Kelsey's office in Muskogee, May 3, June 7, and Aug. 7, 1912. Eq-N67, f. 12, contains a sixty-five-page document dated June 7, 1912, which includes part of the Apr. 29 and May 7–9 testimony; the Aug. 7 hearing before Dana Kelsey at the Union Agency, Muskogee, is in the "Transcript of Testimony Taken in Matter of Conflicting Leases Nos. 22449 and 22863, Aug. 7, 1912" (hereafter, "Transcript of Testimony").

6. Bolwer and O'H testimony, Apr. 29, 1912, 1018 Probate, Eq-N67, f. 11;

O'H, Gooch, and Cornelius testimony and Kelsey's cross-examination, Aug. 7, 1912, "Transcript of Testimony," f. 12. Bolwer (also spelled Bollwar) was the mulatto husband of Jackson's great-neice Winey Fish, daughter of Little Fish, with whom Jackson lived from 1905 to 1908.

7. "A Ten Thousand Dollar Oil Lease Practically Given Away," *Okmulgee Chieftain*, May 9, 1912, p. 1; Randall testimony, "In the Matter of Guardianship of Jackson Barnett, Incompetent," May 3, 1912, 1018 Probate, Eq-N67, f. 10; Farrar dep., Apr. 23, 1925, in Riggs case documents, Eq-N67, f. 13; *Survey*, 1675.

8. Randall testimony, May 3, 1912. Bartlett kidnapped JB and took him to Colorado for three weeks on the advice of his attorneys to get Jackson "out of the way" during the hearings on Jackson's competency. Bartlett testimony, "Transcript of Testimony."

9. Winnie Bollwar Fish and D. Barnett testimony, Apr. 29 and May 7, 1912, and Charley King testimony, May 8, 1912, 1018 Probate, f. 11. Winey Bonilla (Fish) dep., Apr. 17, 1925, and D. Barnett dep., Apr. 14, 1925, f. 13.

10. Randall, Fisher, Seaborn, William Sullivan, J. M. Patterson, and Clinton Summers testimony of May 8, 1912, 1018 Probate, f. 11.

11. Farrar testimony, ibid.

12. Farrar to Kelsey, May 10, 1912; Kelsey to Farrar, May 10, 1912; clippings from *ODT* and *Okmulgee Chieftain*, Eq-N67, f. 12; *Survey*, 1633–1634.

13. "Statement of Facts and Findings."

14. Farrar testimony, June 7, 1912, Union Agency transcript, 29, Eq-N67, f. 12; Farrar dep., Aug. 29–30, 1932, Eq-N67, f. 21.

15. O'H testimony, June 7, 1912, Union Agency transcript, 13, Eq-N67, f. 11.

16. Testimony of McDermott (p. 37); Fields (p. 39); Josiah Looney and Johnson (p. 44), Union Agency transcript, Eq-N67, f. 11.

17. Randall testimony, 48, Union Agency transcript, Eq-N67, f. 11. In 1932, Randall stated that, in some ways, JB had the mind of a child. Randall dep., July 28–29, 1932, 13:95, Eq-N67, f. 23/2.

18. JB testimony, 64, Union Agency transcript, Eq-N67, f. 11.

19. "Transcript of Testimony."

20. "Statement of Facts and Findings," 11.

21. Judge Wade Stanfield's district court decision, June 24, 1912, *Survey*, 1660–1661; "Barnett Case Got a Set Back in District Court," *Okmulgee Chieftain*, June 27, 1912.

22. "Statement of Facts and Findings," citing report to D/I, July 6, 1912.

23. "Transcript of Testimony," 24–25; *And Still*, 61.

24. "Statement of Facts and Findings," 6–14. Bartlett lease, No. 22449; Gooch and Cornelius, No. 22863. The lessees each paid half of the bonus set by the oil inspector.

25. On JB subleases, see Eq-N67, ff. 13 and 22; and *Gilroy v. Burgess*, deeds and quit claims, 1912–1917, RG118-FW, f. 2446.

26. *Barnett v. Barnett*, 252 Pac 414 (1926).

27. *And Still*, 192–193. Sec. 25 of the April 20, 1908, act was amended by D/I on Nov. 29, 1912, to give federal authority over guardians. According to O'H, first he petitioned the court for a sum of money, then transmitted the court-approved request to the Union Agency, then returned with the voucher to the county court for approval before the check would be issued to him. O'H dep., Aug. 8, 1932, Box 13, RG118-FW.

28. Kelsey to Farrar, Sept. 12, 1912; Kelsey to Randall, Sept. 12, 1912, Box 15, RG118-FW; *Gilroy v. Burgess* file, f. 2446.

29. Kelsey to Farrar, Oct. 4, 1912; field clerk to J. C. Smock, Nov. 5, 1912; Farrar to Kelsey, Nov. 30, 1912, ibid.

30. Isom Beams dep., July 28–29, 1932, vol. 14, Eq-N67, f. 24; O'H dep., Aug 8, 1932, 156, 161–164, Box 13, RG118-FW.

31. O'H dep., ibid., 166, 170.

32. Deps. of Charles Wilson (quoted), Isom Beams, W. H. Casey, J. O. Hamilton, July 28–29, 1932, vol. 9, Eq-N67, f. 23/1; cf. the depositions of the same Henryetta clerks in Box 13, RG118-FW.

33. Casey dep., Eq-N67, f. 23/1; O'H dep., Aug. 8, 1932, 163–166, Box 13, RG118-FW.

34. Frank F. Hinton dep., 43 (quoted), and Wilson dep., 14, 22, 27, vol. 13, Eq-N67, f. 23/2; Walter R. Wilson dep., 22, 27 (quoted), and Ed Kersting dep., RG118-FW, Box 13; Kincaid and John Stuart deps., Aug. 12, 1932, vol. 9, Eq-N67, f. 23.

35. Willie Griffin dep., 1932, 166–169 (quoted), Box 13, RG118-FW; George Washington testimony, NALC; Blend, 54; *Survey*, 1549.

36. JB accumulated $755,893.06 by May 1917. For the fifty-two months from Jan. 1913 to May 1917, he averaged $14,536 per month. Beginning in Jan. 1917, his income was $47,082 per month. See Sells to Mr. Bradley, May, 1917, in Chronology; Blend, 55; and John J. McCluster, "Comparing the Purchasing Power of Money in the United States (or Colonies) from 1665 to Any Other Year including the Present," downloaded Sept. 23, 2002, http://www.eh.net/hmit/ppowerusd/.

37. *MTD*, Feb. 9, 1916.

38. Unmarked clipping, Sept. 2, 1917, 1, Dora Brady Exh., Box 677, RG21-FW, f. Dec. 16, 1939.

39. D/I memorandum, c. 1917, Chronology.

40. *MTD*, May 10, 1917; *NYT*, June 4, 1917.

41. *NYT*, June 4, 1917, called JB the "wealthiest Indian in the world"; *MDP*, June 8, 1917, labeled Jackson the "world's richest Indian."

42. *NYT*, June 5, 1917; *MTD*, May 10, 1917; index card entries for JB, June 19 and June 20, 1917, BIA card catalog, RG75, NA I. Senator Ashurst of Arizona introduced a resolution authorizing the secretary of the Interior to deposit tribal funds in Liberty Bonds; shortly afterward O'H put JB's $640,000 into bonds. Blend, 54–58; Charles Fettretch to Burke, Jan. 11, 1927, *Survey*, 6137.

43. D/I to O'H, telegram, June 22, 1917, BIA card catalog, RG75, NA I, *Survey*, 6147. Sells referred the question of whether an investment could be made "without the consent of an adult allottee" or without the consent of probate court in the case of minors or incompetents to a D/I solicitor, as Burke would do later. Judge John C. Pollock, later decisively standing by federal authority to take such action in the McGugin case, was consulted on this question in 1917. Sells to Bradley, May 22, 1917, Chronology. An act of May 25, 1918 (40 Stat. 561) gave statutory authority for investing Indian money in U.S. bonds, but exempted the Five Civilized Tribes and the Osage because Oklahoma state banks protested the loss of their deposits from wealthy Indians.

44. Wiley dep., *Survey*, 1653–1654; JB's sworn statement, Aug. 25, 1919, *In the Matter of the Estate of JB, an Incompetent* (hereafter, *In the Matter, 1919*), transcript

of evidence at the hearing upon application for a writ of mandamus upon guardian to file a petition requesting leave to make a donation to the church. Rec. Pro., Mina Book 15, Okmulgee County court, Eq-N67, f. 10; transcript is in Exh. A, f. 11.

45. *MTD*, July 25, 1919; Joe H. Strain to C. L. Fleshmen, July 28, 1919, *In the Matter, 1919*; Mary Petersdorf (O'H's granddaughter) to Lance Hall, e-mail, July 11, 2001.

46. Testimony on Aug. 30, 1919, included the Henryetta mayor Ira Martin, Dr. Robertson (quoted, 463), lawyer Morgan, bank clerk G. W. Burroughs, Creek Indians Wadley Kelly and W. H. Bonard, and Rev. Cameron. *In the Matter, 1919*, and *Survey*, 1635–1636.

47. *In the Matter, 1919*. See J. G. Woerner, *A Treatise on the American Law of Guardianship of Minors and Persons of Unsound Mind.*

48. *In the Matter, 1919*; Exh. A, Okmulgee County court Finding of Competency, Sept. 1, 1919, Eq-N67, f. 13.

49. *MDP*, Sept. 7, 1919.

50. Index card entries for JB, 1919, BIA card catalog, RG75, NA I.

51. J. O. Hamilton went to Billy Sullivan to interpret, and he said, "No, that Indian ain't got any sense," and then went to Charlie King, another interpreter, and he said, "Jim, I wont do that. . . . He is an imbecile. . . . We better not try it . . . forget it and let it go." Watson dep., vol. 9, 36–37, Eq-N67, f. 23/1; Wilson dep., Box 13, RG118-FW.

52. *In the Matter, 1919*, Exh. A; and *Survey*, 1676.

53. *Survey*, 1074, 6147; Gabe Parker to Sells, Dec. 12, 1919; O'H to Parker (unknown date), quoted in Att. Gen. McNabb's petition, Apr. 7, 1928, Eq-N67, f. 14. McNabb also cites a D/I memorandum, dated June 26, 1919, saying no legal authority for such gifts exists, but as a matter of policy, "the securing of donations from rich, incompetent, Indians" will be launched with "wonderful prospects"; *NYT*, Nov. 19, 1926, p. 27.

54. Sells testimony and dep. in *Barnett v. Equitable*, Box 1772 (123785) 914759-60, RG21-NY; *Survey*, 1640–1642, 1710; and James Davis to CIA, Apr. 15, 1920, 2, Eq-N67, f. 15. JB's income in 1918 was $125,471.69, and for the first eleven months of 1919, it was $104,603.21. Exh. A, Eq-N67, f. 15.

55. Walker dep., Oct. 10, 1932; Hall dep., July 28–29, 1932, Eq-N67, f. 21.

56. *Barnett v. Equitable*, 21 F2d 325, 326, 329; *NYT*, Nov. 19, 1926, p. 27.

57. Sells dep., 62, 68, RG21-NY; Beams dep., vol. 9, Eq-N67, f. 23/1.

58. James C. Davis brief, c. Feb. 24, 1920, quoted in Charles Burke's memorandum to D/I secretary Work, Sept. 23, 1925, Chronology; *Survey*, 1655.

59. Kelly, "Charles Henry Burke," 259.

60. *In the Matter, 1919*.

Chapter 4

1. *Survey*, 882; J. J. Johnson dep., Sept. 12, 1932, vol. 4, Eq-N67, f. 18. Court testimony is the major source for these events, especially the depositions of J. J. Johnson, Willie Griffin, N. F. Jacobs, M. C. Jones, AB, and James W. Rogers in Eq-N67. Copies of Selby depositions taken in 1932 for Eq-N67 are in boxes 3 and 13, RG118-FW. Another important source is the testimony of AB and JB before a Senate subcommittee on Nov. 22–23, 1928, and Feb. 4, 1929, *Survey*, 235, 634–646,

1576–1577 (AB), 882–888, 1542–1575, 1643–1645 (JB). Details vary about who proposed marriage to whom and when, how many meetings before the marriage, and the time of the first meeting and the marriage. See *United States v. McGugin*, 31 F. Supp. 498 (1940). Newspapers covered the romance and elopement in detail with romanticized spins; cf. *DO*, Sept. 29, 1931.

2. J. J. Johnson dep., Box 3, RG118-FW.

3. Ibid.; Fixico, *Invasion of Indian Country*, 14.

4. M. C. Jones dep., Aug. 26, 1932, Eq-N67, f. 20; Judge James's opinion, *United States v. [Anna Laura] Barnett* (1934), Eq-N67, f. 16.

5. Johnson dep., Box 3, RG118-FW.

6. N. F. Jacobs, Tom Francher, and James W. Rodgers deps., Aug. 15, 1932, vol. 14, Eq-N67, f. 24.

7. *MTD*, Jan. 31, 1920.

8. Francher dep., Eq-N67.

9. Johnson dep., Box 3, RG118-FW; *Survey*, 882–888.

10. Thumbmarked donation dated Feb. 11, 1920, *Barnett v. Equitable*, 21 F2d 325, 326. See B. D. Weeks to George Hovey, Feb. 24, 1920, Box 53, ABHSA, f. 3, for details of the lobbying of southern senators by Dr. Gambrell and Dr. Truitt of the Southern Baptist Convention for a $200,000 donation. Sells was in Henryetta in early 1920, dispensing Jackson's money like Santa Claus, making a list and stating emphatically that all requests would be approved. At JB's personal request, the $50,000 donation to the Murrow Orphans home was added. *MTD* and *DO*, Feb. 14, 1920; *MTD*, Oct. 14, 1921; see Creek tribal Attorney, James Davis's briefs, Feb. 4 and Feb. 24, 1920, prepared for Sells and sustaining his authority to make the distribution.

11. O'Hornett estimated the fortune at $2 million. In 1917, Jackson had roughly $800,000 in Liberty Bonds and private accounts, with accrued interest at 4–4.5 percent and roughly $50,000 in monthly income; income tax refunds of 1917 yielded an additional $200,000. For 1918 and 1919, his income was approximately $125,000 yearly—JB's royalty income having declined to $9,509.36 per month in 1919—a sizable decrease from his $50,000 a month in 1917. O'Hornett's fees and Jackson's expenses for 1917 were well under $40,000, assuming that O'Hornett's monthly fee was approximately $500, JB's allowance of $50–150 was increased to $650 per month only at the end of 1919, and adding in the extra expenditures on the car, road, and garage.

12. *MTD*, Feb. 2, Feb. 14, and Feb. 23, 1920.

13. Johnson dep., Box 3, RG118-FW; Griffin dep., Box 13, RG118-FW; and Judge James's opinion, *United States v. Barnett*, Eq-N67, f. 16. The Mooreheads persisted in trying to collect their promised share and ultimately tried to blackmail AB. See Eq-N67, f. 10.

14. *LAT*, Feb. 10, 1933; *Survey*, 1039–1044; O'H dep., Bos 13, RG118-FW.

15. *MTD*, Feb. 26, 1920; *ODT*, May 30, 1934; Charles Bickett dep., Aug 19, 1932, Eq-N67 f. 17.

16. *MDP*, Feb. 27, 1920.

17. AB's testimony, Mar. 13, 1920, in Topeka. *Carl J. O'Hornett v. Anna Laura Lowe*, Supreme Court of the State of Kansas, No. 22,897, transcript, Eq-N67, f. 11. *DO*, Feb. 26, 1920 (quoted), and Feb. 27, 1920; Bickett dep., Eq-N67. *MDP*, Feb. 25, Feb. 26, and Feb 27, 1920.

18. Marriage license, Montgomery County, Kansas, Feb. 23, 1920, in Eq-N67, f. 16; the Mar. 1, 1920, McGugin-Keith-AB contract is in Eq-N67, f. 13. See Fixico, *Invasion*, 14.

19. *MTD*, Feb 26, 1920.

20. *MTD*, Feb. 25, 1920; unmarked clipping, Feb. 24, 1920 (quoted); *DO*, Feb. 29, 1920.

21. Blend, 69, 19; *Survey*, 1554.

22. *MDP*, Mar. 13, 1920.

23. O'H Affidavit of Warrant, Mar. 11, 1920, *O'Hornett v. Anna Lowe*, Eq-N67, f. 11. The expenses of Cameron, O'H, and others to Washington, D.C., in late March of $1,409.35 were charged to Jackson's account.

24. Cross Petition of McGurgin and Keith, Mar. 16, 1920, *O'Hornett v. Anna Lowe*, 20. Payment of $1,000 was allowed by Judge Dudley Monk, See *MDP*, Mar. 18, 1920, and *MTD*, Mar. 18, 1920. A $300 payment plus $2,500 for attorney's fees was mandated by the Kansas Supreme Court in 1920.

25. *O'Hornett v. Anna Lowe*, Eq-N67, f. 11.

26. Blend, 9–10.

27. *O'Hornett v. Anna Lowe*, Eq-N67, f. 8.

28. *MDP*, Apr. 7, 8, 9, 1920.

29. *MDP*, Mar. 2, 1920. County court judge Enloe Vernor agreed with Kansas judge A. M. Jackson of Winfield. *O'Hornett v. Anna Lowe*, A. M. Jackson Referee Report, Oct. 2, 1920, Eq-N67, f. 11.

30. *Shelby v. Farve*, 126 Okla 764 (1912); Oklahoma code—section 3334 of the 1910 revised statutes—and the California code share this legal definition of incompetency. "Confidential Inspection Report on Kidnapping of Jackson Barnett," Special Supervisor W. L. Bowie to Cato Sells, Apr. 25, 1920, RG75-FW, micro, vol. 2 (hereafter, Bowie Report). There are numerous copies in different archives including the General Enclosures section, Box 3331, Entry 112, RG60-CP, f. 207695.

31. Bowie Report. Vital details about Anna have been verified, corrected, and supplemented with census records and her own testimony. She was born in McDonald County, Missouri. Anna's five older brothers were Wirt, James, John, Willie, and Sydney.

32. Jerry Fink, *Tulsa World Sunday Magazine*, downloaded Aug, 28, 2002, http://www.rootsweb.com/~okmcinto/Married/barnettj.htm.

33. Bowie Report; Maxine (who died Feb. 1968) was born Jan. 31, 1904, according to automatic vital statistics records: Social Security no. 364-10-8566; marriage to Sturgis, May 20, 1904–Feb. 1912; marriage to Lowe, July 15, 1913–Nov. 21, 1913.

34. Bowie Report, 5–8.

35. The 1900 census lists her father, James, as having no occupation and as a boarder. *Survey*, 882–888.

36. Bowie Report; the phrase "devil . . . woman" is taken from book by Carol F. Karlsen, *Devil in the Shape of a Woman*.

37. R. C. Mason dep., c. 1932, Box 13, RG118-FW; *MDP*, Mar. 4, 1920. Case law forbade a non-Indian from inheriting a full-blood's property in the Five Civilized Tribes. Mason, twice convicted of whiskey sales, was an unreliable witness, but Alvin Moorehead confirmed the story. *Barnett v. Equitable*, 21 F2d 325; Mason letters to Elmer Thomas, Nov. 9, 1933, and Nov. 12, 1934, in Box 59, ET.

38. Weeks to Hovey, Jan. 8, 1921, Box 53, ABHSA, f. 1; *Barnett v. Equitable*, 21

F2d 325, 326; W. H. Casey dep., Aug. 12, 1932, vol. 9, Eq-N67, f. 23.

  39. McCrory to Sells, Feb. 12, 1921, Eq-N67, f. 10.

Chapter 5

  1. *MDP*, Aug. 7, 1921.

  2. *MTD*, Sept. 15, 1921; Peter Deichman to Burke, Sept. 24, 1921, quoted in McNabb petition to the Att. Gen., Apr. 7, 1928, 15–18, Eq-N67, f. 14.

  3. Ibid., Amasa Ward to Burke, Jan. 11, 1922 in McNabb petition, Eq-N67, f. 14.

  4. The petition written by Edwin Motter, Harding's Republican friend and D/J appointee, was intensely disliked by the Okmulgeans, who suspected he was part of the federal plot; Murphy accused him of trying to personally profit by selling his Muskogee home to the Barnetts at an inflated price. He served as the Barnetts' counsel while in his D/J position, creating a conflict of interest. He retired from the case in 1922. *CR* (Jan. 22, 1925), 2338.

  5. Deichman to Burke, Sept. 24, 1921; Murphy to Burke, telegram, Sept. 24, 1921, both quoted in McNabb petition, 15–18, Eq-N67, f. 14.

  6. Burke to Locke, Sept. 28, 1921, Eq-N67, f. 14.

  7. The request was rejected on July 13, 1921. See *Survey*, 1097, 1647–1648. The Oklahoma Baptist Convention viewed President Weeks of Bacone as a traitor and crook who had stolen their endowment and threatened to bring suit against D/I.

  8. John Williams and Howard L. Meredith, *Bacone Indian University*, 11, 46, 57–59; *American National Bank v. ABHMS*, 106 F2nd 192, 194, 195. Additional donations were given by Richards's daughter, Jeanetta Richards Barnett, and Lena Cosar.

  9. Burke to Reed, Oct. 5, 1921, Eq-N67, f. 14.

  10. *MTD*, Oct. 7, Oct. 10, and Nov. 7, 1921.

  11. Ward to Burke, Oct. 12, 1921, in McNabb petition, 20–22; and Burke to Ward, Oct. 16, 1921, both in Eq-N67, f. 14.

  12. *MTD*, Oct. 12 and Oct. 14, 1921.

  13. *MTD*, Oct. 24, 1921; Ward to Burke, Oct. 14, 1921, Eq-N67, f. 14; Barnetts to Burke, Oct. 17, 1921, *Survey*, 6101. On Oct. 27, 1921, Ward and Locke went to confer with Murphy on a "peace mission."

  14. Ward to Burke, Oct. 14, 1921, Eq-N67, f. 14.

  15. Creeks Wilson Clinton, Lessy Yarhola, and Barney Thlocco sought release from guardians as did wealthy freedwoman Audrey Barnett. With Edwin C. Motter as her attorney, Barnett took her case to the district court for arbitration. *MTD*, Dec. 20, 1921, and Mar. 23, 1922. Thlocco, as Daniel F. Littlefield, Jr., writes, was "a circus performer, fire eater as I recall, afraid to go back to Oklahoma because his attorney, J. Coody Johnson, Creek freedman and owner of Black Panther Oil Company, told him he would be put in the penitentiary for horse stealing. Coody, of course, was in cahoots with bigger fish; Barney had his roll number tattooed on his arm so that if he was found dead, people would know he was a Creek Indian." Declared dead in 1919, Thlocco was actually murdered in Mexico in 1929. E-mail communication, Littlefield to author, May 2, 2001. For Osage testimony regarding guardianship in 1921, see William G. Shepherd, "Lo, the Rich Indian!" 734.

  16. O'H to Burke, Dec. 12, 1921, Box 9, RG118-FW.

  17. Locke to Burke, Jan. 28, 1922; Ward to Burke, Mar. 1, 1922; Ward to Burke,

Jan. 11, 1922; Burke to O'H, Dec. 16, 1921, all in Box 9, RG118-FW; *MTD*, Dec. 13, 1921, p. 10.

18. Barnetts to Burke, Oct. 17, 1921; Burke to Barnetts, Oct. 21, 1921, Eq-N67, f. 14; *MDP*, Oct. 24, Oct. 25, Dec. 6, 1921; and O'H dep., Box 13, RG118-FW. Three thousand dollars was allowed for construction of a garage and road in Mar. 1922; $500 was allowed for a Kansas City trip in addition to other expenses.

19. *MTD*, Dec. 19, 1921. The new home was located at 4801 West Okmulgee. Payments on the 8 percent loan were $500 per month. On the Barnetts' Muskogee home, see Box 9, RG118-FW.

20. *MTD*, Dec. 19, 1921; Locke to Burke, Jan. 28, 1922; Burke to Ward, Jan. 16, 1922; Burke to McGugin, Jan. 16, 1922, all in Eq-N67, f. 14.

21. Ward to Burke, Jan. 11, 1922; McGugin to Burke, Jan 11, 1922; Burke to Ward, Jan. 16, 1922; McGugin to Burke, Jan. 19, 1922; McCrory (to Ward?), Feb. 27, 1922, all in Eq-N67, f. 14. AB to Burke, Jan. 10, 1922; Burke to McGugin, Jan. 23, 1922, *Survey*, 6101. Ward to Burke, Jan. 20, 1922; Locke to McGugin, Jan. 23, 1922; Locke to Burke, Jan. 28, 1922, all in Box 9, RG118-FW. *MTD*, Feb. 8, 1922; *Survey*, 1680.

22. Burke to Locke, Mar. 4, 1922; Ward to Burke, Mar. 14, 1922; Burke to Ward and Ward to Burke, Mar. 16, 1922; Burke to Reed and Burke to Ward, Mar. 31, 1922; Locke to Burke, Mar. 29, 1922; Reed to Burke, Apr. 17, 1922; Burke to Secretary of D/I, June 9, 1922, all in Eq-N67, f. 14. Burke to Locke, Mar. 16, 1922, *Survey*, 6102.

23. Edwin Booth, "Jurisdiction of State Probate Courts," 56–64. Booth's opinion was approved by Fall, Feb. 6, 1922. Ward to Burke and Burke to McGugin, Sept. 20, 1922, Eq-N67, f. 14.

24. *MTD*, June 22, 1922; Weeks to Hovey, June 21, 1922, Box 53, ABHSA, f. 1. According to Weeks, $350,000 would be given by "the Government" to AB, plus a $100,000 home. A $50,000 trust would go to her daughter, and attorneys would be paid $25,000. The remainder of the $1.125 million would go to AHMS to hold in trust for Bacone. Drafts of the agreement were being reviewed at the time by D/I and D/J. *Survey*, 1076.

25. McCrory to Burke, June 27, 1922; Burke to Ward, June 10 and July 1, 1922, Eq-N67, f. 14; *MDP*, July 9, 1922.

26. Burke to McGugin, Aug. 17, 1922; Ward to Burke, telegram, Sept. 20, 1922, Eq-N67, f. 14; *MTD*, Sept. 30, 1922.

27. Burke to Fall, Sept. 28, 1922, Eq-N67, f. 14. Discretionary power was granted to the D/I by acts of Congress, Apr. 24, 1906, and May 27, 1908. Act of Feb. 14, 1920, sec. 24, was amended Oct. 7, 1922.

28. JB to Albert Fall, Dec. 15, 1922, Eq-N67, f. 20; *Survey*, 1074–1075.

29. The division was made by McGugin on a blank envelope from the Burlington Hotel, Washington, D.C. Burke likely had no knowledge that lawyers would get this sizable share. See Exhibits 4, 5, and 7, Eq-N67, f. 7.

30. Weeks to Hovey, Sept. 30, 1927, Box 53, ABHSA, f. 1.

31. The Union Agency cashier, D. Buddrus, fearing being served with an injunction, refused to release these funds as he saw the distribution to be in violation of the law. Burke disagreed, saying the Booth opinion was binding. Buddrus referred the matter to the comptroller general for a final decision. Assistant CIA Meritt assured the comptroller that D/I had this authority. In January, Burke requested transfer of $250,000 of JB's funds held by the Union Agency to Washing-

ton, D.C. to be converted to Liberty Bonds, and Buddrus complied on Jan. 10, 1923. Buddrus to Burke, Dec. 9, 1922; Burke to Buddrus, Dec. 14, 1922; Buddrus to Burke, Dec. 22, 1922; Burke to Fall, Jan. 6, 1923; Booth to Burke, Jan. 10, 1923; Meritt to Booth, Feb. 9, 1923, all in Eq-N67, f. 14.

32. *Survey*, 1074–1075.

33. Ward to Burke, Jan. 29, 1923, Exh. B, *Barnett v. Equitable*, Eq-N67, f. 14.

34. Ibid.; Peter Deichman report to Ward, Dec. 27, 1922; cited in Fixico, *Invasion*, 24, n. 26.

35. Ward to Burke, Jan. 29, 1923, Eq-N67, f. 14.

36. JB to Fall, Dec. 15, 1922, Eq-N67, f. 20; Burke to Fall, Jan. 29, 1923, Eq-N67, f. 14. The trust contracts of AB with Riggs and AHMS with Equitable, both dated Feb. 1, 1923, are in Eq-N67, f. 7 and f. 5, respectively. *Survey*, 1082.

37. Brief of Defendant, *Barnett v. Equitable*, AHMS, 47, Minutes, Box 1773, RG21-NY, 208.

38. *MDP*, Feb. 9, 1923.

39. For the infamous Dance Order, D/I Circular No. 1665, see Edward Spicer, *A Short History of Indians of the United States*, 241–242.

40. *MTD*, Feb. 2 (quoted) and Feb. 15, 1923.

41. *MDP*, Feb. 15 and Apr. 4, 1923, and June 14, 1922, p. 2; Ward to Burke, Feb. 15, 1923, *Survey*, 6104.

42. The Barnett home was at 1410 Norman Way. AB testimony, 31–33, Eq-N67, f. 15.

Chapter 6

1. *And Still*, 342; Blend, 85–86, 205.

2. US Board of Indian Commissioners report (1917), 17, quoted in Wilson, *Underground Reservation*, 127.

3. "Findings of Fact and Conclusions of Law," Oct. 20, 1941, *Leona Richards Fox et al. v. H. G. House and R. L. Simpson*, No. 49-Civil, Box 679, RG21-FW, f. Testimony of June 18, 1945; Accounts and Auditors to CIA, Dec. 20, 1940, Box 6, RG118-FW.

4. The U.S. Supreme Court closed the loophole in the act of Mar. 3, 1921 (41 Stat. 1249) delivering Osage funds into the hands of guardians. Wilson, *Underground Reservation*, 138–142; Osage Agency, *Osage People and Their Trust Property*, viii–ix, 55; Schmeckebier, *Office of Indian Affairs*, 113 (quoting Vaux), 114; Sherman Rogers, "Red Men in Gas Buggies," 629–632; Shepherd, "Lo, the Rich Indian!" 728–730; *And Still*, 323–324.

5. For revealing case studies of manipulations in status, see Osage Agency, *Osage People and Their Trust Property*, 50–62; Tanis C. Thorne, "Indian Beverly Hillbillies," 5–12.

6. Schmeckebier, *Office of Indian Affairs*, 115.

7. Carnegie, *The Gospel of Wealth and Other Timely Essays*, 1–15. This was originally published in 1889. George's widely read *Progress and Poverty* was published in 1879.

8. Ward to Burke, May 9, 1922, in McNabb petition, Eq-N67, f. 14.

9. Weeks to Samuel Bryant, Mar. 1, 1925, *Survey*, 6130; Weeks to Hovey, Jan. 8, 1921, June 21, 1922, Oct 3, 1922, and Nov. 8, 1924, Box 53, ABHSA, f. 1; Lemeul Call Barnes, *Baptist Work among the American Indians*, 20. Also see CIA, "Official Announcement of Gifts Made," *AR* (1923).

10. White to Weeks (quoted), Feb. 14, 1923, *Survey,* 6129; Hovey to Weeks, Nov. 13, 1924 (quoted); Weeks to Hovey, Nov. 8, 1924, and Jan. 12, 1925; White to Weeks, Feb. 14, 1923, all in Box 53, ABHSA, f. 1. By October 1922, Weeks obtained donations from Jeanetta Richards Barnett ($100,000), Susanna Butler ($50,000), Russell Thompson ($5,000), Liza Sewell ($500), Walter Starr ($50,000), Salina Starr ($10,000), and Lena Cosar ($6,500). "Official Announcement by U.S. Indian Office of Gifts Made by Indians to the ABHMS," Feb. 8, 1923, Box 53, ABHSA, f. 1. In 1924, $287,700 was donated for Bacone and $176,500 for the Murrow Orphans Home with D/I approval. "Summary of Donations to Churches and Schools Paid Out of Restricted Individual Funds . . . by Members of Five Civilized Tribes," July 6, 1925, 37, Box 3331, RG 60, f. 207695-17.

11. *Missions* (International Baptist Magazine) (May 1927): 303. The source quoted was likely Secretary Work. Weeks to Hovey, Sept. 13, 1922, and June 29, 1926, Box 53, ABHSA, f. 1; *And Still,* 341.

12. *MTD,* Feb. 23, 1923; p. 14 (quoted), and Feb. 22, 1923; V. Berry? to Work, Mar. 20, 1923 (quoted), Chronology.

13. *Carl J. O'Hornett, Guardian of Jackson Barnett v. Victor M. Locke, Jr., and D. Buddrus; Jackson Barnett by Prochien Ami O'Hornett v. Equitable Trust; Jackson Barnett by Prochien Ami O'Hornett v. Riggs Trust Bank.*

14. *DO* and *MDP,* Apr. 4, 1923. The sum of $216,000 in JB's taxes was recovered.

15. McCrory and Monk to E. K. Burlew, Apr. 28, 1923; Work to McCrory and Monk, May 29, 1923 (quoted), Chronology; Mary Petersdorf (O'Hornett's granddaughter) to author, e-mail correspondence, Dec. 2, 1998.

16. Ward and Edwin Booth to Burke, Nov. 2, 1923, Eq-N67, f. 14.

17. Ward to Burke, Jan. 11, 1922; Booth by D/J Special Assistant O. H. Graves to Burke, Nov. 22, 1923; Burke to Booth, Nov. 27, 1923; Burke to Wallen, Dec. 19, 1923, all in Eq-N67, f. RG-21-LN, f. 14.

18. Booth to Burke, June 11, 1924; Graves to Burke (quoted), June 14, 1924; Wallen to Work and Burke, July 24, 1924, Eq-N67, f. 14; *MTD,* June 21, 1924. Foster and Hummer were Bailey's lawyers. Wallen sent $144,480.54 of JB's funds from the Union Agency to the D/I, July 24, 1924.

19. *Los Angeles Daily Times,* Mar. 2, 1925; *LAT,* Feb. 24, 1933. AB still owed $25,000 on the Rossmore lot; her contractors were Sam Mortenson and G. A. Johnson. Eq-N67, ff. 13, 9.

20. Earlier, O'H successfully blocked Commissioner Burke's directive to Buddrus to release $51,000 for a Barnett home purchase. *MTD,* May 31, 1923; Assistant CIA E. B. Meritt to Secretary of the Interior, Oct. 8, 1923; Goodwin memorandum to Meritt, Oct. 9, 1923; will of JB, Aug. 24, 1923, Chronology.

21. Mott to Burke, Oct. 7, 1924, Eq-N67, f. 14. *Anna Barnett v. Riggs Bank* and *Anna Barnett v. Equitable* were filed in 1924.

22. Mott to Burke, telegram, July 31, 1924, Eq-N67, f. 5; "In the Matter of the Estate of JB," Eq-N67, f. 10; "Declaration of Incompetency," Los Angeles Superior Court, July 31, 1924, Chronology.

23. Harry Chamberlain to E. B. Finney, Feb. 16, 1925, Eq-N67, f. 14.

24. AB to Burke, Aug. 11, 1924, Eq-N67, f. 14; Jackson Barnett guardianship document, Los Angeles Superior Court, and Assistant Secretary of the Interior to B. R. Creer, Security Trust and Savings Bank, both Oct. 8, 1924, Chronology; *Survey,* 636–641.

25. A. D. Cochran dep., Sept. 16, 1937, 4, Eq-N67, f. 2. Hummer and Foster, Bailey's Henryetta attorneys, made a subcontract with the Okmulgee firm of Cochran and Ellison in November 1924.

26. *MTD*, Aug. 20, 1923. Superintendent of the Union Agency, *AR* (June 1923), strongly recommended corrective legislation that would confer *exclusive* jurisdiction by D/I over the guardianship of minors and incompetents. See Mott, *Act of May 27, 1908*, 44.

27. The Wallen report is quoted in *And Still*, 326–328. Wallen examined 14,229 probate cases in six eastern Oklahoma counties. Of a total of 2,866 cases, in 8.8 percent of the cases, fees were more than 50 percent; in 4 percent, 40–50 percent; in 9 percent, 30–40 percent; in 17 percent, 20–30 percent; in 29 percent, 10–20 percent; in 32 percent, 10 percent or less. Superintendent of the Union Agency, *AR* (1924), 26.

28. *MTD*, June 12. 1924.

29. Bonnin, Fabens, and Sniffen, *Oklahoma's Poor Rich Indians*, 8–11, 39. John D. Rockefeller paid for printing. Mott, *Act of May 27, 1908*, 9, 11; Kelly, *Assault*, 313.

30. Work, "Our American Indians," 92.

31. Goodwin to Att. Gen., June 5, 1924, Chronology; Booth to Burke, June 11, 1924; Graves to Burke, June 14, 1924, all in Eq-N67, f. 14.

32. *And Still*, 322–324; *Survey*, 1534, 1232–1233.

33. *MTD*, Feb. 16, 1924.

34. Committee on Indian Affairs, HH 348, "Investigation of the Administration of Indian Affairs in Olkahoma" (1924), 448–455, 460–463; see also HRep 1527, "Investigation of the Administration of Indian Affairs in Oklahoma" (1924–1925).

35. *CR* (Dec. 9 and Dec. 10, 1924), 438.

36. Work to Hummer and Foster, Jan. 1, 1925; Work to Stone, Feb. 7, 1925, *Survey*, 6159.

37. Adding to congressional doubts was JB's testimony in Jan. 1925 before the Snyder subcommittee. Foster and Hummer to D/I, Feb. 14, 1925; BIA card catalog, RG75, NA I; Rayburn L. Foster dep., Sept. 16, 1937, Eq-N67, f. 2.

38. Stone to Work, Feb. 9, 1925, *Survey*, 1087–1088; Cochran dep., Sept. 16, 1937, Eq-N67, f. 2.

39. Cochran dep. (quoted); Burke memorandum to Work, Mar. 3, 1925; HRep 1527, 448–455, 460–463; *CR* (Mar. 4, 1925), 5570–5572.

40. HH on House Bill 6900 [Burke Bill]: "For Protection of the Five Civilized Tribes" *Survey*, 6624–6628. Hastings introduced Bill 11856 as an alternate to the Burke Bill to amend sec. 9 of the Act of May 27, 1908. Also see [Osage] Act of Feb. 27, 1925, 43 Stat L. 1008; Thorne, "Indian Beverly Hillbillies." 16. In Angie Debo's words, Oklahoma Indians were divided over whether to seek refuge in the bureau from state courts or to seek deliverance from the bureau "for its stupid routine, its unimaginative and arbitrary control, and its financial muddling" (*And Still*, 331 (quoted), 332–338).

41. Mott to White, Dec. 30, 1926, Eq-N67, f. 13.

Chapter 7

1. Ted Thackery, Jr., "Richest Indian's LA Mansion Bites the Dust."

2. *And Still*, 346. For a digest of the twenty-one pending actions in the Bar-

nett case, see the 1929 Pierce Butler report for the D/J in *Survey*, 1718–1727. Extensive records are in RG60-CP; Lexis-Nexus has a number of major cases online as does FindLaw.com.

3. *Barnett v. Locke; National Surety Co. v. O'Hornett; Barnett v. Equitable Trust; Barnett v. Riggs.*

4. *Jackson Barnett by R. B. Drake* [Five Civilized Tribes' probate attorney] *v. W. A. Barnett* [Okmulgee County judge] *and E. S. Bailey* [putative guardian].

5. *Jackson Barnett by Bailey v. Equitable Trust and the American Home Missionary Society* (United States intervened in 1926); *Jackson Barnett by Bailey v. Riggs National Bank, Anna Barnett, and Maxine Sturgis; Elmer S. Bailey v. Harold McGugin, Walter Keith and C. M. McGugin; Barnett by Bailey v. Marshall Mott; Barnett by Bailey v. Anna Barnett and Bank of Italy.*

6. *Jackson Barnett, an Incompetent, by Fred T. Hildt as Next Friend v. Gypsy Oil Co. et al.*

7. Hummer and Foster, Cochran and Ellison, and McCrory and Monk were the legal firms prosecuting the Bailey suits and defending the guardianship in the Drake case. On June 19, 1923, O'H's attorney, C. B. McCrory, and the law firm of Cochran and Ellison of Okmulgee entered into contingency contracts with David Barnett and other Siah Barnett descendants for fees between 30 and 50 percent. *Survey*, 1708. There were many subcontracted firms fighting for both sides in cases in separate states, e.g., Carroll Walter of the New York firm Patterson, Eagle, Greenough and Day led the *Equitable* defense for Bailey. The New York firm contracted to receive one-third of the recovered funds.

8. Parmenter to Selby, Dec. 21, 1925, RG60-CP, f. 207695-1.

9. Burke memorandum for Secretary D/I Work, Mar. 3, 1925, Chronology.

10. Hoxie, *Final Promise*, 215, 224, 155–174; Miner, *The Corporation and the Indian*, 151–153; Melissa Meyer, *White Earth Tragedy*, 151–159. The act of Feb. 15, 1901 (31 Stat. L. 790) gave D/I discretionary authority to issue permits for rights of way across Indian land with or without the Indians' consent.

11. Carroll Walter opening statement, Nov. 1926, court transcript, bound volume, Box 1772, RG21-NY.

12. Conspicuous examples are Secretary Lane's New Policy, in which Interior exercised its prerogative, the Oklahoma Closure Act of 1908, and the Osage Act of Feb. 27, 1925 (43 Stat. 1008). In the latter two examples, the federal government sacrificed its jurisdiction over mixed-bloods in order to gain stronger federal controls over full-bloods. Commissioner Vaux declared it was "unreasonable and immoral" that these mixed-bloods "should be tied to the apron strings of the Indian Bureau." Quoted in Wilson, *Underground Reservation*, 136.

13. Burke to President Coolidge, Mar. 11, 1925; Chronology.

14. *NYT*, Apr. 11, 1925, p. 3; a parallel argument was made in the *Riggs* case.

15. Bailey's amended bill of complaint, May 2, 1925, Eq-N67, ff. 19, 20.

16. Ibid.

17. Ibid.; Walter used the phrase "stupidity or cupidity" in his opening statement. Court transcript, 216, 218, Box 1772 RG21-NY.

18. *Survey*, 1331; Work to Att. Gen., Feb. 27, 1925, Chronology. Bailey's lawyers named Work and Burke as "nominal defendants" in the *Equitable* and *Riggs* cases. AB named Work and Burke as defendants in her countersuits in these cases, for failing to sustain the trusts. D/J assigned Lacy to the *Equitable* litigation in Feb. 1925. Walter's brief of Jan. 22, 1925, made no suggestion of fraud.

19. Mott to Burke, Mar. 2, 1925 (quoted); Mott to Burke, Mar. 11, 1925; Burke to Mott, Mar. 14, 1925, all in Eq-N67, f. 14.

20. Mott and Lytle prepared the motion filled in the Okmulgee County court on Mar. 7, 1925. Rogers, Lytle, and Mott collaborated all the way to the Oklahoma Supreme Court on the guardianship case. Rogers to Charles White, June 17, 1925, Box 52, ABHSA, f. 1; see appendix III for further details on the Oklahoma Supreme Court case. Bailey's lawyers were awarded $9,500 by the courts for their prosecution of the cases. Raymond Foster dep., Eq-N67, f. 2.

21. Burke to Weeks, Mar. 12, 1925, Eq-N67, f. 14. On Mar. 24, 1925, the AHMS filed to intervene in the prohibition case but otherwise took no active part. Weeks to Bryant, Mar. 21, 1925, Survey, 6131. Charles Fettretch dep., Eq-N67, f. 19; Mott dep., Eq-N67, f. 22.

22. Cochran dep. (quoted), Eq-N67, f. 19; [?] to Assistant Secretary D/I Edwards, Nov. 5, 1925; G. Lee Phelps, telegram, to D/J, Dec. 10, 1925, and D/J reply, Dec. 14, 1925, RG60-CP, f. 207695-1. Superintendent of Indian Missions to President Coolidge; D/J to Superintendent, Dec. 14, 1925; Survey, 1089.

23. Charles Selby was first assigned to the Barnett prohibition case on Nov. 13, 1925; he was appointed as special assistant to the attorney general on May 14, 1928. MDP, Nov. 29, 1925.

24. Work to D/J, Apr. 30 and June 5, 1925, RG60-CP, f. 207695-1; Survey, 6107.

25. Blend, 95–96. The assistant secretary of the D/I made the flimsy argument on Nov. 5, 1925, that D/I lacked authority to withdraw Drake, as he had begun the lawsuit independent of the Indian office. MDP, Nov. 29, 1929.

26. Burke's memorandum to D/J, Sept. 23, 1925, Chronology.

27. Parmenter to Work, Nov. 16 and Nov. 24, 1925; Work to Parmenter, Nov. 17, 1925; Burke to Drake, Nov. 27, 1927, Chronology; Burke to Mott, Burke to Lytle and Rogers, telegrams, Nov. 16, 1925; Burke to Rogers, Nov. 17, 1925, all in McNabb petition, Eq-N67, f. 14; D/J petition to intervene, Box 1771, RG21-NY; Parmenter to Solicitor Patterson, Nov. 1926, Survey, 1335–1336.

28. Judge Thatcher opinion, 3974, Jan. 1, 1926, Box 1772, RG21-NY.

29. DO, Nov. 29, 1925; MDP, Nov. 29, 1925; Survey, 694, 1331–1332, 1335–1336, 1697, 1702–1703. In nearly identical amendments, D/J and Bailey's lawyers alleged that AB, McGugin, Ward, and Mott were coconspirators.

30. "Burke Throne Shaken Again in Money Row," unmarked clipping, RG60-CP, f. 207695.

31. Foster dep., 6, Eq-N67, f. 2.

32. Survey, 645, 1153; Rogers to White, Dec. 9, 1925, Box 53, ABHSA, f. 1; Parmenter to Selby, Dec. 21, 1925, RG48-CP, f. 207695-1-47.

33. Survey, 1725–1726; United States v. Barnett, Eq-N67, f. 14.

34. LAH, Aug. 21, 1926; LAT, Feb. 18, 1933. AB was quoted: "By god you don't take him. I will go and get my Winchester gun and shoot hell out of you."

35. S. E. Lefko and Oscar Luhring testimony, Eq-N67, f. 14; Fiske to Burke, Aug. 24 and 25, 1926, Survey, 6111–6112. Luhring stated that it was "pathetic" that the wealthy JB was not "permitted to have the very simple pleasures which are all that can possibly mean anything to him." Survey, 1555–1558, 1295.

36. Parmenter to Work, Sept. 18, 1926, Chronology; Fixico, Invasion, 17–19.

37. J. F. Turnbull to Hovey, Sept. 6 (quoted) and Sept. 7, 1926, Box 53, ABHSA, f. 1.

38. AB to Coolidge, Sept. 6, 1926. Chronology; *MDP*, Sept. 17, 1926; *DO*, May 30, 1934.

39. Burke to Work, June 23, 1926, Chronology. JB was returned to custody on Oct. 4, then released to AB's custody when AHMS gave assurances that JB would appear at the *Equitable* trial.

40. Frank Knox to President Coolidge, Oct. 25, 1926, *Survey*, 6172. Knox was Coolidge's advisor and intermediary.

41. *Survey*, 6113, 1110–1111; Blend, 98–99; Selby dep., Box 1771, RG21-NY. Parmenter said Selby "never quite understood it" before early 1928. Parmenter is quoted in a statement, Jan 7, 1928, RG60-CP, f. 207695-1-04.

42. *Survey*, 1696–1697; Weeks to Hovey, June 29, 1926, Box 53, ABHSA, f. 1.

43. Court transcript, Box 1772, RG21-NY; *NYT*, Nov. 17, 1926, p. 42; Nov. 18, 1926, p. 10; Nov. 19, 1926, p. 27; Nov. 20, 1926; and Nov. 28, 1926, p. 18.

44. Opening statements in court transcript, RG21-NY.

45. Ibid.

46. Ibid., 9–10, 16, 27, 39–40; amended answer, c. Oct. 1926, Box 1771, RG21-NY, f. Jan. to Nov. 1926; amended answer of defense, Eq-N67, ff. 19–20.

47. Hovey's notes re: Burke conference, Jan. 10, 1928, Box 52, ABHSA, f. 1.

48. Blend, 100–106; Fettretch brief, point V, Box 1773, RG21-NY.

49. Court transcript; *NYT*, Nov. 25, 1926–1927.

50. Fettretch to John W. Davis, Jan. 24, 1928, *Survey*, 6126; Hovey's notes, Jan. 10, 1928; Fettretch to Rogers, Jan. 21, 1927; Fettretch dep., all in Eq-N67, f. 19.

51. AHMS counsel Fettretch met with top-ranking D/I officials in Feb. 1925. Fettretch to AHMS, Feb. 4, 1925; Burke to Weeks, Mar. 12, 1925, Eq-N67, f. 14. Weeks to Bryant, Mar. 21, 1925 (quoted), *Survey*, 1144, 6131; H. G. House to Hovey, Sept. 17, 1926, Box 52, AHMSA, f. 1.

52. Bryant to Burke, June 17, 1925; Hovey to Weeks, July 1, 1926; Rogers to White, July 8, 1926, *Survey*, 1144, 6107, 6113, 6174. Rogers to Fettretch, Oct. 15, 1926; Rogers to White, Dec. 7, 1926; Fettretch dep., Eq-N67, f. 19. Rogers contracted with the AHMS on Apr. 20, 1925, and with AB on Feb. 9, 1926, and May 24, 1927. See AB testimony, Nov. 22, 1928, *Survey*, 880. Fettretch moved to have AHMS costs paid out of JB's funds in *Equitable* litigation on Jan. 17, 1927; the motion was denied on Jan. 27, 1927, Box 1771, RG21-NY.

53. If not for "the moral stench attached to the names of Rogers, Mott and House," Weeks wrote in 1927, we [Baptists] could get some favorable newspaper publicity. Weeks to Hovey, Jan. 25, 1927, Box 53, ABHSA, f. 1.

54. Fettretch dep., Eq-N67, f. 19; Burke to White, June 10, 1925; White to Burke, June 11, 1925, Box 52, ABHSA, f. 1; Burke to Bryant, June 18, 1925, Box 53, ABHSA, f. 1; "Expenses in Connection with [JB] Litigation from Apr. 20, 1925, to Jan. 17, 1928." Box 163, ABHSA, f. 1. Rogers received $20,578, Fettretch about $3,000 of $27,173.56 expended.

55. See appendix III for details.

56. Ibid. The Okmulgee County court and the Oklahoma district court decisions of July 16, 1926, were reversed on Nov. 30, 1926, and Dec. 7, 1926. *Survey*, 1662–1668.

57. *DO*, Dec. 1, 1926; Board of Directors IRA, AR (1927), p. 5, in Box 53, ABHSA, f. 1.

58. *DO*, Dec. 2, 1926.

59. Burke to Ellis, Dec. 9, 1926; Burke to Fettretch, Nov. 30, 1926; Burke to

Rogers, Dec. 3, 1926, *Survey*, 6114–6115; Burke to White, Dec. 6, 1926 (quoted), Box 53, ABHSA, f. 2.

60. George Riley Hall and H. G. House asked to be appointed guardians in Okmulgee and Muskogee counties, respectively. Fred T. Hildt became Jackson's Creek County guardian. D/I filed a motion to dismiss Hall's petition, saying, "It adds an expense which the Indian has to pay and interferes with the jurisdiction of the Department" (Eq-N67, f. 14). Petitions of Feb. 3 and Feb. 26, 1927, "In the Case of JB, an Incompetent," No. 2722 Probate, Okmulgee County court, Box 3331, RG 60; Weeks to Hovey, Feb. 16, 1927, Box 53, ABHSA, f. 1.

61. *DO*, Dec. 1, 1926, p. 1; *Hildt v. Gypsy Oil.*

62. The Creek County court found JB incompetent on Feb. 28, 1927. Burke to Fettretch, Feb. 1, 1927, *Survey*, 1062–1070, 1144–1149; Burke to Hovey, Feb. 2, 1927; Rogers to Burke, Feb. 19, 1927; Burke to Rogers, Apr. 29, 1927; Burke to Work, June 16 and July 8, 1927; Burke to Rogers, July 21, 1927, *Survey*, 6118, and Eq-N67, f. 7.

63. Jelliffe testimony, Eq-N67, f. 11; Blend, 144–146.

64. Rogers to Fettretch, May 24, 1927, Box 53, ABHMS, f. 1; D/I decision, Mar. 1927, Box 52, f. 1. Burke to Rogers, Jan. 4, June 16, June 20, and Dec. 29, 1927; Rogers to Burke, Jan. 1 and June 13, 1927; Burke to Fettretch, Jan. 10 and Jan. 13, 1927; Burke to White, Mar. 7, 1927, *Survey*, 6116–6118, 6125.

65. See Appendix III and *Barnett v. Barnett*, July 13, 1926, 247 Pac 1117.

66. In early 1927 Rogers prepared a brief for Fettretch to review; Fettretch found it weak and rewrote it, but Rogers had already sent the original version to Knox. Burke to Fettretch, Jan. 10, 1927; Fettretch to Burke, Jan 11, 1927; Burke to Rogers, June 23, 1927, *Survey*, 6116, 6119; Weeks to Hovey, Feb. 16 and June 30, 1927; Hovey to Weeks, Jan. 26 and Feb. 5, 1927, Box 53, ABHSA, f. 1.

67. Opinion of Knox, 173, *Barnett v. Equitable Trust*, 21 F.2d 325.

68. [New York] *Tribune*, n.d., Box 53, ABHSA, f. 1.

69. Weeks to Hovey, Sept. 23 and Sept. 30, 1927, Box 53, ABHSA, f. 1; Burke to Fettretch, Aug. 12, 1927, *Survey*, 6121.

70. Burke to Fettretch, Aug. 10 and Aug. 12, 1927; Rogers to Burke, Dec. 17, 1927, *Survey*, 6121, 6125.

71. Weeks to Hovey, Sept. 23 and Dec. 16, 1927, Box 53, ABHSA, f. 1.

72. Allin to Fettretch, Sept. 28, 1927, *Survey*, 6122.

73. Burke to House, Aug. 12, 1927, *Survey*, 6122; Burke to Rogers, Sept. 24, 1927; White to Burke, Sept. 26, 1927; Burke to White, Oct. 17, 1927; Allin to ABHMS Board, Oct. 24, 1927; White to Rockefeller, Mar. 7, 1928, all in Box 53, ABHSA, f. 2; Weeks to Hovey, Sept. 13, 1922, Box 52, ABHSA, f. 1.

74. Allin to White, (quoted) Dec. 30, 1927, *Survey*, 6125. Weeks to Inspector Blair, Sept. 9, 1927, *Survey*, 6121. Allegations of duplicitious and shady dealings by Rogers, Mott, and House included AB's $50,000 contract with Rogers to maintain the trusts and House's boast of a 50 percent contingency contract with some heirs of Barnett.

75. White to Burke, Oct. 18, 1927; Allin to Fettretch, Oct. 22, 1927; Hughes to Fettretch, Nov. 7, 1927; Burke to White, Dec. 8, 1925; Rogers to White, Dec. 24, 1927; Burke to Diggs, Jan. 11, 1928; Burke to White, Jan 24, 1928; Burke to Rogers, Mar. 23 and Mar. 30, 1928; Rogers to Burke, May 18, 1928; Allin to Bryant, June 5, 1928; Rogers to AHMS, Oct. 30, 1927, all in *Survey*, 1070, 6124, 6126–6128, 6142; court transcript, Mar. 16, 1928, RG21-NY, f. 10408.

76. Blend, 1019–1111; *Survey*, 1053.

77. *United States v. McGugin*, No. 293-N, 28 F.2d 76, District Court of the United States for District of Kansas, 3d division (1928); Rogers to Burke, Apr. 20, 1928, *Survey*, 6127, 1677–1678.

78. Burke to Rogers, Aug. 27, 1928, *Survey*, 6128; *United States v. Mott*, No. 343, 33 F.2d 340, U.S. District Court, Northern District of Oklahoma (1929). The D/J amended bills of complaint against McGugin and Mott in Sept. 1928, which corrected some of the deficiencies of the earlier bills; however, they still lacked the essential element of fraud or deception. *United States v. Mott*, No. 136, Circuit Court of Appeals, Tenth Circuit, 37 F.2d 860 (1930) reversed the Pollock decision.

79. Parmenter to Att. Gen. Sargent, 1929, *Survey*, 1632, 6147.

80. Weeks to Hovey, July 11, 1928; Hovey to Allin, Dec. 29, 1929, Box 53, ABHSA, f. 3. Pierce Butler report, *Survey*, 1719–1721.

Chapter 8

1. David Wilkins *American Indian Sovereignty*, 4–5, 9, 14, 24; *Heckman v. United States*, 224, US 413 (1912); *Barnett v. Barnett*, 24 Pac 1115 (1926).

2. Burke to Fettretch, Jan. 12, 1927; Rogers to Burke, Dec. 17 and Dec. 27, 1927, *Survey*, 6117, 6125.

3. *CR* (Mar. 18, 1924), 4460–4464, 4463 (quoted), and (Feb. 2, 1924), 233.

4. HR 1527 (1924–1925) (Snyder report); U.S. Board of Indian Commissioners, unpublished report, Jan. 26, 1926; Randolph C. Downes, "A Crusade for Indian Reform," 341.

5. Hauptman, *Tribes and Tribulations*, 74. Congressman Snyder introduced the Indian Citizenship Act of 1924; See Philp, *John Collier's Crusade*, 51.

6. Vine Deloria and Clifford Lytle, *The Nations Within*, 42; Tanis C. Thorne, "On the Fault Line," 190–196; W. W. Breedlove to Harrell, June 17, 1925; Breedlove to Coolidge, June 16, 1925, *Survey*, 6712–6714; *And Still*, 330.

7. Downes, "Crusade for Indian Reform," 331–354. See Kelly, *Assault*, and Philp, *John Collier's Crusade*, for the best analyses of 1920 reform.

8. Frear to Collier, May 6, 1929 (quoted). Collier to Frear, Jan. 5, Jan. 29, Feb. 4 (quoted), Feb. 18, and Apr. 6, 1926: Frear to Collier, Feb. 21, 1926, all in reel 2, Collier Papers. Collier would later deny he had any role in the preparation of Frear's speeches, but this correspondence suggests otherwise. Also see Philp, *John Collier's Crusade*, 78–80.

9. *CR* (Mar. 4, 1926); 5034–5035, 5041–5042, 5034 (quoted). Kelly, *Assault*, 370; "Leasing of Allottee Lands," Hearing before a Subcommittee on Indian Affairs, HH 887 (Apr. 11, 14, 15, 1926); Deloria and Lytle, *The Nations Within*, 43. The Indian courts were controversial, as they were used in Indian communities to enforce bureau policies. Hearings on the bill evoked opposition testimony from many tribes. Burke claimed he knew of no instances in which any Indian complained of justice meted out by the Indian Court of Offenses, but this was absolutely untrue.

10. Atwood to Collier, Mar. 24, 1926 reel 1, Collier Papers.

11. HH 887, "Leasing of Allottee Lands" (Apr. 11, 14, 15, 1926), 7, 22–25.

12. For Burke's administrative style as a pragmatist, master of detail, planner, and enforcer of Victorian values, see his BIA circulars for 1922–1923, e.g., 1737, 1665, 1819, and 1846, and his letter to Henry Tidwell, Sept. 23, 1922, reel 12, BIA Circ.

13. Burke to Atwood, Apr. 17, 1926; Collier to Atwood, June 15, 1926, reel 1, Collier Papers. On May 26, 1926, Wheeler presented a formal reply to Burke's accusations of misrepresentation and false propaganda. See Mrs. Stella M. Atwood and Dr. Haven Emerson (AIDA), "Reply to Commissioner Burke's Accusations of Misrepresentation and false propaganda," Hearings before a Senate Subcommittee on Indian Affairs, SR341 (Feb. 23, 1927), 52; and Blend, 122 (quoted).

14. Collier to Atwood, Apr. 8 and Apr. 28, 1926, reel 1, Collier Papers. The reformers' alternative oil bill, the Frear-Cameron-La Follette bill to safeguard title to executive order reservations, passed in 1927. Kelly, *Assault*, 358–364.

15. Kelly, *Assault*, 375, identifies 1926–1927 as the turning point in Indian policy reform. Harrell-Hastings Act, Apr. 12, 1926, 44 Stat. 239, 240. Collier pushed hard behind the scenes for Congress to authorize an investigation of Burke. Collier to Atwood, May 10, 1926, reel 1; Collier to Frear, July 24, 1926; Collier to Frear, Dec. 2, 1926, reel 2, Collier Papers.

16. *CR* (Dec. 13, 1926), 384 (quoted).

17. *CR* (Jan. 4, 1927), 1066, 1072–1073, 1078; Blend, 148–150.

18. Collier to White, Feb. 16, 1927; Allin to S. Keese, Mar. 8, 1927; Collier to White, Feb. 15, 1927, Box 53, ABHSA, f. 1; White to Burke, May 19, 1925, *Survey*, 6160; Burton Wheeler, *Yankee from the West*, 315. Grorund to Collier, Aug. 24, 1927; Congressman W. H. Sproul to Frear, Aug. 27, 1927, C-A, carton 3, Bancroft Library. Collier's AIDA papers at the Bancroft Library include Barnett clippings from the 1920s and 1930s and the 1927 Knox decision. Collier to Frear, Sept. 5, 1927, reel 2, Collier Papers.

19. Senate "Survey" (Jan. 10, 1928), 17, 28.

20. Ibid., 23, 27, 32, 34, 38 (quoted); cf. Senate "Survey" (Jan. 10, 1927), 1403; Blend, 145, 148.

21. Senate Resolution (SR) 341, *CR* (Feb. 3, 1927), 2856–2857; Hearing before Senate pursuant to SR 341 (Feb. 23, 1927), 3, 87–90, 92–97; Senate "Survey" (Jan. 10 and Jan. 13, 1928), 2, 8–9, 39, 46–49. A number of other hearings relating to JB were conducted by Senate subcommittees in the 69th through the 73d Congresses: S545-1-D, S346-0-A, and S545-1-C.

22. Senate "Survey" (Jan. 10 and Jan. 13, 1928), 2, 6–7 (quoted), 8–9, 12; Blend, 148–150; W. H. Sproul to James Frear, Aug. 27, 1927, Bancroft Library, C-A, carton 3; John Collier, *American Indian Life Bulletin* 12 (June 1928): 16.

23. "Survey" (Jan. 10 and Jan. 13, 1928), 43 (Frazier quoted), 88–90 (Bonnin quoted); Blend, 122.

24. Meriam et al., *Problem of Indian Administration*, viii, 100–101 (quoted), 104, 471–472, 479, 484–485 (quoted), 486, 747–748, 756, 779–798, 803–804. One bureau error was the issuance of competency certificates to wealthy Osages, who were again brought under federal supervision after 1925. See Osage Agency, *Osage People and Their Trust Property*, 50–57.

25. Meriam et al., *Problem of Indian Administration*, 8, 480–481, 483–484 (quoted), 754–755 (quoted), 756; the phrase "unearned increment" to refer to leasing income was still being used in the 1950s, suggesting its institutionalization within bureau culture. The Osage argued that their land had not been "given" to them, so this justification for controlling their oil income did not apply. See Osage Agency, *Osage People and Their Trust Property*, 41, 78, 159; and Board of Indian Commissioners report to D/I, Jan. 10, 1929, 25–27.

26. Deloria and Lytle, *The Nations Within*, 44.

27. House of Representatives, Subcommittee of the Committee on Indian Affairs, HR 7204, "Creation of Indian Trust Estates" (Mar. 26, 1928).

28. Ibid., Mar. 26 and Apr. 21, 1928; Work to Frazier, Mar. 7, 1928, in SR 982, "Extension of Restrictions for Five Civilized Tribes" (1928), 4, 11, 20. D/I "Regulations of Indian Service Individual Indian Moneys" (1928).

29. HH on 7204; "Creation of Indian Trust Estates" (Apr. 21, 1928); 28. After much discussion in Congress, an act of May 10, 1928, 45 Stat. 495, extended restrictions an additional twenty-five years from Apr. 26, 1931, for the Five Civilized Tribes; the act of Mar. 2, 1929, 45 Stat. 1478, extended the period for the Osage to 1959.

30. Senate "Survey" (Jan. 13, 1928), 61 (quoted), 62–64. Littlefield, *Posey*, 244; Also see *United States v. Sandoval* (1913) in which Pueblo Indians are described as "a simple, uninformed and inferior people."

31. *Barnett v. Barnett*, 247 Pac 1115 (1926). Davis brief, Feb. 24, 1920, *Survey*, 1655.

32. *Survey*, 6207; Jelliffe's testimony, Apr. 29, 1929, Eq-N67, f. 11. To ascertain Jackson's mental age, Jelliffe used a series of questions devised by Binet and Simon. JB was not an "idiot" (defined as a person with the mental age of a two-year-old), not an "imbecile" (under age four), and not a "high grade defective" (under eight to ten). Jelliffe used the Ziehen blank in a second series of tests. See Stephen Jay Gould, *The Mismeasure of Man*, 196 and Chap. 2.

33. The initial suits filed by the guardian had been dismissed after Bailey's guardianship was voided. Blend, 107–108, 118; *Survey*, 1707. *United States v. Harold McGugin et al.*, a suit brought in U.S. District Court for the District of Kansas, commenced Apr. 11, 1928; *United States v. Marshall Mott* commenced Apr. 10, 1928, in the U.S. District Court for the Northern District of Oklahoma; *United States v. Anna Laura Barnett, Leslie R. Hewitt, Bank of Italy National Trust and Savings Institute* commenced Apr. 11, 1928, in U.S. District Court for the Southern District of California.

34. *Survey*, 1252–1253; McGugin's testimony, Box 3311, RG60-CP, f. 207695-1.

35. Burke to Work, June 23, 1928 [misfiled as 1926], Chronology; *Survey*, 1721–1727.

36. Work to Sargent, telegram, *Survey*, 6128 (quoted), 1190, 1215, 1218–1219.

37. Testimony of Thomas D. Lyons, Tulsa attorney, regarding a 1928 conversation with Bailey's lawyer, Cochran, *Survey*, 1836–1387.

38. Parmenter to Selby, May 28, 1928, telegram, *Survey*, 6146, 1245, 1351, 1354, 1359; *Harlow's Weekly*, June 23 and July 8, 1928, in Box 3331, RG60-CP, f. 207695-17.

Chapter 9

1. *Survey*, 1:1. The formal survey began in Nov. 1928 in Yakima, Wasington, and Klamath Falls, Oregon, Nov. 12, 13, and 16, 1928.

2. *Washington Daily News*, Jan. 11, 1929, quoted in *CR* (Jan. 12, 1929), 1612–1613.

3. AB testimony, Nov. 22, 1928, 635–644; JB testimony, 644–646, *Survey*. Cf. *CR* (Dec. 13, 1928), 538–542 (AB and JB give testimony in part 2, San Francisco, Riverside, and Salt Lake testimony). *Survey*, 6100–6194, is a catalog of JB documents compiled by D/J.

4. Among those present were CIA Charles Burke; E. O. Patterson, solicitor of

D/I; Carroll G. Walter, counsel for Elmer S. Bailey; and Charles Rogers of Tulsa, counsel for AB. See Selby's testimony, *Survey*, 1039–1047; David George Kin, *The Plot against America*, 126; and Wheeler, *Yankee from the West*, 293, 246.

5. *Survey*, 1039–1040.

6. *Survey*, 1042, 1048–1054, 1092–1096, 1117. Thomas corresponded with AB from 1929 to 1935, Box 9, ET, ff. 17 and 19.

7. *Survey*, 1056.

8. Ibid., 1190.

9. Ibid., 1070, 1062, 1066.

10. Ibid., 1071–1072, 1210, 1330, 1334–1341, 1348–1359.

11. Ibid., 1343–1344, 1171–1172, 1541–1542.

12. *And Still*, 324, 344–345; Blend, 115; Kelly, "Charles Henry Burke," 259–260; Kelly, "John Collier and the Indian New Deal," 372–373; and *Survey*, 1099, 1340–1341, 1377.

13. *Survey*, 1049.

14. Ibid., 1219. Parmenter too described JB as an "idiot."

15. Ibid., 1237–1238.

16. Ibid., 1077, 1188–1189.

17. Ibid., 1092–1096, 1117, 1281, 1290. Lacy did not think it was a crime for a woman to marry an Indian man, even if she had done it solely for the money.

18. Ibid., 1062, 1066.

19. Ibid., 1070, 1165, 1226–1227. See the balanced and knowledgeable testimony of W. E. Foltz, Nov. 18, 1930, *Survey*, 6638–6641, on dual guardianship.

20. Ibid., 1268, 1271.

21. Ibid., 1639, 1641, 6196–6207.

22. Ibid., 1259–1260, 1261, 1266, 1267.

23. Ibid., 1625, 1627–1631.

24. Ibid., 1281, 1290.

25. Ibid., 1300, 1302.

26. Ibid., 1542, 1550, 1555–1557, 1567.

27. Ibid., 1562, 1566, 1568, 1571, 1573.

28. *NYT*, Feb. 5, 1929, p. 13; *Survey*, 1558–1559.

29. *Survey*, 1573–1574.

30. Ibid., 1575–1576.

31. Blend, 89–90, 122; *Survey*, 1690. Chain of approval: Locke, Meritt, Dawson, Burke, Booth, Goodwin, Fall.

32. *Survey*, 1653–1731, 1788–1801, 6713.

33. "Interior Scandal Due for Inquiry by Senate," unmarked clipping, c. May 1929, Chronology.

34. *Time*, Feb. 18, 1929, p. 13, and Feb. 20, 1929, p. 219.

35. *Latta's Fortnightly Review* (c. Feb. 1929), pp. 5, 12, Box 53, ABHSA, f. 1; Thomas entered it in the *CR* on Mar. 2, 1929, Chronology.

36. *Tulsa World* editorial, Jan. 16, 1929, entered into *CR* (Jan. 30, 1929), 2480; copy in ET, Box 9, f. 17.

37. *Indian Truth* 6, no. 2 (Feb. 1929): 1–2.

38. *NYT*, Mar. 13, 1929; *Survey*, 1716, 1655.

39. *Survey*, 1716–1717; Wheeler, "Is It the End of the Road?" The same day, May 16, 1929, Senator Thomas had documents favorable to Burke entered into the *CR*'s appendix.

40. *New York Herald Tribune*, Mar. 13, 1929; Kelly, "Charles Henry Burke," 260–261. Collier, in *Indians of the Americas*, says Burke resigned because he failed to substantiate the allegations he made against Collier. Other historians underestimate the stigma of Burke's handling of the Barnett case in his decision to resign, citing health problems instead. Kelly, *Assault*, 372; Philp, *John Collier's Crusade*, 90n; and Donald Parman, *Indians and the American West in the 20th Century*, 87.

41. Hovey to Weeks, Apr. 26, 1929, Box 53, ABHSA, f. 1. The Baptists' worst fears were not realized. In *American National Bank v. ABHMS*, 106 F.2d 192, 195, 198 (2d Cir., 1939), two Creek women tried to recover $150,000 they'd donated to construct buildings on the Bacone campus, using identical arguments to those that struck down the JB donation, and failed.

42. Wilkins, *American Indian Sovereignty*, 127–129. *Mott v. United States*, 283 US 747, 752 (1931). *United States v. Equitable Trust of New York*, 283 US 738, 746 (1931). Both cases are available online at FindLaw.com.

43. David Wilkins and K. Tsianina Lomawaima, *Uneven Ground*, Chap. 2, "The Trust Doctrine," 64–98, esp. 69–72.

44. In the measured judgment of historian Angie Debo, "He was an illiterate with an illiterate's limited concepts, but he spoke intelligently of matters within his experience" (*And Still*, 347).

45. Holm, "Indians and Progressives," iv, 143, 154.

46. "Survey" (Jan. 10, 1928), 88–90. On Feb. 28, 1929, the Senate adopted two resolutions, 303 and 308, authorizing the continuation of the investigation of the Indian bureau.

Chapter 10

1. AB testimony, Mar.–Apr. 1937 in Equity 4556, Box 686, 462–463, RG21-FW. *LAT*, Sept. 28, 1932, and Feb. 24, 1933; *LAH*, Nov. 25, 1926; *Los Angeles Daily Times*, Mar. 2, 1925; newspaper clippings in Boxes 199–201, MIA-LN, Jackson Barnett clippings file, *Los Angeles Herald Examiner*, and indexed Barnett clippings, *LAT*, History Room, LAPL.

2. Bert Van Tuyle, *Know Your Los Angeles: An Unusual Guide Book*. *LAT*, Jan. 25, 1987, sec. 8, p. 1; Cecilia Rasmussen, "'Richest Indian' and Battles for His Wealth," B3; *LAH*, Dec. 16, 1962, pp C1, p. 1.

3. Charles Bickett dep., Aug. 1932, Eq-N67, f. 17.

4. AB testimony, Equity 4556, 491–492.

5. Interview with Robert Hine, Irvine, California, Dec. 7, 1999; e-mail communication from Hine to author, Dec. 22, 1999.

6. *ODT*, Jan. 1, 1963.

7. "Mrs. (Pale Face) Barnett's Struggle to Hold Millionaire (Red Skin) Husband," *San Francisco Chronicle*, May 20, 1934, Jackson Barnett folder, C-A 360, Box 3, Bancroft.

8. *Survey*, 1270.

9. McGugin served as a Kansas congressman 1931–1935 and ran for governor of Kansas in 1938. See "A Poor Old Indian," *Winners of the West* 15, no. 8 (Aug. 1938), OCHS.

10. *LAT*, Sept. 27, 1932; McGugin quoted in undated clipping, *LAH*, LAPL; AB quoted in *MDP*, June 6, 1934.

11. AB spent $143,000 by 1926 on various properties.

12. *Survey*, 638. AB's lawyers, Miller and Chavalier, were replaced by Jerry A.

Mathews and Josephus G. Trimble in the *Riggs* and *Gypsy Oil* litigation. Herbert House and L. O. Lytle worked under Rogers and Mott. AB-Mott contract, Aug. 22, 1923; AB-Rogers contract, Feb. 9, 1926; Charles Ellis to Burke, Jan. 30, 1927; Weeks to Inspector Blair, Sept. 9, 1927, all in *Survey*, 6119, 6121.

13. *NYT*, Oct. 31, 1926, p. 12; JB to Burke and Work, Sept. 18, 1926; AB to Burke, Oct. 4, 1926; JB to Work and Burke, Oct. 4, 1926; Ellis to Burke, Oct. 5, 1926; Burke to Rogers, June 10, 1927; Rogers to Burke, Dec. 20, 1927; Burke to Rogers, Apr. 27, 1927; JB to Work and Burke, May 23, 1927; AB and JB to Rogers and Lytle, May 24, 1927; Burke to Rogers, June 10, 1927; JB to Work, June 23, 1927; Rogers to Ellis, July 11, 1927; Lytle to Work, Aug. 8, 1927; Burke to Graves, Sept. 20, 1927; AB to Burke, Jan. 30, 1928, all in *Survey*, 6112–6113, 6117–6120, 6122.

14. Burke to Ellis and Burke to Rogers, Dec. 9, 1926; Burke to Ellis, Nov. 2, 1926; JB to Work, June 23, 1927; Rogers to Ellis, July 11, 1927, all in *Survey*, 6113–6115, 6119–6120, 6124; Burke to Work, Nov. 23, 1927, Chronology.

15. On May 10, 1927, Burke authorized $5,000, Chronology. Burke to Ellis, Mar. 14, 1929; Burke to Work, Mar. 30, 1929; Burke to Ellis, Dec. 5, 1927; Burke to Ellis, Nov. 28, 1928, all in *Survey*, 6124, 6128.

16. Burke to Ellis, Nov. 2, 1926, *Survey*, 6114, 1056–1058.

17. D/J's suit in Sept. 1926 blocked guardian Leslie Hewitt from dispensing funds to the Barnetts, either allowances or extra expenses. *Survey*, 881, 1706, 1727, 6127; Acting CIA Meritt to Pine, Dec. 13, 1928. Assistant Secretary D/I Edwards and CIA Rhoads approved extra Barnett expenditures, Sept. 1929; Nov. 28, 1930; Apr. 29, 1931; May 23, 1931; Dec. 9, 1931; and Nov. 16, 1932, Chronology.

18. *NYT*, Oct. 31, 1926; JB to D/I, Oct. 6, 1926; JB to Ellis, Oct. 7, 1926; JB to Work, Dec. 3, 1926; Burke to Ellis, Dec. 8, 1926; Ellis to CIA, Dec. 17, 1926, and Feb. 8, 1927; George Ramsey, telegram to Burke, Nov. 13, 1926, all in Box 9, RG118-FW.

19. Security Trust sued AB in the Superior Court of Los Angeles on Nov. 29, 1926, for failure to meet contractual obligations. *Survey*, 638, 1726–1727; Anna to D/I?, Jan. 26, 1928. Interior paid $25,516 from Jackson's funds on the Coldwater assessment bond in 1930. Chronology; *LAH*, Nov. 24, 1930.

20. Burke to Rogers, June 23, 1928, *Survey*, 6119.

21. MIA Superintendent Ellis and Anna did a trust agreement for the Hancock Park home on Sept. 26, 1928; AB to D/I, Jan. 26, 1928. On June 29, 1929, Interior authorized a payment to meet mortgages and taxes on the home. Chronology.

22. *Survey*, 634, 635, 641, 881.

23. Butler report, Mar. 4, 1929, in *Survey*, 1722–1723, 1726, 1717 (quoted). AB's sale of a $200,000 property (the Brentwood home) in May 1926 alerted D/J to the urgency of tracking her financial dealings. A suit filed June 3, 1926, by D/J was dismissed. On April 11, 1928, the last day allowed by the statute of limitations established by the Harreld-Hastings Act, the United States commenced its suit in federal court in Los Angeles. Raymond Foster and Cochran deps., Eq-N67, f. 2.

24. Jan. 4, 1932; Apr. 16, 1932; Oct. 13, 1932, Chronology; Wilbur to AB, Oct. 27, 1932, Box 201, MIA-LN, f. 30.

25. Rhoads to Wilbur, Nov. 15 and Nov. 22, 1932; D/I memorandum, Jan. 3, 1933, Chronology.

26. Wilbur to Att. Gen., Apr. 16, 1932; Att. Gen. Mitchell to Wilbur, Apr. 18,

1932, Chronology; AB to Wilbur, June 23, 1932, Wilbur to AB, Oct. 27, 1932, Box 201, MIA-LN, f. 30.

27. Tax bills of Nov. 2, Nov. 5, and July 7, 1932, Chronology; *LAT*, Feb. 23, 1933; JB to D/I, telegram, July 5, 1932 (quoted) in MIA, Box 201, RG75-LN, f. 30.

28. *LAH*, Mar. 9, 1933, and Feb. 10, 1937; AB to Wilbur (quoted), Jan. 9, 1933, Chronology.

29. AB's brief on motion to dismiss, Jan. 2, 1930; AB's brief of Apr. 17, 1930; Hewitt's amended brief, July 10, 1930, Eq-N67, ff. 8, 9, and 10; *LAT*, Mar. 11, 1933.

30. *LAH*, Feb. 8, 1933.

31. *LAT*, Feb. 9, 1933, and Mar. 4, 1933.

32. *LAT*, Sept. 28, 1932 (AB quoted); *LAT*, Feb. 8, 1933 (Thomas P. Cruce quoted); *LAT*, July 7, 1934.

33. White to Rhoads, Nov. 2, 1932; Rhoads to White, Dec. 10, 1932, Box 9, ET, f. 59; Selby's testimony, *Survey*, 1190; *LAT*, July 7, 1934.

34. Unmarked clipping, Box 200, MIA-LN, f. 23 3/3.

35. *LAT*, Sept. 30, 1932.

36. Ickes to JB, Jan. 24, Jan. 21, Feb. 21, 1933; E. K. Berlew to Rhoads, Mar. 21, 1933, Chronology.

37. Ickes to Judge DeVries, Apr. 8, 1933; Ickes to JB, Apr. 14, 1933, and Mar. 7, 1933, Chronology. Since July 1, 1932, $52,000 had been paid out to the Barnetts.

38. Ickes to AB, Mar. 24, 1933; AB to Ickes, Mar. 30, 1933 (quoted); Ickes to JB, Apr. 14 and June 22, 1933; JB to Ickes, June 22, 1933; JB to Ickes, telegrams, May 11, May 20, and May 25, 1933, Chronology.

39. JB to D/I, telegram, June 1929; Ickes to Barnetts, July 1, 1933; Ickes to Att. Gen., July 10, 1933, Chronology; Graham White and John Maze, *Harold Ickes of the New Deal*, 92–93.

40. *LAT*, May 13, 1933; E. K. Berlew to Rhoads, Mar. 31, 1933; AB to Ickes, Mar. 30, Aug. 7, Aug. 28, Sept. 4, Sept. 14, 1933, and May 8, 1934, Chronology.

41. AB to Ickes, Jan. 7, Jan. 11, Feb. 16, Mar. 21, Apr. 3, 1934; Nathan Margold report to Work, Mar. 17, 1933, Chronology.

42. *LAH*, Dec. 4, 1933.

43. AB to Thomas, Jan. 9 and Jan. 13, 1933; Thomas to AB, Jan. 24, 1933, Box 9, ET, f. 59. Claude Porter, guardian of Lewis Fisher, made the proposal to AB in Dec. 1933, "In the County Court of Okfuskee County," No. 2174, 39–43, RG75-FW.

44. The term "comedy-tragedy" originated with AB's attorney. James opinion and decree, Mar. 31, 1934, *United States v. Barnett*, Eq-N67, f. 16.

45. Ibid., 4, 22.

46. Ibid., 12, 15, 20, 25–27.

47. *LAT*, Apr. 4 and Apr. 5, 1934 (quoted).

48. Chris Fahey to Work, May 28, 1934, Chronology.

49. Ickes to Landman, Apr. 3, 1934; AB to Ickes, Apr. 20, 1934, Chronology; Thomas to Collier, May 18 or May 29, 1934; Rogers to Thomas, June 28, 1934, Box 9, ET, ff. 65 and 80.

Chapter 11

1. *ODT* and *NYT*, May 30, 1934; *MDP*, June 3, 1934 (quoted); Jackson's death certificate gives advanced chronic myocarditis as cause of death, Eq-N67, f. 16.

2. *MDP*, May 31 (quoted), June 1, June 2, and June 3, 1934; *Riverside Daily Press*, June 1, 1934, in Box 199, MIA-LN, f. 23. Dady originally agreed to authorize $825 for the Forest Lawn plot; AB purchased two adjoining sites for $220.

3. *NYT*, June 1, 1934; *MDP*, June 2 and June 3, 1934; *Okmulgee Sunday Times-Democrat*, June 3, 1934; *LAT*, June 5, 1934. Anna appeared before the Los Angeles Superior Court on June 6, 1934, asking for a permanent injunction against releasing the body to the federal government. *MDP*, June 7, 1934.

4. *MDP*, June 8 and June 9, 1934; Charles West to John Simpson, Oct. 22, 1935; Eva Warren to FDR, Oct. 21, 1938, Chronology. At the request of Maxine Sturgis, JB's body was moved to section 14 of Hollywood Memorial Cemetery (now, the Hollywood Forever Cemetery, 6000 Santa Monica Boulevard) in 1952, presumably so AB could be buried next to JB; "Sachem" used in *LAT*, July 5, 1934.

5. *MDP*, May 31 and June 13, 1934; *LAT*, Aug. 7, 1934; AB to "Ikie" [Ickes], May 8, 1934; AB to Ickes, May 21, 1934, Chronology.

6. *LAT*, July 9, 1934 (quoted), June 30, 1934, and May 10, 1935; *Washington Evening Star*, June 30, 1934; AB, *Truth: A History of Jackson Barnett*, 17; Chronology; Dady to CIA, Nov. 6, 1946, Box 199, MIA-LN, f. 23 2/3.

7. *LAT*, July 10, 18, and 19, 1934, Box 200, MIA-LN, f. 23 3/3.

8. *Washington Evening Star*, July 17–19, 1934; *MDP*, July 19, 1934; *LAT*, July 27, 1934; AB to Superintendent Landman, June 8, 1934, Box 3331, RG60-CP, 207695-16(4); Hutchinson to Ickes, July 27, 1934, Chronology; *ODT*, Oct. 16 and Oct. 26, 1934.

9. Hutchinson to Harry Blair, Nov. 24, 1934; E. K. Burlew and Dawson D/I memorandum for Collier, Dec. 8, 1934, Box 3331, RG60-CP, f. 207695-16(4) and f. 592; AB to Ickes, Aug. 29, Oct. 15, and Dec. 17, 1934; Ickes to Att. Gen. Cummings, Dec. 8, 1934, Chronology.

10. Cummings to Ickes, Feb. 28, 1935, Chronology.

11. AB to Ickes, May 6 (quoted), May 1, May 2, May 17, and May 23, 1935; Ickes to AB, May 2, 1935; AB to FDR, May 29, 1934; Ickes to Att. Gen., Dec. 17, 1934; D/I memorandum, Feb. 28, 1935; Hutchinson to FDR, June 1935, Chronology.

12. AB to Thomas, Nov. 1 and Nov. 5, 1935, Box 9, ET, f. 80; Hutchinson to FDR, May 27, 1935, Chronology.

13. McGugin to Hutchinson, Sept. 20, 1934, quoted in AB, *Truth: A History of Jackson Barnett*; Chronology.

14. *LAT*, July 15, 1935 (quoted) and July 1, 1935; William James to Harry Blair, July 19, 1935, Chronology.

15. AB to Ickes, telegram, 1936, Chronology.

16. *LAT*, Oct. 27, 1934; Hutchinson brief, 1936, 59, Box 696, RG21-FW; *Barnett v. United States*, No 7962, Circuit Court of Appeals, Ninth Circuit, 82 F.2d 765 (1936).

17. *LAH*, Feb. 3, 1938; *LAT*, July 12, 1938, Box 200, MIA-LN, f. 23 1/3; AB to Ellis, June 3, 1937, Chronology.

18. "Widow of JB Placed in Solitary Cell," *LAT*, June? 1938, Box 200, MIA-LN, f. 23 2/3; *LAT*, June 7, 1938.

19. *LAH*, and *Los Angeles News*, June 14, 1938.

20. *LAT*, July 12, 1938.

21. Unmarked clipping, Dickson File scrapbook, Folio, California Room, LAPL; N-67-J, Box 201, MIA-LN, f. 100.

22. *Los Angeles Evening News*, Aug. 12, 1938; *LAH*, Aug. 12, 1938.

23. *LAT*, July 26, 1938, and Aug. 8, 1938. There are about four dozen letters regarding the eviction, mostly written by women and overwhelmingly sympathetic to AB. Most were written in July–Aug. and Oct. 18–Nov. 7, 1938. AB index cards in the BIA file, D/I, NAI; *LAH*, Oct. 13, 1938; Congressman Charles Kramer to Att. Gen. Cummings, Oct. 13, 1938, Box 3331, RG60-CP, f. 207695-22. Bill introduced by Thomas, Mar. 30, 1939, S. 2002 (76-1), Box 43, ET, f. 38.

24. Ickes to Mrs. S. A. Merken, July 11, 1938, Chronology.

25. Collier to Dady, Aug. 31, 1938; Report for Land Division Claims, 38479-38 44, 17, Box 202, MIA-LN, f. 108.

26. *LAH*, Oct. 31, 1938.

27. Devitt Vanech to Att. Gen., Oct. 13, 1938, RG60-CP, Box 3331, 207695-16(4); *LAT*, Aug. 13, Aug. 14, and Aug. 30, 1938; Los Angeles Att. Gen. Office to Att. Gen., telegram, Oct. 23, 1938, Land Division, Box 3331, RG60-CP, f. 207695-22.

28. Maud Ward to Att. Gen., Sept. 3, 1938, Box 3331, RG60-CP, f. 207695-22.

29. Sherman Jackson to Cummings, Oct. 19 and Oct. 21, 1938; Eva Warren to FDR; L. Stewart to [?], Oct. 26, 1938, all in Box 3331, RG60-CP, f. 207695-22.

30. *LAH*, Oct. 20, 1938, Box 199, MIA-LN, f. 23; Merriam to FDR, telegram, Oct. 22, 1938; unmarked clipping, Oct. 24, 1938, Box 82, Indians file, Haynes Collection, Special Collections, University of California, Los Angeles.

31. *LAT*, Oct. 21, 1938.

32. *LAT*, Oct. 31 and Nov. 1, 1938.

33. *Riverside Press*, July 11, 1938; *LAH*, Aug. 12, 1938.

34. *LAT*, Oct. 19 and Oct. 31, 1938.

35. *LAH*, Oct. 19, 1938.

36. *LAH*, Oct. 21 and Oct. 22, 1938.

37. *LAT*, Oct. 31, 1938.

38. Ibid.

39. *LAT*, Nov. 1, 1938; *Los Angeles Evening Express*, Oct. 31 and Nov. 1, 1938.

40. *LAT*, Oct. 31 and Nov. 1, 1938.

41. *LAT*, and *LAH*, Nov. 2 and Nov. 3, 1938; *LAH*, Nov. 11, 1938; *NYT*, Aug. 10, 1952; *LAT*, July 31 and Aug. 11, 1952; Equity K-44 through K-48, Box 213; Civil Cases 8353-8364, Box 1224, both in RG21-LN.

Chapter 12

1. *MDP*, June 6, 1934; June 2, June 3, June 7, 1934; *Okmulgee Sunday Times-Democrat*, June 3, 1934; *ODT*, June 16, 1934, and July 11, 1934; *Tulsa Tribune*, July 17, 1934; *DO*, June 5, 1934.

2. Proceedings commenced in the Muskogee County court, but as probate proceedings had begun in other counties for the JB estate, the attorney general applied to have the cases combined and removed to the federal district court for the Eastern District of Oklahoma. The D/I filed a petition, asking the court to determine Jackson Barnett's true heirs after publicizing a call for claimants to appear. *In the Matter of the Estate of Jackson Barnett*, Equity 4556, Consolidated, Boxes 674–696, RG21-FW, and Equity 4556, RG118-FW. Records from pre-1935 Barnett litigation (depositions collected by Selby and others), used by the federal court as reference material, are also stored at NARA-FW.

3. The equity testimony is a rich source for Indian and African-American experiences from before the Civil War to Oklahoma statehood.

4. Judge Bratton's comment is in *Scott v. Beams*, 122 F.2d 777 (10th Cir., 1941), 783. See this case for a good synopsis of the evidence and conclusions in 4556 Consolidated.

5. "Findings of Fact," May 14, 1943, Box 678, Equity 4556, RG21-FW, f. 1943.

6. Lance Hall to author, Oct. 23, 2002, e-mail correspondence; Chilli Barnett testimony. See also the census card of Trump Barnett—enrolled as a Creek freedman and formerly the slave of William Sullivan—who was a son of Siah by a third woman. John Roberts (aka John Cat) testified that Siah, son of Thomas Barnett, was the slave of William Sullivan. NALC, 14, 43–44.

7. "Claim of Bennie Barnett Scott," Box 677, RG21-FW, f. 1939.

8. "Synopsis in Opposition to Wesley Barnett Claim," Sept. 7, 1938, Box 677, RG21-FW, f. Sept.–Oct., 1938.

9. Joseph C. Stone and Howell Parks? to Cleon Summers, Jan. 17, 1941, Box 2, RG118-FW.

10. Equity 4556 testimony, Mar. 22–24, 1937, 417, Box 686, RG21-FW.

11. Ibid.; Blend, 184.

12. Assistant Superintendent, Five Civilized Tribes, to William Fisher, Oct. 10, 1932; William C. Lewis to Fisher, May 9, 1934; C. W. Miller, Assistant Att. Gen., to Fisher, Dec. 7, 1936, all in Lance Hall Papers, Fort Worth, Texas; Blend, 28–31; Lance Hall to author, e-mail communication, Oct. 29, 2002.

13. Blend, 27–28, 206; *LAH*, Apr. 6, 1937, and Dec. 18, 1939; *MDP*, June 6, 1934; *And Still*, 349–350.

14. "Synopsis in Opposition to Wesley Barnett Claim," Sept. 7, 1938.

15. Claims of Joe H. Tiger, Annie Ponds (née Tiger), and Peter Hamilton (known as the Tiger group), Box 677, RG21-FW.

16. *Scott v. Beams*, 783; Littlefield, *Africans and Creeks*, 117, 129, 162, 167–168, 239, 241.

17. Tuckabatchee Town payrolls, Curns-Gentry Exhibits of 1857, 1859, 1882 and 1890. RG21-FW; Lance Hall to author, March 6, 2003, e-mail correspondence.

18. NALC, 41, 42, 50.

19. Caroline Henry testimony, Box 688, 24–25, 28–29, RG21-FW; brief against family pact, US Circuit Court of Appeals, Tenth Circuit, Box 3, RG118-FW.

20. Findings of fact and conclusions of law, filed July 18, 1938, Box 677, RG21-FW; downloaded Oct. 15, 2002, http://freepages.genealogy.rootsweb.com/~texlance/jackson/findings2.htm.

21. Order approving the family settlement, June 30, 1936. The petition was filed May 3, 1937, and approved by the D/I on Sept. 2, 1937. *Survey*, 1708. These persons comprised the core of those who signed contracts with lawyers McCrory, Hummer, and Foster in 1923. In the trial, there were 422 witnesses for adverse claimants and 115 for the three consolidated; several hundred exhibits were presented.

Fourteen descendants of JB's half siblings on his father's side were in Family Compact, Group I. These were the descendants of the offspring of Siah Barnett and Mary Beams: Hannah (Fisher) (Creek Roll Number [CRN] 4513), David Barnett (CRN 4955), Eliza "Lizzie" Fish (CRN 4754, married to Little Fish), Ellen Barnett Grayson, and Sissie (or Mariah) Barnett Davis. The children of half sister

Hannah were Seaborn Fisher (CRN 4517), Mariah Fisher Thomkins (CRN 4515), Lewis Fisher (CRN 4516), and William Fisher (CRN 4514). The children of half brother David Barnett were Jimmie (CRN 4497), Annie Barnett Beams (CRN 4504), Melviney Barnett Ditzler (CRN 4953), Nellie (CRN 4498), Tom (CRN 4502), Wesley (CRN 4955), and Hettie Barnett Smoot (CRN 4954). Tom and Wesley, deceased, had no heirs who claimed shares. The five heirs by half sister Lizzie and Little Fish were Katie Fish Litsey (CRN 4750), Winey Fish Lewis (CRN 4748), Mahaley Fish Hickman (CRN 4749), Milley Fish Gilroy (CRN 4752), and Frazier Fish (CRN 4751). An heir by half sister Ellen Barnett Grayson (deceased) was Charity Buckley née Smith (identified as a half-Creek; CRN 5824).

22. On Jackson's maternal side, there were sixteen claimants in Group II, who claimed shares through Jackson's putative grandfather. Old Man Conner's nine children were alleged to be Thlesothle's siblings, including William (Seminole Roll 215), Hannah (Wolf) (CRN 6641), and Thomas (CRN 8593). Conner's daughters Jenny and Lydia died without heirs. Descendants received fractionalized shares of 1/72, 1/108, or even 1/216. William Conner, Thlesothle's alleged brother, was married twice and had four daughters: Wynie Conner Hendrix (Seminole Roll 223), Susie (Seminole Roll 216), Emma Conner Burgess (Seminole Roll 217), and May (or Hanna) (Seminole Roll 219). Thomas Conner's children were Thomas Jr. (CRN Minor 226), William (CRN 9212), Nellie Conner Bear (CRN 9211), and John (CRN 9215). Hannah Wolf (deceased) had surviving children Rebecca Baker (CRN 5833), Nathan Williams (CRN 6637), and Susie Williams (CRN 6645). Group III heirs consisted of four persons, who were the children of Jackson's maternal half brother Haryaryeche: Susie Lowe (CRN 8358), Leona Lowe (CRN 8355), Liza Lowe Gouge (CRN 8356), and Kizzie Lowe (CRN 8818). Leona, Liza, and Kizzie died without issue before Jackson Barnett, leaving the Group III share of the estate to be divided among the heirs of Susie Lowe.

23. Findings of fact and conclusions of law, filed July 18, 1938 but appeals delayed the final resolution until 1939; appeals continued until 1943; Fact and conclusions, Jan. 2, 1940, 6–15, Equity 4556, U.S. Circuit Court of Appeals for 10th Circuit, Box 3, RG118-FW; findings of fact, 1943, JB index Box 199, MIA-LN.

24. Findings of fact and conclusions, 1938, 1940, and 1943. Box 3 and Box 5, RG118-FW. Bertha Barnett findings, Box 677, RG21-FW.

25. Alleging fraud, Dora Brady and Lucinda Watashe made an appeal to disqualify Williams and retry the case in 1942. Their appeal was rejected by a federal circuit court on Sept. 2, 1941. Cf. *Scott v. Beams*; final brief by opponents of family compact, Box 677, RG21-FW, f. 1939.

26. *United States v. McGugin*, No. 293, 31 F. Supp. 498 (District Court of Kansas, 3d Division, 1940); McGugin litigation, May 10, 1938, to Feb. 9, 1940, RG60-CP, f. 207695-3; J. B. Walker's claim, rejected by U.S. Circuit Court of Appeals, 10th Circuit, Sept. 1941, Box 11, RG118-FW.

27. Group I had expenses of approximately $14,000; Group II, roughly $9,500, and Group III, $10,000; findings of fact, 1943, 14, 16.

28. Findings of fact, 1943. *LAH*, May 11, 1945; Accountants and Auditors to CIA, Dec. 20, 1940, Box 6, RG118-FW.

29. "Distribution of 50% of Balance of Account of JB, July 14, 1943," Equity 4556, No. 5917, Box 5, RG118-FW; 36 heirs collected shares from 1/216 to 1/20 in 1943. Inheritance Tax Appraiser William Daggett, Jr., produced this estimate on July 27, 1948. The estate of $1.3 million minus debts, $13,848 in attorney's fees, and

federal estate tax, totaled $1 million. "Estate of JB," Box 5, RG118-FW, f. 1386.

30. Tunney Litsey Graff, interviews with author, Nevada City, California, Mar. 27 and 29, 2001; Claude Porter report, No. 2174, "In the Matter of the Guardianship of Lewis Fisher," FW-Micro.

31. Bill Graff to author, May 21, 2001, e-mail communication.

32. Lance Hall to author, Oct. 24, 2002, e-mail communication.

33. HR 4186, "To authorize sale and conveyance . . . of JB's estate," (1944); SRep 820, "JB, Deceased, sale of property," (1944). *NYT*, Aug. 13?, 1945; *Thomas Kuchel, Controller of the State of California v. John Dady and Heirs*, No. 527628, RG21-LN, f. 16; Tom Anglin to Francis Stewart, Dec. 16, 1949, Box 5, RG118-FW, f. 386; "Richest Indian's LA Mansion Bites Dust," *LAH Examiner*, Dec. 16, 1962. C1-4. Act of Congress, Dec. 13, 1944 gave authority to sell. Box 1224, RG21-LN.

34. Maxine and AB's home was at 1277 West Boulevard. *NYT*, Aug. 10, 1952; *LAT*, July 31 and Aug. 11, 1952. Anna was survived by Maxine and two brothers, William Randolph of Davis, Oklahoma, and James Randolph of Pineville, Missouri. *Los Angeles Herald and Express*, Aug. 14, 1952.

35. Collier to Dady, Aug. 31, 1938, 17, Report for Land Division Claims, 38479-38, Box 202, RG75-LN, f. 108. Oil royalties, which began in January 1913, averaged $13,310.92 a month over a 208-month period. By the end of 1929, royalties totaled $2.7 million. Oil royalties from 1929 to 1934 were estimated at approximately $240,000. Interest on U.S. bonds was estimated at $250,000, and the Equitable and Riggs trusts accrued approximately $200,000 in interest, plus rental income of $2,000. This brought his total life income to roughly $3.5 million, or $350 million in 2002 dollars. The lawyers' share was $329,000 in Equity 4556; $55,000 in *Equitable*; $20,000 in *Riggs*; and an estimated $50,000 in other litigation. Guardians collected roughly $125,000; $116,000 was disbursed between 1934 and 1943 for taxes and court costs; "Distribution of 50 percent of account of JB, July 14, 1943," Eq-4556, Box 5, RG118-FW.

Epilogue

1. *And Still*, 93.

2. See *American National Bank v. ABHMS*; 103 F.2d 192 (1939).

3. *Quick Bear v. Leupp*, 210 US 50 (1908).

4. See, for example, Thomas Krainz's study of the Utes in "Indian Rights or Poor Relief: Progressive-Era Indian Policy," 3–8.

5. The 1933 legislation to create private Indian trust agreements proved inadequate to prevent grafting, and in 1938, Ickes recommended that D/J cancel eleven trusts. *And Still*, 362–367, 374–377; Blend, 196–205. Both Debo and Blend give considerable attention to the legislative reforms of the Oklahoma probate system in the wake of the JB scandal.

6. SH on SR 2047, "To Promote the General Welfare of Indians of Oklahoma"; Blend, 193, 197, 205–206. The 1933 Thomas-Rogers bill, seen as a corrective to the crazy quilt of divided administrative and judicial responsibility in Oklahoma, failed to pass Congress. John Collier worked to transfer heirship from the county to the federal courts in Oklahoma and to limit exorbitant lawyer's fees. In 1935, Congress again investigated and made another futile effort to reform the Oklahoma probate system.

7. Winona LaDuke and Ward Churchill, "Native America: The Political Economy of Radioactive Colonialism," 107.

8. Clyde Warrior, "We Are Not Free," 1967, quoted in Colin C. Calloway, *First Peoples*, 468. See Osage Agency, *Osage People and Their Trust Property*, 67–73, for evidence that Oklahoma courts continue to drain Indian estates in probate proceedings.

9. Quoted in Timothy Egan, "Poor Indians on Rich Land Fight a U.S. Maze," A1, 20.

10. Ibid.; Suzan Shown Harjo, "A Matter of Trust: The Trust Funds Case and How Two Native Lawyers See It," 50.

11. Harjo, "A Matter of Trust," 48.

12. Ibid., 48–49; *NYT*, Jan. 7, 2003, A17.

13. Peter Maas, "The Broken Promise/She Seeks Justice," 4–6.

14. Ibid.: Michael Kennedy, "Truth and Consequences on the Reservation," 14–16.

15. Egan, "Poor Indians on Rich Land," A20.

16. Valerie Taliman, "Standing Strong: Elouise Cobell's Siege of Interior," 52–54 (quote on 52); Harjo, "A Matter of Trust," 48.

17. "Norton Takes Trust Fund from Indian Bureau," LAT, Nov. 16, 2001, p. A35.

18. Taliman, "Standing Strong," 52–54 (quote on 52); Harjo, "A Matter of Trust," 48.

19. Quoted in Harjo, "A Matter of Trust," 50.

20. Quoted in Robert Jackson, "Norton Contempt Trial Opens over Indian Trust," *LAT*, Dec. 11, 2001, p. A23; Egan, "Poor Indians on Rich Land," A20.

21. Harjo, "A Matter of Trust," 48.

22. Taliman, "Standing Strong," 52–54.

23. "Worst Federal Agency," *US News and World Report*, Nov. 28, 1994, p. 151–152; Louis Sahugun, "Tangled Trust Funds Earn Wrath of Native Americans," *LAT*, Nov. 10, 1996, p. A13; *The Indian Report* (Jan. 1997): 4–6; "Indian Trust Inquiry Stalls, Lawyer Says," *LAT*, Feb. 14, 2001, p. A17; "Interior Eyes Sample Indian Trust Accounts," *LAT*, Mar. 1, 2001.

24. Maas, "The Broken Promise/She Seeks Justice," 5.

25. "Promise to Fix Indian Trust Fund Finds Skepticism" *LAT*, Feb. 14, 2002, p. A16.

26. Elizabeth Shogren, "Indians Who Sought Billions Owed $60.94, Report Finds," *LAT*, Mar. 27, 2003, A19.

27. Davis, "Chitto Harjo," 139.

28. "Remarks of Kevin Gover, Assistant Secretary, Indian Affairs," downloaded Nov. 12, 1002; http://rosecity.net/cherokee_trails_newsletter/links/kevin_gover_statement.html.

Appendix III

1. Thomas Crawford dep., Dec. 27, 1928; U.S. Court Appeals for the Second Circuit, Case 10404–10408. Feb. to Dec. 1928, Box 1771, RG21-NY.

2. U.S. Court of Appeals for the Second Circuit, Box 1771, f. Jan. to Sept. 1929, 123785 and 914759–60; f. July 1931 to Feb. 8 and 9, 1932.

3. Selby testimony, *Survey*, 1053.

4. Opinion filed on Nov. 30, 1926, *Survey*, 1661–1668.

Bibliography

Manuscript and Archival Collections

American Baptist Historical Society Archives. American Baptist Archives Center, Valley Forge, PA.

Bancroft Library. University of California, Berkeley.

Collier, John. Papers. Correspondence, 1922–1928 Microfilm rolls 1–3. Yale University, New Haven, CT.

Costo, Jeanette and Rupert. Collection. University of California, Riverside.

Federal Records Center, College Park, MD. (aka National Archives II, National Archives Record Administration).

    RG48: Records of the Department of the Interior, Office of the Secretary, esp. Box 11445-1, Chronological List of Correspondence re: Jackson Barnett 1907–1936.

    RG60: Records of the Department of Justice.

Federal Records Center, Fort Worth, TX, NARA, Southwest Region.

    RG21: Records of the District Court for the Eastern District of Oklahoma, Equity 4556, Consolidated. Boxes 674–696, "In the Matter of the Estate of Jackson Barnett."

    RG75: Selected Records relating to Jackson Barnett. 2 microfilm rolls. 7RA-99.

    Tribal Rolls, 1852–1964, Records of the Bureau of Indian Affairs, Muskogee Area

    Office and Five Civilized Tribes Agency, Entry 54, 7RA23 and 7RA43.

    RG118: Records of the U.S. Attorneys and Marshalls, Equity 4556, Boxes 1–15, "In the Matter of the Estate of Jackson Barnett."

Federal Records Center, NARA, Pacific Region, Laguna Nigue. CA.
    RG21: Records of the District Court of the United States for the Southern
        District of California, Southern Division. 1907–1929. Equity N-67;
        Boxes 314–318. *United States v. Anna Laura Barnett,* "In the Matter of
        Guardianship of Jackson Barnett, Incompetent," No. 1018 Probate, Ok-
        mulgee County Probate Minutes, Book 10; May–August 1912, Lease
        Dispute Hearings re: Conflicting Leases 22449 and 22863; 1919 Church
        Building Fund Litigation: "In the Matter of the Estate of Jackson Bar-
        nett, an Incompetent," Okmulgee County, September 1, 1919; 1920
        Habeas Corpus Case to Annul Marriage, *Carl J. O'Hornett v. Anna
        Laura Lowe,* No. 22,897, Supreme Court of the State of Kansas. Box 213,
        Equity K-44 through K-48; Box 1224, civil cases 8353–8364.
    RG75: Records of the Office of Indian Affairs, Mission Indian Agency, Boxes
        199–203: Records Relating to Jackson Barnett estate, 1934–1947.
    RG118: Records of the United States Attorneys and Marshalls. Eastern and
        Western Districts. File Copies of Equity-4556 documents.
Federal Records Center, NARA, Northeast Region, New York.
    RG21: Records of the District Court of the Southern District of New York.
        Boxes 1771–1774. *Barnett v. Equitable Trust* and *United States v. Equitable
        Trust of New York,* E31–91, and *Anna Barnett v. Equitable,* Equity 31–193.
Federal Records Center, Washington, DC (aka National Archives I)
    RG75: Records of the Office of Indian Affairs. Central Classified Files, Box
        33: Correspondence re: Jackson Barnett; Records of the Commissioners
        of Indian Affairs, Box 2: John Collier Papers. Bureau of Indian Affairs,
        Card Catalogue File of Jackson and Anna Barnett.
Federal Reporter and Supreme Court Reports. California State Law Library, Sacra-
    mento, CA.
Hall, Lance. Papers. Fort Worth, TX.
Haynes, John Randolph. Collection. Special Collections, University of California,
    Los Angeles. CA.
Los Angeles Public Library, Los Angeles, California.
        Los Angeles Herald Examiner. Newspaper Clippings and Photo Archive.
        Los Angeles Times. Index Reel 124, 1927–1945.
National American Legal Collection. "Depositions Taken in a Suit to Determine
    the Heirs of Jackson Barnett [Abstracts of Testimony in Equity 4556]."
    Part I, Title 1162, 79–400, 1934–1936. Microfiche.
Oklahoma Historical Society. Western Historical Collection, Oklahoma City.
Okmulgee County Historical Society, Okmulgee, OK.
Thomas, Elmer. Collection. Carl Albert Center, Congressional Archives. Univer-
    sity of Oklahoma, Norman.

Government Documents and Publications

Atwood, Stella M., and Haven Emerson. *Reply to Commissioner Burke's Accusations
    of Misreprentation and False Propaganda.* Washington, DC: Government
    Printing Office, 1926.
Board of Indian Commissioners. *Annual Reports.* Nos. 48–50 (1917–1920), 1927,
    1929, 1932. Microfilm.
Booth, Edwin. "Jurisdiction of State Probate Courts, Aug 2, 1922." Interior De-

partment Indian Rulings, *Indian Law Survey*. Washington, DC: Department of the Interior, 1939.

Bureau of Indian Affairs. Records, Procedural Issuances, Orders, and circulars, 1854–1955. Washington, DC: National Archives and Records Service, 1980. Microfilm.

Commissioner of Indian Affairs. *Annual Reports*. 1913–1914, 1917, 1919, 1921, 1923, 1926–1934.

Congress. House. Hearings and Reports of Committees and Subcommittees on Indian Affairs.

——. House Hearing on House of Representatives Bill 181. 68th Cong., 1st sess. (1924).

——. House Hearing on house Resolution 348. "Investigation of the Administration of Indian Affairs in Oklahoma. 68th Cong., 1st sess. (1924–1925).

——. House Hearing on House Bill 6900 (Burke bill). "For Protection of the Five Civilized Tribes." 68th Cong., 1st sess. (1924).

——. House Report 1527. "Investigation of the Administration of Indian Affairs in Oklahoma." 68th Cong., 2d sess. (1924–1925).

——. House Hearing on House Bill 887. "Leasing of Allottee Lands." 69th Cong., 1st sess. (1926).

——. House Hearing on Appropriation Bill, Fiscal 1928. 69th Cong., 2d sess. (1925–1926).

——. House Hearing on "Survey into Conditions of the Indians of the United States." 69th Cong., 1st sess. (1926).

——. House Hearing on House Bill 7204. "Creation of Indian Trust Estates." 71st Cong., 1st sess. (1928).

——. House Report 4186. "To authorize the sale and conveyance of certain property of the estate of Jackson Barnett, deceased Creek Indian." 78th Cong., 2d sess. (1944).

Congress. Senate. Hearings and Reports of Committees and Subcommittees on Indian Affairs.

——. Senate Report 1998. "To Amend the Act Providing for Allotment of Lands to Indians." 59th Cong., 1st sess. (1905–1906).

——. Senate Report 5013. "Affairs in Indian Territory with Hearings." 59th Cong., 1st and 2d sess. (1906).

——. Senate Report 575. "Removal of Restrictions from Part of the Lands of the Five Civilized Tribes." 60th Cong., 1st sess. (1907–1908)

——. Senate Subcommittee Hearing on Senate Resolution 341. "Survey into the Conditions of the Indians of the United States." 69th Cong., 1st sess.; 69th Cong., 2d sess. (1926–1927).

——. Senate Hearing Pursuant to Senate Resolution 79. "Survey of Conditions of Indians of the United States." 70th Cong., 1st sess. (1927–1928).

——. Senate Report 982 on House Bill 504-3. "Extension of Restrictions for Five Civilized Tribes." 70th Cong., 1st sess. (1927–1928).

——. Senate Hearing pursuant to Senate Resolution 79. "Survey of conditions of the Indians in the United States." 70th Cong., 2d sess. (1928–1944).

——. Senate Hearing on Senate Resolution 2047. "To Promote the General Welfare of Indians of Oklahoma." 74th Cong., 1st sess. (1935).

———. Senate Report 820: Jackson Barnett, Deceased; Sale of Property. 78th Cong., 2d sess. (1944).

Congressional Record. 1906–1908, 1926–1928.

Department of the Interior. *Annual Report of the Secretary of the Interior.* 1914, House Document, no 1475, 63 Cong., 3d sess. Serial 6814 (1914–1915) 1932.

Department of the Interior. "Regulations of the Indian Service Individual Indian Moneys," Approved by the secretary of the Interior Jan. 30, 1928 (Washington, D.C.: Government Printing Office, 1929.

Osage Agency. *Osage People and Their Trust Property.* Field Report of the Bureau of Indian Affairs, Andarko Area office, Osage Agency, 1953.

Superintendent of the Five Civilized Tribes. *Annual Report.* 1916, 1923, 1924, 1926.

Newspapers
Daily Oklahoman, 1916–1938.
Los Angeles Herald (later merged with *Los Angeles Herald Examiner*), 1926–1938.
Los Angeles Times, 1926–1938.
Muskogee Daily Phoenix, 1917–1938.
Muskogee Times-Democrat, 1917–1938.
New York Times, 1925–1927.

Unpublished Theses and Conference Papers
Blend, Benay. "Jackson Barnett and the Oklahoma Indian Probate System." Master's thesis, University of Texas at Arlington, 1978.

Holm, Thomas Mark. "Indians and Progressives: From Vanishing Policy to the Indian New Deal." Ph.D. diss., University of Oklahoma, 1978.

Krainz, Thomas. "Indian Rights or Poor Relief: Progressive-Era Indian Policy." Paper presented at the Western Historical Society Conference, October 16–19, 2002, Colorado Springs, CO.

Thorne, Tanis. "The Indian Beverly Hillbillies: The Migration of Oklahoma's Wealthy Indians to Southern California in the 1920s." Paper presented at the Western Historical Society Conference, Oct. 16–19, 2002, Colorado Springs, CO.

Books. Pamphlets, and Articles
Baird, W. David, ed. *A Creek Warrior for the Confederacy: Autobiography of Chief G. W. Grayson.* Norman: University of Oklahoma, 1988.

Barnes, Lemuel Call. *Baptist Work among the American Indians.* 2d ed. [n.p.] 1922.

Barnett, Anna. *Truth: A History of Jackson Barnett.* Rev. ed. Los Angeles, CA: privately printed, 1935.

Beaulieu, David L. "Curly Hair and Big Feet: Physical Anthropology and the Implementation of Land Allotment on the White Earth Chippewa Reservation." *American Quartely* 8 (Fall 1984): 281–314.

Bolt, Christine. *American Indian Policy and American Reform.* London: Allen and Unwin, 1987.

Bonnin, Gertrude, Charles Fabens, and Matthew Sniffen. *Oklahoma's Poor Rich Indians: An Orgy of Graft and Exploitation of the Five Civilized Tribes—Legalized Robbery.* Philadelphia: Office of the Indian Rights Association, 1924.

Braund, Kathryn. *Deerskins and Duffles: Creek Indian Trade with Anglo-America: 1685–1815.* Lincoln: University of Nebraska Press, 1993.

Carnegie, Andrew. *The Gospel of Wealth and Other Timely Essays.* Garden City, NY: Doubleday, Doran, 1933.

Carter, Nancy Carol. "Race and Power Politics as Aspects of Federal Guardianship over American Indians: Land-Related Cases, 1887–1924." *American Indian Law Review* 4, no. 2 (1976): 197–248.

Collier, John. *Indians of the Americas.* New York: Norton, 1947.

———. "The Indian Bureau's Record." *Nation* 135 (1932).

———. "Are We Making Red Slaves?" *Survey,* Jan. 1, 1927. 453– 455, 474–480.

Corey, Herbert. "He Carries the White Man's Burden." *Collier's,* May 12, 1923.

Davis, Mace. "Chitto Harjo." *Chronicles of Oklahoma* 13, no. 2 (1935): 139–145.

Debo, Angie. *And Still the Waters Run: The Betrayal of the Five Civilized Tribes.* Princeton, NJ: Princeton University Press, 1940, repr. 1984.

———. *History of the Indians of the United States.* Norman: University of Oklahoma Press, 1970.

———. *Road to Disappearance.* Norman: University of Oklahoma Press, 1941.

Deloria, Vine, and Clifford Lytle. *The Nations Within.* New York: Pantheon, 1984.

———*American Indians, American Justice.* Austin: University of Texas Press, 1983.

Downes, Randolph C. "A Crusade for Indian Reform, 1922–1934." *Mississippi Valley Historical Review* 32 (Dec. 1945): 331–354.

Draper, William. "Depression in the Osage." *Outlook and Independent* 160, no. 4 (1932): 113–114.

Egan, Timothy. "Poor Indians on Rich Land Fight a U.S. Maze." *New York Times,* March 9, 1999, pp. A1, 20.

Epple, Jess. *Honey Spring Depot, Elk Creek, Creek Nation.* Muskogee, OK: Hoffman, 1964.

Ferber, Edna. *Cimarron.* Garden City, NY: Doubleday, 1929.

Finny, Thomas. *Pioneer Days with the Osage Indians West of '96.* Bartlesville, OK: privately printed, 1925.

Fixico, Donald L. *The Invasion of Indian Country in the Twentieth Century,* Niwot: University Press of Colorado, 1998.

Foreman, Carolyn. "The Yuchi: Children of the Sun." *Chronicles of Oklahoma* 37, no. 4 (1959–1960): 480–496.

Forman, Grant. *A History of Oklahoma.* Norman: University of Oklahoma Press, 1942.

Foulke, William Dudley. "Despoiling a Nation." *Outlook* 91, no. 40 (1909): 40–44.

Franks, Kenny. *Oklahoma Petroleum Industry.* Norman: University of Oklahoma Press, 1980.

Franks, Kenny, Paul Lambert, and Carl N. Tyson. *Early Oklahoma Oil: A Photographic History, 1859–1936.* University College Station: Texas A and M Press, 1981.

George, Henry. *Progress and Poverty.* 1879. Reprint. New York: Schalkenbach Foundation, 1955.

Gideon, D. C. *Indian Territory: Descriptive, Biographical and Genealogical* New York and Chicago: Lewis, AZ: 1901.

Glassock, C. B. *Then Come Oil.* Indianapolis, IN: Bobbs-Merrill, 1938.

Gould, Stephen Jay. *The Mismeasure of Man.* New York: Norton, 1981.

Graebner, Norman. "Public Land Policy of the Five Civilized Tribes." *Chronicles of Oklahoma* 23, no. 2 (1945): 107–118.

Green, Donald. *Creek People*. Phoenix, AZ: Indian Tirbal Series, 1973.

Greenberg, Jonathan. *Staking a Claim: Jake Simmons, Jr., and the Making of an African American Oil Dynasty*. New York: Atheneum, 1990.

Haas, Mary. "Creek Inter-town Relations." 1940. Reprinted in *A Creek Source Book*. edited by William C. Sturtevant. New York: Garland, 1987.

Hagan, William. *American Indians*. Rev. ed. Chicago, IL: University of Chicago Press, 1979.

Harjo, Chitto [Crazy Snake]. "The Plea of Crazy Snake." In *A Short History of Indians of the United States*. edited by Edward Spicer, 165–170. New York: Van Nostrand Reinhold, 1969.

Harjo, Suzan Shown. "A Matter of Trust: The Trust Funds Case and How Two Native Lawyers See It." *Native Americas* 18, nos. 3–4 (Fall–Winter 2001): 48–51.

Hauptman. Laurence M. *Tribes and Tribulations: Misconceptions about American Indians and Their Histories*. Albuquerque: University of New Mexico Press, 1995.

Hawkins, Benjamin. *A Sketch of the Creek Country in the Year 1798 and 1799*, 1848. Reprint. Spartanburg, SC: Reprint Company, 1982.

Hitchcock, Ethan Allen. *A Traveler in Indian Territory: The Journal of Ethan Allan Hitchcock*. edited by Grant Foreman. Cedar Rapids, IA: Torch, 1930.

Hogan, Linda. *Mean Spirits*. New York: Atheneum, 1990.

Hoxie, Frederick E. *A Final Promise: The Campaign to Assimilate the Indians, 1880–1920*. Lincoln: University of Nebraska Press, 1984.

The Indian Report. (Jan. 1997): 4–6. Friends Committee on National Legislation, Washington, D.C.

Indian Rights Association. *Forty-Fifth Annual Report*. Phildelphia: Indian Rights Association, 1927.

Kappler, Charles, comp. and ed. *Indian Affairs: Laws and Treaties*. Reprint. New York: AMS Press 1972.

Karlsen, Carol F. *Devil in the Shape of a Woman: Witchcraft in Colonial New England*. New York: Vintage, 1989.

Kelly, Lawrence. *Assault on Assimilation: John Collier and the Origins of Indian Policy Reform*. Albuquerque: University of New Mexico Press, 1983.

———. "Charles James Rhoads, 1929–1933." In *The Commissioners of Indian Affairs, 1824–1977*, edited by Herman J. Viola and Robert M. Kvasnicka, 263–271. Lincoln: University of Nebraska Press, 1979.

———. "John Collier and the Indian New Deal: An Assessment." In *Indian-White Relations: A Persistent Paradox*, edited by Jane F. Smith and Robert Kvasnicka, 227–241. Washington, DC: Howard University Press, 1976.

———. "Cato Sells, 1913–1921." In *Commissioners of Indian Affairs*, 243–250.

———. "Charles Henry Burke, 1921–1929." In *Commissioners of Indian Affairs*, 251–262.

Kennedy, Michael. "Truth and Consequences on the Reservation." *Los Angeles Times Magazine*, July 7, 2002, pp. 14–17, 31–32.

Kin, David George. *The Plot against America: Senator Wheeler and the Forces behind Him*. Missoula, MT: Kennedy Publishers, 1946.

LaDuke, Winona, and Ward Churchill. "Native America: The Political Economy of Radioactive Colonialism." *Journal of Ethnic Studies* 13, no. 3 (Fall 1985): 107–132.

Leupp, Francis E. *The Indian and His Problem.* New York: Scribner's, 1910.

Littlefield, Daniel, Jr. *Alex Posey: Creek Poet, Journalist and Humorist.* Lincoln: University of Nebraska Press, 1992.

———. *Africans and Creeks: From the Colonial Period to the Civil War.* Westport, CT: Greenwood, 1979.

"Lo the Rich Indian, How He Blows His Coin." *Library Digest* 67 (1920): 62.

Maas, Peter. "The Broken Promise/She Seeks Justice." *Parade,* Sept. 9, 2001, pp. 4–6.

McDonnell, Janet. *The Dispossession of the American Indian, 1887–1934.* Bloomington: Indiana University Press, 1991.

Mackay, Richard. *Guardianship Law: The Law of Guardian and Ward Simplified.* New York: Oceana, 1948.

Magee, Carl C. "Removal of the Restrictions," *Sturms Statehood Magazine,* no. 15 (1906): 10–11.

Martin, Joel. "Rebalancing the World in the Contradictions of History: Creek/Muskogee." In *Native Religions and Cultures of North America,* edited by Lawrence F. Sullivan, 85–103. New York: Continuum, 2000.

Mathews, John Joseph. *Sundown.* Norman: University of Oklahoma Press, 1934.

May, Katja. *African Americans and Native Americans in the Creek and Cherokee Nations, 1830s to 1920s.* New York: Garland, 1996.

Meriam, Lewis, et al. *The Problem of Indian Administration: A Report of a Survey Made at the Request of Sec'y of the Interior Hubert Work on June 12, 1926, and Submitted to Him, Feb. 21, 1928.* Brookings Institution. Baltimore, MD: Johns Hopkins University Press, 1928.

Merserve, John B. "Chief Samuel Checote with Sketches." *Chronicles of Oklahoma* 16 (1938): 401–409.

———. "Chief Isparhecher." *Chronicles of Oklahoma* 10 (1932): 52–76.

———. "Chief Opotheyhola." *Chronicles of Oklahoma* 9 (1931): 439–453.

———. "Chief Pleasant Porter." *Chronicles of Oklahoma* 9 (1931): 318–334.

Meyer, Melissa. *White Earth Tragedy.* Lincoln: University of Nebraska Press, 1994.

Miner, H. Craig. *The Corporation and the Indian: Tribal Sovereignty and Industrial Civilization in Indian Territory, 1865–1907.* Columbia: University of Missouri Press, 1976.

Moorehead, Warren K. *Our National Problem: The Sad Condition of the Oklahoma Indians.* Andover, MA: Privately printed, 1913.

Mott, Marshall L. *The Act of May 27, 1908 Placing in the Probate Courts of Oklahoma Indian Jurisdiction: A National Blunder.* Washington, DC: Privately printed, 1925.

O'Brien, Sharon. *American Indian Tribal Governments.* Norman: University of Oklahoma Press, 1989.

Opler, Morris. "Report on the History and Contemporary State of Aspects of Creek Social Organization and Government." 1937. Reprinted in *A Creek Source Book,* edited by William C. Sturtevant. New York: Garland, 1987.

Parman, Donald. *Indians and the American West in the 20th Century.* Bloomington: Indiana University Press, 1994.

Philp, Kenneth. *John Collier's Crusade for Indian Reform.* Tucson: University of Arizona Press, 1977.

———. "John Collier, 1933–1945." In Viola and Kvasnicka eds., *The Commissioners of Indian Affairs,* 273–282.

Posey, Minnie H., comp. "On the Capture and Imprisonment of Crazy Snake." In *The Poems of Alexander Lawrence Posey.* Topeka, KS: Crane, 1902.

Prucha, Francis Paul. *The Indians in American Society.* Berkeley, University Press, 1985.

———. *The Great Father.* Abridged ed. Lincoln: University of Nebraska Press, 1984.

Rasmussen, Cecilia. "'Richest Indian' and Battles for His Wealth." *Los Angeles Times,* Aug. 28, 1995, p. B3.

"Red Man's Burden." *New Republic,* Oct. 19, 1927, pp. 224–226.

"Reverend William McCombs." *Chronicles of Oklahoma* 8 (1930): 137–140.

"Richest Indians." *Literary Digest* III (1936): 14.

Robinson, Edgar E., and Paul C. Edwards. *The Memoirs of Ray Lyman Wilbur, 1875–1949.* Stanford, CA: Stanford University Press, 1960.

Rogers, Sherman. "Red Men in Gas Buggies." *Outlook* 134, no. 14 (1923): 629–632.

Sahugun, Louis. "Tangled Trust Funds Earn Wrath of Native Americans." *Los Angeles Times,* Nov. 10, 1996, p. A13.

Schmeckebier, Lawrence F. *Office of Indian Affairs: Its History, Activities and Organization.* Baltimore, MD: Johns Hopkins University Press, 1927.

Shattuck, Petra, and Jill Norgren. *Partial Justice: Federal Indian Law in a Liberal Constitutional System.* New York: Berg, 1991.

Shepherd, W. G. "Lo, the Rich Indian!" *Harper's Monthly Magazine,* Nov. 1920, pp. 723–734.

Slosson, Edwin. "Lo the Rich Indian." *Independent,* Sept. 18, 1920, pp. 337–338.

Sniffen, M. K. *A Man and His Opportunity.* Philadelphia: Indian Rights Association, 1914.

Spicer, Edward. *A Short History of Indians of the United States.* New York: VanNostrand Reinhold, 1969.

Sturtevant, William, ed., *A Creek Source Book.* New York: Garland, 1987.

Swanton, John R. "Modern Square Grounds of the Creek Indians." Reprinted in *A Creek Source Book,* edited by William Sturtevant. New York: Garland, 1987.

Taliman, Valerie. "Standing Strong: Elouise Cobell's Siege of Interior." *Native Americas* 18, nos. 3–4 (Fall–Winter 2001): 32–39.

Thackery, Ted, Jr. "Richest Indian's LA Mansion Bites the Dust." *Los Angeles Herald Examiner,* Dec. 16, 1962, C1–4.

Thorne, Tanis. "On the Fault Line: Political Violence at Campo Fiesta and National Reform in Indian Policy." *Journal of California and Great Basin Anthropology* 21, no. 2 (1999): 182–212.

Underhill, Lonnie E. "Hamlin Garland and the Final Council of the Creek Nation." *Journal of the West* 10, no. 3 (1971): 514–515.

Van Tuyle, Bert. *Know Your Los Angeles: An Unusual Guide Book.* 2d ed, Los Angeles: Ahlrich, 1940.

Viola, Herman, and Robert M. Kvasnicka, eds., *The Commissioners of Indian Affairs, 1824–1977.* Lincoln: University of Nebraska Press, 1979.

Wahrhaftig, Albert. "Making Do with the Dark Meat: A Report on the Cherokee Indians in Oklahoma." In *American Indian Economic Development*, edited by Sam Stanley, 409–510. Hague, Mouton, 1978.

Wallace, Anthony F. C. *The Long and Bitter Trail: Andrew Jackson and the Indians*. New York: Hill and Wang, 1999.

Warde, Mary Jane. *George Washington Grayson and the Creek Nation, 1843–1920*. Norman: University of Oklahoma Press, 1999.

Warrior, Clyde. "We are Not Free." In *First Peoples: A Documentary Survey of American Indian History*, edited by Colin Calloway, 467–471. Boston: Bedford/St. Martin's, 1999.

Wheeler, Burton, with Paul F. Holts. *Yankee from the West*. Garden City, NY: Doubleday, 1962.

———. "Is It the End of the Road?" Wheeler Remarks in Senate, May 1, 1929. Washington, D.C.: Government Printing Office, 1929.

White, Graham, and John Maze. *Harold Ickes of the New Deal*. Cambridge, MA: Harvard University Press, 1985.

Wiebe, Robert. *Search for Order*. New York: Hill and Wang, 1967.

Wilkins, David. *American Indian Sovereignty and the U.S. Supreme Court: The Masking of Justice*. Austin: University of Texas Press, 1997.

Wilkins, David and K. Tsianina Lomawaima, *Uneven Ground: American Indian Sovereignty and Federal Law*. Norman: University of Oklahoma Press, 2001.

Williams, John, and Howard L. Meredith. *Bacone Indian University: A History*. Oklahoma City, OK: Oklahoma Heritage Association, 1980.

Wilson, Terry. *The Underground Reservation: Osage Oil*. Lincoln: University of Nebraska Press, 1985.

Woerner, J. G. *A Treatise on the American Law of Guardianship of Minors and Persons of Unsound Mind*. Boston: Little, Brown, 1987.

Woodward, Thomas S. *Woodward's Reminiscences of the Creek, or Muscogee Indians*. Montgomery, AL: Babrett and Wimbish, 1859.

Work, Hubert. "Our American Indians." *Saturday Evening Post*, May 31, 1924, p. 92.

"Worst Federal Agency." *US News and World Report*, Nov. 28, 1994. 61–64.

Wright J. Leitch, Jr. *Creeks and Seminoles: Destruction and Regeneration of the Muscogulge People*. Lincoln: University of Nebraska Press, 1986.

Wright, Muriel. *A Guide to Indian Tribes of Oklahoma*. Norman: University of Oklahoma Press, 1951.

Wright, Peter. "John Collier and the Indian Welfare Act of 1936." *Chronicles of Oklahoma* 50, no. 3 (1972): 347–371.

Young, Mary. *Redskins, Ruffleshirts and Rednecks: Indian Allotments in Alabama and Mississippi, 1830–1860*. Norman: University of Oklahoma Press, 1961.

Interviews and E-mail correspondence

INTERVIEWS

Tunney Litsey Graff, Nevada City, CA, Mar. 27 and Mar. 29, 2001.
Robert Hine, Irvine, CA, Dec. 7 1999.

E-MAIL CORRESPONDENCE

Bill Graff to author, May 21, 2001.
Lance Hall to author, Oct. 13, 24, 25, 2002. March 6, 2003.
Robert Hine to author, Dec. 22, 1999.
Daniel Littlefield to author, May 2, 2001.
Mary Petersdorf to author, Dec. 2, 1998.
Mary Petersdorf to Lance Hall, July 11, 2001.

Internet Sources
Bowie Report.
    http://freepages.genealogy.rootsweb.com/~texlance/jackson/1920report.htm
FindLaw.com. *Mott v. United States,*
    http://laws.findlaw.com/us/283/747.html *United States v. Equitable Trust Co,*
    of New York.
    http://laws.findlaw.com/us/283/738.html
Fink, Jerry. "Jackson Barnett." *Tulsa World Sunday Magazine*, June 20, 1982.
    Downloaded Mar. 14, 2002.
    http://www.rootsweb.com/~okmcinto/Married/barnettj.htm
Gover, Kevin. "Remarks of Kevin Gover, Assistant Secretary, Indian Affairs, De-
    partment of the Interior, at the Ceremony Acknowledging the 175th Anni-
    versary of the Establishment of the Bureau of Indian Affairs, September 8,
    2000." Downloaded Nov. 12, 2002.
    http://rosecity.net/cherokee_trails_newsletter/links/
    kevin_gover_statement.html
Hall, Lance. "Jackson Barnett, the 'Richest Indian.'" Downloaded Aug. 17, 2002.
    http://freepages.genealogy.rootsweb.com/~texlance/jackson/jackson.htm
———. "Barnard Family Genealogy: Descendants of Thomas Barnett." Down-
    loaded Oct. 4, 2002.
    http://freepages.genealogy.rootsweb.com/~texlance/my/barnett/pafg03.htm
———. "Some Miscellaneous Testimony Taken 1935–1937." Downloaded Oct. 28,
    2002.
    http://freepages.genealogy.rootsweb.com/~texlance/jackson/testimony.htm
———. "Jackson Barnett photos."
    http://users3.ev1.net/~lancehall/jackson/photos.htm
———. Rg21. District Court, Eastern District of Oklahoma. Equity Case 4556.
    Case Filings for Boxes 674–679.
    http://freepages.genealogy.rootsweb.com/~texlance/jackson/fillings.htm
McCusker, John J. "Comparing the Purchasing Power of Money in the United
    States (or Colonies) from 1665 to Any Other Year including the Present."
    Economic History Services, 2001. Downloaded Sept. 23, 2002.
    http://www.eh.net/hmit/ppowerusd/

Web Addresses for Lexis-Nexis Barnett Cases On-Line
Appeal of Barnett, et al. (1926), 122 Okla. 169, 252 P. 418 (Lexis 232)
Appeal of Jackson Barnett (1926) 122 Okla. 160, 252 P. 410 (Lexis 231)
Barnett v. Barnett, County Judge, et al. (1926), 121 Okla. 142; 247 P. 1115 (Lexis 79)
Barnett v. Equitable Trust Co. (1927), 21 F.2d 325 (Lexis 1374)
[Anna] Barnett v. United States (1936), 82 F.2d 765 (Lexis 3108)

McGugin v. United States (1940), 109 F.2d 94 (Lexis 1904)
Mott v. United States (1931), 283 US 747 (Lexis 858)
United States v. Equitable (1931), 283 US 738 (Lexis 857)
United States v. McGugin (1928), 28 F.2d 76 (Lexis 1441)
United States v. McGugin (1940), 31 F. Supp. 498 (Lexis 3628)
United States v. Mott (1929), 33 F.2d 340 (Lexis 1309)
United States v. Mott (1930), 37 F.2d 860 (Lexis 2655)

Index

Printed in the United States
142531LV00002BA/10/A